Renoir's Dancer

Also by Catherine Hewitt

The Mistress of Paris:
The 19th-Century Courtesan Who Built an Empire on a Secret

Renoir's Dancer

The Secret Life of Suzanne Valadon

CATHERINE HEWITT

St. Martin's Press
New York

www.stmartins.com

Library of Congress Cataloging-in-Publication Data

Names: Hewitt, Catherine, author.
Title: Renoir's dancer : the secret life of Suzanne Valadon / Catherine Hewitt.
Description: First U.S. edition. | New York : St. Martin's Press, 2018. | Includes bibliographical references and index.
Identifiers: LCCN 2017041095 | ISBN 9781250157652 (hardcover) | ISBN 9781250157645 (ebook)
Subjects: LCSH: Valadon, Suzanne, 1865–1938. | Painters—France—Biography. | Women painters—France—Biography.
Classification: LCC ND553.V3 H49 2018 | DDC 759.4 [B]—dc23
LC record available at https://lccn.loc.gov/2017041095

Our books may be purchased in bulk for promotional, educational, or business use. Please contact your local bookseller or the Macmillan Corporate and Premium Sales Department at 1-800-221-7945, extension 5442, or by email at MacmillanSpecialMarkets@macmillan.com.

First published in the United Kingdom by Icon Books Ltd

First U.S. Edition: February 2018

10 9 8 7 6 5 4 3 2 1

Contents

List of illustrations

COLOUR PLATES

Renoir's Dancer

Prologue

When dawn broke on 2 October 1949, a thick mist had descended over the wooded valleys of the Limousin countryside, obscuring the little town of Bessines-sur-Gartempe and its 4,000 hectares of fields and hamlets.[1] In the pastures, the warm russet of Limousin cattle appeared muted; from street level, chimneys and steeples were all but lost. Yet from the peaks of the surrounding granite hills, a milky autumn sun could be seen rising slowly against a cloudless sky. It promised to be a fine day.

The cobbled *place* at the heart of the town was still deserted. Not one of the surrounding buildings showed signs of life. The doors of the *mairie* were firmly bolted and not a soul entered the medieval church. Silence reigned.

But behind painted shutters, the people of Bessines were stirring. Already in the stillness, the sense of expectation was almost palpable.

Coloured bunting had been stretched across the streets, cheering the grey and beige stonework of the buildings as it flapped and fluttered in the gentle breeze. A short walk from the *place*, at a house especially brave in banderols, a section of 17th-century wall was concealed by a curtain. Nearby, a kind of platform had been erected, and several chairs covered in red velvet upholstery had been arranged on top. And right in the middle of this makeshift stage, there was a marvel to behold. The trickle of spectators who had now started arriving stopped to gaze in awe at the quintessence of modern innovations: there stood a microphone in dazzling metallic white paint. Many houses in Bessines still did not have running water.[2]

The annual festival of Saint Léger, the town's patron saint, was always a great event. It was celebrated with all the enthusiasm generated by a year spent awaiting its arrival. When it came round, music, dancing and gaiety became the residents' guiding principles for one glorious day. But this year, the people of Bessines were expecting a very important guest – a famous guest. The whole town was poised in anticipation. The main road had been closed, the press had been alerted and someone even said that they had heard an American accent among the crowd. Bessines was a rural community which took altruism as its unspoken ethos and where hard work earned respect. The cult of celebrity was at once bewildering, wonderful and entirely out of the ordinary.

Before long, the men of the local band were arranging themselves in a corner by an arched doorway. With their top hats, trumpets and polished shoes, the group lent a sense of pomp and ceremony to the occasion. The testing of brass and the impromptu rehearsal of the drum signalled that it would not be long now. They were a jolly group, known as 'Les Gueules Sèches' or 'Dry Mouths' – an ironic choice, locals could not help observing, considering the guest they were about to receive.

The people of Bessines were now filling the streets in droves, and the band struck up a cheerful number to set the mood for the day. The crowd looked quite the part. Best shirts had been pressed, women had curled their hair; young boys had been made to scrub their knees and little girls permitted to wear frocks reserved for special occasions.

The school term had only just resumed, so the event was a welcome sweetener to a bitter pill. Young necks were craned in curiosity as children edged their way to the front of the crowd.

'Let me tell you,' one little girl solemnly informed the boy standing next to her, 'the plaque is under that curtain. You'll see soon enough. I know what it says by heart. My father fixed it in place.'

Older spectators looked on with battle-weary eyes. The war was still chillingly fresh. Just a few miles away, the similar-sized town of Oradour-sur-Glane had found unsought fame when Nazi troops stormed in one Saturday afternoon and locked the town's women and children in the church and its men in the barns and outbuildings. Grenades and machine guns were turned on the men and the church set on fire. 642 people were massacred. That was just five years ago. For the townsfolk of Bessines, celebration still felt a surreal concept. They participated apologetically.

All at once, the church bell struck half past eleven. The ceremony commenced.

The light-hearted melodies ceased, and as the band shifted register, the crowd recognised the triumphant opening bars of *La Marseillaise* as a stirring call to patriotism. Older residents liked to boast that, at halfway between Paris and Toulouse, Bessines was at the centre of the world. Today, it really felt true.

Emotions ran high as an official-looking group stepped forward *en masse*. More cultured spectators could recognise notable personalities among them, including the local poet Jean Rebier and the painters M. Edmond Heuzé and M. Rosier. There was the secretary of the 'Friends of the Municipal Museum of the Limoges', Robert Daudet, as well as some more familiar local faces such as M. Donquiert, the newly appointed *sous-préfet* of the nearby town of Bellac, and M. Duditlieu, Bessines' own mayor. They made an impressive group. But one figure in particular held the people's attention. All eyes were fixed on the man in the centre of the group, right at the front.

He was slim, in his mid-60s and visibly uneasy in his smart suit and tie. As the group advanced, he tottered slightly as he walked. An attempt had been made to tame his dark hair, but some unruly strands had escaped, giving him a wild appearance. A whole lifetime of suffering and experience was etched on his weathered face, while the creases of skin around his eyes told of a thousand dramas lived and emotions endured. His dark eyes darted about him rapidly, like those of a startled quarry. And when for a moment they came to settle on another person, his penetrating stare seemed to read their very soul. Never had a man looked so ill at ease before a crowd. And this was the celebrity everyone had come to see.

He had not come to Bessines for the attention. These days, his life was structured around a strict routine; this trip upset it. But he had had no choice. A woman had drawn him here.

By his side marched a formidable female. Matronly in appearance, her robust frame had been squeezed into a tailored dress and jacket, while a matching beret had been carefully positioned on her head. Two strings of pearls around her neck brought a touch of glamour, and her jewelled brooch bespoke wealth as it glinted in the mid-morning sunlight. She moved with confidence, supremely self-aware, as comfortable in the limelight as the man next to her appeared out of place. It was a curious contrast; they were husband and wife.

But it was not for the woman next to him that the man had made this trip. He was haunted by another, a woman not even his wife could rival. 'A Goddess,' he had once called her, 'a sublime creature full of goodness, integrity, charity, selflessness, intelligence, courage and devotion.'[3]

There was indeed something rather mythical about this woman.

His 'Goddess' had come from nothing. Born into poverty, the illegitimate daughter of a humble linen maid, her very birth was clouded with disgrace. Nothing in her genealogy had predestined her for greatness. But determination causes the most stalwart of obstacles to crumble. Refusing to accept that the opportunities she most desired were those least open to her, she surmounted the constraints of class and gender. At a time when 'respectable' women did not even work, she entered one of the most precarious professions possible, attempting to live by her creative gifts alone. This poor countrywoman's daughter found fame and unimaginable fortune. With her golden hair, dramatic eyebrows and intense, blue-eyed stare, her beauty bewitched the Impressionists. She was courted by famous painters, she befriended a prime minister, she became mistress of her very own château and her private life caused a scandal. She even danced for Renoir. But most importantly, she revolutionised the art world and irreversibly altered the place of women within that world.

Her dramatic tale begins here in the rural backwater of Bessines 100 years earlier. It starts with another woman and a seemingly insignificant decision which was to alter the course of history.

CHAPTER 1

Life-cycles

Ne pura pu, bravo novio, rizio dounc!
Faras pa maû sechâ to grimaço, rizio dounc![1]
(Do not cry, sweet young bride, laugh;
You would not be unwise to dry your eyes, laugh!)
<small>COUPLET FROM A TRADITIONAL LIMOUSIN WEDDING SONG[2]</small>

hen eighteen-year-old Madeleine Valadon awoke on
13 February 1849, she knew to expect a thick morning
fog to have enveloped the town of Bessines, while the
frosty air would sting and redden her bare hands once she stepped
outside.[3] It was a Tuesday; soon, the deserted *place* in the town
centre would spring to life, as labourers, shopkeepers, artisans,
seamstresses and laundresses hurried across the cobbles in all direc-
tions to take up their posts. The tap of wooden clogs on stone was
a familiar sound as men in blue smocks made their way through the
streets. White bonnets bobbed in time with female footsteps, subtle
variations in each cap silently declaring its wearer's social standing
and origin. The skirts and capes beneath them were sombre, often
being worn for mourning.[4]

The festivities of Christmas had now long passed; calls of *Boun
Anado* in the local patois which resounded through the streets on
1 January were just a memory; Easter was late that year and the

colour of Mardi Gras would pass all too quickly.[5] February days were short and the nights could be bitter. And in just a few weeks, the truly hard work would begin. The following month, the whole town would be absorbed as the task of preparing the fields and then planting the year's turnip crop commenced.

In one way or another, everyone in Bessines was affected by agriculture and the rearing of livestock. Most households were self-sufficient, and those individuals who did not work the land themselves had a husband, brother or son who surely did.[6] All would need meals prepared and clothing mended. Then there were the associated trades, so vital in the struggle to turn out bountiful yields of crops and herds. Born as she was to the local cartwright, Madeleine belonged to one of the many families whose livelihoods were dependent on the town's dominant commercial activity.

Moneyed, upper-class families were in a minority in the Limousin and countryfolk led a rude existence.[7] Poor soil and a variable climate made it difficult to obtain good crops. Spring frosts could bring tragedy to farms and winters were glacial; hamlets were frequently cut off by snow, and heating the stone-walled cottages was a relentless task. Better off families might boast a home of two or three rooms with adjoining outbuildings, such as a barn, stable and bread oven (for most households had to be able to bake their own; often they would take turns with neighbours to bake for the whole hamlet for the week). There might also be a dryer for chestnuts, that important Limousin staple. Even the poorest peasants owned a shelter for the pig kept in readiness for sacrifice at Christmas. However, the less fortunate among them could be reduced to just one room. For many families, the chief objective was simply to survive.[8]

In such circumstances, the spectre of death cast a shadow over everyday life. The Limousin was a region steeped in folklore and ruled by superstition. All manner of rituals and customs were employed to anticipate and forestall death's arrival. Placing a jar of honey in the stable was reputed to be a good way of protecting a cow, while a nut shell containing a live spider worn round the owner's neck was said to safeguard the wearer from the fever. Rural superstition held that a creaking piece of furniture presaged an imminent death, while a hen that crowed like a cockerel was an equally sinister omen; the creature should be dispatched without further delay and served at table.[9]

But such methods did not always prove reliable deterrents. Indeed, death was an uninvited visitor Madeleine knew only too well. That winter, it had plunged the Valadon household into despair. In early October, just days before his 44th birthday, the young girl's father had died.[10]

Aside from the emotional distress, Mathieu-Alexandre's death had sobering practical implications for Madeleine, her mother and her brother Clément, who at fifteen was still a minor. That Valadon owned several parcels of land gave a deceptive impression of affluence. He was proprietor of some ten plots besides the family's house and garden, which included heathland, grazing and even a small chestnut wood. Yet with some fields located several miles away from the family home, Valadon's property betrayed a patchwork estate of land acquired and reapportioned through inheritance. Such plots were often financially inconsequential; the Valadons were not a wealthy family.

Madeleine had already been put out to work as a linen maid by the time her father died. It was a low-paid, physically gruelling profession, liable to attract sniggers and disdainful looks from the daughters of better-off families. Every channel of income available to the Valadon family was already being exploited, and Madeleine was still unmarried. The loss of the household's head and main breadwinner would have terrifying repercussions.

Even for Limousin girls who had not lost a father, finding a husband was a primary goal from adolescence. Whereas a single man could work and make a living, a woman, with her sphere accepted as the domestic environment and wages meagre even when they were earned, was dependent on male income. Women enjoyed little status outside marriage. The daughters of artisans and peasants alike felt the same sense of urgency when it came to the question of matrimony. Much was at stake, and for many more people than the young couple directly concerned. The family remained the basic social unit in the 19th century, and the marriages of its younger members was its principal means of shaping its identity. The fortunes and future of the entire family rested on the kind of marriage made by its teenagers. This was because marriage determined the distribution of that scarce resource: land. In selecting (or, as was increasingly common in the 19th century, approving) a partner for their offspring, parents needed to feel confident that the match ensured that their own needs in old age would be met. Then there was the question of status; opportunities for social advancement were limited, so it was vital that a youngster did not marry below his or her station. A *mésalliance* could shatter reputations and squander resources where they could never be reciprocated. The burden of duty and expectation weighed heavily on young shoulders. Personal pride naturally came into the equation, too. And living in small, isolated communities, the range of marital options was painfully restricted.[11]

For all these reasons, life for the typical Limousin girl became a veritable man hunt once she reached marriageable age. With such limited pickings, competition between village girls could be fierce. And no means were considered too outlandish when it came to ensnaring a husband. Mystical legends, magic and ancient traditions were still a very real part of everyday life in the Limousin. Many villages and towns had their own ritual practices which young girls were advised to adopt if they wanted to be sure of finding a husband. In the village of La Villeneuve near Eymoutiers, gaggles of single girls were to be found dancing wildly in the mud at the January fair, and the more soiled their skirts became, the better; they would undoubtedly secure a husband within twelve months. Meanwhile, seamstresses in the town of Ambazac, a short distance from where Madeleine lived, swore by a different technique. Whenever they were commissioned to make a wedding dress, they would stitch a lock of their own hair into the hem of the garment to guarantee that they too would become a wife before the year was out.[12] Every community defended the unparalleled efficiency of its own method. But the girls of Bessines had the advantage of a very special tool for performing their ritual, an object few other villages could rival. It took the form of a vast monolithic stone basin, which locals had baptised Pierre Belle.

Nobody could explain how the enormous circular stone of 5m diameter and 80cm depth had arrived on the north bank of the Gartempe river.[13] Some believed it was an ancient fountain, others insisted that it was a monument from Druid culture, perhaps some kind of sacrificial stone. It had a curious lean on one side, which one legend attributed to the occasion when six fairies had tried to move it. Only three of them called on the Virgin for assistance, and the other three were crushed under its massive weight as punishment for their impiety. But however conflicting the explanations of Pierre Belle's origin, its talismanic properties were undisputed. The townsfolk maintained that all a single girl needed to do was to visit the stone on the night of the full moon, hoist herself up onto its rim and run round it seven times. With a rim of little more than 15cm in width, simply staying upright was an achievement worthy of requital. But if a girl took the trouble (and kept her balance), she would be rewarded with a husband within twelve months.

But despite the persistence of these traditions, the Limousins were steadfastly practical people. Where divine intervention failed, rural ingenuity often triumphed.

With marriage paramount and chances to form new acquaintances scarce, every opportunity was taken – or engineered – to propagate meetings and nurture potential relationships. There was the *veillée*, that timeless rural custom, when family and neighbours would gather together and while away the long winter evenings.[14] Huddled around a crackling fire, a whole cross-section of generations could be found laughing, singing, playing cards, passing on traditions and telling stories, tales of ferocious werewolves and gruesome murders and supernatural happenings. The square after Mass was another valuable place to share news and foster connections. With its welcoming heat and constant flow of customers, the blacksmith's was also a hive of social interaction and a breeding ground for gossip.[15] In all instances, family had a key role to play in encouraging auspicious romantic unions. It was in the group's interest. And when a young man had set his sights on a particular girl, he nervously awaited his first meal with her family; if he arrived to find coq au vin cooking, it was a sure sign that he had been approved.[16]

Though the father was the undisputed head of the Limousin family, in cases of this figure's untimely death, his wife would assume this role, and with just as much authority.[17] Hence, when Mathieu-Alexandre died, Madeleine's mother Marie automatically acquired the right to manage the family's money and estate, oversee the distribution of responsibilities, and crucially for Madeleine, to make decisions concerning the choice of spouse of the younger generation. But even if Marie faltered in her new task, the wider family could be counted on to provide vital support.

The extended family was considered deeply important in rural Limousin society, with several generations often living together under the same roof. It was quite usual to find married couples and their offspring living in the paternal home. Children were used to living with grandparents, and while the average household in the 1830s contained five people, at the upper extreme it was not uncommon to find as many as fifteen people packed into the same house. Even when family did not live together, the bonds were typically ferociously strong. Aunts, uncles, and in particular, godparents, played an important role in the lives of the family's younger members. This was especially true in cases where a father had died, when a youngster was advised to *far sounar soun peiri* (or to 'call one's godfather close').[18] Madeleine's grandfather, Martial Dony, was also a dependable presence, there for all his granddaughter's important rites of passage. In short, Madeleine was not going to be left without the sound guidance of a mentor or a paternal figure in her father's absence.

So it was that despite the early morning chill and the bleakness of a season made even more melancholy by the still recent loss of her father, the young girl had every reason to feel full of hope and expectation that February morning. It was no ordinary Tuesday; that day, she was to be married to one of the most eligible young men in the village.

Léger Coulaud was a man many a girl would be proud to call her husband. A local lad from a respectable family, he plied one of the most highly prized trades in the town: he was a blacksmith. In an agricultural town like Bessines, *lu faure* (as he was known in the local dialect), commanded universal respect.[19] Not only did he repair the shoes of both horse and rider; he fixed broken machinery, mended farm equipment and could turn his hand to any task where welding was required. It was a valuable skill – a potentially lucrative skill. Without *lu faure*, the very heart of the town would stop beating.

For Madeleine, that mattered. Urgent though securing a match might have been, her family were not the kind of people to accept any man for their latest marriageable member.

While they were not rich, Mathieu-Alexandre Valadon and Marie Dony were a good, honest couple with estimable ancestral heritage.[20] Mathieu-Alexandre's father was a military man, and his grandfather had enjoyed the honour of being one of the town's first municipal officers. Marie Dony's family tree boasted all manner of figures considered 'notable' in rural society, such as master masons, millers and notaires.[21] Though they were by no means bourgeois, the Valadons came from good stock.

Nor would Madeleine make an undesirable wife. She had high cheekbones, and though she was plain and her face rather angular, and she was hardly the prettiest girl in Bessines, her features were at least even. Furthermore, she could read and write, and being trained as a linen maid, she could boast a skill. Etiquette manuals stipulated that linen maids should be quick, strong, neat and above all, keen to please – attributes which rendered a woman equally appealing as a spouse.[22]

However, in Léger Coulaud, Madeleine could feel confident that she would be taking a husband whom her family considered worthy. Strength and physical stamina were a professional requisite in Léger's trade, important considerations when selecting a spouse on whose income a female would come to depend; no right-minded young girl wanted a husband who was incapable of work.[23] And besides his profession, Léger too benefited from favourable family connections; the names of two Coulauds appeared on the list of teachers approved by the local council in the 19th century.[24] One of them was also called Léger, a name passed down the male line in the Coulaud family, so undoubtedly a relative. To possess even the rudiments of education was considered impressive at the time, particularly in a rural community like Bessines. 'Public instruction,' wrote the new *sous-préfet* or sub-prefect to the mayor in 1816, 'wisely directed, is the seed of social virtues; the sowing of pure morality, the tie that binds together all citizens, the guarantee of happiness and the glory of nations.'[25] Educated men and their associates were looked on with respect. And as if those attributes did not suffice, Léger shared his name with the town's patron saint and was born in the nearby hillside commune of Le Mas Barbu, where Madeleine's family hailed from. Those facts alone surely boded well. What did it matter if the young girl's fiancé was thirteen years her senior, and the civil ceremony, the legally binding part of the marriage contract, was to be performed on the 13th of the month? Superstition was surely immaterial when set against such auspicious circumstances. Besides, the presence of a white hen throughout the proceedings and a pinch of salt in the pocket, both traditional amulets said to bring marital harmony, would allay the concerns of the most paranoid of wedding guests.[26] The match was decided.

Following the Revolution of 1789, marriage had been secularised, and couples were obliged to officialise their union at the *mairie* as well as having a religious ceremony. Sometimes the two ceremonies took place on the same day, but more usually there was a day or two between them. According to custom, Léger Coulaud and Madeleine Valadon's banns had been read twice outside the *mairie*, first on 28 January and then on 4 February at ten in the morning. None of the locals had made any objection, and so on 12 February, a small ceremony had been conducted in the local church. Then at 11 o'clock on 13 February, Madeleine officially became the wife of Léger Coulaud. Two of the couple's mutual friends stood as witnesses along with one of Madeleine's cousins, while the bride's mother and grandfather also signed the register. So did Léger's father, Léger senior, but his mother, Thérèse Thoumassonet, did not; like so many women in rural society, she could neither read nor write.[27]

Limousin weddings were big affairs. Once the formalities were complete, a copious meal was traditionally offered to guests in one

The Place and Saint-Léger church in Bessines.

or other of the family members' barns, which would be decorated with swathes of white sheet and laurel leaves.[28] Normally sparse tables strained under the weight of steaming pot-au-feux, meat pies, veal and mutton casseroles, roast pork and spit roasted poultry. Then came apple tarts, prune tarts and clafoutis (the region's cherry and batter dessert), and the whole meal was washed down with formidable quantities of wine. Once all the guests had eaten their fill, there would be singing, which would be opened by the maid of honour, before the rest of the diners joined in to congratulate the bride and groom. But under no circumstance were the couple to lend their voices to the throng: that was bad luck. After the singing came dancing, which would often take the form of special regional dances (of which there were several in the Limousin). The bride and groom would take the lead, and it was not unusual for the dances to continue into the small hours of the morning. The physical exertion was sufficient to rekindle waning appetites, so the dancing was invariably followed by more feasting. By the time the revellers were ready to begin the next round of dancing, the bride and groom would be preparing to make their discreet exit. But even if they managed to escape unnoticed, the couple would be subject to all kinds of teasing and pranks, the next day if necessary.[29] And they would also be compelled to partake in some more serious rituals, not least walking beneath the requisite loaf of bread, held aloft as they passed through the doorway of the new marital home, while good fortune was invoked on the household with the words '*Qué jamais vous manca!*' (May bread never be lacking).[30]

After the deluge of rituals and festivities, it was often a relief for couples to begin their new life together in peace and establish their routines, all the while hoping that the measures taken to ensure happiness and prosperity would prove effective. M. Coulaud and his new wife moved into a property in Bessines and began to settle into married life. With Madeleine continuing to work, as well as having to keep house and make sure that her husband was well fed, there was much to do. But both husband and wife working meant that there was money coming in, and as they began their first year of marriage, fortune seemed to smile on the newlyweds.

Still, however, Madeleine's happiness was not yet complete. Something was missing. The dearest hope of every young Limousin wife was to provide her husband with a healthy son to continue the family name. As with marriage, there were a number of different methods at a woman's disposal if she wanted to ensure she became a mother. Bessines had its own sacred fountain named after the town's patron saint. Drinking its water was said to guarantee that a woman would give birth to an attractive baby and that the labour would be free of complication.[31] Whether due to unearthly powers or just good luck, within a year of their wedding, the couple's joy was complete. By the end of the summer, Madeleine had fallen pregnant and the following April, she gave birth to a baby boy, who was named after his father.

In a society where the best guarantee of autonomy was work, a son was considered the ultimate boon. Baby girls were frequently referred to pejoratively as *no charamello* (the whiner) or *no pissouso* (the pisser). The baptism of a girl would be announced with a single bell; for a boy, the joyous peals would go on and on.[32]

Madeleine could not ignore what a blessing the child was. In impoverished rural areas like the Limousin, the loss of a child was all too common, so common in fact that at the time Madeleine gave birth to her infant, throughout France, parents still did not wear mourning following the death of a child.[33] Generalised poverty in the Limousin led to its mothers acquiring a reputation for breast-feeding their babies well beyond the time deemed appropriate by women in other regions – up to twenty months in some cases.[34] With children being raised on a diet that became less nutritionally sufficient as they grew, those very early years were fraught with risk. Still, there was no shortage of country wisdom available to an anxious new mother like Madeleine when it came to safeguarding her precious newborn baby. She should not show the child a mirror; that was to summon the devil. On no account should he be allowed to kiss a girl of similar age, for his speech would surely be retarded. And mothers should never cut their babies' fingernails in the first year unless they wanted the child to become a thief. Only once the child began toddling could a parent start to have a little more confidence in his or her physical stamina.[35]

To Madeleine's relief, two years passed without significant problems. The Coulaud family grew more and more used to each other's company. But a week before Madeleine's 22nd birthday, her little boy, aged just two and a half, died unexpectedly.

People who knew the family were horrified. For all that infant mortality was common, losing an only son seemed a particularly cruel blow. A glimmer of hope came to lighten an otherwise dark period in the New Year, when Madeleine became pregnant again. The baby was delivered safely in October 1853, but the joy of the second child's arrival could not match that of the first: it was a baby girl. That meant not the promise of a second male income, but another mouth to feed, then a dowry to find, and it was far more difficult to marry off a daughter than a son. By this time Madeleine was no longer working; the growing family were having to survive on a single income.[36]

Madeleine had another grievance, too. All was well so long as things worked in Coulaud's favour, but Madeleine soon learned that when displeased or intoxicated (or both), her husband was inclined to fly into a fearful rage. On one occasion, a violent outburst had resulted in his arrest, and Madeleine was forced to cope alone for two months as Coulaud served a short prison sentence.[37] His volatility boded ill. After such an auspicious beginning, the family's future now looked decidedly bleak.

❧

While the Coulaud family struggled to adapt to their altered circumstances, broader changes were taking place on a national scale. On 2 December 1852, Louis Napoleon made himself emperor, promising to repair the damage left in the wake of the Second Republic by restoring the authoritarian order of the Bonapartist regime. By the 1850s, agriculture had become stagnant in the Limousin and the region's industry was concentrated in Limoges.[38] Disillusioned by the Second Republic, eager for change, the people of the Limousin showed overwhelming support for the new emperor.[39] Three days after the coup, the Empire was officially declared in Bessines. The announcement was greeted by enthusiastic calls of '*Vive l'empereur!*', thunderous applause and sincere hopes for a brighter future.[40] Napoleon's mission to boost internal prosperity found keen support in the region.[41] Few recognised his campaign as an ingenious ploy designed to deflect attention from the staggering loss of liberty. The people of Bessines found it impossible not to be swept up in the heady allure of the new Empire. Indefatigable Republicans made themselves scarce. On 13 February 1853, the municipal council voted on a congratulatory message for his Highness following his recent marriage, and it was agreed that the town should find 45 francs to fund a bust of the emperor.[42] As the new Empire started to thrive, religious sentiment withered in the Limousin, and a distinctly materialistic mindset took its place.[43]

Léger Coulaud was not the only man swayed by the prevailing mood of optimism and possibility. Disguising its structural flaws with a gloss of gaiety and frivolous living, the Empire fostered a climate where self-improvement and prosperity seemed not only desirable but achievable. Coulaud found a kindred spirit in his neighbour Pierre-Louis Planchon, a watchmaker and jeweller.[44] The two men established a firm friendship. Madeleine had every reason to feel alarmed. Planchon was a confirmed scoundrel in his business dealings, and had already served a six-month prison sentence in 1845.[45] But the Limousin wife had no business telling her husband with whom he could and could not mix. She knew her place.

Sure enough, one impassioned bar-side conversation led to another, and before long, Coulaud and Planchon had devised a plan to guarantee a better future for themselves and their families. With their combined skills and business nous, they could surely fashion a coin which would pass for authentic currency. It needn't be a large operation, just the odd coin here and there in lieu of genuine payment to the innkeeper's wife, and soon their families could be enjoying comforts previously unknown to them. The risk seemed small. But one fateful day, Coulaud and his companion were caught.

Towards the end of October 1856, Coulaud and Planchon decided to visit the village fair in the nearby town of Ambazac.[46] Afterwards, they stopped at one of the local inns for dinner, and once they had eaten, Coulaud produced a 40 franc coin to pay their small bill, which only amounted to 5 francs. Growing suspicious, the landlady objected that she did not have enough change, and when one of the regulars entered the inn, she whispered to him to take a look at the coin which still sat in the middle of Coulaud and Planchon's table. Coulaud immediately leapt on the coin, determined that it should not be examined. Planchon had to think quickly to explain his companion's haste; Coulaud was not from the area and did not speak the local dialect, Planchon told them. The friends attempted to persuade the landlady a second time to take the coin, but by then, her trusted regular was certain: Coulaud's 40 franc payment was merely a 2 franc coin on which an attempt had been made – unsuccessfully – to alter the figures. It was a shoddy counterfeit, and the man gestured to the landlady not to accept the payment. Coulaud and Planchon were outraged. They became aggressive. Ambazac was a poverty-stricken town indeed, the men declared, for the sight of a 40 franc coin to cause such a stir!

In rural society, a slight on a countryman's *pays* was taken as a personal insult. Defensive, the regular suggested that the mayor be asked to check the coin, upon which Coulaud and Planchon hastily settled the bill with legitimate currency and left. But their concession came too late. The pair had already aroused concern. The police were promptly alerted, and the friends were stopped before they could leave the town. Coulaud was found to have more false coins on him, and it transpired that the pair had attempted the same ruse in another inn at lunchtime. Things quickly spiralled. Madeleine was startled when the authorities arrived at the couple's home to carry out a full search. Their personal belongings were ransacked, and in their bedroom, further damning items were found, including a receipt for the chemicals needed to carry out the forgery and the instructions for fashioning medals. Coulaud and his companion were certainly determined; from the evidence found in Coulaud's workshop, it became clear that they had attempted three different methods to produce their counterfeit currency.

In a small community like Bessines, such a crime was considered appalling. That it was committed by one of their number – an ostensibly respectable family man no less – rendered it particularly shocking. The authorities were severe. Léger Coulaud and Pierre-Louis Planchon were taken to trial in February 1857, where they were found guilty and banished to a penal colony in French Guyana to begin a sentence of hard labour.[47]

Separated from her husband, Madeleine Valadon was left in Bessines to bear the shame of Coulaud's offence and to bring up their three-year-old daughter, Marie-Alix, on her own without the support of her husband's income. It was at such times that the strength of the Limousin family network proved invaluable. But however much pity Madeleine's family felt for her plight, nobody had the resources to support an entire family. What they could offer was care for little Marie-Alix and employment for her mother.

By chance, one of Madeleine's distant cousins ran an inn at the centre of town. Although it was not an official coaching inn, when the nearest auberges at Morterolles and Chanteloube were full, Catherine le Cugy's establishment provided travellers with a comfortable alternative.[48] Separated from the road by a small courtyard, the 17th-century stone building did not appear vast from the outside. However, once a traveller stepped through the heavy front door, they would find that the rooms, divided over four floors and linked by a sprawling warren of dimly-lit corridors and passageways, were considerably bigger than those of the competitors. They were also reputed to be better kept, and the horses more spirited. Widow Guimbaud, as Catherine was known, ran the inn with a firm and capable hand, and she was helped by her childhood friend, Jeanne Dérozier, also a widow. To her mind, it was

The former Auberge Guimbaud in Bessines.

hardly heroic to assist a family member in difficulty; it was the natural thing to do. Besides, Madeleine's training as a linen maid gave her instant value to the business. Widow Guimbaud needed someone younger and fitter than herself with Madeleine's skills. And Madeleine needed employment which provided accommodation. It was a simple calculation.

Entrusting the care of Marie-Alix to the child's paternal grandparents in Le Mas Barbu, Madeleine began her new employment.

In a large establishment, the linen maid's role would have taken on a more administrative character, and consisted largely of checking in and distributing laundry, making minor repairs and ensuring all linen was in good order. But in a small enterprise like Widow Guimbaud's, the linen maid's responsibilities often encompassed those of a laundress and a chamber maid, too. These duties demanded far more physical stamina. Washing was done in huge vats known as *bujardiers* or *bujadous*, and women used a hot solution containing ash to clean the clothes.[49] The linen was then rinsed in the Gartempe river before being heaped onto a cart. Heaving great bundles of soaking linen resulted in aching limbs and the task became even more arduous when the weather turned cold. However, the shared experience of this onerous duty turned the riverside into an important space of feminine sociability. As they toiled by the water's edge, the women shared news, gave advice and gossiped to their hearts' content. It was a place to make companions and form alliances. Madeleine was not an extrovert, and many found her taciturn.[50] But if not friends, she made acquaintances, which was just as well. Madeleine needed the support of her peers now more than ever, for early in September 1859, a shocking piece of news reached Bessines: Léger Coulaud was dead.

How Madeleine's husband was killed remained a mystery. All she was told was that he had died on Montagne d'Argent (Silver Mountain) at five o'clock on 26 April.[51] The news had taken four months to reach Bessines. Now, Madeleine was truly alone.

But neither creditors nor hunger would show deference to grief. Madeleine had to continue working, and at Widow Guimbaud's, there was plenty of physical labour to divert melancholy thoughts.

❧

Limoges had long been treated as a convenient halfway point to break the journey between the South of France and the capital. And by the mid-19th century, painters like Corot were frequenting the region in search of landscape subjects.[52] Then in 1856, the Châteauroux–Limoges train line had opened, bringing with it an influx of engineers while it was worked on, and drawing even more visitors to the region once it was complete.[53] Situated as it was on the main route through Bessines, the Guimbaud inn attracted many passing travellers. There was no shortage of company for Madeleine while she worked – and much of it was male.

Madeleine turned 30 in 1860. Though a mother and a widow, she had retained the fresh-faced complexion so often associated with countryside youth, while her work had kept her body lean and supple. She was not unattractive, and as one of the younger women working at the inn, it was often on Madeleine that the roving male gaze first alighted.

'Don't go drawing attention to yourself,' Jeanne Dérozier warned when she noticed the interest her colleague was attracting.[54]

But Madeleine had no time for interference. And, just as she was inclined to become stubborn and quick-tempered when she felt cornered, it was not her way to meekly comply when others interfered in her business.[55] Why should anyone begrudge her pleasure? After all she had suffered, did she not deserve the flattery of male attention if the opportunity presented itself? Madeleine was defiant. She would do as she pleased.

❧

The winter of 1864/65 was especially cold. Snow first fell in early December.[56] For much of January 1865, the sky was dreary, the snow flurries persistent and the cold unrelenting. And by February, Madeleine was pregnant.

'If only you had not drawn attention to yourself,' Jeanne lamented.[57]

The riverside was soon abuzz with Madeleine's news. A widow's pregnancy six years after the death of her husband was a titillating scandal. But by far the most intriguing question remained: who was the father?

Stories began to circulate. It was some local Don Juan; no, it was a painter, visiting from Paris; certainly not, it was one of those travellers who had been staying at the inn. With limited staff, a variable client base and all those dark, shadowy corners, the auberge was fertile ground for sordid affairs.

Madeleine steadfastly refused to satisfy curiosity. Intrusion annoyed her. As her pregnancy advanced, she enjoyed goading the village gossip machine by baiting it with red herrings. She had been seduced that cold winter by a miller, Madeleine would tell some people, later adding that the offender had subsequently been crushed under his own millstone, which she felt to be suitable penance for his crime.[58] Then, she would assure someone else that her seducer was a construction engineer, and that justice had been served when he fell from a bridge.

Accounts varied so widely that locals had to resign themselves to ignorance. And when all was said and done, Madeleine was a local girl, and village loyalty took precedence in such cases, particularly if the culprit was an outsider as people suspected. Nobody ostracised the cartwright's daughter, and Widow Guimbaud stood firmly by her cousin, allowing her to stay on at the inn and to see out her labour and convalescence there.

Finally, after months of struggling up and down the hefty, dark stairs to complete her chores under the weight of her swollen belly, at six o'clock in the morning on 23 September 1865, Madeleine gave birth to a baby girl.

That poignant first encounter between mother and child was intensified by circumstance. The baby had a strong little body, clear blue eyes and a well-defined chin – a tiny person already.[59] Motherhood was familiar territory to Madeleine, but this time she was an only parent. There would be an inherent closeness to this helpless infant, a bond different from that which she had previously experienced. And yet now more than ever, Madeleine needed her child to be capable of surviving without her constant attention.

As Madeleine lay contemplating the new bundle of life in her arms, her mother's cousins François Peignaud and Clément Dony went to the *mairie* to make the requisite declaration of the child's birth, and a neighbour, Armand Chazeaud, agreed to join them to act as a witness.[60] Peignaud and Dony had performed the same service after the birth of Marie-Alix. But the sisters' birth certificates had crucial differences. Where Marie-Alix was a Coulaud, Madeleine's new baby took her maiden name, Valadon. She was given the forename Marie-Clémentine, combining the names of the two godparents Madeleine already had in mind, Clément Masbey and Marie-Céline Coulaud.[61] But those names could not efface the significance of two other words: 'father unknown'.

So much importance was placed on the father's role in the Limousin, that some parts of the region upheld the custom of the father taking to bed and receiving visitors following his wife's safe delivery of a child.[62] From the very first, Marie-Clémentine was a social deviant. Fatherless, her identity was incomplete, unstable, mercurial.

And the only parental bond the little girl had was about to be put to the test.

CHAPTER 2

Places to Call Home

*Si l'un pourtàvo sà penà ô marcha per là vendre, obe
là changeà, chacu s'en tornario en la souà.*

(If everyone took their troubles to market to sell or
exchange, each would return with his or her own.)

<small>OLD LIMOUSIN PROVERB[1]</small>

Marie-Clémentine Valadon spent the first few months of her life in a cradle, tucked discreetly out of view at the busy Guimbaud inn. As soon as she was able, Madeleine resumed her duties, stopping every so often to breastfeed her newborn daughter before returning to her work. She tried as best she might to engineer a seamless blend between her new, unplanned role as a mature single mother and her old life as a capable linen maid without obvious attachments. But it soon became clear that Marie-Clémentine's place at the Guimbaud inn could only be a temporary solution. A sleeping baby, recently fed and satisfied, might pass unnoticed; a tearful, hungry infant was less easily concealed. No longer the energetic girl just out of her teens who had given birth to little Léger and Marie-Alix more than ten years ago, Madeleine could not help but feel the strain. It was decided that as soon as she was weaned, Marie-Clémentine must be found an alternative home and carer.

The little girl's grandmother, Marie Dony, seemed the obvious choice. *Lo grando-maï*, the grandmother, commanded infinite respect in Limousin families. Even when she was not the primary carer, the grandmother was typically consulted on all matters relating to the successful rearing of the family's younger members.[2] In addition, Marie Dony lived nearby, and she was widowed and did not work, so would surely be glad of the company and distraction.

And so, no sooner was she weaned from breast milk than Marie-Clémentine was separated from her mother and sent to live with her grandmother.

At times, it seemed as though Madeleine courted tragedy. Marie-Clémentine had barely been living in her grandmother's home a few months when the old lady died.[3] Madeleine had now lost both her parents – and at only one-and-a-half, Marie-Clémentine became homeless for the second time in her life.

Becoming a full-time mother was not an option, and so Madeleine took the only choice available to her: Marie-Clémentine would have to be sent to Le Mas Barbu to be cared for, just like her half-sister. Little Marie-Clémentine would be looked after by Madeleine's 'cousins', a deceptive term, since it was often applied loosely in rural society to refer to a relative so distant that nobody could recall the precise connection.[4] The move would take Marie-Clémentine even further from her mother. Le Mas Barbu was situated only two miles out of Bessines, though working long hours and lacking transport, daily trips down the winding roads between the town and the commune were out of the question. Still, Madeleine's determination to keep her child, even at the cost of physical separation, was valiant under the circumstances. In the first half of the 19th century, there was one infanticide every 320 births in the department of the Haute-Vienne, and one in 24 infants was abandoned.[5] Those figures were startlingly high by comparison with the neighbouring departments of the Corrèze and the Creuse. The offenders were nearly always impoverished single mothers. Poverty and shame could be a deadly combination, enough even to override the usually unshakeable Limousin sense of family. But Madeleine held firm. She would not give Marie-Clémentine up.

Marie-Clémentine's new home was a substantial commune, a cluster of stone cottages, farmhouses and barns clinging to a steep hillside. At the entrance to the village was an ancient stone cross, an edifice used in times gone by to mark the first stopping point of both funeral processions and the ceremony of Rogations, when the priest would bless the crops before Ascension.[6] The main road running through the village twisted and turned its way up the hillside, weaving around the buildings and creating a network of sloping streets and narrow passageways. It could be perilous underfoot when the first frosts arrived, but on fine days, the views down into the valley below were glorious, while the steep incline of the streets provided the perfect terrain for simple children's games. Buttons, stones, marbles, and for the more fortunate, even coins, could be rolled down the hill.[7] Streams provided hours of entertainment when frozen in the winter and refreshed hot little feet in the summer. Boys would play catch around the buildings and in the road, while girls sat in doorways nursing crude corn dollies. This was where Marie-Clémentine would take her first uncertain steps, where she would be introduced to many local peasant foods and would make her first social encounters.

The toddler had a rounded face with clear skin, a pretty little mouth with soft, rosebud lips, and that firm jawline. Her enormous eyes were an exquisite shade of light blue, becoming darker at the edge of the iris, and above them, her jet black eyebrows gave her a dramatic appearance. Her hair soon settled into delicious tones of golden brown, which fell in soft, loose curls about her face. Though still only small, it was already clear: Marie-Clémentine was going to be a striking child.

As Marie-Clémentine grew and discovered more of the world, Madeleine continued to toil to pay for the upkeep of her two daughters. Had the girls been closer in age, Madeleine might have had the consolation that they would offer each other companionship. But the twelve-year age gap was a frontier between two distinct worlds. Increasingly, the family was functioning as three individuals, with separate lives and concerns. For Madeleine, all other immediate family ties had expired, while her work, already irksome, was only becoming more so with age and growing resentment. Madeleine was tired and embittered. She longed for some relief.

It came as no surprise, then, when word began to spread in Bessines that Madeleine had been seen with one of the engineers employed to work on the new railway in the nearby town of Saint-Sulpice-Laurière.[8]

❧

At the end of 1865, an influx of some 50 able-bodied men had given cause for great excitement among the single women of Bessines.[9] The following year, the number of employees had increased to 500.[10] It was a matter of considerable interest among locals. Everybody was talking about the new railway.

Since the first tracks were laid in France in the early 19th century, the railway had revolutionised national travel and transformed conceptions of space and time. Until that point, a man could not conceive of travelling any faster than his horse might gallop. Now, suddenly, huge steaming monsters of iron could take him to towns and cities that he had heard of, but never dreamed he might one day visit.[11] In just a few hours, a train could travel the distance it would take a *diligence* or stagecoach more than two days to cover. Although the French rail network was slower to develop than its British counterpart, steadily, surely, the capital was reaching arms of modernity out to the comparatively regressive provinces, beckoning country folk with the promise of opportunities, advancement and adventure.[12] Of course, like any newfangled invention, the railway had its adversaries. Being subjected to such a rapid change of climate would be catastrophic for the respiratory system, doctors warned.[13] And that was to say nothing of the detrimental effect of the change of diet. Some peasants too remained incredulous; what use was the railway to them when they only need travel as far as the next town? What business did they have going any further?

But for many, the possibilities opened up by the railway were simply marvellous. Everyone in the Limousin had heard retold the tale of Martin Nadaud, the humble stonemason from the neighbouring department of the Creuse. As a young boy, Nadaud would travel every year on foot to Paris; by 1849, he dressed as a gentleman and was elected member of Parliament.[14] The story served as a glittering reminder that in Paris, peasants really could become kings. It was said that even women could hope for a better lot – more freedom – in the capital. So when the Limoges–Poitiers line via Saint-Sulpice-Laurière finally opened just before Christmas in 1867, it was greeted with widespread enthusiasm in the Limousin.[15] The railway was a symbol of possibility and progress, and anyone involved in its construction or maintenance was venerated and seen to radiate an aura of glory.

For many country folk, the railway was Paris. Its gleaming tracks brought tales of success, prosperity and realised dreams to the provinces, qualities with which the capital was increasingly seen as synonymous. For a countrywoman like Madeleine, short on money and luck, overworked, and whose future appeared only to offer more of the same, those dazzling steel tracks represented a chance. All at once, resignation turned to hope. Suddenly, Madeleine could see clearly. If she stayed in Bessines, her future was mapped out – and it was bleak. But if she boarded the train to Paris, anything was possible – perhaps even happiness.

Jeanne and Widow Guimbaud were horrified when, not five years after Marie-Clémentine's birth, Madeleine announced that her mind was made up: she was going to start a new life in Paris.

'What on earth will you do in Paris?' Jeanne exclaimed, 'It's like a moth to a flame. The grass is no greener up there, you know.'[16]

But her colleagues' objections merely strengthened Madeleine's resolve. She had an aunt on her father's side living in the capital on the Ile Saint-Louis, she told them.[17] It was not a permanent solution, but Madeleine felt sure that Marie-Anne Valadon would put her and her girls up until she could make alternative arrangements.

When word got out about Madeleine's plan, people suspected her new beau to be at the root of her decision. But Madeleine had loftier aspirations. She envied those she had seen escape the monotonous, suffocating existence to which she felt condemned. Now, at last, Madeleine felt that she too could have a fresh start. Wages in the city were higher – a powerful incentive now that Marie-Alix too was old enough to work – and she and her daughters could be a proper family.

For all that the railway symbolised progress, making use of it came at a cost. A linen maid in the provinces could seldom expect to earn more than 2 francs 50, perhaps 3 francs a day.[18] Being under seven, Marie-Clémentine could travel half price; but even then, at nearly 25 francs a full price ticket, relocating the family to Paris would cost Madeleine at least a month's wages.[19] And then a journey undertaken in one of the cheapest seats was tedious and deeply uncomfortable. Third-class passengers were squeezed into cramped carriages, where they would be obliged to perch on hard wooden seats as the steam train trundled through the countryside. A train leaving Saint-Sulpice-Laurière at 9.15 in the morning would not arrive in Paris until shortly before midnight, an exhausting journey for Madeleine and the teenage Marie-Alix, still more so for the four- or five-year-old Marie-Clémentine.[20] But

Madeleine knew countless traditional country songs and tales if little Marie-Clémentine needed to be entertained en route. The mother considered the fatigue, discomfort and expense a price worth paying, for of one thing she was certain: she was never coming back to Bessines.

'I never saw anything more beautiful and gay than Paris,' Queen Victoria had declared when she visited the capital in 1855.[21] For a small, impoverished child of the country like Marie-Clémentine, accustomed to the green hills and cattle-studded pastures of the Limousin and for whom the bright colours and noise of Bessines' modest weekly market was the only highlight, that first glimpse of Paris's spectacular skyline through the carriage window could only be more marvellous. Paris was vast.

The capital's population had doubled in the first half of the 19th century, so that by 1850 it had reached 1 million.[22] Under the Second Empire, it merely continued to expand. At Baron Haussmann's command, the Parisian landscape had been radically transformed, while the Empire continued to project an enviable image of glamour and carefree pleasure. For hopeful provincials, the draw was irresistible.

In reality, by the 1860s, cracks were forming beneath the Empire's lavish veneer. The working classes were growing more fretful, the Emperor's foreign policy struck many as ill-advised and since the spectacular climax of the 1867 Exposition Universelle, everyday life had felt flat and uneventful. But Madeleine, like so many other migrants from the countryside, was blissfully unaware of the widening fault lines. Paris remained a utopian emblem of good living and possibility.

For a newcomer to the city in search of a better life, ignorant (or at least dismissive) of wider problems, the Ile Saint-Louis was an ideal destination to seek shelter. Comprising a network of narrow streets lined with tall, 17th-century buildings, it felt like a miniature, self-contained city, and was seemingly immune to the rumblings of discontent now sounding in the world outside. It exuded a near puritanical aura, having remained largely unaffected by the revolts which had plagued the rest of Paris over the last 150 years.[23] It was little wonder that it had become a favoured haunt of such bohemian literary and artistic figures as Baudelaire and Delacroix. From this peaceful vantage point, a person could lose themselves in the hypnotic rhythm of barges and laundry boats drifting, unhurried, up and down the Seine.[24]

But if at first the Valadon family's temporary home offered protection from the troubles that were brewing, they could not be shielded indefinitely. In bringing her girls to Paris at the dawn of the new decade, Madeleine had sorely mistimed their move. In the summer of 1870, daily life in the capital was turned on its head.[25]

In July 1870, a Prussian prince came forward as a candidate for the vacant Spanish throne, placing France's southern frontier under immediate threat.[26] A fierce French reaction led to the Prussian candidacy being withdrawn. But fearing a second attempt to seize power, France declared war on Prussia on 19 July 1870. It was an ill-judged decision. On 1 September 1870, Napoleon III was defeated at the battle of Sedan and captured. The Empire was officially over.

With the Emperor gone, people assumed that life would return to normal. But they were wrong. The Prussians stormed Paris, and a full-scale siege set in. The provisional government, now based in Tours, continued to fight, but in vain. For four months, daily life in Paris was in uproar. Communications were cut off, food shortages spiralled into starvation. The rich defiantly turned sewer rats into patés; the poor were reduced to eating cats and dogs. Once a glamorous capital famed for luxurious living, Paris was now a war zone scarred by poverty and hunger.

'You talk only about what is eaten, can be eaten, or can be found to eat,' wrote Edmond de Goncourt on 8 December 1870.[27]

'Conversation does not go beyond that.' Madeleine and her daughters' first Christmas in Paris should have been a happy, hopeful occasion. Instead, it was grim. As one Parisian remarked, that 25 December:

> No one had the heart to amuse himself. With what melancholy bitterness one remembers the sparkling quality of Paris, of our Paris, in those days that led up to the 1st of January? What animation on our boulevards and streets! How the carriages rolled joyously by the thousand along the macadam! What gaiety in the lights in the windows of the department stores decorated for this holiday! ... And the long, the interminable line of small booths which imprinted on all our boulevards such a charming character of popular joy! Alas! All that was far in the past! A grey sky, full of snow weighed down on a mournful city![28]

By mid-December, even horsemeat had been rationed.[29] In the New Year, the already poor quality bread was rationed as well, while the price of un-rationed foods rocketed. Butter was eight times its normal price. The cost of eggs increased fourteenfold. 'We are moving fast towards starvation,' Edmond de Goncourt exclaimed.[30]

The capital was in chaos – and Madeleine's situation was becoming desperate. Though Marie-Alix was now of working age, Marie-Clémentine was entirely reliant on her mother. All around Madeleine raged the pervading belief that women offered inadequate protection for the capital's children in their men's absence.[31] For many, the Prussian offensive could only be thwarted with physical strength, something the weaker sex was ill-equipped to provide. Deceived in her vision of Paris, urgently needing work and affordable accommodation in a strange, war-ravaged city, Madeleine, like so many migrants before her, frantically sought out something familiar.[32]

Then, at last, Madeleine's luck turned. She came across Montmartre.

With its windmills, its clear air and the old-fashioned, village feel of its higgledy-piggledy houses perched on a slope, few places recalled the Limousin countryside so vividly as Montmartre.[33] It was up to 129 metres above sea level at the highest point. Why, with its narrow, winding streets and alleys, and its cottages clinging to the hillside, a person could have believed themselves in Le Mas Barbu. The bustling Rue Lepic and the Place des Abbesses readily called to mind Bessines' town square on a busy market day. And all around, steep, grassy banks rose up protectively, hillside homes bloomed with flowers, old men installed in wrought iron chairs sat outside doorways and set the world to rights, children played in the street and women chatted and gossiped as they made their way to fill baskets with provisions. At last, Madeleine had found somewhere familiar, reassuring, comforting. Montmartre felt like home.

❧

Madeleine could not have fully comprehended the intricacies of the area's history at the time, but like herself, Montmartre had had a chequered past.

The area took its name, the most popular legend held, from one of Paris's first martyrs. Around AD 250, an old man named Denis, the first bishop of Paris, was arrested for refusing to accept the Roman Emperor's divinity. He and two of his colleagues were decapitated on the hill of Montmartre, and the story went that afterwards, he picked up his own head, washed it and continued walking for 6,000 paces (or six miles, depending on which version of the legend was recounted). A pious woman took pity on him and, taking the severed head out of his arms, enabled Denis to die. A chapel was built where he finally fell and the area became known as 'Mont des Martyrs', then 'Montmartre'.

In 1133, Louis VI acquired the site and the now derelict chapel, and built the church of Saint-Pierre de Montmartre, as well as founding an abbey, whose buildings and gardens came to occupy most of Montmartre. A chapel was also built on the site where Denis's murder was believed to have taken place. For many years, an order of Benedictine nuns reigned over Montmartre, owning most of its buildings and land (which included vineyards), while pilgrims flocked to its summit to pay homage to the cult of martyrs. Over time, however, the nuns' wealth increased and through their questionable use of these funds, the sisters earned themselves a reputation for frivolity and corruption. Still, despite popular jokes about their doubtful morals, the nuns ruled until the Revolution, when the abbey and its chapel were destroyed. At the same time, Montmartre (which was still administratively considered outside the limits of Paris) became more clearly defined in Parisian eyes when it was officially re-categorised the 'commune' of Montmartre.

But aside from its religious associations, Montmartre's elevation and strategic position had also seen it play a pivotal role in numerous military exploits. It was used variously by the Normans, Otto II, and Henry IV, and had acted as a lookout point for Joseph Bonaparte, the former King of Spain, in 1814 when Prussian, Austrian and Russian armies invaded Paris. The Russians too recognised Montmartre's tactical advantages, and occupied the area using the hill for their artillery as they bombarded the city. It was then fortified in 1815, but escaped further attack.

Over the course of the nuns' rule, the number of pilgrims had gradually dwindled as rumours spread that the summit of the Butte was haunted by evil spirits. But by the 18th century, Montmartre was attracting interest for other reasons, namely its vineyards and its mills. The windmills first started appearing in the 16th century, and were used for grinding wheat and pressing grapes.

The conical landmarks with their elegant sails soon came to symbolise Montmartre and enterprising owners set up sideline businesses in the hospitality trade. Henceforward, a new kind of pilgrim could be found in Montmartre: every Sunday, people would climb the steep slopes to the windmills where they could relax beneath the shade of the mills' sails, and enjoy a glass of cheap wine, since as a 'commune libre', Montmartre was exempt from city taxes.[34] (During the 1814 siege of Paris, Montmartre's mills found further, unsought fame when the miller M. Debray was killed defending his property against the Russians, who nailed his quartered corpse to the wings of his mill.[35]) At one time, more than 30 of these triumphant edifices imprinted their proud silhouettes against the Montmartre skyline. If by the time Madeleine arrived their number had significantly reduced, their memory continued to shape perceptions of the area.

Le Moulin de la Galette.
Collection Société le Vieux Montmartre/Musée de Montmartre

The operation of gypsum mines to provide the material necessary for the world-famous plaster of Paris added yet another layer to Montmartre's character. The earliest mining activity dated back to Gallo-Roman times, and by the 19th century a substantial industry had built up. An unsavoury consequence of this was the proliferation of thieves and drunks, who came to seek shelter in the great cavernous pits, tainting Montmartre's reputation. But by mid-century, the quarries' closure restored Montmartre's respectability, and in 1860 Paris embraced the northern 'commune' as part of its own identity, by annexing Montmartre to the city and turning it into the 18th arrondissement. The wall of the *Ferme générale* tax operation erected in the 1780s (which imposed a tax on merchandise being brought into the city) was torn down and the sparkling new Boulevard de Clichy and the Boulevard de Rochechouart rose up in its wake. The boulevards made the area more accessible, but they also reiterated its independence by physically segregating it from the rest of the city.[36] From then on, Montmartre was both part of Paris, and clearly separate; at one with the quickly modernising city, yet retaining its own, distinct identity and otherworldly feel. It was a *quartier* lost in time.

Like Montmartre itself, Madeleine had come to have an ambivalent relationship with the capital; she was at once attracted by its novelty, yet anxious; hungry to taste its opportunities and its buzz, but wary of relinquishing the traditional way of life she knew so well.

The Montmartre Madeleine first discovered extended a rural welcome in an otherwise hostile metropolis. She soon learned that the lower part of Montmartre was dominated by cabarets, dance halls and entertainment venues, a legacy of the fiscal wall, which had caused a vibrant leisure and entertainment industry to blossom on the Montmartre side where wine was inexpensive.[37] But besides the cheap rents (which could be found throughout the former commune), the upper part of Montmartre also boasted a peaceful atmosphere and so had begun to attract workers and artists. The former had found themselves driven out of the city centre, unable to afford the elevated living costs of Haussmann's grand, multi-storey apartment buildings. The artists, who frequently shared the workers' precarious financial situation, found cheap studios and spectacular views to paint. But more than that: by the mid-19th century, paint and politics had become indissociable. Montmartre provided a perfect forum for aesthetic polemics.

Increasingly, a new generation of artists were finding the creative projects which so excited them systematically rebuffed by the official art bodies.[38] It was exasperating. Did the jury of the Salon, that 'great event' of the artistic world, never tire of the tedious repertoire of historical events and myths that had formed the mainstay of Salon paintings for so long? Did they not feel ridiculed being sold the blatant lie of highly finished paint surfaces, of bodies without a blemish, of landscapes stripped of all signs of modernity? Was contemporary life, the sweat and odour of real men and women, not deserving of a place on the Salon walls?

Young artists huddled around tables in Montmartre's cafés, sharing their deepest frustrations, breathing life into their most keenly held ideas. Just a few streets away from the Cimetière de Montmartre, Édouard Manet, the *enfant terrible* of the contemporary art world, could be found at his regular table in the Café Guerbois surrounded by reverent confrères, who would in time become famous in their own right.[39] When Manet spoke, his blue eyes sparkled, his body leant forwards persuasively, and an artistic revolution felt achievable. The atmosphere was electric, the conversation passionate – often heated, but always exciting. The discussions 'kept our wits sharpened,' Claude Monet later recalled, 'they encouraged us with stores of enthusiasm that for weeks and weeks kept us up.'[40] And though the war caused many of the artists

Young women in the Rue Cortot, c. 1900.
Collection Société le Vieux Montmartre/Musée de Montmartre

to leave the capital, it proved merely a temporary migration. At the time Madeleine and her daughters arrived in Montmartre, the artists had firmly marked their patch.

Hence by the mid-19th century, Montmartre had become known as a pleasure-seeker's paradise, a common man's refuge and a crucible of creativity. It was a district infused with quaint rustic charm, at once affordable, lively in parts, tranquil in others and seemingly free from the constraints that stifled the rest of Paris. The spirit of revolution felt ingrained in its very soil. In Montmartre, anything seemed possible.

Madeleine was lucky. When the roads which had paralleled the old fiscal wall had fused creating the Boulevard de Clichy and the Boulevard de Rochechouart, business-minded landlords spotted an opportunity to increase their assets.[41] Cheap studios and apartments began to spring up on either side of the boulevard. And it was here, on the Boulevard de Rochechouart, that Madeleine eventually found modestly priced lodgings in one of the newly constructed tenement buildings.

Running along the southern edge of Montmartre, the Boulevard de Rochechouart catered to all Madeleine's needs. There, she could enjoy the reassurance of being close to the traditional way of life which characterised Montmartre, while still tasting all the colour and vibrancy that had initially tempted her to Paris. Throughout the siege, the Boulevard de Rochechouart remained a lively street. There was always something happening: movement, people, the rumble of carriage wheels, voices – life. Just a short walk from the apartment was the Elysée-Montmartre, a popular dance hall, where, at only 1 franc entrance, the 'eccentric clientele' included hordes of young bachelors and a good helping of the quartier's *grisettes* (low-paid, working-class girls who turned to casual prostitution to make ends meet).[42] Even during the siege, and despite the constraints imposed on public entertainment, the Elysée-Montmartre remained active, serving as both a workshop for producing the balloons used to fly post out of the capital, and as a hospital.[43] It was also the site of many ostensibly 'non-political meetings', as was the nearby Folies-Bergère, where crowds had gathered in the middle of September 1870 to listen to a stirring speech by General Gustave Cluseret.[44] There may have been little dancing in the music halls, but the street was bustling and full of people. 'Since Paris has become a prisoner, it lives on the boulevard,' commented Juliette Lamber Adam.[45] 'The whole boulevard is like a fair,' seconded Edmond de Goncourt.[46]

For Marie-Clémentine, it was an extraordinary time to discover her country's capital. And as Madeleine, to her relief, finally found work as a charwoman, and the heady draw of city life and boys kept the teenage Marie-Alix otherwise disposed, the concierge became Marie-Clémentine's intermittent supervisor, and the street her playground. 'The streets of Montmartre were home to me,' she recalled many years later. 'It was only in the streets that there was excitement and love and ideas – what other children found around their dining-room tables.'[47]

Not yet six, Marie-Clémentine was already an assured tomboy. Small and impressively agile with her unkempt, cognac-coloured hair and her huge, wide-set blue eyes, she turned heads as she darted about the street. Those enormous eyes coupled with her broad forehead gave her an appealing look of innocent sweetness. It was deceptive. She was a wilful child and ran barefoot whenever possible, revelling in the dirt of the streets and doing just as she pleased. The little girl was always getting up to mischief, though mostly preferred to conduct her escapades alone. She was a sensitive child and found solace in her vivid imagination, inhabiting a world of which only she seemed aware. Notwithstanding, she talked to strangers unselfconsciously, and was perfectly at ease sharing her opinions and advice in a matter-of-fact manner quite in advance of her years. However, when displeased, she was in possession of a fearsome temper, and had been known to fling stones or scratch when consumed by one of her rages. Neighbours called her 'the little Valadon terror', though few could suppress a respectful tone when they did.[48]

Marie-Clémentine's wild behaviour was hardly surprising. A naturally headstrong child left to discover new surroundings in a city which was itself in chaos was bound to grow even more unruly. Meanwhile, the capital was no closer to seeing order restored.

❧

Finally, at the end of January 1871, the Prussians' bombardment of the city forced France's president, General Trochu, to concede that he must ask Bismarck for an armistice.[49] France had to surrender Alsace and Lorraine, and pay 50 billion francs of war indemnity. But by far the most painful loss was that of national pride.

Towards the end of the siege, the government had established an artillery park of over 200 guns at Montmartre, weapons which were funded by public subscription.[51] When the government now asked for the guns to be returned, they met with vehement opposition. At the end of February, detachments of the National Guards seized the guns, and when loyal French Army troops tried to reclaim them at the end of March, their opponents fought back viciously. The breaking point came when, in a courtyard in the Rue de Rosiers, the National Guards lynched and shot two elderly generals. The case of the Montmartre guns was a final straw to topple an already overloaded beast of burden. Suddenly, the whole balance of power was upset. Paris was no longer fighting the Prussians – it was fighting itself.

Revolutionaries set up a rival regime in Paris which assumed the title of the Commune de Paris. The Commune united disgruntled members of a number of different parties. There were Jacobins, radical feminists, Proudhonians, veterans of the revolutions of 1851, 1848 and even 1830. The interests varied, but they shared a single grievance: all were deeply unsatisfied with the government of Paris. The Commune set up its headquarters in the Hôtel de Ville. Immediately, in Versailles, Thiers' party began planning the reconquest of Paris. And then there broke out one of the bloodiest civil wars France had ever seen.

Still smarting from the Prussian siege, citizens watched in horror as the streets of Paris were again reduced to a scene of devastation. Thiers' private house was demolished. The Vendôme column, erected by Napoleon Bonaparte to celebrate the victories of 1805, was torn down. Violence swept across the city. Barricades were erected and buildings mercilessly burned to the ground. Paris was in chaos. Finally, Thiers' army succeeded in entering the capital, and for a week which became known as '*la semaine sanglante*' (the bloody week), a horrific confrontation played out.

Just streets away from the Valadons' home, the radical feminist Louise Michel, dressed in a National Guard's uniform, headed the Women's Battalion as it confronted the Versaillais Generals de Ladmirault and Clinchant.[52] The Rue des Rosiers was again the scene of bloodshed when around 50 Communards were shepherded together and shot. One evening, Parisian blood ran cold when people noticed the sky lit with a furious glow and realised the cause: it was the burning edifice of the Tuileries Palace. Wild *pétroleuses* (lower-class, female supporters of the Commune and arsonists) hurled fireballs through the windows of bourgeois homes; Parisian turned on Parisian. Then came one of the most sickening acts the Communards had yet committed: the Archbishop of Paris, who had been taken hostage, was executed.

Thiers' army eventually emerged victorious against the Communards and by the end of May, the conflict was over. But the toll was horrifying; some 20,000 Parisians lost their lives and the city's landscape was unrecognisable.

The Paris that Madeleine beheld in 1871 was as far removed as could be imagined from the ideal she had anticipated. Buildings were in ruins. In the smoking, barricade-littered streets, the sounds were alarming. Edmond de Goncourt described 'frightening noises: fusillades and collapsing houses'.[53] Paris was a pitiful shadow of the marvellous city it had been. 'In the wind this evening the Commune's notices, which have been pulled off the walls, make a sound like dead leaves chased by an autumn whirlwind on the pavement,' de Goncourt observed. But from the ashes of the Commune, the seeds of hope were undeniably breaking through, for amid the moans of a haggard city, 'you hear the stiff flapping of brand-new tricolor flags.' Paris was bruised, but it was not beaten. Soon, the capital's emigrants were flooding back. 'Parisian life [...] is being reborn,' triumphed de Goncourt on 29 May 1871.[54] All at once, the streets were filled with Parisians, 'taking possession of their city once again'. Life and energy were being breathed back into the glorious city. Parisians had returned, defiant and proud.

Madeleine was not a politically minded woman. In Bessines, politics was something that got the men fired up and occasionally caused a heated dispute in the café. There, Madeleine's life had a more immediate and practical focus: how many beds needed changing that day? Was it so cold that morning that she would have to break the ice off the surface of the river, only to feel the ache and chill of the glacial water on her fingers as she rinsed the clothes? And most of all, where would the next meal be coming from?

By contrast, in Paris, it seemed impossible to escape politics. As Napoleon III strode across the battlefield at Sedan, on street corners, workmen muttered about flawed military strategy. As the Prussians were planning their next move, the women in the queue outside the butcher's offered a commentary on the action. When word spread along the Boulevard de Rochechouart that innocent blood had been shed in a street just like Madeleine's, when barricades obstructed the route to work, when the grocer was asking ten times the usual price for a bag of potatoes and milk was unavailable, politics suddenly seemed very real and very tangible indeed.[55]

Madeleine was utterly dismayed by the Paris she had discovered. Even before the atrocities of the Commune – unimaginable for a woman raised in the small rural community of Bessines – she had found the employment situation far less utopian than she had been led to believe. An experienced linen maid was a valuable asset. It was an estimable skill. And Madeleine had years of experience. But acquiring such a position in Paris required good interpersonal skills and the ability to promote oneself; Madeleine boasted neither.

She was overqualified to take the job that she did. Cleaning and scrubbing offices was demeaning.

Marie-Alix had adapted admirably to her new life. She had attracted the attentions of a young man named Georges; there was already talk of marriage.[56] Madeleine had no cause to worry about her eldest daughter. But in all other respects, Madeleine was feeling demoralised, disenchanted, betrayed.

With heavy heart, Madeleine discovered that neighbourhood gossips thrived as much in Paris as they did in Bessines. Before long, Madeleine's name was being whispered in immoral connection with a number of local widowers.[57] Several swore they had smelled alcohol on her breath as she passed them on the boulevard. That Madeleine Valadon was simply crazy, children hissed, a village fool, come to Paris thinking she could make a fortune. And nobody could recall ever having seen her express affection towards Marie-Clémentine, nor respond kindly to the youngster's approaches. People felt certain that, behind closed doors, the mother must issue the most terrible beatings. It was little wonder, neighbours concluded, that the daughter behaved so badly. For many, Madeleine was as far removed from the maternal ideal as could be imagined.

It seemed everything in Madeleine's conduct gave rise to suspicion. In the wake of the Prussian siege and the Commune, Parisians harboured a profound distrust of that which could not be seen. And Madeleine was quiet, docile and discreet.[58] She worked steadily and kept her opinions – and her disappointment – to herself. Physically too, she was a pitiful figure.[59] Her body was hunched, her shoulders stooping, and her furrowed brow gave her a permanently fraught expression. Her centre-parted hair was swept back and severe, while her heavy-lidded, blue-eyed gaze seemed designed to keep the world at a distance. And though she was just 40, work had now given her once-supple body the appearance of one half that again.

Marie-Clémentine's unruly behaviour was a burden too many. It was not that Madeleine lacked maternal empathy. Though the mother appeared a sour-faced and embittered contrast to her vigorous daughter, the pair shared a complex bond, both invisible and indivisible. More than once, Madeleine had had the opportunity to deny her daughter. She could have given her up as a baby or abandoned her and gone alone to Paris. Every time, she had recognised her responsibility towards the youngster and stood by her, quietly, assuredly, claiming her as her own. Years later, few could deny that Madeleine was probably the only human being who truly understood the will-o'-the-wisp, elfin creature she had given birth to.[60]

But now, Madeleine had seen the very worst side of Parisian street life. She could not work and supervise her daughter as well. More than anything, she had seen only too clearly how miserable a woman's life could be when she lacked appropriate skills. If Marie-Clémentine was to be spared the same fate, she must have what Madeleine had been denied: structure and a formal education.

So it was that Marie-Clémentine made her first encounter with an institution.

CHAPTER 3

Testing the Line

L'un ne po pa tropà lo luno en là den.
(You can't catch the moon with your teeth.)
OLD LIMOUSIN PROVERB[1]

'A woman's greatest error is to attempt to be a man,' proclaimed the late 18th- to early 19th-century moralist and Christian philosopher M. de Maistre, 'and wanting to be a man is wanting to be wise. A woman should not pursue any knowledge which interferes with her duties; a woman's merit is to make her husband happy, to raise her children and to make men [...] as soon as she seeks to emulate man, she is no more than a monkey; women have never produced any great works in any genre [...] there are few things more dangerous for a woman than science [...] It is far easier to marry off a tart than it is a wise woman.'[2]

While de Maistre's opinion was not universally held in such an undiluted form in the 19th century, his principle was widely accepted: women were physiologically, intellectually and emotionally different from men, and for many, that meant inferior. In the 1870s, French society was underpinned by a deep-seated gender bias. Conservative social discourse maintained that female brains were smaller (ergo substandard), more prone to emotion and sentiment, and that women were therefore best suited to bearing and raising children, no more. To develop a woman's intellectual faculties was to jeopardise her breeding capacity – a school of thought which found keen endorsement in the fields of science and history.

In such a climate, few issues caused blood to boil more fervently than that of female education. Even those considered more liberal thinkers were inclined to agree that a woman's place was in the home, that her proper role was that of wife and mother, and that academic and serious artistic pursuits were neither her priority nor her strength. 'What is a man's vocation?' asked philosophical writers Jules and Gustave Simon, before answering: 'to be a good citizen. And a woman's? To be a good wife and a good mother. One is called into the outside world; the other is retained inside.'[3] Few disputed social theorist Paul Janet's view that: 'in the life of men, instruction plays an important role' but that 'for girls, learning is far less important. [...] besides, let us not forget, where is a woman's place? In the domestic interior. [...] A young girl is raised for the family. Does it not follow that she should be taught at home?'[4]

It had not been until the 17th century that concern had started to be raised about girls' education, and then only because it was decided that it might be practical for a woman to have a basic grasp of arithmetic if she were expected to run a household and keep accounts.[5] Schools for girls had not been at all common until the 19th century.[6] The Guizot law of 1833 relating to primary education failed to deal with girls.[7] Eventually, it was decided in 1850 that communes of more than 800 people should provide a school for girls, and in 1867, the criterion to qualify for that facility was reduced to communes of more than 500.[8] But it was still a paltry gesture.

However, as the 19th century unfolded, the case for women's education gathered momentum. It was conceded that the ability to add and subtract and make intelligent conversation might assist a woman in her primary role as wife and mother. But the real question remained: just what should she know, and more importantly, how much was safe for her to know?

'I do not ask that women be wise,' clarified Archbishop Félix Dupanloup, 'but rather intelligent, judicious, attentive, well-informed in everything that it is useful for them to know, as mothers, mistresses of households and women of the world.'[9] 'I am quite in agreement that a woman should not know too much,' seconded Janet, 'I do not think that it is necessary for a young girl to learn a lot, the important thing is to learn it well.'[10] But while such vagaries circulated, there was still no such thing as compulsory secondary education for girls, and where girls' primary schools were established, the emphasis remained firmly on homemaking skills such as needlework, music and cooking. For among champions of female learning, one view remained virtually uncontested: 'the basis of women's education should be domestic economy'.[11]

Madeleine was no stranger to society's inherent gender bias. 'A woman who knows Latin will never make a good end,' one Limousin proverb declared.[12] 'The written word is for men, the spoken word, for women,' maintained another.[13] But Madeleine had seen the admiration literate women received in rural society. She had felt that frisson of pride whenever she had the chance to demonstrate that she could sign her name; women who could not never quite fostered the same degree of respect. There was no school for girls in Bessines when Madeleine was young.[14] Any teaching girls received was issued on a casual basis by a knowledgeable relative, a family friend or a sympathetic elder. How different things might have been for Madeleine had it been otherwise. But there was another reason Marie-Clémentine's education was important now: language.

Until the 19th century, it was accepted that rural communities would communicate in their local dialect or patois. However, from the Revolution, schools were made to encourage the use of French, and from the 1870s, patois speakers would become the quarry in a veritable linguistic witch-hunt.[15] Nonetheless, Limousin had remained the main form of social communication in Madeleine's region in the mid-19th century, and 105 defiant communes in the Haute-Vienne still functioned primarily in patois.[16] But in Paris, speaking in patois was the ultimate betrayer of rural archaicism and social inferiority. 'We tried to transform our pronunciation,' recalled migrant Martin Nadaud; 'to speak coarsely, without our natural accent, seemed the height of distinction.'[17]

If Marie-Clémentine were to fit in in Paris – and ultimately be independent – she must have a sound grasp of French.

In 1857, the sisters of Saint Vincent de Paul had established themselves in Montmartre and with support from the legacy of a Russian noblewoman, the late Mme Sophie Swetchine, had begun running classes for poor and orphaned little girls in the area. As the pupil intake swelled, the sisters were obliged to move premises several times. Finally, in 1876, the year Marie-Clémentine turned eleven, construction commenced on the sisters' ultimate location, and soon, their new school, orphanage and sewing room opened in the Rue Caulaincourt, just a few minutes' walk from the Valadons' apartment.

Enrolling Marie-Clémentine in the new establishment would lift any concern that played on Madeleine's mind about the young-ster's antics when she was not there to supervise her. And while Madeleine was not an especially devout woman, the rigour and dis-cipline of the nuns' approach would surely have a desirable impact on her daughter. Even if Marie-Clémentine did not emerge from the experience a confirmed Catholic, she would undoubtedly learn good manners, along with a host of practical skills such as needlework. If she applied herself, she might even master some scholarly expertise. Madeleine began to arrange the formalities.

Charitable religious primary schools or *petites écoles* had begun to appear in the 17th century in Paris when priests started founding free schools for the children of the poor.[18] To begin with, these catered mainly for boys, but before long religious orders such as the Ursulines were also founding schools to meet female education needs. These welcomed day girls as well as boarders and were free or cost very little to attend.[19] A wave of social discourse and novels like Adolphe Belot's *Mlle Giraud, Ma Femme* (1870) criticised convent education, holding the claustrophobic environment in which the girls were taught responsible for all manner of female ills, not least lesbianism. Nonetheless, with the Virgin Mary held up as the exemplary model of femininity, and religious teaching widely seen as an essential part of every respectable girl's education, in 1870, 60 per cent of girls attending school were still being taught by sisters.[20] And to the founders' surprise, these charitable organisations attracted not just the poor and destitute, but the middle classes as well, whose confidence in clerical education – and enthusiasm that it should be free – unwittingly turned these schools into great social levellers.[21]

So it was that one morning, Marie-Clémentine found her bare feet forced into suffocating stockings and imprisoned in tight-fitting boots. Once made as presentable as possible, she was ushered outside, not to bound through the streets unchecked as usual, but to begin the solemn walk towards a new life, one governed by timetables and rigorous discipline. From that moment, her freedom of expression was curtailed, her private world invaded.

Religious schools lived by strict rules and regulations, and were staunch advocates of traditional methods of discipline and punishment when their policies were not complied with.[22] From the middle of the 19th century, they had become even stricter. The nuns taught modest comportment and self-restraint. Discretion and industry were rewarded, spontaneity and natural impulses suppressed; from the outset, Marie-Clémentine's relationship with the sisters of Saint Vincent de Paul was ill-fated.[23]

Once a girl stepped through the school gates, every minute of her day was structured, each activity monitored with the utmost scrutiny. It was considered unwise to leave a child unsupervised for long periods, and liberty – the kind Marie-Clémentine had been used to – was systematically eradicated. Nothing passed unnoticed. The slightest movement was watched, judged, assessed, the theory being that constant surveillance would negate entirely the need for punishment.[24] 'In the seminary,' complained the 19th-century writer Stendhal, 'there is a way of eating a boiled egg that reveals the progress made in the devout life.'[25] Henceforward, Marie-Clémentine's day was framed by morning Mass and evening prayer, and the time in between was heavily regimented and closely observed.

Though convents claimed not to groom girls in readiness to join their order, in practice, religious education formed a large part of the convent syllabus.[26] French, history, geography, music and botany were all subjects highly regarded by convent administrations. However, at primary level, the main objective was simply to ensure that the girls could read, write and count.[27] Even so, the time allotted to these academic pursuits was usually minimal. A good portion of the school day was given to fashioning socially respectable young ladies. This meant cultivating the important arts of sewing and embroidery. Girls were taught to stitch, knit, make stockings and gloves, and launder, for manual tasks were revered.[28] 'You would do well to employ your leisure time undertaking manual work,' stipulated a student handbook in 1865. 'It is the occupation most fitting to your sex: your health, your character, your heart and your spirituality will be all the better for it.'[29] For if the sisters could not transform their charges into nuns, they were determined to turn out good wives and mothers.

Teaching included instruction in good conduct, self-presentation, politeness, and how to make intelligent conversation. Girls were told to adopt moderation in all things. Dress should be simple, food plain and sufficient. Classic works of literature were accepted, but 'frivolous' novels, much poetry, songs with doubtful lyrics and anything that excited the emotions, was banned.[30] Excessive movement without purpose was condemned and in many convents dancing was prohibited; a girl's very walk should be slow and considered.[31] Passion and sensitivity were repressed, curiosity calmed. In the convent, perfect obedience and docility were the order of the day.

Marie-Clémentine's ebullient nature was in direct conflict with the sisters' ethos. From the moment she set foot in the school, the young girl proved herself a social deviant.

Not that all the nuns inspired animosity. Few could dislike the cheerful Sister Geneviève, whose happy disposition and sheer delight in language was contagious. But a sister was still a figure of authority, and though Marie-Clémentine enjoyed words and language, she was always too distracted to apply herself to the repetitive exercises used to instil linguistic competence.[32] Her writing was wild and impassioned. Text and writing lacked the immediacy she craved. Ideas caught her imagination more than text. Jean de La Fontaine only secured her attention because his vivid fables appealed to her love of the fantastic. Similarly, when Marie-Clémentine was introduced to the renegade 15th-century poet François Villon, it was as much his dramatic life story as his verse that earned her admiration.[33] She understood confrontation with authority figures and appreciated rebellious measures taken to outsmart them. She fancied what it might be like to know such a man, and with utter disregard for temporal continuity, solemnly told people that she was his daughter, insisting that they address her as Mlle Villon, and adopting the walk and gestures she imagined such a character might have used.

Marie-Clémentine lived entirely in her mind. 'I was haunted,' she explained years later. 'As a child, I thought far too much.'[34]

Moreover, she had the physique and agility to support her mental acrobatics and live out her daydreams. Marie-Clémentine was petite, shorter than most of her classmates, and physically fearless. As a result, the sisters of Saint Vincent de Paul soon found they had no wall high enough, nor gate secure enough to contain her. 'I am a monkey. I am a cat,' she would call down from the top of a wall or fence, before springing nimbly to the ground and speeding off.[35] Institutional repression propagated brazen rebellion. She became one of the most artful truants the school had ever known.

When she was in class, there was one matter on which the sisters were particularly firm: hygiene.[36] Marie-Clémentine's contemporary, Anne-Marie Chassaigne, who would grow up to become the famous courtesan Liane de Pougy, recalled arriving for her first day at a convent, 'at the age of nine, with filthy fingernails and head lice.'[37] The youngster was instantly rejected by her classmates and she returned 'clean, washed, gleaming and worthy of association, not dangerous [...] Naturally, I was teased for the rest of the term.' For Liane, 'the lesson was hard, but it served me well for the rest of my life'.[38] Marie-Clémentine was less responsive to such uninvited teaching. 'Water is for washing pigs!' she hurled back when one of the more biddable students criticised her cleanliness.[39] Her appearance bothered her not at all; she was unmoved by social exclusion. 'Solitude suited me,' she explained, years later.[40]

Despite Madeleine's and the Mother Superior's best efforts, Marie-Clémentine was definitively a child of the streets. Her Montmartre was a marvellous playground. Where there were bars, she saw apparatus to climb; handrails were not aids, but irresistible poles to slide down. She went jumping, leaping, tumbling just where her mind took her, talking to people she encountered on the way, and picking up coarse expressions and vulgar songs, of which she was fond of giving raucous performances. 'I was a devil,' she conceded. 'I behaved like a boy.'[41]

Once, she was seen swinging from an upstairs window and passers-by stared up aghast and hollered as she called down assurances that they need not worry, the fire brigade were on their way.[42] On another occasion, a horse broke loose in the Place Blanche, causing terrified pedestrians to dive this way and that for cover; people were amazed when Marie-Clémentine succeeded in catching and then gently calming the wild creature. The pomp, ceremony and emotion which could be observed at funerals fascinated the youngster, and she took to attending the burials of complete unknowns at Père Lachaise. One day, she gave such a convincing impression of a tearful mourner that the deceased's widow came to comfort her and slipped her some money, concluding that the child must be a consequence of one of her late husband's extramarital dalliances. She bantered and chatted with anyone she came across who happened to interest her, though never seemed to demand closeness from any of these contacts. 'I had just one friend, an old girl of 78 who could speak seven languages,' she recounted.[43] Some years later, she recalled one particular encounter she made in the Rue Lepic when she stopped to watch an artist working at his easel. After observing his industry for a little while, she approached him, convinced that her advice would be pertinent. He should not feel discouraged, she assured him. Why, she could see real potential in his work; he certainly had a future in it. As it turned out, her prophecy proved accurate: the artist was Pierre-Auguste Renoir.

In her conversations, Marie-Clémentine showed utter disregard for the truth. Sometimes her father was an aristocratic baron, the Empress Eugénie her godmother and Madeleine merely an adoptive mother who was doing the best she could. She took each experience, every exchange as she found it, with no thought of the consequences. Dates, times, names, were all immaterial and perfectly changeable. The past was irrelevant, and so was the future. All that mattered was the present.

And by the time her care was entrusted to the sisters, she had discovered a uniquely gratifying way to engage with the present: drawing.

At first, her attempts to capture the world around her were crude. Using pencil stubs, she traced the outline of flowers and trees on any scrap of paper that she could find.[44] One of her chance encounters was with a coalman, who gave her some lumps of charcoal. Madeleine was outraged to discover cats, dogs and all sorts of exotic creatures drawn here and there on the walls of the apartment. Then, charcoal sketches of nude figures started appearing on nearby pavements, to the titillation of passing workmen and the outrage of well-bred ladies. Marie-Clémentine's toys were few and shabby; drawing became both her passion and her principal entertainment.

Not that she drew with any kind of regularity; she abhorred routine, and would sometimes go for long spells without committing anything at all to paper or pavement. Then, all at once, the desire to draw would take her over, and she would work frantically as though possessed. 'It seized me so young,' she remembered. Already 'at eight years old I was hooked; I recorded what I saw, I would have liked to possess, to demonstrate the very essence of the trees and limbs so that I could keep hold of them'.[45] By the time she was presented to the sisters, Marie-Clémentine was positively addicted to drawing. She had always been at odds with the sanctioning frameworks of the world around her. Now, for the first time in her life, there was something she could control. She had power. With a pencil or piece of charcoal in her hand, she suddenly moved from passive servant to active master.

Capturing the world on paper demanded good observational skills, heightened sensitivity and being highly attuned to surroundings and stimulus. Marie-Clémentine boasted all those traits. On Sundays, she would climb to the roof of the tenement building where she lived and lie on her stomach for hours at a time, watching the people and carriages in the street far below moving about like tiny ants.[46] She noticed the flashes of colours which seemed to merge from such a distance, and listened to the continual hum of faraway activity. It was the world in miniature, and from such a height she felt like a divine creator, empowered by omniscience. When night fell, obliging her to return to the cramped apartment, she would climb into the confined space of her bunk with her observations of the day still racing through her mind, and would draw arms, legs, anything which sprang to mind, on the wall. 'How did I do it?' she wondered years later. 'I really don't know when I think about it, because I couldn't draw a sugar bowl from memory now.'[47]

But the world around her was changing. In February 1874, when Marie-Clémentine was nine, Marie-Alix had accepted Georges Merlet's proposal of marriage, and the following year, the couple had moved to the coastal town of Nantes.[48] Since then, Madeleine and Marie-Clémentine had been alone together, and now that she had started school, Marie-Clémentine's unruly behaviour was thrown into even sharper relief. The tolerance of the sisters of Saint Vincent de Paul began to wane, and Madeleine decided a short stay with her half-sister in Nantes and the firm hand of an authoritative male presence might succeed where the sisters had failed. The project proved no more effective. Marie-Clémentine seemed to thrive on naughtiness; she could not be tamed, and though Marie-Alix at least felt tenderly towards her younger sibling, her husband was under no obligation to show the same degree of patience. The arrangement was agreed unworkable, and Marie-Clémentine sent back to Paris.

Before long, the sisters of Saint Vincent de Paul were also obliged to admit defeat, and the convent doors were closed firmly behind the youngster forever. Now, there was only one course possible: Marie-Clémentine would have to get a job.

It was not unusual for the children to start work as young as seven or eight in the country, so from Madeleine's perspective, the timing of Marie-Clémentine's entry on to the job market before she was fourteen was perfectly reasonable, and if anything a little late.[49] Her first job was that of apprentice seamstress at an *atelier de couture* not far from where she lived.[50] Her training at the convent had equipped her with all the skills necessary to excel in such a position. And she proved herself an adept employee, quick and competent in all the fine motor skills required to apply ribbons and trimmings. But Marie-Clémentine loathed the work. The artificiality of all those frills and all that frippery exasperated her.[51] And she was no more inclined to adhere to routine and kowtow to authority than she had been at the convent. She took to disappearing when she felt the whim, and her relationship with her employer soon soured. Before long, she was looking for another job.

One day, she returned home and told Madeleine that she was to begin 'looking after rich children in the Tuileries'. But that did not last long either. There followed a series of menial positions: waitress and dishwasher at a cheap café; fruit and vegetable seller at Les Halles des Batignolles; factory worker making funeral wreaths. Then, she took a position as stable hand at a nearby livery. It seemed the best-fitting post to date, and people later recalled seeing her ride, despite having no formal training, with natural dexterity and skill. Some even said they had seen her perform handstands on horses' backs. But she was still answerable to somebody and ruled by time. Marie-Clémentine took against authority and routine. Her very nature was in discordance with the role of employee, or at least that was how it seemed. Until, that is, a very unique employment opportunity presented itself.

By the time Marie-Clémentine was approaching her fifteenth birthday in 1880, Paris was on the cusp of a golden era.[52] The Exposition Universelle of 1878 had seen the capital reclaim its position as a great European city. For the first time in decades, politics appeared stable, while scientific and technological progress were fashioning a world which would have been unrecognisable to Madeleine's forefathers back in Bessines. Industry was booming, communications improving and proliferating transport links expanding mental and geographical horizons as never before. Public telephones started appearing from the 1880s, electricity made it possible to illuminate a room with the mere flick of a switch, and improving literacy levels meant that newspaper circulation continued to rise.

In practical terms, the upper and middle classes found that they now had money to spare once the cost of basic necessities had been met, and decadent department stores guaranteed that they never ran short of commodities on which to spend it. Mass consumerism was on the rise. But more than anything, whether they sought to distract themselves in their spare time or to colour the dull monotony of the working week, both classes craved entertainment. Paris's flourishing leisure industry was quick to oblige. An eruption of café concerts, balls, music halls, theatres and sporting events ensured boredom had no place in the city.[53]

Montmartre was already peppered with such entertainments, and they thrived in the 1880s. There were two dance halls on Marie-Clémentine's street. In the evenings, they would come to life, bringing a tide of catchy melodies, jovial bachelors and happy-go-lucky girls in frothy skirts spilling out on to the streets in an effluence of pleasure. For indeed, Montmartre had two faces; during the day, much of it remained the quaint rustic haven which had first tempted Madeleine to settle there. But when the sun began to set, the windows of hundreds of entertainment venues lit up, twinkling seductively and drawing a nocturnal population of artists, prostitutes and anarchists out of hibernation. At night, Montmartre became the illuminated playground of Paris's marginalised, its smoky pleasure palaces a forum for sharing grievances and ideas.

Of the myriad of entertainments on offer, few appealed to such a broad social spectrum, nor promised the same surge of adrenaline, as the circus. Paris had a long history of passionate circus attendance. Philip Astley first brought the modern circus from England to Paris in the 18th century, before the Italian Antonio Franconi transfixed the city's audiences with his breathtaking feats of horsemanship. By the 19th century, the circus was a well-established feature of the Parisian social scene. In 1860, the Cirque de l'Impératrice had fed Paris's insatiable hunger for all things death-defying when the acrobat Léotard had inspired gasps as he leapt through the air to catch the flying trapeze.[54] 'In Paris, the man who risks his life [...] is sure to start a general infatuation,' proclaimed Henri Dabot the same year.[55] In the 1880s, Paris's enthusiasm for the circus showed no signs of dwindling. One contemporary review summarised popular opinion: 'The proliferation of circuses [...] is a blessing!'[56]

The circus was familiar to Marie-Clémentine. While the thought of spending money on such frivolities as leisure was unthinkable in the Valadon household, Marie-Clémentine could hardly ignore the brightly coloured circus posters pinned to walls as she tried to edge her way through the throng of eager spectators queuing on her very own street. For in 1875, when Marie-Clémentine was ten, a new circus had come to town and set itself up at 63, Boulevard de Rochechouart, on the corner of the Rue des Martyrs.

The Cirque Fernando was a curious wooden building whose posters promised all manner of wonders and delights: there were acrobats, jugglers, tightrope walkers, performing animals and a fine equine section with skilled equestriennes.[57] Bright lights made exotic costumes sparkle, while breathtaking gymnastic feats were performed to the crack of the whip and the triumphant sound of brass. 'The horses are magnificent,' raved one review. 'The performers could rival the best in the profession. The clowns are the most original to be found. The inhabitants of the west of Paris no longer have far to travel to see such a popular show: they have the Cirque Fernando.'[58]

Of all Montmartre's temptations, it was the circus that most captured Marie-Clémentine's imagination. It seemed the very antithesis of the existence she was being urged to accept, and encapsulated everything she wished her life would become. The circus was unusual and exhilarating, colourful and exciting. It pleased the eye, roused the emotions and lifted the soul. And above all, the circus showcased the extraordinary capabilities of the human body, a distinguishing feature which made it eminently attractive to artists. It certainly had everything to appeal to Marie-Clémentine. And it just so happened that now she was a teenager and in need of work, a new circus was about to open. By chance, the owner was a man with a soft spot for amateurs, a keen eye for potential and a nose for new talent.

Round-faced with a spectacular moustache, Ernest Molier was the 36-year-old son of a wealthy treasurer and magistrate from Le Mans.[59] He had arrived in Paris in his twenties with a passion for horses that was greeted with disdain by members of the Haute École, on the grounds that he was no more than a rich, eccentric amateur. The charge was difficult to dispute; but as for his skill, Molier's critics had sorely underestimated his capabilities. Molier schooled himself in equestrian science, and through sheer determination and hard work, by his mid-twenties, he had become an outstanding horseman and a competent trainer.

In 1880, Molier's equine skills, combined with his eccentric streak and backed up by his personal affluence, were mustered to launch one of the most outlandish entertainment ventures Paris had ever seen: a superb private circus, run entirely by amateurs. Having bought terrain on the Rue Bénouville near the Bois de Boulogne,

Molier constructed his very own circus, with a 13m-diameter ring and seating for some 100 spectators. Then, he sought out performers, initially among his friends (many of them aristocrats like the Comte Hubert de La Rochefoucauld), who practised boxing, fencing and gymnastics in their extensive leisure time. His acquaintances also included a number of actors, actresses and singers whose regular performances took them to the capital's most esteemed stages, such as the Opéra and the Palais Royal. Molier had all the ingredients for success.

The first performance was by invitation only. And just before 9pm on 21 March 1880, the tiered wooden seating at Molier's circus began to fill up with curious guests. Men in best suits craned their necks, chicly dressed women chattered excitedly. And all around the ring, posters whetted the appetite with illustrations of the remarkable feats about to be performed, heightening the sense of expectation.

Given the vogue for equestrian acrobatics and gymnastics (inspired, critics sneered, by fears over the degeneration of the privileged classes), the opening performance was a wild success. 'A private circus!' one review exclaimed. 'You have to admit, it's a highly original and brilliantly funny idea [...] quite English [...] I declare M. Molier an utterly unique circus director.'[60]

Unique the circus certainly was. Like all circuses, there were acrobats, jugglers, clowns, monkeys, horses and pretty young girls in revealing costumes performing gymnastics on their steeds' backs. There was music, there was humour and there was dancing. But the show also included a horse that would hunt – and retrieve – objects on command. And one of the most popular acts proved to be a rabbit assault course. 'We have all heard of dressed rabbit. Now, M. Molier has launched dressaging rabbits! It's the maddest thing!'[61]

Before long, all high society was clamouring for a ticket. Everyone wanted to see this much-hyped Parisian folly. Molier's background and social position made him uniquely placed to appreciate the subtleties and delicate balance of Paris's complex social strata. The inaugural show proved so popular that Molier decided that henceforward he would give two or three performances a year, and that there would be two sittings for each show: one for his eminent friends and another for their mistresses. Molier was thoroughly in tune with the desires of his public, and Paris loved him for it. The cream of Paris society, from financiers to physicians, began eagerly awaiting the shows, each of which was followed by a sumptuous dinner accompanied by fine champagne.

The performances went from strength to strength. 'The first performance was a great success,' declared *Le Figaro*.[62] 'The next year [...] the Molieros surpassed themselves.' The following year 'marked a new era for the Molieros'. The multi-talented Comte de La Rochefoucauld in particular received endless plaudits. His trapeze work 'was enough to make a person forget the great Léotard', his routine agreed to 'surpass the very best seen at the Hippodrome'.[63]

Molier's circus was the show all Paris was talking about.

Always passionate about the circus, Marie-Clémentine's ears pricked up when she overheard two painters discussing the circus in one of Montmartre's popular bars one evening.[64] She quickly joined the discussion, from which it transpired that the men knew the owner of the circus. Marie-Clémentine was clearly enthusiastic, claimed to enjoy amateur gymnastics and believed she could handle a horse. Now a ripe adolescent poised on the threshold of womanhood, she was undeniably alluring. And she needed work. The men could introduce her to Ernest Molier. For they did know him, very well indeed – one of them was the Comte de La Rochefoucauld.

Molier was only too conscious of the power of a pretty young girl to arrest an audience's attention: he also staged pantomimes for his friends where scantily clad women were the main attraction.

Suzanne Valadon (Marie-Clémentine),
Paris, c. 1880.
Collection Jean Fabris

In addition, he was a keen benefactor where young talent was concerned and had acquired a reputation for training up protégés
who would earn a small wage for their efforts.[65] Marie-Clémentine
was hired.

At last, her passion for acrobatics had an outlet where it would
be appreciated. She would perform as a multi-skilled gymnast and
try her hand at a variety of circus skills. Working for Molier was
exhausting, but Marie-Clémentine loved every minute. Each experience provided rich material for her drawing. Besides, Molier had a
refreshing approach to established convention which appealed to
Marie-Clémentine. He even shunned the tradition of women riding
side-saddle, which was widely agreed to be the only decorous way
for a lady to travel on horseback.

Much of Marie-Clémentine's time was spent in the stables, where quick banter with upper-class, older men and matronly warnings from women more worldly-wise than herself matured her fast and exposed her to a side of life which was still new to her. But Molier worked his trainees hard, his favoured teaching methods alternating between patience and the horse-whip.[66] Marie-Clémentine had to put in innumerable hours perfecting the art of the trapeze. It was strenuous, but the rewards – and the applause – were well worth the exertion. It was not unheard of for trainees to be picked out for special praise in the press. At one show, a young female protégé of Molier's 'was especially applauded' when, standing on a horse's back, her performance 'would have made any of M. Loyal's students envious.'[67]

For six glorious months, Marie-Clémentine's physical stamina and suppleness impressed her fellow performers.[68] The toned muscles of her tiny limbs became taut as she stretched out, bent and wrapped her body around the unforgiving steel bar of the trapeze.

And then one day during a rehearsal, something went wrong.

There was a slip, a gasp, a thud. And then nothing. Marie-Clémentine's body lay crumpled and motionless on the floor of the arena.[69]

CHAPTER 4

Inspiring Painters

L'un ne po pà essei a lo proucessi e sounà lo clocho.
(You can't follow the procession
and sound the horn.)

OLD LIMOUSIN PROVERB[1]

Physical fearlessness like Marie-Clémentine's can seldom be attributed simply to reckless self-neglect. More often, it results from an unconscious, intuitive understanding of the body, of its capabilities and limitations; from a self-knowledge so instinctive that the owner herself is barely conscious of it. Marie-Clémentine had just such an innate understanding of her body. She knew how it behaved and responded. Without realising, she had trusted it, believed in it, based her dreams on it. She had relied on its support, and taken that support for granted. But it had let her down. Now, all she could think of was the pain.

Marie-Clémentine's fall left her with acute back pain – the kind of deep, sickening ache which cuts straight to the soul, tears at the emotions and seems to alter the very character of the sufferer. Marie-Clémentine had flown, and she had soared. Her body had sprung lightly and done just as she commanded. Suddenly, it was not responding as it used to. It was impossible to ignore its weight, its very earthly quality.

There were no more bright lights, music, people, excitement, energy. The scents of horses and straw, of body odours mingled with cigarette smoke, had evaporated. Everything was still and quiet, colours sober and muted. The walls of the dingy bedroom became the teenager's unchanging horizon; while outside the distant sounds of life going on without her were a constant reminder of what she had lost. Even the prancing creatures drawn in her own hand on the walls of the apartment seemed to mock her. The girl who had finally found happiness in movement among people had been grounded, confined, isolated.

And it soon became clear that while her back would improve, she would not be able to perform acrobatics again – and she would not be returning to Molier's circus. All that had been pleasure and light suddenly became dark and serious. Eventually, denial was impossible – her body was fallible. It was a chastening realisation, a brutal confrontation with physical vulnerability at such a young age. And all the while, the pain persisted.

Of course, Marie-Clémentine could still draw. While she recovered, she continued to sketch and reluctantly tried for the first time to paint; it made her uneasy. There was something committal about the medium which unsettled her. 'I was so wild and proud that I did not want to paint,' she explained. 'I tried to make my palette so simple that I wouldn't have to think about it.'[2] And conservative 19th-century artistic discourse projected colour as feminine, line as masculine.[3] Drawing was a way of brazenly rejecting established artistic – and gender – conventions. Besides, decent pigments were expensive and hard to come by. 'I painted with whatever I had, indiscriminately,' she remembered.[4] Then there was the question of subject matter. She could always paint her mother, but her efforts seemed little use when there was nothing new to commit to paper. Memory was not a limitless source of material. To create, Marie-Clémentine needed to experience.

Madeleine, meanwhile, was preoccupied with a more pressing concern. When all due sympathy had been paid, for them to survive, Marie-Clémentine needed to earn.

Marie-Clémentine eventually agreed to take on some sewing work. It exasperated her. To be confined to the apartment engaged in such tedious industry felt like taking a step backwards – towards imprisonment and away from freedom. The only paid employment she had ever enjoyed had been in Molier's circus. Now that opportunity had been snatched away, she had just one passion: art.

If a woman must work, painting was hardly a reasonable or lucrative employment option. A lady amateur's nonchalant interest in art or music was considered enchanting, a sign of good breeding; painting as a serious female profession, on the other hand, was nothing short of scandalous. It was viewed as deeply unfitting.

Certainly, there were recognised female artists who had made a successful career – as much as it could be called one – out of painting. Acceptance at the prestigious Paris Salon remained the ultimate testimony of painterly attainment in the 19th century. This huge exhibition was the most important event of the artistic world, for it was here that reputations were made, commissions earned, and skill showcased and assessed. Gradually, the conservative Salon jury was growing more receptive to women artists, and even went so far as to award fourteen women first-class medals in 1879.[5] But a skilled woman artist had to expend an inordinate amount of energy to gain even a fraction of the recognition that a man of similar talent might readily enjoy. American Mary Cassatt had her first Salon piece accepted in 1868.[6] Throughout the 1860s and 1870s, Berthe Morisot had been a regular exhibitor at the Salon. But both those women came from wealthy families with contacts and the capital to back what were widely perceived to be their daughters' flights of fancy. Even then, each had to suffer the critical rebuffs of their immediate circle. Berthe Morisot and her sister's painting teacher

Joseph-Benoît Guichard underlined the danger of nurturing female artistic talent when he wrote to their mother: 'With characters like your daughters', my teaching will make them painters, not minor amateur talents. Do you really understand what that means? In the world of the *grande bourgeoisie* in which you move, it would be a revolution, I would even say a catastrophe.'[7]

The Salon jury tolerated women artists. It condescended to acknowledge exceptional female talent where there was no alternative, but praise was rarely offered ungrudgingly. When Morisot's and Cassatt's paintings were shown in public, they were shielded from the most biting criticism precisely because their pictures conformed with the main tenets of Impressionism. They worked on small canvases, used a delicate palette, and drew their subject matter from their immediate environment. Their canvases often showed women, children and domestic scenes, all of which were considered appropriate subjects for their sex, although too inferior to be seriously considered in the context of high art. Clearly, conservative critics reassured themselves, Cassatt's and Morisot's paintings were those of women who knew their place. In 1881, J.K. Huysmans described Mary Cassatt's paintings as 'impeccable pearls', before adding: 'but of course, a woman is equipped to paint childhood. There is a special feeling men would be unable to render unless they are particularly sensitive and nervous.'[8] Marie-Clémentine's brushstrokes and charcoal lines were already bolder, more defiant – far less feminine.

If a girl from a poor family like Marie-Clémentine truly wanted to make a living in the art world, there was only one way she could be sure of doing so. She needed to approach the business from the other side of the canvas: she would have to become a model.

One of the friends Marie-Clémentine had made in Montmartre was an Italian girl named Clelia.[9] Clelia knew all about the rigid, gendered framework of the art world and the business of modelling.

She was one of the countless Italian immigrants (many of whom originated from the countryside around Naples), who had settled in Paris and found work as an artist's model.[10] It was a problematic career choice. Models were shrouded in a dark cloud of social stigma. Popular stereotype cast the artist's model as little better than a prostitute, as happy to satisfy her employer's sexual urges as she was his creative impulses. So ingrained in the Parisian psyche was the connection between posing and prostitution that artist's models were frequently referred to as *grisettes*, the name also used to designate working-class girls who supplemented their income through prostitution.[11] But when the most coveted asset in rural Italy was a piece of land and given that meagre wages were typically paid in kind, not coin, the Parisian model market was a deeply attractive option.[12] In Paris, a female model could make ten and sometimes up to twenty francs per day, more than a peasant – or a charwoman like Madeleine – could ever dream of earning.[13] Whole Italian families would be uprooted and migrate to Paris, where just one or two of their number could secure the future of all.

When Marie-Clémentine found herself incapacitated, despondent and in desperate need of work, Clelia good-naturedly suggested that she too try modelling. It seemed a perfect solution. Marie-Clémentine was passionate about art, and her fall had not altered her physical appearance – or her appeal. Besides, models had to be resilient, flexible and have total command of their body, all skills Marie-Clémentine had perfected in the circus. The model must have the stamina to hold a pose for as long as a painter required, and above all, remain absolutely still – an ideal job description for a pretty girl who had to avoid excessive movement. At the very least, Marie-Clémentine could accompany Clelia to some of her assignments and see for herself.

Marie-Clémentine did – and a whole new world was opened up to her.

When Italian models like Clelia arrived in Paris, they flocked to the quartier around the Place Jussieu on the left bank.[14] However, to secure work, they had to venture further north to where the lively model market took place every Sunday morning around the fountain in the Place Pigalle – which, conveniently for Marie-Clémentine, was located just off the Boulevard de Rochechouart.

The model market was essentially a large, rather chaotic beauty pageant where the competition was fierce, for the prize was unsurpassed: paid work – and perhaps even fame if a girl was lucky enough to be selected by a painter whose work appeared at the Salon.[15] The shrewdest girls had taken note of the 1880s vogue for paintings of peasants and rural life, subjects which had become convenient messengers of four key bourgeois values: work, family, religion and patriotism.[16] The themes were guaranteed crowd-pleasers. Bourgeois Salon-goers seemed never to tire of them and painters were only too happy to pander to their audience's tastes. In response, the Italians wisely arrived at the weekly market dressed in their picturesque traditional costume. Doe-eyed girls with olive skin draped themselves provocatively around the fountain, batting their thick eyelashes, hoping to secure a commission and their future.

It was daunting competition for Marie-Clémentine. She did not boast a picturesque peasant's costume or the sultry features of her Italian counterparts. She had never taken much time over her appearance. She wore plain, dark clothes with high collars and not so much as a smear of makeup. But her clear, blue eyes, well-defined bone structure and natural complexion were striking. In many ways, Marie-Clémentine had the advantage over the Italians: she was a blank canvas. The Italian girls offered themselves up as pre-determined subjects; with Marie-Clémentine, a painter could make her whatever he wished. It did not take long for a prominent artist to spot that versatility.

Marie-Clémentine had inherited Madeleine's scornful disdain towards public curiosity; she playfully allowed a number of stories to circulate about the circumstances of her first commission.[17] She was seen by the artist as he looked down on the model market one Sunday morning from his upstairs window, one tale ran. Not at all, countered another; Madeleine had taken on some odd jobs doing laundry for private clients, and on one occasion, had asked Marie-Clémentine to deliver a basket of linen to the said painter's address. In an elaborated version of that story, Marie-Clémentine had to wait in the hallway for the artist to return before she could deposit her laundry basket. The artist's colour grinder was also waiting for the master of the house, and he started making unwanted advances towards Marie-Clémentine in the interim, only to have his attempts dramatically thwarted by the entrance of the artist who chivalrously came to Marie-Clémentine's rescue, demanding in his booming voice: 'Who is this charming person?'.[18] Theories abounded, but on one fact, opinion was unanimous: when Marie-Clémentine was spotted, she landed one of the most enviable commissions imaginable. For the artist who first noticed her was none other than the eminent Pierre Puvis de Chavannes.

Tall and corpulent with a long face, hoary beard and moustache, and receding hairline, at nearly 60 years old, Puvis de Chavannes had firmly established himself as a figure of authority in the art world. He had a steady gaze, an erect stature and a nose which he self-deprecatingly described as 'colossal'.[19] Impeccably dressed, well mannered and eloquent — the *bonhomme*, Berthe Morisot's daughter Julie Manet called him — Puvis presented as an old-fashioned gentleman who knew all the turns of phrase to compliment a lady.[20] His endless philosophising, pompous demeanour and readily shared opinions both amused and exasperated his closest companions. Edgar Degas delighted in comparing him to the condor in the Jardin des Plantes, and sometimes referred to him as 'the peacock'.[21] 'You have no idea how formal and complicated he is,' Berthe Morisot once groaned to Claude Monet.[22] Nonetheless, few could dispute Puvis's talent or experience.

The son of a successful mining engineer from Lyon, Puvis was expected to pursue his father's career.[23] However, a trip to Italy in the 1840s altered his thinking, and he returned to France determined to become a painter. He studied under Eugène Delacroix, Thomas Couture and Henri Scheffer, but quickly realised that he was more comfortable working alone. And when he did so, he started to excel. Puvis made his Salon debut in 1850 and reappeared there in 1859 after a series of rejections. By the 1860s, he had settled comfortably into producing the epic decorative work that was to become his trademark. By the time he met Marie-Clémentine, Puvis had made his name producing vast, often allegorical compositions (frequently murals), which bore the influence of classical art, and depicted Grecian and antique figures in statuesque poses. His success was due in no small part to his sensitivity to popular tastes and his ability to satisfy a diverse array of ideologies simultaneously. As the French grappled to redefine national identity in the aftermath of the Franco-Prussian war and the Commune, Puvis's carefully planned, meticulously executed compositions appealed to multiple schools of thought. 'I have great power of evocation,' he once informed Berthe Morisot, 'and I often live in the past.'[24] Indeed, Puvis could boast that rare achievement of being admired by academics and moderns alike. Zola wrote that Puvis's art was characterised by 'reason, passion and will'; the description might just as easily have been applied to the man.[25]

While Puvis's apartment was situated near Pigalle, he disliked interruption when he was working, and so had taken a large studio to the west of the city at Neuilly.[26] It was here that Marie-Clémentine unbuttoned her high-collared dress to have her bare skin exposed and her body scrutinised by an older man for the very first time.

During the winter season (understood to run from September through to the opening of the Salon in May), a good model could expect to work a long day.[27] Many were booked for two sittings. The morning began at eight o'clock and ran through until mid-day. Afternoon sittings started at one o'clock and finished at five. With models rarely allowed more than ten minutes rest from a pose every hour, Marie-Clémentine soon realised that she had embarked on a physically gruelling profession. There was no such thing as a school for modelling; a girl learned on the job, and the lessons could be harsh. Marie-Clémentine gradually began to understand the expectations, and the protocol to adopt if she wished to please her employer.

Puvis's studio was vast and airy – suffocating in the summer, its bitter contrast in the winter.[28] But the good model would know better than to ask for more coal.[29] She must be punctual and able to hold the desired pose for as long as necessary, and without appearing fatigued or needing continual reminders and corrections. A successful model was creative and bright, and worked in collaboration with, not against, the authoritative presence of the artist. It was not a role in which Marie-Clémentine was inherently comfortable. But once she stepped through the doors of the Neuilly studio, the secret world she discovered was awe-inspiring. Dazed by the novelty, she complied with all Puvis's demands.

Models posed either for parts (the head, a clothed torso, for example), or, more controversially, for *l'ensemble* – the full (often nude) figure. The girls who offered this service earned more but fell victim to the very harshest social opprobrium. In a society which prized female propriety, accepting money in exchange for one's naked body seemed the ultimate sin. For girls who succumbed to such an act would be inspected not only by the professional eye of the artist; they would be explored by the untrained gaze of the Parisian public.[30] Models for *l'ensemble* were thus widely agreed to be sexually available, a common mid-19th century perception that George du Maurier reflected in his novel *Trilby* (1894). When a mother learns that her son is in love with an artist's model, she enquires: 'A *model* [...]? What *sort* of model – there are models and models, of course [...] A model for the *figure*?' A reply to the affirmative incites the reaction: 'Oh, my God! my God! my God!'[31]

But Marie-Clémentine had inherited a peasant's stoicism regarding the human body. She harboured a curiosity in its form rather than a self-conscious embarrassment over its social implications. She had no scruples about exposing her own body, no concern when it came to society's opinion.

In the early 1880s, Puvis had been commissioned to decorate the monumental staircase in the Palais des Arts in Lyon.[32] His giant *The Sacred Grove of the Arts and Muses* (1884) was consequently one of the first works Marie-Clémentine sat for. Painters seldom found their ideal beauty in a single model, and so were often obliged to take features from several different models and attempt to merge them into a seamless – flawless – whole. Likewise, one model could provide material for several figures and accordingly, a number of the characters in *The Sacred Grove*, male and female, borrowed parts of Marie-Clémentine. With her restrictive clothing shed and her hair released to come tumbling down her back, Marie-Clémentine provided Puvis with just the human material he needed to compose his cast for the ethereal scene he had envisaged in *The Sacred Grove*.[33]

Puvis could be stubborn when he had fixed his mind on something, 'as difficult as a plough to set in motion,' Berthe Morisot observed.[34] But once he had begun a piece he felt passionately about, the artist worked methodically. At such times he was fond of routine. As soon as Marie-Clémentine had taken her pose, he set to work. The artist worked steadily in silent concentration, inhaling on his pipe from time to time, while Marie-Clémentine was left to ponder her surroundings. With its high ceilings, the quiet studio was elegant and refined, qualities new to Marie-Clémentine, while all around the workspace, ladders, brushes and canvases were carefully arranged. Puvis abhorred disorder and was, in character, quite a different breed from the bohemian artists Marie-Clémentine had seen lounging around café tables in Montmartre. Marie-Clémentine absorbed everything she saw.

A creature of habit, Puvis worked carefully until lunchtime when he and Marie-Clémentine would stop to revive themselves on bread and fruit, and the sitting would resume in the afternoon. On one occasion, Puvis required a second figure, and Marie-Clémentine suggested an older model she knew. And then there were the occasional visits of the Princess Marie Cantacuzène, a Romanian noblewoman who, despite her marriage, had continued a love affair with Puvis for more than twenty years.[35] The eldest child of Prince Nicolas Cantacuzène, the Princess was a slender, sad-looking woman in her sixties by the time Marie-Clémentine made her acquaintance. She had a pallid, oval face with small yet intense brown eyes. Graceful and dignified, her grey, centre-parted hair was scraped back off her face severely, and her entire persona exuded an air of melancholy. She had first met Puvis in the 1850s, before Marie-Clémentine was even born, in the studio of the painter Théodore Chassériau.[36] Theirs was a chivalrous, elegant relationship for all its illicit nature. Throughout their extended courtship, Puvis showered her with gifts, letters and flowers. The Princess was, in appearance, age, background and demeanour the very opposite of Marie-Clémentine. Her whole, regal person was an object of intense curiosity and fascination for the spirited young model and daughter of a pauper. Whenever the Princess arrived, the silence in the studio was broken and the sitting abruptly ceased.

But most of the time, the painter and his model were alone.

While models in private *ateliers* escaped the ritual teasing inflicted on girls by merciless male students at teaching *ateliers*, the enforced intimacy between painter and model increased the potential for erotic encounters.[37] With Marie-Clémentine regularly baring her nubile young body before the older painter, rumours that Puvis had given in to temptation and taken his young model to be his lover were inevitable. Like so many outwardly decorous pillars of society, Puvis was the subject of a lewder portrait among Paris's gossips. Incidents of lecherous behaviour, quite the antithesis of the gentleman presented, had been recounted. Soon, stories about the artist and the girl young enough to be his granddaughter were being whispered around Montmartre.[38] It was said that Puvis took Marie-Clémentine to restaurants and plays; she had moved out of the apartment she shared with her mother and was living with him in sin; he had given her a little pearl ring. Someone even said Marie-Clémentine had been heard to drop his name into conversation and casually refer to him as her lover.

The extent of their physical relationship remained a matter of conjecture. But when gossip and a star-struck teenager's careless chatter with peers were laid aside, there remained a spiritual chasm between model and painter which could never be bridged. Even when, at the end of each day, Puvis paternally accompanied his charge on foot on the long walk back to Pigalle, they drew tantalisingly close but failed to connect. As they walked through the twilit streets, Marie-Clémentine remembered: 'He was as charming as could be. He talked and talked, quietly, slowly, but constantly, chatting about this or that. He was as curious as a woman. I listened to him, walking close by without uttering a word. Besides, I would not have known what to say. I was so impressed with him. I would never have dared admit to him that I had been trying to draw.'[39]

Unbeknown to her employer, Marie-Clémentine was using her sittings at Neuilly to train herself, not just in how to be a model, but in how to be an artist. Quietly, but attentively, Marie-Clémentine watched and absorbed every detail; from the artist's way of working, the mixing and handling of paints, the ordering of a composition, to the public relations of the business, including preparing for exhibitions and negotiating with dealers. Nothing escaped her attention.

Artists usually kept a log, however crude, with the names of models they could use on future projects. Eugène Delacroix's address book served as a useful aide memoire whenever the painter needed a model: 'Mme Carbon, 44, Rue Fontaine-Saint-Georges; elegant model, quite tall, good with drapery. Mme Eléonore, 40, Rue Notre-Dame-de-Lorette; very pretty model, little Venus.'[40] The 19th-century art scene was a close-knit community; everyone knew (or at least knew of) everyone else, even if they were not formally acquainted. Painters often passed on the name of a good model when she was not being used. Although Puvis was a ponderous worker when absorbed with a commission, he did not need full days from Marie-Clémentine for all of that time. And as Marie-Clémentine was blossoming into a woman, others were starting to notice how enticing she was too. Plump and radiant with good health, her brilliant blue eyes sparkled whenever she smiled, which was often.[41] She was light-hearted and seductive, sometimes cheeky, always spirited. Then when her long, golden-brown hair was released and fell loose, cascading over her shoulders down to her waist, she looked the very image of country vitality. Added to which, she was now acclimatised to the demands of the profession, comfortable with exposing her body and expert at holding a pose. Living in Montmartre, the heart of Paris's art community, and with Puvis's name on her résumé, Marie-Clémentine soon established an enviable modelling career.

She sat gazing wistfully for hours so that Prix de Rome winner Jean-Jacques Henner could create his painting *Melancholy*, and even the artist had to compliment her on her physical stamina and mature approach to the sittings.[42] The painter, caricaturist, illustrator and graphic artist Jean-Louis Forain, a good friend of

Degas, employed her. She posed for Théophile-Alexandre Steinlen, as well as the Italian Giuseppe de Nittis, the American painter Cornelius Howland and even the Emperor's cousin, Princesse Mathilde, who hosted an acclaimed painting and literature salon. One day, Marie-Clémentine was 'Truth' in the Czech artist Vojtěch Hynais's *Truth Emerging from the Well* (*c.* 1880–1890). The next, she was a siren clinging to a sailor in Gustav Wertheimer's *The Kiss of the Siren* (1882).[43] Every time, Marie-Clémentine was created afresh. Each new environment demanded a different identity, and like an actress, she changed herself accordingly. It therefore seemed only natural that she should alter her name to something more manageable for the artists now employing her. So from the 1880s, Marie-Clémentine became the more convenient – the more Italianate, exotic and sacred – Maria. She had always lived for the present and adapted herself to circumstance. At last, she had found a profession in which she truly excelled.

Maria's job was engrossing, but the efforts required to maintain a modelling profile were immense. After long periods sitting, standing or reclining, motionless and in silence, trying not to shiver, or else struggling to bear sweltering heat, her teenage vitality remained repressed and unspent. To return home to the cramped apartment and her ageing mother after such a day was too much. For to Maria, it seemed as though Madeleine, now in her fifties but appearing older, merely grumbled continuously about her own sorry lot and the monotony of her cleaning work. Maria longed for some release. Fortunately, she was now mixing in circles with people who craved the same. And they could show her just where to go to satisfy that urge.

CHAPTER 5

Dancing in the City

Quand lo jorn es tròp cort, fau li apondre la nuech.
(When the day is too short, you have to add the night.)
OLD LIMOUSIN PROVERB[1]

For an unconventional, creatively minded teen in search of fun, there were few grounds more fertile in which to blossom than Montmartre. If the entertainment industry was thriving and democratising across Paris in the last quarter of the century, Montmartre boasted the particularity that it catered primarily to – and attracted, in droves – Paris's working classes and artistic types, all the while retaining its unique ambience of casual rustic charm. The mood was relaxed, the drinks cheap and the people as diverse and interesting as could be found anywhere in Paris.

The area's nightlife was renowned, and now, being of the age and inclination to appreciate it, Maria was soon swept up by its heady lure. Once a solitary child, painfully aware of her difference, she was now surrounded by creative, artistic people, people with imagination and ideas and passion – people just like her. It was liberating. At last, she was accepted just as she was. And whatever the hour and the night of the week, there was an activity on offer in Montmartre and acquaintances desperate that she should participate.

On the nights when Maria had not been invited to a studio party by one or other of the contacts she had made through modelling, there were dance halls, cabarets, cafés, bars and taverns to spoil even the most ravenous of social gastronomes. Each had its own unique character and distinct clientele.

The Elysée Montmartre was a familiar landmark to Maria. It was open all year round, and in the 1880s it was responsible for launching the craze of the French cancan.[2] Determined thighs kicked their way out from under swathes of lace and gauze, in ribald defiance of popular notions of propriety. Only occasionally did the management impose its authority, 'when a girl who had left her briefs behind so raised her leg that everybody was invited to appreciate *de visu* [with one's own eyes] that this oversight was a trifling matter'.[3] There was also the Boule Noire, a 'second or third class' establishment, sniffed a contemporary tourist guide, but one which nevertheless acted as an irresistible magnet to swarms of eager dancers.[4]

But of all the dance halls, it was undoubtedly the Moulin de la Galette that best epitomised Montmartre's inimitable blend of bucolic nostalgia and carefree sociability. The mill-turned-dance hall had its detractors, but for its converts it remained the sunny idyll of conviviality and good feeling which Renoir captured in his *Dance at the Moulin de la Galette* (1876).[5] The mill took its name from the small cereal-based flat cakes or pancakes which its owners, the Debray millers, served to visitors, originally with milk before their innocuous offering was exchanged for a far more palatable glass of mulled wine from the 1830s.[6] By the 1870s, the Sunday dances had turned the Moulin de la Galette into a hub of social activity. From mid-afternoon, excitable working-class girls in home-made dresses and boastful lads in shirtsleeves flocked to the mill, where in fine weather, dances moved to the courtyard outside. The cares of the week evaporated as giggling couples spun round and round to the cheerful melodies of the band, while exhausted stragglers rested and whetted their whistles at tables erected in the shade of the surrounding acacia trees. Chatter and laughter bubbled out from the venue until midnight, and the whole atmosphere was that of a lively village fete.

However, a teenager did not need to appreciate dancing to have a good time in Montmartre. Paris's burgeoning café scene was an intrinsic part of the social fabric by the 1880s. Cafés had suffered severe repression in the 1870s under then president Marshal MacMahon's harsh 'moral order' regime.[7] Viewed as hotbeds of political opposition, they were monitored with suspicion. Added to which, in 1873, the *Loi Roussel* had imposed controls on alcohol consumption in a bid to quash incidents of public drunkenness. Hence, when the formal controls were relaxed in the summer of 1880, café culture emerged into a golden era.

'In Paris, cafés are an important resource for everyone,' declared one contemporary guidebook, but 'particularly for the *flâneur*', that cool, aloof observer of urban society.[8] In a city whose population included a swelling number of migrants, cafés provided an environment which afforded proximity without prior acquaintance and where new connections could be formed. Moreover, Haussmann's wider pavements now brought café life spilling out on to the street.[9] All at once, public life overshadowed private, strangers shared spaces and relationships became uncertain. The café terrace offered a strategic vantage point from which to assess the city and its inhabitants. 'Sat outside, you can philosophically judge Paris in all its animation and contemplate a new and constantly changing world as you savour your *demi-tasse*,' explained a popular tourist guide.[10] In order to sample this delight, visitors were advised to stroll along to the café 'in the evening, at about 10 o'clock', or more particularly, 'around five, absinthe o'clock'.[11]

It was a loaded reference. Absinthe, or wormwood, the liquorice-flavoured, plant-based liqueur, had been popular in France throughout the 19th century. Though the drink was of Swiss origin, heavy tax on import had encouraged H.L. Pernod to start producing it commercially in France at the end of the 18th century.[12] It was a tremendous success, and as the 19th century unfolded, its popularity soared. Exceedingly potent, it was closer to a soft drug than a drink. 'The drunkenness it gives does not resemble any known drunkenness,' bemoaned Alfred Delvau. 'It makes you lose your footing right away [...] You think you are headed towards infinity, like all great dreamers, and you are only headed towards incoherence.'[13] In excess, absinthe could have a fatal effect on the nervous system, and by the time Maria started attending the bars and cafés where it was served, it had become a national curse. A favourite drink among the working classes precisely because of its relative cheapness for the effect produced, absinthe became the scapegoat for a host of social ills, not least the Commune. But in a supreme illustration of the vicious circle of capitalism, producers (both legitimate and crooks who would cut or substitute the drink with other, cheaper substances), could not resist its lucrative potential, just as addicts fell victim to the liquid's power to lift their earthly worries, if only temporarily.

Absinthe found a dedicated following among artists, writers and poets (including Charles Baudelaire), for whom the liquor became the entrancing 'green fairy'. Its popularity in these circles was due primarily to its intoxicating effect, but also because its consumption was accompanied by a curious ritual which appealed to quirky individuals with a taste for the extraordinary. To counteract the drink's inherent bitterness, a sugar lump was placed on a special spoon with a hole in it, which was held above the glass while water was poured over it, with the effect of sweetening the absinthe. Not surprisingly, absinthe flowed freely through the bars and cafés of Montmartre.

However, even where absinthe was not involved, for a single bourgeois woman to attend a café unaccompanied would have had catastrophic repercussions in the 19th century. Her reputation would have been irretrievably tarnished – only *demi-mondaines* and working-class girls with no regard for morals attended such places. And yet it was in the café that prominent male artists like Manet held court, where the most revolutionary and exhilarating aesthetic debates took place, and where the deepest artistic friendships were formed. Berthe Morisot and Mary Cassatt had to forge careers around this glaring absence in their résumés. But Maria was not a member of the bourgeoisie. Her lower-class status earned her entry to the café, while her work as a model gained her access to an even more exclusive club: the world of the artists and their conversation. Modelling thereby handed her the key to unlock a door which remained firmly bolted to the likes of Morisot, Cassatt and even many lower-class women.

Maria soon discovered the café which was to become her favourite. The Lapin Agile was a rustic hillside tavern-cum-café on the corner of the Rue des Saules.[14] It had green-painted shutters, a charming little terrace with wooden picnic tables, and a swashbuckling history. It had begun life as the Rendez-Vous des Voleurs, in triumphant recognition of all Montmartre's outlaws, before becoming the Cabaret des Assassins in the 1860s. The name change was part of an ingenious marketing strategy by the innkeeper, which predicted that a nod to the area's history of gruesome crimes would be good for business, particularly in view of the mood aroused by the recent trial of the serial killer M. Troppman. But when Maria first started taking her seat at the long stretch of joined-together tables by the bar, or in the shade of the trees on the leafy terrace, the inn had just undergone its final transformation. In 1875, humorist and cartoonist André Gill had been asked to redesign the sign, and drawing inspiration from the inn's list of specialties, he painted an ungainly rabbit springing out of a saucepan balancing a bottle of wine on its paw, with a cap sliding drunkenly off its head. Perpetuating Gill's wit, the Lapin à Gill soon contracted into the Lapin Agile. Locals jealously guarded their seats at the venue, but in its new guise and with its relaxed ambience and music, the inn quickly became the un-missable evening haunt of students, writers and artists, as well as pimps, prostitutes and Montmartre's full cast of eccentrics. For regulars – which is what Maria became – the inn was something of an institution, and one patron fondly remembered, 'you could sit for the whole evening into the small hours with the same drink.'[15]

But if Maria felt like a change of scene and company, just a short walk down the hill past the rising silhouette of the Sacré-Coeur (which had been climbing steadily up the Montmartre skyline since its construction began in the mid-1870s), she could take a seat for the evening in the Café de la Nouvelle Athènes. Conveniently located on the Place Pigalle, it was to this café that Édouard Manet and his Impressionist companions had switched allegiance from the Café Guerbois in the 1870s.[16] It was also the café whose unremarkable interior Edgar Degas used as the setting for his *In the Café* (*The Absinthe Drinker*) (1875–1876). Of an evening, a visitor could expect to find Manet surrounded by artists such as Degas, Claude Monet, Pierre-Auguste Renoir and Camille Pissarro, and writers like Émile Zola and Edmond Duranty. As Irishman George Moore explained, attendance at the café was not so much an entertainment – it was an education. 'I did not go to Oxford or Cambridge,' he proudly announced, 'but I went to the Nouvelle Athènes.' He vividly remembered:

the white face of that café, the white nose of that block of houses, stretching up to the Place, between two streets. I can see down the incline of those two streets, and I know what shops are there; I can hear the glass door of the café grate on the sand as I open it. I can recall the smell of every hour. In the morning that of eggs frizzling in butter, the pungent cigarette, coffee and bad cognac; at five o'clock, the fragrant odour of absinthe; and soon after the steaming soup ascends from the kitchen; and as the evening advances, the mingled smells of cigarettes, coffee, and weak beer [...] The usual marble tables are there, and it is there we sat and aestheticized till two o'clock in the morning.[17]

The fruit of these discussions changed the course of art history; it was here that the idea of the first independent Impressionist exhibition was born.[18]

Maria adored lengthy conversations with kindred spirits and creative minds. But when fatigue or lethargy rendered a less partici-patory entertainment appealing, Montmartre also boasted several café-concerts. Like alcohol and coffee, song had been cast as the faithful servant of political opposition when Louis-Napoleon came to power.[19] Singing in cafés was consequently one of the first forms of expression outlawed under his regime. However, when a series of decrees in the 1860s had lifted many of the restrictions imposed on entertainment venues (notably by permitting the use of props, costumes and music), café-concerts had begun to flourish. By the 1880s, there were over 200 such venues belting out hearty songs about working-class life across Paris. Along with the usual facili-ties of a café, café-concerts also offered a small indoor stage or a covered pavilion outside where singers, and sometimes acrobats and comedians, performed for an often raucous audience. Patrons paid more than they would in a standard café, either in the form of an entrance fee or through elevated drinks prices. But many judged the supplement worthwhile; the atmosphere was relaxed, the singers, though not first rate, were undeniably 'of the people', and unlike theatre-goers, audience members could also smoke. And as one guidebook writer exclaimed with surprise, 'sometimes, one can actually hear quite good music.'[20]

But most of the time, after a long day spent holding a pose, Maria simply wanted somewhere she could meet with like-minded individuals, a place where her aching limbs could relax and her mind would be inspired. In 1881, she found the perfect venue. It was a place where creative expression was not just permitted – it was positively encouraged.

Rodolphe Salis was a tall, red-headed bohemian with a coppery beard and boundless charisma.[21] He had tried and failed to make a success of several different careers, including painting decorations for a building in Calcutta.[22] But by 1881 he was listless and creatively frustrated, uncertain where his niche might lie. More pressingly, he was desperate to secure a steady income. But then he had the ingenious idea to turn the studio which he rented, a disused post office on the resolutely working-class Boulevard de Rochechouart, into a cabaret with a quirky, artistic bent. He was not the first to attempt such a venture: La Grande Pinte on the Avenue Trudaine had been uniting artists and writers to discuss and give spontaneous performances for several years.[23] But Salis was determined that his initiative would be different – and better. A fortuitous meeting ensured that it was.

Poet Émile Goudeau was the founder of the alternative literary group the Hydropathes ('water-haters' – meaning that they preferred wine or beer). After meeting Goudeau in the Latin Quarter and attending a few of the group's gatherings, Salis became convinced that a more deliberate form of entertainment than had been offered at La Grande Pinte would create a venue that was truly innovative – and profitable.[24] The Hydropathe members needed a new meeting place, and so Salis persuaded Goudeau to rally his comrades and convince them to relocate from the Latin Quarter to his new *cabaret artistique*. They would be able to drink, smoke, talk and showcase their talents and their wit. Targeting an established group like the Hydropathes was a stroke of genius on Salis's part. Baptising his cabaret Le Chat Noir after the eponymous feline of Edgar Allan Poe's story, he made certain that his ready-made clientele were not disappointed.

Everything about the ambience and the decor reflected Salis's unconventional, anti-establishment approach, an ethos which the Hydropathes shared. A seemingly elongated room with low ceilings was divided in two by a curtain.[25] The front section was larger and housed a bar for standard customers. But the back part of the room (referred to as 'L'Institut') was reserved exclusively for artists. Fiercely proud of his locality, Salis was adamant that he could make Montmartre glorious. 'What is Montmartre?' Salis famously asked. 'Nothing. What should it be? Everything!'[26] Accordingly, Salis invited artists from the area to decorate the venue. Adolphe Léon Willette painted stained-glass panels for the windows, while Théophile-Alexandre Steinlen created posters. And all around, a disorientating mishmash of antiques and bric-a-brac gave the place a higgledy-piggledy feel. There was Louis XIII furniture, tapestries and armour alongside rusty swords; there were stags' heads and wooden statues nestled beside coats of arms. It was weird, it was wonderful and it was utterly bizarre – the customers loved it.

Salis was outrageously mean when it came to paying his staff, but with his customers he was the perfect gentleman *cabaretier*.[27] A smooth talker, he made a point of welcoming guests with gushing hyperbole. Patrons were not 'Sir' or 'Madam' but 'Monseigneur' or 'Your Highness', and were greeted with a bow.[28] A consummate showman, Salis soon had artists, writers, poets, journalists, actors, singers and their associates pouring through the doors of his unlikely studio. Maria was one of them.

Her drinking companions included budding talent from the musical world, such as Paul Verlaine, Claude Debussy, Charles Gounod and Yvette Guilbert.[29] There were artists, some established, many up-and-coming: Édouard Manet, a certain Henri de Toulouse-Lautrec, Henri Rivière, Willette, Steinlen and Caran d'Ache. And a person could guarantee that they would meet with writers, for Salis's guests included such names as Jean Lorrain, Léon Bloy, Maurice Donnay, Jean Richepin, Jules Renard, Maurice Rollinat, Jules Jouy, Émile Zola, Alphonse Daudet, Guy de Maupassant, Victor Hugo and Alphonse Allais. There were also statesmen like Léon Gambetta, and actresses, notably Sarah Bernhardt.

On a typical evening, guests were greeted at the door by a Swiss guard, brilliantly adorned in full uniform, complete with halberd, who had the professed mission of ushering in poets and painters while expelling members of the clergy and the military.[30] Tables were then served by waiters disguised as academicians. Once equipped with a drink (distinctly mediocre wine in the early days, or Salis's famous beer, 'hydromel'), visitors could take a seat at one of the oaken benches and while away an evening in the dimly lit, smoky tavern, drinking, laughing, chatting and joining in raucously with familiar old songs while someone accompanied on a guitar or violin.[31] There were recitals and performances of all kinds, and sometimes even a shadow show. Friday evenings were wildly popular.

Salis made the extraordinary both his raison d'être and his selling point. The bourgeoisie eyed the cabaret and the image of bohemian life it projected with bemused curiosity; the proprietor made sure that ferrets of eccentricity were never disappointed. Salis made a flamboyant show of subverting convention wherever possible, and his militant rejection of modernity in favour of a childlike wonder at the absurd found a sympathetic following in

Montmartre. Little could rival Salis's charisma – save perhaps the stage presence of one of his performers, a square-jawed singer named Aristide Bruant, who took the stage with a flourish wearing a broad-brimmed felt hat, cape, scarlet scarf and boots.[32] His lyrics about familiar perils of working-class life always drew an enthusiastic response.

An 1881 press law laid the ground for a boom of humorous publications, and, ever the opportunist, early in 1882 Salis founded a journal with the same name as the cabaret.[33] The proprietor turned to his artist and writer friends for amusing contributions to crystallise Le Chat Noir's ethos and publicise its exploits, and their writings, poems and illustrations were paid in hospitality (for Salis was loath to part with money).

Public hoaxes and practical jokes were wholeheartedly encouraged and the journal played an active part in these pranks; in April 1882, *Le Chat Noir* published news of Salis's death.[34] A sign was placed outside the tavern explaining that the premises were open for mourning, and inside, a cello case was concealed under a black cloth to imitate a coffin. Horrified mourners were invited to pay their respects and then console themselves with beer. On another occasion, a well-known actor from the Variétés was recognised by Salis's clientele as he passed the tavern.[35] Drinkers came rushing out into the street clutching props seized from the cabaret in order to serenade the star in a mock ceremonial worship, with Salis reverently kneeling to present the bewildered actor with an honorary beer in an antique vase.

Maria delighted in such hysterical revelry. As a child, the only people she had been tempted to befriend were the unusual characters she came across while playing truant; the sole activities that had held her attention were the strange or the daring. Now, everyone around her had their share of eccentricities and the bizarre was a universal pastime. The wild but withdrawn and awkward little girl blossomed into an outgoing social butterfly with dozens of friends and a taste for fun. Maria was in her element. One night, she surpassed even the most brazen of Montmartre's extroverts by sliding down the banisters at the Moulin de la Galette wearing nothing but a mask.[36]

In the liberal, bohemian village that Montmartre had become, a pretty teen seldom kept her chastity for long. To the rumours that Maria was sleeping with her employer Puvis were added countless others. By the time she was sixteen there were enough stories of promiscuous behaviour for Montmartre's gossips to have branded Maria with a prodigious reputation; there was the Breton waiter at Père Lathuile's, the postman Léconte, the sailor Guichet and a growing list of artists.[37] Maria proudly refused to confirm or deny the stories. She had grown impervious to criticism. Besides, she was having fun. And in 1880s Montmartre, social boundaries and relationships were rarely clear or stable. A late-night party might only end when a girl fell into bed with somebody, and it happened so frequently that memory could seldom recall the episode clearly. When removing clothes before an observer had become a natural part of the daily routine, making love was merely an extension if a good time was being had. Physical intimacy was no index of spiritual closeness.

But on one of her ventures out into Montmartre's vibrant social scene, Maria met a man with whom she could share both.

Miguel Utrillo y Morlius was a dashing, dark-haired Spaniard with intense brown eyes and an infectious zest for life. He was tall and slender with a neat moustache, and he cut a fine figure in his velvet jacket and broad-brimmed hat. Three years older than Maria, Miguel came from a well-to-do family from Barcelona who first brought their son to Avignon in 1880.[38] Besides his good looks, energy and intelligence, Miguel had the enviable knack of excelling at any creative pursuit to which he turned his hand. He could paint, draw, sing and dance spectacularly. But so numerous were his talents that Miguel found it impossible to settle on one of them. He had returned to Barcelona briefly to sit his science-based baccalaureate, but he also received some artistic training alongside his studies. That he demonstrated skill in both areas only made choosing one of them more difficult. Eventually, Miguel came back to Paris in 1880 and took up the offer of a place to study at the Institut Agronomique, where he began to train as an engineer. However, with his creative streak unsatisfied, he was gaining as much satisfaction from the lively social life attached to Montmartre's art scene as he was from his studies, and was often seen out enjoying himself with his great friends, fellow Catalan painters Santiago Rusiñol and Ramon Casas.

Le Chat Noir was a natural habitat for Miguel, and when he and Maria met, they immediately warmed to each other. Though she was surrounded by artists, Maria was elusive about her own drawing, often destroying sketches she was unsatisfied with; that she shared her hidden passion with Miguel stands testimony to their closeness. Miguel (who Maria insisted on calling Michel, using the French version of his name) was amazed at her skill. Praise from a man as talented as him made Maria radiant with pride. From the early 1880s, they seemed inseparable, taking their meals together and, like a pair of naughty children, partaking in all manner of outrageous practical jokes, often with Rusiñol and Casas (who had also both succumbed to Paris's charms) joining in. Miguel was known for having ridden into the Moulin de la Galette on the back of a donkey and having staged a mock bullfight in the lobby of the Boule Noire dance hall.[39] One evening, he trundled a cart full of pungent fish into the Elysée-Montmartre, with Maria close by struggling to suppress her giggles.[40] It was naturally assumed that Miguel and Maria were lovers, not just cheeky playmates. Maria's memories of their relationship left many in little doubt. 'At a time when barely anyone paid me any attention, he encouraged me, strengthened me and supported me,' she said. 'You should have seen him chatting with the famous artists [...] He was studying at the Institut Agronomique [...] And on top of that, he painted and drew.'[41] She expanded: 'With Michel [Miguel] I spent the best years of my youth [...] We lived an artistic and bohemian life.'[42]

The bond between Maria and Miguel was unique, but with both of them being impulsive and passionate, their relationship was peppered with explosive rows. Moreover, the climate in Montmartre was such that even when a young couple were lovers, monogamy was the exception, not the rule. Maria drifted. There were too many fascinating characters in Montmartre for a girl to spend all her time in the company of one man. And then conversations at the bar could always lead to lifelong friendships or interesting work. Maria's meeting with Italian painter Federico Zandomeneghi brought both such rewards.

The son of a Venetian sculptor, Zandomeneghi had associated with members of the Macchia movement in Florence, a group who, like the Impressionists, had adopted the innovative practice of painting entire canvases outside and who used patches of colour to capture the effects of light.[43] In 1874, 'Zando' became convinced that a move to Paris would bring him the professional recognition he hungered for and from the late 1870s he was a regular at the Café de la Nouvelle Athènes. With a long face, large nose and dark features which betrayed his Mediterranean origins, Zando's quizzical expression gave him an interesting appearance which made a person yearn for closer acquaintance. He was fiercely proud of his Italian origins, and was not long in Paris before he was drawn to Degas, who also boasted Italian heritage. Degas took the young Venetian under his wing, and persuaded his grudging protégé to exhibit in four of the Impressionist exhibitions between 1879 and 1886. Zando worked with zeal, focusing on figure subjects for which he experimented with unconventional angles and framing.[44] But by the early 1880s, with success not forthcoming, he had had to resort to illustrating fashion magazines to supplement his income. Zando was increasingly bitter and he laid the blame firmly at the feet of the French.

Maria and Zando formed a close and long-lasting friendship, and when busy routines rendered face-to-face meetings impossible, they took to writing to each other, particularly when a notable date like New Year fell. Zandomeneghi's name soon joined the list of Maria's presumed lovers. Indeed, for a girl with an appreciation of painting, Zandomeneghi was a most respectable beau. But in the middle of 1882, when Maria was sixteen, she was offered a modelling assignment with an artist who far overshadowed Zandomeneghi. It was then that Maria was recommended to Pierre-Auguste Renoir.

By 1882, Renoir was widely agreed to be one of the most sought after, fashionable portrait artists in Paris. Though he had been painting most of his life (beginning decorating porcelain at the age of thirteen, before enrolling at the École des Beaux-Arts in 1862 and soon after being accepted to study under the prestigious painter Charles Gleyre), it was not until the end of the 1860s that Renoir started to gain public recognition.[45] His portrait of his lover Lise Tréhot attracted attention at the Salon of 1868, but his real triumph came when he entered a portrait of the wife of his patron Georges Charpentier at the Salon of 1879. An influential hostess of a highly regarded literary salon, Mme Charpentier enjoyed all the right connections to ensure that her portrait was prominently displayed. Renoir's reputation soared, and his financial situation was 'transformed, virtually overnight'.[46]

Quite apart from his talent, earning potential and renown, Renoir had a magnetic appearance despite his 40 years. He had changed little since the time Maria claimed to have encountered him as a child. He was slim, with light brown hair, even features and an aquiline nose. But most of all, it was his eyes that stopped ladies in their tracks. 'His eyes were light brown, bordering on amber,' remembered his son, 'and they were sharp and penetrating. He would often point out a bird of prey on the horizon, flying over the valley, or a lady-bird climbing up a single blade in a tuft of grass [...] They had the look of tenderness mixed with irony, of merriment and sensuousness. They always seemed to be laughing, perceiving the odd side of things. But it was a gentle and loving laughter.'[47] Women adored him. And with that intense gaze, magnetism and almost Mediterranean allure, Renoir possessed all the qualities for which Maria had already demonstrated her weakness.

Still, although his career (particularly as a portrait artist) was flourishing, by the 1880s, Renoir was unsettled. He was universally branded as a member of that revolutionary group, the Impressionists. But he had become concerned about exhibiting with them as an independent artist, particularly once Degas introduced a clause in 1878, which stipulated that participants could not simultaneously exhibit at the Salon.[48] Renoir found himself unable to espouse the notion that the Salon did not matter; he knew he needed it. He had consequently refused to exhibit in the Impressionist exhibitions since 1879. Moreover, he believed that he had not yet reached the pinnacle of all he was capable of, that there was still more he could achieve. At the same time, he was conscious he had reached an impasse in his work as an Impressionist. It was not so much the style he had perfected which bothered him; rather, he longed to transform his treatment of the figure. The question was: how?

Much of the company he was keeping now was of the upper-class variety, that tranche for whom lengthy trips to foreign lands were almost a rite of passage.[49] And so with the savings to spare and

Pierre-Auguste Renoir, c. 1875,
Musée d'Orsay, Paris.

Photo © Musée d'Orsay, Dist. RMN-Grand Palais/Patrice Schmidt

a creative solution to find, following the example of his associates, early in 1881, Renoir set off on an epic journey.

He travelled first to Algeria, then back to France for a few months, and then off to Italy.[50] He took in Venice and Rome, and marvelled at the Raphaels; he went to Naples, and gazed in amazement at the frescoes. He returned to France briefly early in 1882, fell ill, but refused to let this hamper another trip to Algeria, where he spent just a few months more before returning to Paris. By the summer of 1882, he was back in the capital, physically ailing, financially depleted, but creatively revitalised – and excited: he had a new idea.

Renoir had in mind a pair of paintings and a third canvas which would be shown separately. All would continue the sequence of urban recreation he had already started and would depict a couple dancing. But these canvases would be distinctly different from much of his previous work, and would draw on his new discoveries, particularly those made in Italy.

But first he needed models. His good friend Paul Lhote would be perfect for the male figure. He had modelled for Renoir before, so knew the routine, even if his flirtatious behaviour needed to be kept in check around the ladies.[51] But the female dancer must be selected more carefully; it was she, after all, on whom attention would inevitably fall. Maria's acquaintances would later recall that it was Puvis de Chavannes who recommended Maria when Renoir made his need known.[52]

Maria later explained that their actual face-to-face meeting was orchestrated by another of Renoir's models, a buxom blonde named Nini Gérard.[53] When Renoir beheld Maria, he could see just the young woman he had been looking for.

'I loved women even before I learned to walk,' Renoir confided, and as the son of a tailor, he had very clear ideas regarding what did and did not become them.[54] He despised the fashion for tight-fitting corsets, which restricted movement and distorted the body's shape.[55] He preferred his women natural and voluptuous, their hair flowing free, their figures ripe and healthy. Maria embodied his ideal.

For the painting which became known as *Dance in the City*, Renoir wanted Maria dressed in a sweeping satin ballgown with a train and long, elegant gloves. Painters sometimes borrowed dresses for their models, but while Maria was shapely, she was especially petite, and the clothes had to fit to perfection.[56] There was nothing for it: like a real-life Cinderella, Maria was whisked off to couturiers to transform her from a linen maid's daughter into a high society lady.[57] Sourcing the costume was a ponderous task, but eventually Renoir found the gloves which would slip over her delicate fingers. The sittings commenced.

Maria had to make her way to one of Renoir's studios, usually the workspace located in the narrow Rue d'Orchampt, for the sittings would take place indoors.[58] As the painter explained to his patroness, Mme Charpentier, his travels had brought him to the conclusion that: 'by studying outdoor effects, I have ended up by only seeing broad harmonies without preoccupying myself with the small details which extinguish sunlight instead of lighting it up.'[59] He wanted to rectify this oversight.

So there in the studio, her hair held up loosely by a single pink blossom, the white lace ruffles of her virginal ballgown kissing the creamy skin of her naked shoulders, Maria stood for hours with a powerful male arm holding her possessively close, its owner's breath warming her cheek at intervals. And as she stood, an experienced hand traced her every curve, lingering over each limb in turn, as Renoir did what he did best.

Renoir's weakness for women was well-known. He had a lover, the rotund and well-scrubbed countrywoman, Aline Charigot. However, he was putting off officialising their union, and remained cagey about the affair, presenting himself as a bachelor in public. To his mind, he was not married. And, as he said himself, 'before marriage, you do whatever you please.'[60]

The circumstances were propitious for even the mildest physical attraction to blossom into a passionate affair. Maria was candid about the relationship. She was heard to insist that he had fallen in love with her.[61] Though young of spirit, Renoir was already rheumatic and Maria conceded that there were men more handsome to be found. But when she was there with him in the studio, none of that mattered; the great painter found her attractive. That was enough.

And when Renoir laid down his brushes at the end of a long, hot session in the studio, there was more to sustain a relationship between painter and model than crude sexual chemistry. Like

Maria, Renoir came from a lower-class family and had started life in the Limousin, where infants were raised on a wholesome diet of simple produce, traditional customs and fantastical stories.[62] As a child, he too had experienced hardship. The couple also shared a single-minded approach to drawing and painting, which often flew in the face of social expectation and dismissed popular notions of propriety. When Renoir stayed with the painter Jacques-Emile Blanche and his mother, Mme Blanche was appalled by his unrefined manners and insistence on painting in all weathers: 'if it were a matter of more than five or six days, I might have been led to violence,' she exclaimed, 'because he is not a man to be stopped by the mud in our neighbourhood, there is no reason for us to let our nice new rooms get soiled, with their fabric upholstery and mats underfoot'.[63] Then Renoir and Maria's mutual love of François Villon provided ample source of conversation.[64]

For the period Renoir was perfecting his canvases, the world Maria inhabited transformed into a blissful sunlit idyll blossoming with romantic interludes and sweet-perfumed flowers. There were rapid sketches and protracted studies, swift strokes in charcoal and gentle, tantalising blending of oils. Renoir worked quickly, puffing on a cigarette, sometimes singing. As she watched him, Maria noticed that he was eager to progress to colour as soon as possible.[65] With his three canvases, Renoir wanted to explore the multiple hues of pleasure's glorious rainbow.

From the ballroom of *Dance in the City*, Maria was transported to a sunny afternoon by the waterside with dappled light penetrating through the trees for the work which would become known as *Dance at Bougival*.[66] Bougival was a pretty riverside village 18km west of Paris which had become a lively hub of middle- and working-class entertainment at the weekends. Renoir clothed Maria in a pale pink, ruffled dress edged with red, an example of the very latest summer fashion.[67] It was fitted at the waist, and fanned out at the base, cleverly accentuating the idea of movement as she was spun round and round, discarded matches and a bouquet of violets abandoned by her feet to underscore the mood of carefree spontaneity. Renoir tried dozens of hats on Maria's head before settling on one: a vibrant red bonnet or *chapeau Niniche*, whose ribbons he painted flying out behind her as she moved, while her gaze bashfully refused to meet that of her insistent partner.[68] For the finishing touch, Renoir teasingly placed a wedding ring on her finger.

But when the third painting, *Dance in the Country*, was revealed, something peculiar became apparent.

'Do you recognise me? I am a dancer who smiles as she abandons herself in the arms of her partner,' Maria declared years later, purportedly in relation to this picture.[69] And yet it was clear that the woman in *Dance in the Country* had a figure which was plumper, a face which was fuller – an appearance closer to that of Aline.

One story ran that Aline, jealous of her commitment-shy lover's closeness to his model, became furious when she saw *Dance in the Country* showing Maria and smudged out her younger competitor's face.[70] People whispered that her anger had come to a climax on a subsequent visit to the studio when she caught Renoir and Maria locked in a passionate embrace, and that she seized a broom and attempted to beat Maria to the door.[71] It was said that Renoir had sheepishly repainted the smeared canvas using the victorious Aline as the model. The tale would explain Maria's determination to stake her claim and her insistence that the painting resulting from the studies for which she had posed was her. At least one of Renoir's preparatory drawings shows a face which clearly has Maria's features.

However, when it was concluded that she was referring to her role in *Dance in the Country*, none of her audience seemed to recall that *Dance at Bougival* was also originally titled *Dance in the Country*, first when it was deposited with dealer Paul Durand-Ruel in April 1883 and then again in the dealer's records in 1891.[72] Moreover, when *Dance at Bougival* was used to illustrate model Paul Lhote's short story, *Mademoiselle Zélia*, in 1883, it accompanied the description of a young female dancer 'waltzing, deliciously abandoned in the arms of a fair-haired man with the air of an oarsman' – an expression repeated by Maria.[73] The 'composition at Bougival' which Maria also spoke of having posed for could refer to any number of works inspired by the time Renoir spent painting there in the summer of 1882.[74] Either way, anyone acquainted with Renoir's lover or his model could see that the figure in *Dance in the Country* was not Maria. And there was another difference between the three dance canvases, too. In *Dance in the City* and *Dance at Bougival* – the two works depicting Maria – the face and, notably, the eyes of the male character were almost entirely concealed. Like a Rembrandtian self-portrait, Renoir made his male dancer's identity uncertain, malleable – illicit. The painter could almost imagine his own face into the pictures with Maria.

One day, Maria was at home and had become so engrossed in the drawing she was working on that she had lost all sense of time. She was due for one of Renoir's sittings. When she failed to appear, Renoir set out to find her, and called at her home. The scene he found came as a total shock: his model was drawing – and with assurance. 'You too,' he exclaimed, 'and you hide it!'[75] But he offered no further critique or encouragement.

Maria was unfazed. She could feel when a drawing was good. As a model and budding artist, Maria could not fail to respect her employer, but in later years, she gained the confidence to critique him in her turn. She called him *le peintre à la tomate*, an insult many took to signify the 'tomato sauce' (i.e. superficial) painter.[76] But the expression, which could also be understood as 'the painter with the tomato', might simultaneously have been a snide allusion to the rosy complexion and round-faced person of Aline. He was, Maria said, a 'fine painter', but 'all brushes' and 'no heart'.[77] Besides, Renoir's conviction that a woman's purpose was to please the eye and keep the home was not a view she could tolerate for long.[78] In any case, by the spring of 1883, when Renoir finally submitted his finished dance canvases to Durand-Ruel, Maria had a more pressing concern. She had just made her own discovery: she was pregnant.

CHAPTER 6

Not Just a Pretty Face

Ce que se vei ne po pà se cochà.
(You can't hide what everyone can see.)

OLD LIMOUSIN PROVERB[1]

The stigma attached to falling pregnant outside marriage had altered little since Madeleine had given birth to Maria eighteen years earlier. The devastating label *fille-mère* (girl-mother) was applied to a female who found herself in such a predicament.[2] 'No, we are not married,' mother of two Gervaise admits in Émile Zola's novel *L'Assommoir* (1877), published just five years before. 'I don't try to hide it,' she declares.[3] All the same, Zola has his anti-heroine draw closer to her listener to say it.

The spread of more varied forms of contraception brought some assurance.[4] From the 1880s, latex condoms were beginning to replace more primitive versions made of sheep or pig gut. But they were not yet widely used. The standard contraceptives remained coitus interruptus, the vaginal sponge or the douche. But whichever method was used, all required foresight or swift reparatory action – neither of which harmonised with Montmartre's prevalent mood of carefree living and spontaneity.

In the circles Maria was mixing in, premarital pregnancy was considered, at best, a costly inconvenience. At its most extreme, it was a financial wound and an indelible social blight which could destroy a girl's chance of making a good marriage – or indeed any marriage at all.

But when news of Maria's dilemma was leaked on the Butte, the question on everyone's lips was not what the possible repercussions of the pregnancy might be but rather: who was its author? And that was a far more opaque matter.

It could only be Miguel Utrillo, many Montmartrois reasoned. The pair were rarely apart. Why, just months before, Maria had been seen enthusiastically applauding the lecture Miguel had given at Le Chat Noir on the Bal del Ciri, a Catalan candle dance.[5] He had spoken eloquently on the dance and associated folklore, sung, and even broken into an empassioned demonstration of the rapid footwork involved, with its contrapas and sardanas. Maria had been mesmerised and had often been heard to eulogise the evening since. More ominously, Miguel had recently left Paris to work abroad, embarking on an extensive tour of Belgium, Germany, Bulgaria, Russia and Spain.[6] For cynics, no further evidence was required; those were indisputably the actions of a man fleeing responsibility, anxious to safeguard his family name.

However, others were convinced that Renoir was the father. Everyone had heard the rumours, and the opportunities for business to blossom into pleasure would have been all the greater as Renoir raced to complete his *Dance at Bougival* in time for the exhibition at the Dowdeswell Gallery in London that April. Eventually, the painting had arrived for the show – five days late.[7] (By way of evidence of an ongoing relationship, it would subsequently be said that when Renoir and Lhote travelled to Guernsey later that year, Maria accompanied them and was all set to stay until word reached the party that Aline was on her way to join them – whereupon Renoir hastily ordered his model to return to France.[8] The fact that Maria was heavily pregnant at the time did nothing to dissuade purveyors of the myth, which soon became woven into the rich tapestry of Montmartre's social history. As if to endorse the story, Renoir's *Seated Bather* (1883–1884), which was said to have been inspired by studies the artist completed during his stay on the island, bore an uncanny resemblance to Maria.[9])

Yet a third school of thought subscribed to the theory that Puvis de Chavannes was the baby's father. The painter's ponderous working method was legendary. His eyes would roam Maria's scantily clad body for longer than many younger artists. And how often time had been shown to increase the chances of sexual liaisons – and misdemeanours.

But there was another, more sinister possibility, too. While the Sunday afternoon dances at the Moulin de la Galette were cheerful, good-humoured affairs, on Monday nights, women and girls were admitted free of charge, and as a result, on those evenings the venue transformed into the playground of a far less salubrious crowd.[10] This included a good helping of local drunks, thieves and hooligans. Rumour had it that one night, Maria had ventured out to one of these events when there was a drunken brawl. The music stopped, the lights went out briefly, someone pulled out a knife and people screamed. Terrified, Maria fell into the arms of the lecherous, alcoholic insurance clerk and amateur painter, Adrien Boissy. In the confusion, she found herself accompanying him home. A drink was poured, and then another, and before long, the clear division between right and wrong started to blur. Boissy's embraces became more urgent. He seemed deaf to Maria's objections, oblivious to her struggles. Then it was over. The child Maria now carried was the rotten fruit of a sickening violation, several locals maintained. That the very sight of Boissy around Montmartre seemed to inspire virulent animosity in the usually placid Madeleine only reinforced the story's likelihood.[11]

Then to the distinctive verses of prime suspects was added a predictable chorus of various Montmartrois, artists and local riff-raff who could all be potential fathers.

Maria's standard response when questioned directly was an enigmatic 'It could be' or 'I hope so'.[12] She remained elusive – studiously so. Ultimately, no one on the Butte could say for sure who the child's father was. Some suspected that Maria herself may have been uncertain. She was once heard to rebuff the usual question with the candid reply: 'I've never been able to decide.'[13]

In any case, Maria had a more concerning problem to tackle. Paris's arts scene may have been turning out a new generation of forward-thinking painters, but few would seriously consider a girl swollen with pregnancy to model their Madonnas or their nubile sea nymphs. Without a source of income from outside, Maria's pregnancy would cost her and Madeleine dear. But there was no choice. And once Maria was finally forced to accept that she had become unemployable, she had her drawing to distract her attention.

Maria often destroyed her artwork, but that year, she did something unprecedented: she drew her own self-portrait, and she kept the finished piece.

It was a poignant moment to carry out such a close inspection of the self. As Maria looked into the mirror, the face she saw staring back was not Renoir's blushing dancer with her sweet smile and rosy lips; nor was it the lofty, statuesque muse who had posed so elegantly for Puvis. For once, she was not playing the role assigned to her by a man; she was being herself.

In a near monochrome palette of cool blues and greens with mere highlights of pink and yellow, Maria recorded what she saw with unnerving honesty. With her hair centre-parted and swept back severely off her face, her plain, sombre dress and natural complexion rejected artifice, while her off-centre framing reflected the aesthetic innovations of the art world around her. Considerable industry was required to get the naturally smooth texture of pastel to form the sharp contours of her cheek and jaw. Combined with her unsmiling expression, the effect was dramatic, disconcerting – devastating.

Critics subsequently described the dour-looking girl depicted as pugnacious and proud. Certainly, for an eighteen-year-old who had based a career on her appearance, Maria made surprisingly little effort to flatter herself. Her defiant expression and natur- ally upturned lip seemed instantly to challenge her viewer, as her big blue eyes fixed them with a sideways look, at once suspicious and sad; Maria wore the defensive mask of a girl who had already seen too much of the world. 'I paint people in order to know them,' Maria later explained.[14] The drawing was not an exercise in self-glorification for the benefit of others; it was a curious, quasi- scientific exploration of the woman she was becoming, designed to satisfy no one but Maria. The artist was not looking critically at the viewer; Maria was looking critically at herself.

As Maria's pastel swept across her paper, the very definition of art was being reassessed, the context in which it was consumed changing. That year had witnessed some dramatic shifts and excit- ing new beginnings. At the end of April 1883, the art world had lost Édouard Manet, the pioneer who had brought about a sea change in Western art and inspired a whole generation of enthusiastic young artists. The Impressionists, who had once seemed such a coherent and redoubtable group, had disbanded and as if to reiter- ate their autonomy, dealer Paul Durand-Ruel mounted a series of one-man shows at his gallery during the course of 1883. Even the long-standing dissatisfaction with the Salon was starting to effect tangible change. At the end of 1880, the everyday running of the Salon was finally placed in the hands of the artists, and no longer the state.[15] In the event, the jury proved just as rigorous in its selec- tion process, but the very fact that artists had been empowered heralded change and possibility. The 1863 Salon des Réfusés, where all the works rejected by the official Salon jury could be viewed separately, had already offered a taste of the kind of creative freedom many craved, and demonstrated that taste was diversifying. Now, the concept of an organisation which united independent artists and was entirely free of state control was no longer just a utopian dream; discussions were already under way. Then there was the Brussels group, Les XX, a newly formed organisation of twenty Belgian painters, which also showcased the work of twenty additional avant-garde artists from abroad in its yearly exhibitions. Suddenly, the ceiling on what was realistic and possible for a marginalised talent like Maria appeared less stable. For the first time ever, it was not a preordained fact that her drawings should have no life or impact outside her own four walls. Significantly, from that year she fell pregnant, Maria started keeping more and more of her works.

However, if Maria stood to be affected by the changes taking place in the art world outside, they were of little consequence to Madeleine. Perpetually bewildered by her daughter's creative yearnings, Madeleine's requirements were far more elementary. Her aspirations seldom extended beyond basic necessities. As the pregnancy advanced, Maria used her time to capture the soon-to-be grandmother in a chalk-and-pencil study. The business of sitting still for protracted periods did not come naturally to Madeleine, who had been taught to measure self-worth by industry. In her experience, only purposeful activity yielded results. But she sat and obliged her daughter's whims.

Positioned close to her mother, Maria's eyes darted between sitter and study as her red and white chalk rasped across the paper to fix Madeleine's sceptical expression and timeworn face in a brutally honest profile portrait. Every wrinkle on her mother's forehead was documented, each fold of skin around her eyes patiently recorded. Though neither had foreseen it, by the time the baby was due, circumstance had brought Maria and Madeleine to know each other more intimately than many mothers and daughters would in a whole lifetime.

While Maria's unplanned pregnancy was hardly desirable, Madeleine had retained a peasant's pragmatism when it came to life's unexpected twists. There seemed little value continually chastising her daughter for an act already committed, and one which was, in any case, impossible to repair. Besides, Madeleine had fallen into the same trap herself. She knew the struggle of raising a child alone would be penance enough. The most practical course of action now was to prepare for the baby's arrival.

By the time Maria's due date approached that Christmas, the mother and daughter had moved to a flat in the Rue Poteau.[16] It was a dingy street, higher up the hill of Montmartre, but it was at least removed from the hustle and bustle of the noisy Boulevard de Rochechouart.

That December, the seasonal festivities were overshadowed by the anticipation of Maria's imminent travail. It was just as well that the mother and daughter were well-prepared; no sooner had the Christmas celebrations commenced than Maria's contractions began.

The women never spoke in detail about the delivery, but word had it that it was an extremely difficult labour. Maria was said to have suffered terribly and fallen unconscious once the child was delivered.[17] Fortunately, Madeleine had had the foresight to ensure that there was an experienced midwife on hand, 57-year-old Celinie Elisa Durrez, who was able to oversee the proceedings. The baby finally appeared at one o'clock in the afternoon on 26 December. It was a boy.

Word later reached Maria that the same night, Adrien Boissy was found collapsed on the floor of the Lapin Agile, having bought rounds of drinks in honour of the birth and consumed more than his fair share into the bargain. He subsequently made himself scarce in Maria's life.[18]

On 29 December 1883, the child was registered. Maria was careful not to admit her real profession and offer information which might endorse further social opprobrium. She described herself as a more respectable 'seamstress'. Like her own birth certificate, the document bore the damning qualification 'father unknown'. Maria called her little boy Maurice.

Maurice was not Madeleine's first grandchild. Maria's sister, Marie-Alix, had given birth to a daughter, Marie-Lucienne, shortly after her marriage nearly ten years ago. But with Marie-Alix married and living at a distance, there was no question of Madeleine playing the hands-on role that was now required of her. The family's new composition called for a reassessment of each member's duties and responsibilities.

Madeleine was now in her 50s, and even if there had still been a substantial working life ahead of her, both women knew that of the two of them, Maria stood to earn considerably more once she could resume modelling. She was in demand. 'I'm stuck in Paris,' Renoir complained to Monet just weeks after Maria gave birth and was consequently indisposed, 'where I'm bored to death and running after the unobtainable model, but I'm a painter of figures! Alas! – It's very pleasant sometimes, but not when the figures you find are not to your taste.'[19] Maria's pre-pregnancy physique and professionalism were not easily come by; she could command respectable prices now. With Madeleine looking after the baby, Maria would also save on childcare expenses. It was the kind of strategic use of family resources which had been adopted by Limousin peasants for centuries, an approach that prioritised the welfare of the group over that of the individual.

The new arrangement seemed to suit all parties. But if it was primarily implemented for practical reasons, it also satisfied deeper, spiritual needs. Madeleine's thinking was permeated by the rural mentality that favoured sons, and having lost her own, she found that Maurice filled an aching hole. He offered her a second chance to live the experience she thought she had lost. At last, she could be a mother to a son, and without the full weight of responsibility and pressure to earn experienced by young parents. She could savour that indulgence unique to grandparents of being able to truly enjoy her grandson. And Maria was still beautiful. Even with the child, she could yet ensnare a husband – and security for them all – if she were back in circulation in Montmartre society.

Maria was content too. She had always oscillated between extremes, alternately throwing herself passionately into each new experience and then withdrawing to study the world around her objectively with a quizzical, unforgiving eye. The delicate tenderness of motherhood had no natural resonance for her. Her own relationship with her mother was neither demonstrative nor openly affectionate. The doting mother saw no imperfections; when Maria drew figures, she saw nothing else. The miniature body which suckled her breast was curious and strange, a mass of tiny, writhing limbs, a face made wrinkled and red through howling. But the adoring gazes and gestures she seemed unable to summon, the inane cooing, appeared to come naturally to Madeleine, in whom Maurice brought out a whole new side. So as soon as she was able, Maria left Madeleine and Maurice and returned to work, content that Madeleine would manage the family's private life at home, while she would assume the masculine role as main breadwinner. And to Maria's mind, circulating in the public sphere encompassed a return to the evening repertoire of parties and café visits which had formed such an intrinsic part of her routine before she became a mother.

However, even with Maria's wages from modelling, with only one family member earning, the household income would be radically reduced. Housing and feeding three mouths would leave little money to spare – certainly not enough to afford a move to bigger premises in one of the sparkling new apartment buildings near the centre of Montmartre. And yet mysteriously, that is precisely what the family did.

Zandomeneghi had lately moved to an imposing property on the corner of the steep Rue Tourlaque, which intersected with the Rue Caulaincourt where Maria had gone to school. Ever loyal to his model friend, Zando managed to negotiate three first-floor rooms for the Valadon family. By the time they moved in, the building had become home to a number of artists besides Zando, and so the atmosphere was closer to a bohemian student residence than a standard apartment; it was as though it was designed expressly to Maria's tastes. The Valadons' living quarters were brighter and infinitely more spacious and conducive to work than their previous home. But that Maria could never have afforded it herself was indisputable.

Montmartre's gossips concluded that the apartment must have been paid for by one – or perhaps even several – of Maria's lovers. Miguel Utrillo or Puvis de Chavannes seemed the most likely candidates. Miguel and Maria kept up an active correspondence during his travels abroad; away from Paris and with his honour intact, it seemed entirely plausible that Miguel could improve his finances and send the proceeds back to Maria discreetly.

But many, even those closest to Maria, believed Puvis to be the secret benefactor. Years later, an official document from that period was reportedly found in which Puvis promised Maria a regular maintenance allowance – an odd contract to make if he were not her child's father.[20] The condemnatory evidence was conveniently destroyed, but the theory of Puvis's paternity was sufficiently convincing and widely held for his great-nephew to feel the need to publicly deny the connection, on the grounds that the artist left no legacy to Maria and 'his son' in his will.[21]

However, the apartment was funded, the year 1884 marked the start of a new chapter for Maria, which saw her modelling by day, socialising by night and returning to the apartment in between to find Madeleine engrossed in raising her grandson, drawing on the aeons-old Limousin country wisdom she had gleaned during her youth.

It was an exhilarating time to be involved in the art world, in any capacity. At last, individualism was encouraged, not condemned. By the 1880s, Impressionism was yesterday's news. Artists had already gone beyond it, and were experimenting with new forms, content and techniques. Diversity was the modus vivendi. Accordingly, 1880s Paris became the birthplace of some radically different movements, including Divisionism, Symbolism, Synthesism and Nabis. Furthermore, the proliferation of alternative exhibiting bodies offered real grounds for hope for avant-garde painters and those hailing from the fringes of society. The Salon was no longer the sole and hazardous rite of passage lying between a painter and success. There were now other organisations where reputations could be forged, such as the Société des Aquarellistes Français. But by far the most notable and innovative artistic venture in 1884 was the Salon des Artistes Indépendants.

When his technically daring composition *Bathers at Asnières* (1884) was rejected by the jury of the 1884 Salon, former pupil of the prestigious École des Beaux-Arts Georges Seurat was spurred to retaliate. Joining forces with a number of other disgruntled painters, among them Symbolist Odilon Redon and self-taught artist Albert Dubois-Pillet, Seurat helped found the Groupe des Artistes Indépendants.[22] With Redon acting as chairman, the group proposed to do something unprecedented: they would mount a show whose organisers were not answerable to any official institution, and where there would be no prizes and, significantly, no jury.[23] The venture introduced a radically new concept onto the Parisian art scene:

freedom. The first exhibition, the Salon des Artistes Indépendants, was held from May to July in a temporary building in the Jardin des Tuileries near the Louvre. To critic Jules Claretie's surprise, the 'sub Salon, or side Salon, or Salon margin' was 'neither laughable nor ridiculous'. 'There are many works which would have honoured the Champs Elysées' exhibition,' he exclaimed, perceptively adding: 'You will find more than one young talent who, in years to come, might just be famous.'[24]

Times were changing and Maria was uniquely placed to take advantage of the opportunities now being created. Her modelling career had already proliferated her image across the globe. Now, every night at the Prague National Theatre, audiences were graced with Maria's presence, as the new curtain designed by Hynais and for which Maria had posed, descended to reveal her winged, semi-naked body hovering above a dramatic allegorical scene. Meanwhile, Renoir was hard at work on his vast painting, *The Large Bathers* (1884–1887), painstakingly sketching, reworking and perfecting a voluptuous Maria as she reclined naked to treat viewers to the sight of her radiant skin, firm breasts and sun-kissed hair. But of all Maria's dramatic incarnations, one of the most talked about at that year's Salon was undoubtedly Puvis de Chavannes's *The Sacred Grove of the Arts and Muses* (1884).

Le Figaro's reporter was enraptured. Puvis was 'an inspired artist', the figures for which Maria had posed 'interpreted by a poet', the landscape 'a pure masterpiece of construction, finesse and poetry'.[25] In short, the work was 'hands down, the best piece in the Salon'.

But not everyone shared the reviewer's opinion. Hobbling through the echoing halls of the Salon that year, a bowler hat on his head, a cane in one hand, peering at the artworks through his pince-nez, was a diminutive art student by the name of Henri-Marie-Raymond de Toulouse-Lautrec-Monfa.[26]

Lautrec was different from the majority of students sent to browse the Salon walls. He was of noble birth. The first son of Count Alphonse and Comtesse Adèle de Toulouse-Lautrec Monfa, whose union as first cousins continued the ancient ancestral union of the counts of Toulouse and the viscounts of Lautrec, Henri was part of a magnificent aristocratic dynasty.[27]

He spent the first eight years of his life near Albi in the Tarn. As a boy, he showed an exceptional talent for drawing, and when his father decided on a move to Paris, family friend and painter of animals René Princeteau coached him before encouraging him to train further.[28] Having first been accepted to study under the revered portrait artist Léon Bonnat, Lautrec joined his classmates in soliciting the tutorship of the estimable painter of biblical and pre-historical scenes Fernand Cormon when Bonnat was elected to teach at the École des Beaux-Arts.[29]

Now, in the public mindset, the quintessential modern artist came from humble origins and struggled to appease his gnawing hunger on stale bread and broth; Lautrec was brought up on a rolling estate, where riding and hawking were a gentleman's preferred pastimes and meals were flamboyant, multi-course spectacles of gastronomic decadence. His father was a fearless horseman and an incorrigible eccentric who delighted in dressing up and was inclined to stray from his marital bed. Meanwhile, his mother was a mild, sweet-tempered creature in whose eyes little Henri could do no wrong. Lautrec's childhood had conditioned him to female tenderness, male eccentricity and good living. He gave little thought to money; he did not need to.

Then in addition to his noble heritage, Lautrec was eloquent (despite a marked lisp), witty and charming, and undeniably charismatic. But, also unlike many of his peers, he was, by his own definition, a monster.

Though in the prime of life at twenty, he was the height of a child. His torso was more or less normal in size, but an undiagnosed osteo-related condition had arrested the growth of his limbs and made his bones unusually friable.[30] The startling effect was that of a full-grown man's chest balanced precariously on the legs of a child who was, paradoxically, crippled with age. He waddled as he walked, gripping his cane with short, fat fingers. And the irregularity with which his different body parts had grown seemed even to have affected his facial features. His head was reasonably proportioned for his shoulders, but his nose was uncommonly broad. Lips too enormous and plump for his face caused him to drool as he spoke and impeded his speech, making him roll his 'r's.[31] Beneath his stubbly black beard and moustache, his chin was rounded and upturned like a baby's. By his twenties, Lautrec had grown used to the reaction he typically incited in others: stomach-churning disgust.

But one physical feature redeemed him a little of his unpleasantness. His dark brown eyes were arresting in their beauty. They seemed to laugh when he spoke, betraying his quick mind and enthusiasm for life.[32]

And that joie de vivre was contagious enough to make those who knew him entirely forget his physical shortcomings. Even as a child, Lautrec had demonstrated an eccentric streak and an affected manner of speaking far beyond his years. As an adult, it ripened into a brilliant sense of humour based on the same stringent powers of observation that pervaded his drawing. He could bring a whole room to tears. 'He had a gift for getting on with people and all his fellow students liked him,' remembered his close friend, the painter François Gauzi.[33] 'He never had a harsh word for anyone and never tried to be funny at someone else's expense; he made fun of himself, and fun of the next man with the point of his pencil.'[34]

His clowning and self-deprecation was at once his best defence and a mask to which he clung. Maintaining it was a full-time

Henri de Toulouse-Lautrec,
photograph Paul Sescau, c. 1894.
Photo © RMN-Grand Palais (Musée Picasso de Paris)/image RMN-GP

occupation, for atelier students showed little mercy where phys-ical difference was concerned. But by his twenties, Lautrec was well-practised in the art of affecting a cheerful disposition. When he fell off a chair and fractured his left leg at the age of thirteen (an unusually consequential injury, since his weak bones refused to knit together afterwards), Lautrec never once complained, even when it meant that he could not partake in the outdoor activities he enjoyed with his cousins.[35] When he fractured the right leg the fol-lowing year after falling into a ditch, his response was just as placid. He did not shed a tear, but simply sat clutching his leg while his mother ran off frantically in search of help.[36] 'I hope you won't fret too much about my case,' he implored his godmother, 'because a clumsy fellow like me just isn't worth it.'[37] Though the consequence and not the cause of his condition, the injuries marked a turning point after which he would always feel the need to defend himself against the label he most abhorred: cripple. Few would have seen in his eyes anything besides merriment, but Gauzi remembered: 'I have known them to be desperately sad.'[38]

By 1884, Lautrec was one of Montmartre's most patriotic residents, an enthusiast of all that the 18th arrondissement had to offer. An inherently social creature, he was enthralled to discover the area's vibrant nightlife. A spectacle himself, Lautrec eagerly sought out the more spectacular and the strange. He was delighted when he happened upon a man even shorter than himself, a dwarf named Gustave de Fontanelle, with whom he would always stop and chat when they passed in the street.[39] Montmartre's bars, cabarets and the circus fed his hunger for the extraordinary. He had no need to limit himself on financial grounds either. One characteristically jovial letter to his mother in which he detailed his current expenses ended simply: 'P.S. Send money.'[40]

Part of the area's attraction was that, for all its sloping terrain, every entertainment was close at hand; he could not walk far or for long. So by the time Puvis's epic painting of Maria was shown at the 1884 Salon, Lautrec's days were spent working – and joking – with his fellow students at Cormon's, and his nights supping on the full array of Montmartre's delectable pleasures.

Puvis's great work had divided opinion at Cormon's atelier.[41] Lautrec sided with those who found it ridiculous, the colour insipid and the composition facile. Consequently, for two hysterical afternoons, the students at Cormon's were taken up creating a visual parody of the medal-winning canvas. The muses became popular personalities from Montmartre's cabarets, well-known singers or actresses, and Lautrec even painted himself in, next to a companion who showed his backside to the ladies. When it was complete, a chuckling Lautrec signed it on behalf of everyone and mounted it in his studio.

Maria and Cormon's jester went to all the same bars, knew the same people and embraced the thrill of Montmartre's social scene with the same fervent gusto; that Lautrec should encounter his own, real-life muse was practically inevitable. Whether or not their paths had already crossed at Le Chat Noir or another of their shared haunts of choice, as Gauzi remembered it, it was Zando who took Maria to formally meet Lautrec for the first time when he was struggling to find a model.[42]

Lautrec was immediately smitten. With her circus training, Maria was fascinating to him. He loved the circus, having gone regularly to the Cirque Fernando with Princeteau when he first arrived in Paris.[43] The colour, the noise, the lights, the adrenaline, the physical dexterity of the performers – he loved it all, it was everything he wished his life could be. And besides Maria's association with that spectacular world, Lautrec adored women, for all he knew that he likely repelled them. He had a pronounced sex drive and – one of the happier anomalies of his irregular growth rate – more than ample means of satisfying it when the opportunity arose. Many a girl around Montmartre giggled knowingly when he compared himself to 'a coffee pot with a big spout' on account of this asset.[44] Along with alcohol and art, women were one of his favourite weaknesses; he demanded no further compensation for the hand fate had dealt him. And Maria was unusually beautiful, and there was a strength to her beauty, something he would never possess. She also spoke her mind, a quality he always admired. The crowning glory was that, at only 1.54m tall, Maria was nearly as short as he was.

For her part, Maria was never one to be fazed by an extraordinary physique. She knew the torment when bodily encumbrance frustrated creative dreams. And once she set foot in Lautrec's studio, with its dust and its clutter and, among other bric-a-brac, its parody of the painting by Puvis that she knew so well nailed crudely to the wall, it was clear that she had found a kindred spirit.[45] Lautrec's humour was electric, he seemed permanently excited by life. At last, she had met a painter for whom art was not imperious and stale but vital and energised. It was refreshing.

The more sittings she attended, the closer their acquaintance became. The class gap seemed irrelevant.

Lautrec had in mind an enormous painting of a circus equestrienne on horseback, he told her.[46] She would be preparing to jump through a hoop that a clown held ready. The practical complications of working on such a large scale when he was himself so small bothered Lautrec not at all; he simply clambered up a nine-foot ladder. Such determined chutzpah for the sake of art was just to Maria's taste.

Artists could behave abominably towards their models, but Lautrec treated Maria with the utmost respect. He enjoyed nothing more than lively conversation and sharing delicious refreshments. He also urged her to borrow any of his books that she pleased; Maria's literary knowledge expanded. Through Lautrec, she even came across the contemporary, avant-garde poetry of many of Le Chat Noir's regulars, like Maurice Rollinat.[47]

Sittings usually took place in the afternoon when Lautrec had finished working at Cormon's. He often painted in his studio, but if the painting demanded it and the weather permitted, he would take his model outside. He had become acquainted with an elderly photographer, Père Forêt, who owned a little-used plot of land at the bottom of the Rue Caulaincourt.[48] Forêt gave Lautrec permission to paint there. With its brambles and long grass, it was a barely cultivated little wilderness, and mostly quiet. A small summer house proved an ideal place to keep his equipment, along with a selection of bottles, for as Lautrec would solemnly say: 'One should drink little, of course, but often!'[49]

Suzanne Valadon (Maria), Paris, 1885.
Collection Jean Fabris

For one painting, Lautrec decided that he wanted Maria to be wearing an elaborate hat. The cost being of little consequence, he scoured all the best milliners in Paris. Finally, he settled on an extravagant, tall and winged 'butterfly' hat, whose sharp lines he mirrored by making Maria's face appear more angular and her expression stern.

When the day's sitting was over, Maria often found herself, not returning to Madeleine and Maurice but persuaded to accompany Lautrec on one of his wild jollies to Le Chat Noir or another such drinking den and being proudly introduced to his many friends. And in the year that Lautrec painted Maria in the butterfly hat, there was a brilliant new haunt to patronise.

At midnight on Wednesday 10 June 1885, Rodolphe Salis, dressed in a third-class *préfet*'s uniform, left Le Chat Noir in a noisy and ostentatious torch-lit procession to the sound of beating drums, with a crowd of curious customers and friends following close behind.[50] The Boulevard de Rochechouart premises had become too small, he boasted; Le Chat Noir was to move to a bigger venue on the Rue de Laval.[51] The new cabaret would be even better, Salis assured his customers. And as for their favourite aspects, they would hardly notice the difference. As it happened, drinkers would still be able to enjoy the ambience of the smaller venue: a few days later, the abandoned cabaret reopened as Le Mirliton – and its founder was none other than Salis's own star performer, the magnetic singer Aristide Bruant.

Salis had every reason to feel anxious. Like the Pied Piper of Hamlin, wherever Bruant led, crowds were sure to follow. Lautrec and Maria were among them.

What the place lacked in furniture after Salis's dramatic exit, Bruant made up for in personality. He strode up and down in his felt hat, boots and cape, addressing each drinker in turn. And in counterpoint to Salis's excessive flattery, Bruant gave his venue a unique twist: he systematically insulted customers.

'Here's something fancy coming,' the singer would holler. 'Something choice, three star tarts. And the gentlemen following behind are undoubtedly pimps or ambassadors! This way, ladies, this way! Sit beside the little fat fellow here!'[52] Or else: 'Here you, fatty, place your fat carcass next to Madame. And you, you long sausage, put your skeleton between these fools who are laughing like a couple of idiots at God knows what!'[53]

Incredibly, Bruant's fashionable patrons loved it. For many, to be insulted to their faces was a revelation. It gave a real taste of the legendary Montmartre lowlife. It was quite the thing.

Lautrec thought Bruant's bedside manner terrifically funny and immediately became one of the regulars, often arriving with Maria in tow.

Maria and Lautrec got along famously, and with their individual reputations for promiscuity and wild living, it was naturally assumed that they were lovers. Their behaviour had given firm proof that neither automatically took love-making to imply spiritual attachment. 'He chased me,' Maria confided years later.[54] Lautrec's friends were convinced that he was infatuated with her, and Gauzi defensively maintained that she led him on.[55] Intimately acquainted with Lautrec's personal affairs, Gauzi was also privy to the fiery rows between the painter and his muse. Maria was 'capricious' Gauzi accused, and would fail to arrive for sittings, sometimes disappearing for days at a time with no explanation.[56] She had told Lautrec that she had a two-year-old son, but she could just as easily have been off on some folly for all he knew. An unreliable model made completing canvases an infuriating business.

'My dear Mama,' Lautrec wrote in the spring of 1886. 'My tonsillar troubles are ended, but my model is threatening to leave me. What a rotten business painting is. If she doesn't respond to my ultimatum the only thing I can do is bang out a few illustrations and join you in August.'[57]

Though now a mother, Maria was still wilful. She danced to no one's tune but her own.

It seemed probable that Lautrec would be able to keep better track of her movements when a generous allowance from his family in the second half of 1886 enabled him to lease a studio on the fourth floor of the building in the Rue Tourlaque where the Valadon family lived.[58] But it was not to be.

Gauzi too had an attic studio in the building and one morning he was startled by knocking at his door. It was Lautrec.[59]

'Maria has gone!' he exclaimed. 'She hasn't been home for three days and her mother doesn't know where she is [....] Forain asked me for a model. I sent her along – he might have kept her for himself.'

'Well? Any news of Maria?' Gauzi inquired a few days later.

'She has come back! [...] She never set foot at Forain's. She told me some tall story; she's got plenty of imagination, and lies don't cost anything.'

But there was more binding Lautrec to Maria than her function as a model and her role as a drinking companion. Finally, one day, he discovered her artistic talent. Lautrec was rich, skilled and well-connected in the avant-garde art world. And when he saw Maria's drawing, he was stunned. He had to show somebody.

'Look at that drawing,' Lautrec enthused to Gauzi. 'Isn't it good?'[60]

Gauzi examined a fine profile portrait of a little boy.[61] The infant could not have been more than two or three, but the confident handling of the red chalk, the crisp outline of his profile, the delicate, wispy strokes of his hair, gave the child an indisputable character.

'Not bad,' Gauzi remarked. 'There's delicacy in the line, and sensitivity in the vision. Who did it?'

Lautrec's eyes sparkled when something excited him.[62]

'Maria,' he said.

CHAPTER 7

Talent Laid Bare

Ton vesin t'ajudará si lo sabes apelar.
(Your neighbour will help you if you know
how to attract his attention.)

OLD LIMOUSIN PROVERB[1]

'The weather has turned quite inclement,' announced *Le Figaro*
on the morning of 23 September 1886 – Maria's 21st birthday.[2] The sky above Paris was grey and overcast, the
temperature had dropped and throughout the day, persistent show-
ers drizzled down on pedestrians as they hurried along the reflective
macadam. And there was worse on its way; forecasters predicted
violent storms to come thundering in from North America and hit
the French coast in the next few days.

Maria often suffered with coughs and colds when the weather
turned at the end of the year.[3] However, with Madeleine's Limousin
home remedies to soothe her body and a host of events to occupy
her mind, her birthday that year was a time to look forward.

Lautrec had lately formed a friendship with a fascinating new
addition to Cormon's atelier, a student with whom Maria immediately empathised. Hollow-cheeked and pale, with intense blue eyes
and a shock of red hair, Vincent, as the newcomer insisted on being
called, was the son of a Dutch Protestant minister, and he fittingly

took himself and his art with reverent seriousness. He had arrived in Paris unannounced in March to join his brother Theo van Gogh, who was an art dealer. Theo obligingly took his older brother in. When Vincent appeared for his first day at Cormon's a few months later, the other students soon realised that he was different.

At 33, he was older than most of them. He worshipped Delacroix; the subject of colour aroused in him a passionate reaction; and any artistic theory which ran counter to his own views was liable to provoke a fierce response.[4] 'It is as if two people dwelt within him,' Theo explained, 'one of them marvellously talented, refined and tender, the other selfish and hardhearted! They appear alternately.'[5] His intensity and volatility unnerved many of Cormon's students, who judged it wisest to leave him alone.[6] But the day he first seized a paintbrush, they could not help but watch in astonishment. He painted frantically, furiously, with bold, brightly coloured sweeps of his brush – as though his life depended on it. His classmates were stunned. It was the very antithesis of the academic style they were being taught to follow. Lautrec's interest was immediately piqued.

And Lautrec was not the only student of Cormon's to take notice when an alternative approach was presented. Vincent had arrived just as dissent was reaching fever pitch at the atelier, and his avant-garde style won him at least two other admirers.

Four years older than Lautrec, Louis Anquetin, the son of a Normandy butcher, had arrived in Paris in the early 1880s determined to become a painter.[7] Tall and sturdy with a long face and a crooked nose, Anquetin was an undeniably good painter. Even Cormon prophesied a brilliant career for him However, Anquetin was no more inclined to kowtow to the rigid conventions of academic art that Cormon preached than Lautrec. Innovative in his artwork, he discarded new painting styles nearly as quickly as he picked them up and by the 1880s, he was applying his experiments with colour to modern Parisian scenes. Lautrec had immediately warmed to Anquetin. Besides their enthusiasm for art, their shared love of horses provided ample source of conversation. With a confidence that bordered on self-importance, Anquetin was the unofficial leader of the little group that now frequented Bruant's where Maria and Lautrec drank.

Eighteen-year-old Émile Bernard was the baby of that group.[8] With the slender physique and fine features of a boy, tousled brown hair and a rebellious nature, Bernard had come to Paris from Lille and joined Cormon's atelier a little after Lautrec. Lautrec and Anquetin soon took him under their wings and introduced him to the works of the great masters in the Louvre, as well as the more modern canvases of the Impressionists. Wide-eyed and hungry to indulge on Paris's feast of visual offerings, the teenager embraced the new with all the enthusiasm of youth, devouring theories and experimenting alternately with Impressionism, Pointillism, and later Cloisonnism and Pictorial Symbolism. But for all his love of novelty, the activity of Montmartre's seedier side horrified him. Like Van Gogh, Bernard was deeply religious and took his art extremely seriously. In fact, so firmly did he hold a view once he had settled on it that he was eventually expelled from Cormon's for insubordinate behaviour. As he remembered it, it was when he paid a call on his former classmates that he first met Van Gogh. Despite the age gap, the pair formed a firm friendship, one based on mutual respect.

Now whenever Maria accompanied Lautrec on one of his evenings out in Montmartre, one or several of these artists was sure to be there.

Sometimes the young men shared ideas around a café table, or else they would stroll along to the shop of Julien 'Père' Tanguy, the colour merchant, in the Rue Clauzel.[9] Parisian artists held diverse, often conflicting views on many matters, but on one thing there was universal agreement: the former Communard Père Tanguy was kindness itself. Overwhelmingly generous, calm and serene, Père Tanguy supported struggling artists, gave them credit and allowed the back rooms of his little shop to become at once an informal meeting place and a repository where works could be exhibited and viewed.[10] For Lautrec and his friends, the greatest boon was that it was one of the few places in Paris they could marvel at the work of Cézanne at leisure. Each man came away inspired, his enthusiasm rekindled, with an urgent desire to pursue his own creative vision.

Van Gogh was particularly anxious to promote the work of himself and his friends. Why not mount an exhibition?, he enthused.[11] He had already organised an exhibition of Japanese prints at the Café du Tambourin in the spring of 1887. Now he thought of the Restaurant du Chalet on the Avenue de Clichy where he often ate and which had superb lighting. He could get his new friend Paul Gauguin to join them.[12] They could be the 'Petit Boulevard Group' (in answer to the Impressionists, widely thought of as the 'Grand Boulevard Group'). The others agreed, but none threw himself into the venture more wholeheartedly than Van Gogh. It opened in November 1887, but did little to further Van Gogh's artistic reputation.[13]

Maria watched the Dutchman with sympathy, and Lautrec's renowned parties afforded her an even closer acquaintance.

Lautrec was a party host extraordinaire and his weekly 'at homes' and dinners were legendary. The prospect of being left alone with only his thoughts terrified him. He consequently 'freely invited people', so that on many occasions, his 'studio was so cluttered with visitors […] that there was nowhere to sit.'[14] If it was a dinner he was hosting, a guest could be sure to have their taste buds excited by a gastronomic orgy of the finest delicacies in Paris, while their mind would be stretched and inspired by the most profound debates. For Lautrec, food was an art form as sacred as painting. He was a fearless amateur chef, and he and his childhood friend Maurice Joyant delighted in concocting recipes together which would be generously bestowed on those select friends they deemed worthy of their culinary masterpieces – and oddities. Few who had tasted it could forget Lautrec's chocolate mayonnaise or his port with garlic, which he swore to be an infallible cure for bronchitis.[15] And whether a studio party or a formal dinner, Lautrec took abstinence as a personal affront.[16] He even went so far as to tip goldfish into the carafes of water to dissuade guests from leaving him to drink alone. The American craze for cocktails delighted him, and he perfected the art of mixing them.[17] Friends were invariably presented with a potent glass of brightly coloured liquid; often these were experiments, carried off with varying degrees of success and served with a chuckle.

An incorrigible bachelor, Lautrec was pleased to have Maria as his unofficial hostess at these gatherings. So it was that she came to witness Van Gogh's integration into the world of the Parisian artists.

Born into the claustrophobic environment of a profoundly religious Dutch family, Van Gogh's life thus far had been a tumultuous chain of false career starts, failed love affairs and ill-health. He had worked variously as an art dealer, a missionary and had even trained as a minister. The one constant was his deep conviction in the importance of art and his quest for painterly satisfaction. 'I long most of all to learn how to produce those very inaccuracies,' he wrote the year before he came to Paris, 'those very aberrations, reworkings, transformations of reality, as may turn it into, well – a lie if you like – but truer than the literal truth.'[18] His approach struck a chord with Maria.

She watched as, every week, Van Gogh arrived at Lautrec's struggling under the weight of his latest canvas.[19] As the room hummed with conversation, he would set the piece on an easel in the corner, and wait expectantly for someone to comment. Everyone ignored him. He scrutinised the faces around him in earnest, hoping to spot a reaction which could be interpreted as a critique. Nothing came. Eventually, he would resign himself to his colleagues' indifference and leave, his canvas under his arm, dejection inscribed on his face. And yet he would always return the following week and the performance would be repeated. 'Painters are brutes,' Maria spat after she had witnessed the scene replayed countless times.[20]

But however his guests behaved, Lautrec's cheerful front seemed ironclad. He was a firm believer in the power of humour and practical jokes to lighten a mood.

In March 1887, he moved into an apartment with his friend, the medical student Henri Bourges, whose faithful housemaid Léontine saw to the men's every need.[21]

One night, Lautrec invited Maria over for supper, and when conversation began to dwindle as Léontine was clearing the first course, Lautrec, as usual, started to look elsewhere for entertainment.

'Undress,' he urged Maria, as soon as the servant had left the room. 'Strip yourself naked, and we'll watch Léontine's face.'[22]

Stifling her giggles, Maria did exactly as he said, retaining only her shoes and stockings. Then she sat down primly on the edge of her seat. Once she and Lautrec had summoned sober expressions, Lautrec rang the bell for dessert. When Léontine arrived, she gave a start. Then composing herself, she continued to serve the rest of the meal as though nothing were amiss. Not a word was uttered – until the following day.

It was then that Bourges came to Lautrec, furious. Léontine had been to see him. Monsieur had 'failed' her, she exclaimed. A good, honest woman like herself deserved some respect.

'You conducted yourself indecently,' fumed Bourges. 'In front of servants, one keeps oneself in check [...] Undress your models in your studio to your heart's content, but at table, leave them with something on! If you persist in your jokes, Léontine will leave us and then where will you be!'

Lautrec appeared aghast. 'Léontine is wrong to believe herself offended,' he protested. 'I had no intention of outraging her morals – Maria was the only one naked [...] I was dressed, and the only thing I took off was my hat.'

But Lautrec could see that his flatmate was far from sharing his amusement at the incident.

'Léontine knows very well what shape a woman is underneath,' he grumbled.

The episode was just one of many of Lautrec's practical jokes in which Maria participated. He found her marvellously good fun. And the fact remained that when she was in the mood to work, she was an extremely versatile model.

In 1887, Lautrec began *Poudre de Riz*. The canvas showed a face-on depiction of Maria as a demi-mondaine seated behind a table, the eponymous powder pot by her side. With her pale, wiry arms folded in front of her, she fixed the viewer in the eye, her expression disdainful yet resigned, her face drawn in a near-scowl. Though presented as a woman of loose morals, her appearance, like the table in front of her, paradoxically put up a barrier to intimacy. Thus cast, Maria was at once available yet untouchable. The role was fitting.

As Lautrec was all too aware, Maria was no more likely to show loyalty to a single painter than a demi-mondaine was to show affection to just one man. Nor did she feel the slightest obligation to tell Lautrec how she spent her days when she was not modelling for him. She had posed for Zando's *At the Café de la Nouvelle Athènes* in 1885, and had given a remarkably convincing impression of a young woman thoroughly enjoying herself in a man's company with an array of beverages in front of her. More particularly, Maria's relationship with Renoir was far from resolved. It was difficult to ignore the resemblance between Maria and many of the major figure subjects Renoir tackled between 1884 and 1887. There was *The Large Bathers* (1884–1887), but also *Woman with a Fan* (1886) and *Young Woman with a Swan* (1886).[23] And then in 1887, Renoir painted Maria in one of his most suggestive interpretations yet: *The Plait.*

Curvaceous and healthy, looking much younger than her twenty years, Maria sat plaiting her long, now brunette locks in a lush green garden. Her simple, peasant-like outfit scarcely contained her shapely form and exposed her naked arms, while her bodice could barely hold her firm young breasts. The work, an example of Renoir's so-termed 'Ingres' period, seemed to exude natural vitality, unlike Lautrec's painting, which blatantly exploited artifice.[24] And yet, as Maria later recalled, 'I was caked in make-up.'[25] Renoir openly conceded that the model was merely a starting point, that his brush could mould her to fit a painting and satisfy his bourgeois viewer – and ultimately, himself. 'The painting must not smell too strongly of the model,' he warned. 'But at the same time, you must get the feeling of nature. A painting is not a verbatim record [...] The most important thing is for it to remain painting.'[26]

From Zando to Renoir, and from Hynais to Lautrec – though now in her twenties and a mother, Maria's identity was no less protean, no less transitory, than it had ever been. Each artist saw in her what he wanted, but she belonged to no one. And Lautrec was not the only male pained by the realisation that he must share her.

Every day, waiting for her return at the apartment in the Rue Tourlaque, was a little boy desperate to see his mother.

In 1888, Maurice turned five. His first few years had shown Madeleine and Maria that he was not going to be an easy child.[27] He was tiny, skinny even, and the dark shadows under his deep brown eyes gave him a haunted appearance. His nerves seemed as delicate as his fragile body. People might see him cowering fearfully behind his grandmother's skirts in the streets. But he could just as easily erupt into a furious tantrum, often without warning or obvious cause. It took all Madeleine's ingenuity to calm him down again.

People whispered that Madeleine was weak, that she should use a firmer hand with the boy. But Maurice would have presented an arduous challenge for any woman, let alone one nearing 60. Still, it was impossible not to sympathise with the child; he knew no father and as the main breadwinner, his mother, his only parent, was seldom at home. Most of the time, Madeleine had to deal with his fits alone.

Fantastical stories and incredible legends were the Limousin countrywoman's first resource when presented with an infant who needed pacifying. Many a child raised in Madeleine's region could recall popular tales like that of The Snow Child, in which an old peasant couple unable to have children are elated when a little boy made of snow comes to life one Christmas night, giving them the son they always dreamed of, only to watch him melt before their eyes when their possessiveness spurs him to escape.[28] But in Paris, Madeleine's stories had no context. Maurice knew nothing of the Limousin country ways or people, still less of Bessines. And traditionally, when verbal therapies failed, peasant women resorted to a more measurable tonic.

Alcohol was respected among countryfolk and employed as much for its restorative properties as its recreational purposes. For centuries, working peasants in the Limousin had started their day *en faisant chabrol* (adding red wine to a dish of part-eaten soup), usually starting with a base of *bréjaude*, a cabbage soup prepared with fresh bacon; it was recommended for sustenance.[29] The countrywoman's natural instinct was to give a child a few drops of liquor if they needed calming. Years later, family agreed that this was almost certainly what Madeleine did with Maurice.[30]

Soon, Maria and Madeleine could enrol Maurice in the local primary school at the foot of the Sacré-Coeur; if his moods could not be tempered, at least the responsibility would for a time fall to an outside authority.[31] They might just prove more successful in taming him. In the meantime, only one thing could be relied upon to console him: his mother. Maurice adored Maria and wanted nothing more than to be in her presence.

While Maurice fought to keep his mother close, Lautrec was also struggling to catch hold of her, as only he knew how. In 1889, he completed *The Hangover*. The image showed Maria in profile in a working woman's shirt, her hair held in a loose chignon. She sat alone, propped on her elbow in a near-slump over a bar table. A prominent bottle and a single glass – at once half empty and half full – signalled both the cause of her misery and the promise of its continuation. The sketchy style recreated the distorted lens of drunkenness. Meanwhile, Maria's mournful expression as she gazed into the distance epitomised the overwhelming sense of hopelessness at the heart of the piece.

It was Lautrec's most unflattering portrait yet. But unbeknown to Maria and Lautrec, that humble picture was to provide their first introduction to one of the most influential figures on the 19th-century art scene: Edgar Degas.[32]

Separated from Madeleine Valadon by only four years in age but a chasm in class, Hilaire Germain Edgar Degas presented as the quintessential Parisian gentleman. He was 'an exceptionally distinguished man,' remembered artist Georges Jeanniot, 'a man of subtlety, effortless composure, and irony. His was a most intelligent head, with a very high brow and a pleasing oval shape.'[33] He had 'a few silver threads in his beard and hair, looked hale and hearty, and was dressed neatly, but without ostentation.'[34] Though himself Parisian born and bred, Degas's father was a banker who originated from Naples, while his mother was the heiress of a well-to-do family from Louisiana.[35] As a young man, Degas trained in law, but quickly resolved to make painting his profession. He studied under Louis

Edgar Degas in his library, 1895, Musée d'Orsay, Paris.
Photo © RMN-Grand Palais (Musée d'Orsay)/Hervé Lewandowski

Lamothe, a disciple of Hippolyte Flandrin, from whom he received a full academic training. Degas then travelled to Italy to perfect his artistic skills, he fought in the artillery of the National Guard in the Franco-Prussian war of 1870, and afterwards, journeyed to New Orleans to visit family; his worldly wisdom was substantial. But it was his skill as a figure painter and role as one of the foremost champions of Impressionism and avant-garde art that had earned him his reputation. He had been instrumental in organising all of the Impressionists' group shows to date. By the 1880s, he was relieved to have settled back into the city he considered home, which was proving an inexhaustible supply of modern urban subjects. He painted Paris's café-concerts, racecourses, working women and bathers, but it was his images of ballet dancers for which he had become renowned.

However, besides his professional standing, Degas was equally famed for being blunt, opinionated and (as his vision deteriorated, to a large extent justifiably) hypochondriac.

Life had distilled his inherent cynicism, which found a daily outlet in dry, often caustic wit. His devastating critiques seemed designed for his own amusement as much as that of his audience. 'Now and then,' recalled Jeanniot, 'his usually serious eyes would look amused, especially when he came out with one of those *mots* of his, so carefully crafted and so highly effective, too.'[36] Few things delighted him more than the establishment turning on itself. And the frequent accusations of misogyny were difficult to defend; women were both fascinating and deeply troubling to him.

'I had Forain over for dinner the other day,' Daniel Halévy, son of Degas's friend Ludovic remembered him recounting once. 'He came to keep me company.'[37]

'With his wife?' Halévy enquired.

'She was "out of sorts",' Degas sneered.

'You don't believe it then?'

'How would I know?' the painter retorted. 'Women invented the expression "out of sorts". It has nothing to do with us.'

Degas was particular to the point of compulsion. The dealer Ambroise Vollard never forgot the painter's reply when he invited him to dinner one day.

'Certainly,' Degas agreed. 'Only, listen carefully: will you have a special dish without butter prepared for me? No flowers on the table, and dinner must be at seven-thirty sharp. I know you won't have your cat around, but no one will be allowed to bring a dog, will they? And if there are any women present I trust they shan't come smelling of perfume. How awful all those odours are when there are things that smell so good, like toast! Or even the delicate aroma of s—t! Oh, yes [...] And very few lights. My eyes, my poor eyes!'[38]

But all these quirks merely made Degas's good opinion all the more covetable. For an artist like Lautrec, there could be no higher accolade. For an amateur, lower-class woman artist like Maria, such a prospect was unthinkable.

Lautrec was jubilant when, in April 1889, the *Courrier Français* agreed to publish a drawing of his picture of Maria.[39] Rightly proud, Lautrec made a gift of the image to his old family friends, the brothers Désiré and Henri Dihau and their sister Marie.[40] All three were musicians, and they happened to own an impressive collection of paintings. The Dihau home gallery included works by Degas, who was also a close family friend. In fact, in 1870, Degas had painted Désiré in his role as bassoon player in the orchestra of the Paris Opéra. However, Lautrec had never yet had the good fortune to cross paths with the great man on any of his visits to the Dihau residence.

One day, Degas was visiting his friends when he saw Lautrec's drawing of Maria. He stopped and began to inspect it closely. 'To think,' he muttered at last, 'a young man has done this, when we have worked so hard all our lives!'[41]

Lautrec was exultant when the comment was repeated back to him, and even more so when singer and piano teacher Marie managed to secure him a meeting a few days later. A compliment from Degas was nothing short of gold dust. But to Lautrec's disappointment, he left his introduction with no subsequent meetings to report back to Maria.

Still, by the summer of 1889, there was a new diversion to distract young thrill-seekers like Maria and Lautrec: the Exposition Universelle of 1889.

A world fair was always cause for great excitement in the capital, but this year was symbolically important: 1889 marked the 100th anniversary of the French Revolution. The significance was not lost on European countries still ruled by monarchies, several of whom were uneasy and reluctant to participate. But Parisians were undeterred. The grand opening was awaited with keen anticipation.

For nearly six months, Paris became the host of a brilliant party to which the whole of Europe was invited. Fine arts and industrial exhibits were on show at the Trocadéro and the Champ de Mars, while the Esplanade des Invalides housed a colonial exhibit and several state-sponsored pavilions. The capital's artistic skill was paraded, its architectural prowess showcased and its scientific innovations celebrated. Paris basked in its own glory. But by far the city's proudest exhibit was the Eiffel Tower, that awesome iron structure that Parisians had been watching creep up the skyline of the Seine's left bank over the last few months.

The tallest metal structure in the world at the time, at over 300m high, the tower had its critics. However, few could remain unmoved as, at the monument's inauguration, Burgundian engineer Gustave Eiffel climbed on foot to its summit and raised an enormous Tricolore flag. Parisians and international visitors, common people and celebrities; everyone gazed up in awe as the great masterpiece of engineering glittered and twinkled with the glow of over 20,000 gaslights.

But if a daring architectural statement stole the show, there was no place for innovative contemporary art. Participation in the fine arts section was by invitation only, and the final selection of works was made by a jury as hypercritical as that of the Salon. The colourful Javanese dancers and a homage to Manet in the retrospective exhibition went some way to appeasing older Impressionists.[42] But younger contemporary painters like Lautrec, Bernard and Anquetin were furious.

Then, artist Émile Schuffenecker discovered that Signor Volpini, who had the contract for the Café des Arts opposite the exhibition, had been let down by the Italian supplier of the mirrors intended to decorate the interior of his venue. Thinking quickly, Schuffenecker offered to mount a display of paintings by himself and his friends. Anquetin and Bernard (though not Lautrec) were among the participating artists.[43] Another key exponent and one of the driving forces behind the show was the artist with whom Van Gogh (now relocated to Arles and earless) enjoyed such a fractious relationship: Paul Gauguin.

In his early 40s and well travelled, the former seaman and stock-broker had originally taken influence from the Impressionists.[44] However, his travels had consolidated his desire to create art which was liberated from the constraints inhibiting Western painting. At times, the spatial fragmentation in his work still bore the hall-marks of Degas's influence, but his use of flat areas of colour and bold outlines marked out his difference. He longed to convey not just effects as the Impressionists had done, but the inner, spiritual quality of the exotic scenery and inhabitants he had experienced in Peru, Martinique and Brittany. For Gauguin, that meant a move away from realistic representation and a return to a more primi-tive painting mode. As the leader of the so-called Pont-Aven group, and with his painting silently advocating an escape from urban civilisation, Gauguin had the undivided attention of the young contemporary artists.

In the event, the Volpini exhibition failed to impress the public or the press, and contributed negligibly to the overwhelming suc-cess of the 1889 Exposition Universelle. But that hardly mattered: it represented yet another public statement of artistic rebellion. Rejected young artists were not going to back down quietly, the show declared. From now on, artistic recognition was available to any talent willing to fight for it.

Maria had never been short of fighting spirit. Few people knew that better than Miguel Utrillo. And it just so happened that among the sea of visitors the Exposition brought flooding into the capital was none other than the old flame of Maria's youth.[45]

Suzanne Valadon (Maria), c. 1890.
Collection Jean Fabris

Miguel had landed the opportunity of reviewing the Exposition for various Spanish newspapers, including *La Vanguardia*. He took lodgings with a group of fellow Spaniards, among them Rusiñol and Casas, at the very Moulin de la Galette which had formed the backdrop to so many unforgettable evenings when he was a fun-loving teen. Maria had never been difficult to find if you knew who to ask, and she and Miguel were each soon standing before an older version of their former playmate.

In Maria's clear blue eyes, and with those soft brown tresses falling loosely about her face, Miguel could detect a gentleness and a maturity beneath the defiant mask she presented to others.[46] And Maria could hardly deny that Miguel looked more dashing than ever, sophisticated and confident.[47] His self-assurance was due in no small part to the fact that, in his work as an art correspondent, Miguel seemed finally to have found his niche; indeed, he had now resolved to stay on in Paris and work as an art critic. The Spaniard was delighted to rediscover all the familiar haunts, and in no time he and Maria had fallen into their old pattern: chasing playfully through Montmartre's twisted streets, calling in at its bars and cabarets when dusk fell, laughing, bickering, making up, then repeating the whole dizzying repertoire.

But Miguel had been absent a long time. Maria was not about to abandon her other friends and for all their fallings-out, Lautrec was one of these. Though he had been busy preparing for the Salon des Indépendants and absorbed in the flurry of excitement generated by Montmartre's new dance hall, Moulin Rouge, with its thighs and froth and flounce, he had not forgotten Maria's drawings.[48] He discussed her ability with Zando, and the men agreed that her work showed exceptional skill.[49] Really, someone with more sway and standing should see this – someone like Degas, for example.

But Lautrec had only met Degas recently and while Zando was better acquainted with the great man, there was always a degree of condescension in Degas's treatment of the Venetian he called 'the prince'. The unspoken tension in their relationship was only growing more pronounced as Zando's style crept closer to Degas's own under pressure to sell.[50] They would do better seeking the approval of an artist who was already firmly established in his own field; a person who enjoyed both an intimate acquaintance with Degas and – even more difficult to obtain – his respect. Sculptor Paul-Albert Bartholomé matched the description perfectly.

Like Degas, Bartholomé had studied law and fought in the Franco-Prussian war. Intending to become a painter, he had attended the prestigious École des Beaux-Arts briefly.[51] It was through his involvement in Paris's art world that he had met Degas. Degas soon became a close friend, and was a frequent visitor to Bartholomé and his wife's home for dinner. The friends maintained a regular correspondence through letters in which Degas aired his typic-ally wry opinions on the world and, less characteristically, shared confidences about matters personal to him. The bond had been strengthened by the one's grief and the other's sympathy; in 1887, Bartholomé's wife, Prospérie de Fleury, the ethereally beautiful model of his *In the Greenhouse (Mme Bartholomé)* (*c.* 1881), had died tragically young when she was in her 30s.[52] 'Poor lady, poor man!' Degas wrote as Prospérie's health declined.[53] 'I shall go and see them immediately. My heart of stone breaks.' Bartholomé's move into sculpture and his creation of a monument to commemorate his late wife had been greatly directed by Degas's encouragement. It would have been hard to find someone closer to the revered artist.

Therefore, one day, Lautrec took Maria along to meet Bartholomé and he encouraged her to bring some of her drawings. Bartholomé's reaction when he was shown her work was just as Lautrec had hoped. 'Degas has to see this!' he exclaimed.[54]

So it was that not long after, Maria found herself stand-ing nervously on the doorstep of Degas's apartment in the Rue Victor-Massé, a letter of introduction written in Bartholomé's hand clutched in her sweaty palm.[55]

The door was opened by a sturdy, round-faced, middle-aged woman. Years later, Maria still remembered the beautiful, penetrat-ing doe eyes of Degas's housekeeper, Zoé Closier, whose robust and wholesome country physique, Maria guessed, must have turned many a male head in her youth.

At length, Maria and her portfolio of drawings were shown through to meet the man himself. Outwardly smart and polite, Degas was always deeply suspicious of 'undiscovered talent', never more so than when the 'talent' claimed to have found their voice without formal training. Slowly, carefully, he examined Maria's pic-tures. He uttered not a word. His expression betrayed nothing.

Eventually, his attention shifted from the documents in his hands to the young woman in front of him.

'You are one of us,' he murmured.[56]

The remainder of the meeting passed in a blur. There was praise beyond Maria's wildest dreams, and most of all, questions: had she really no training? Where did she find the courage to dedicate herself so fully to this work? And the money for materials? Might he purchase a drawing? That one, for example, the red chalk study of a girl getting out of a bath?

In moments, Maria's life was transformed. Suddenly, her greatest dream became credible.

'That day, I had wings,' she recalled.[57]

Henceforward, she was welcomed at the Rue Victor-Massé as one of the household and she called in every afternoon to discuss art in general and her art in particular.[58] From now on, her work was informally overseen by the paternal figure she had never had.

Not even Lautrec could have foreseen it.

It was Maria's recurrent pattern of associations with older men that led Lautrec, people said, to quip darkly one day that she should go by the name of Suzanne. The name implied a reference to the tale of *Susanna and the Elders* (*Suzanne et les vieillards* in French) from the book of Daniel. In the story, the Hebrew wife of a noted member of the community rejects the advances of two lecherous older men, only to have them publicly accuse her of adultery. She is consequently threatened with death and saved only by Daniel's intervention.[59]

Maria abhorred predictability. Rather than angrily dismiss the potentially offensive comment, she embraced the suggestion; why not? She would do just that. Her confidence was building. From then on, Maria signed all her artwork Suzanne Valadon, even going so far as to return to old work and sign it with her new name. New contacts would know her only as Suzanne.

But if her artwork was taking flight, the outline of a career starting to take shape, her personal life was as chaotic as ever. For all her liaisons, there was still no secure male presence to underpin the daily routine; no stability – for either herself or Maurice. At a time when women were financially and socially subordinate to men, it made life deeply precarious, even for a spirit as free as Maria's.

However, Gauzi maintained a clear recollection of a pivotal moment in Maria's – Suzanne's – life which took place when she was in her twenties.[60]

One day, he was painting in his studio when his doorbell began ringing frantically.

The caller's impatience allowed him no time to set his brushes and palette down. He hurried to the door. As it was opened, a panting Lautrec near-on fell into the room. Gauzi had no chance to speak.

'You've got to come at once!' Lautrec gasped. 'Maria is trying to kill herself.'

CHAPTER 8

Flavours of Happiness

Lo que se conha la testa dins un bornat
Se deu pas planher d'èsser fissat.
(He who sticks his head in a bee hive
Can't complain about being stung.)
OLD LIMOUSIN PROVERB[1]

Shouting could be heard coming from the kitchen in the Valadon apartment as Lautrec and Gauzi came to a halt at the bottom of the stairs.[2] Lautrec had left the front door ajar when he raced off to fetch Gauzi and the friends slipped inside unheard.

'You've really done it now!' Gauzi remembered Madeleine bellowing at Suzanne. 'He's taken fright and will never come back – then where will you be?'

'He wouldn't play ball,' Suzanne protested, 'and I used every trick I knew.'

'You could wait a bit longer ...' the mother offered.

Lautrec stepped through the kitchen doorway so that the friends could be seen. Suzanne and Madeleine stopped arguing and spun round. Both parties beheld each other in awkward silence. Finally, Gauzi found his voice, and demanded to know what was going on. But before either woman could answer, he had drawn his own conclusion: Suzanne had resolved to shore up her family's material security through marriage – a marriage which, for her part at least, would be entirely one of convenience. But however much he cared for Suzanne and loved company, Lautrec prized his freedom. Gauzi calculated that when his friend's proposal had not been forthcoming, Suzanne had begun using emotional blackmail to corner her prey.

'My poor friend,' he said to Lautrec, 'they have been duping you!'

Lautrec turned his back, and stopping only in the front room to collect his cane and hat, left the apartment with Gauzi, closing the door behind them.

Outside on the landing, Lautrec turned to his friend. 'Goodbye, see you tomorrow,' he said, shaking Gauzi's hand before returning to his room.

Lautrec hated solitude. Gauzi felt sure that had he followed his friend that day, he would have found Lautrec collapsed, 'choking with sobs', nursing his broken heart. And as far as Gauzi was aware, Suzanne and Lautrec never saw each other again.

However sour the note on which Suzanne and Lautrec parted, she could not brood over the loss for long. There were too many other people and problems clamouring for her attention. Maurice's performance at school was causing alarm, Madeleine was fretting, Miguel and countless others were seeking her company. Meanwhile, there were modelling assignments to fulfil, and at every turn, there seemed to be a figure or form just begging to be brought to life in pencil or chalk, committed to paper, captured forever. And then each afternoon, there was Degas expecting her arrival at 37, Rue Victor-Massé. If for any reason she failed to appear, Suzanne could be sure that Zoé would appear on her doorstep to inform her that the master demanded to know the reason for her absence.[3]

Degas had only moved to the spacious three-floor apartment in 1890, largely through necessity as his passion (or obsession) for collecting paintings was then reaching its peak.[4] Until 1892, he could often be found at the opera in the evenings, and was in the habit of going to stay with his friends the Halévys in Normandy or the Valpinçons at Ménil-Hubert in the summer months.[5] But the rest of the time, he was at home. It was therefore important that the apartment – and the landlord – met his every requirement.

'Let's not quibble anymore over details,' he wrote impatiently to the proprietor in the year he took up residence. 'I am a quiet and solvent tenant; ask no more of me.'[6]

Degas had his studio on the fourth floor of the house, and on the second was his 'museum', where Suzanne could marvel at works by great masters including Jean-Auguste-Dominique Ingres and Camille Corot, as well as examples of younger talent such as Paul Gauguin and Paul Cézanne.[7] It was on the third floor that the artist lived. Polymath Paul Valéry recalled the scene a visitor like Suzanne could expect to find when they paid a call on the great man.

'Degas would be milling about, dressed like a pauper in old slippers and loose-fitting trousers that were invariably unbuttoned.' For Valéry, Degas could be described as:

> a man who once was elegant, whose manners, when he chose, could be of the most unforced distinction, who used to spend his evenings in the wings of the Opéra, a frequent visitor in the paddock at Longchamp, a supremely sensitive observer of the human form, a supremely cruel authority on female contours and poses, a discerning connoisseur of the finest horses, the most intelligent, most reflective, most demanding, most ruthless draughtsman on earth ... not to mention being a wit, the guest whose comments, in their sovereign breach of fairness, in their selective truth, could prove lethal ...[8]

It was not unusual for Suzanne to cross paths with other of the artist's close acquaintances on her visits, often Bartholomé or Degas's great friend Henri Rouart.[9] Rouart was an amateur painter who had regularly exhibited in the Impressionists' shows from 1874.[10] But he had made his fortune as an engineer, and since spent it liberally building up an enviable art collection. And whatever the day or the season, all the comings and goings of the household were overseen and catered for by the formidable and rotund person of Zoé.

'She speaks very well,' Valéry observed, 'it seems she was once a schoolteacher. The huge round spectacles she wears lend her broad, frank, invariably serious face something of a scholarly air.'[11] Notwithstanding, Suzanne came to like her enormously.

By the 1890s, Degas was growing more selective about where he exhibited and what he sold. But his output remained steady and consistent, and he experimented voraciously. He claimed to have invented the technique of monotype, and he worked in a range of drawing media as well as oils, but increasingly his medium of choice was pastel.[12] Pastels did not require mixing and so lent themselves to a more spontaneous working method; they also effectively conveyed the elusive, fleeting quality of the scenes Degas wished to capture.[13] Above all, while pastels could be retouched and changed, a mark once made could never be fully erased. As such, they corroborated Degas's conviction in the need for excellent draughtsmanship, his belief in the importance of line and respect for its authority.

That kind of commitment struck a chord with Suzanne. She never used erasers.[14] Mastering a line was like riding on a wave; either you caught it and the drawing came to life, or you had failed and must start again.

Degas was astounded by the pieces Suzanne brought to show him. How a linen maid's daughter with not a day's training could take a pencil and handle it with such assurance, maintain such confident control of a line as to bring a form to life on a flat page, left him speechless. Though there was no formal agreement to their relationship, Degas took his self-appointed role of tutor with the utmost seriousness. And as Camille Pissarro observed, as critics went, 'Degas was one of the harshest'.[15]

Still, merciless self-scrutiny was a familiar bedfellow to Suzanne. 'You have to be hard on yourself,' she warned. 'You should not put suffering into drawings, but all the same, nothing is achieved without pain.'[16]

Degas's style defied categorisation. He refused to let the course of his creative oeuvre be steered by a single aesthetic doctrine and he was never an Impressionist as such (though he was often bracketed together with that group).[17] Similarly, Suzanne abhorred the oppressive bounds of theory. 'I sincerely admire people who have theories on art,' she declared ironically, as though to unsettle those of obverse persuasion. 'I've noticed that the most contradictory theories can be used to justify the same works of art. When all is said and done, I think that the real theory is nature which imposes itself; the painter's nature first of all, then, that of the subject they are representing. Is there really an artist who has ever painted as he would have wished? Everyone paints as they see, which is to say that everyone paints as they are able.'[18] Suzanne could not have chosen a more suitable master.

Degas was a notoriously awkward man to befriend. But in the previous decade he had lost a number of close acquaintances: there was Mary Cassatt's sister, Lydia; the Italian painter Giuseppe de Nittis (for whom Suzanne had posed); his old school friend Alfred Niaudet.[19] And of course, nobody could forget the horrific demise of Édouard Manet who had suffered a slow and agonising death as a result of locomotor ataxia, the gradual deterioration of the spinal column and nervous system, in his case brought on by syphilis. It was a chastening reminder of the unrelenting march of time and it did nothing to ease Degas's morose disposition. 'Oh, where are the days when I thought I was strong,' he had already moaned to Bartholomé in the early 1880s, 'when I was full of logic, full of plans! I am quickly sliding downhill, rolling I know not where, wrapped up in lots of bad pastels, as if in so much packing paper.'[20] There was room in his life for new acquaintances.

A fresh young talent like Suzanne breathed vitality into his dusty existence. She also proved a wonderful source of Montmartre gossip. More importantly, if Suzanne admired Degas, it was clear that she was not prepared to compromise her unique personal blueprint to satisfy him. People must take her as she was. For Degas, such quiet self-assurance and refusal to imitate was refreshing. Degas's attention had often been drawn to Lautrec's idolising tendencies. Years after his initial meeting with Degas, Lautrec was still smitten. On one occasion, having treated some friends to a sumptuous dinner, Lautrec stood to his feet and instructed his bewildered guests to follow him.[21] Going out into the street, he led them to the Dihau residence, where he guided them up and gestured towards one of Degas's pictures. 'There is your dessert,' he announced. In his artwork too, Lautrec had borrowed liberally from his hero, another point that had not escaped Degas's attention. 'The gentleman's wearing trousers that are too big for him,' Degas was once heard to sneer maliciously when the similarity was pointed out.[22]

However, so long as his caustic swipes were not directed at her, Suzanne knew she stood to learn much from this man. When asked, she firmly denied ever having posed for him. But, people probed, was she ever more than just his pupil? The insinuation invariably met with a laugh: no, but she would have slept with him out of gratitude.[23] Their friendship, like their work, defied simple classification. Degas was the spiky mentor Suzanne could not help but admire. And whatever pseudonym she took, she would always be his 'Terrible Maria', the wild gamine of Montmartre who arrived on his doorstep one day and changed his life.

But if her afternoons at 37, Rue Victor-Massé were abuzz with creativity and learning, her home life was growing increasingly fraught. Maurice's behaviour was worsening, his tantrums becoming more frequent. The daily routine at the Valadon residence was a minefield of broken crockery and broken tempers.

Motherhood had been unplanned, and it was a role for which Suzanne was ill-prepared. She was as human as the next inexperienced new mother. Each fresh, explosive outburst required her to learn a new lesson, and quickly. Desperately, she sought to understand the little boy in the only way she knew how: she drew. She studied every limb, watched closely how each sinew and muscle moved, stretched and tightened. With pencil in hand, it seemed she regained control of the situation, because Suzanne truly believed

Suzanne Valadon and Maurice Utrillo, c. 1890.
Collection Jean Fabris

that close observation of the form led to an intimate knowledge of the spirit. 'You must have the courage to look the model in the eye if you want to see into their soul,' she explained.[24]

But there was no escaping the fact that without a father, the boy's personal history was incomplete. Schoolmates could be merciless; neighbours whispered. Suzanne understood well how that kind of uncertainty and stigma could give rise to debilitating self-doubt. It seemed impossible to exclude Maurice's absent father as a factor contributing to his fits and tantrums.

So, really, who was the boy's father? The question was yet again posed as Suzanne, Miguel and a group of their friends sat around a café table meditating over glasses of beer, wine and absinthe one evening. Miguel had lately taken an apartment on the Boulevard de Clichy; Montmartre's watering holes were more than ever his home. 'I don't know if the little fellow is the work of Puvis de Chavannes or Renoir,' Suzanne confessed.[25]

'Why,' Miguel returned, 'I would be honoured to sign my name to either of those fine artists.' The response was bound to arouse titters around the table. But the Spaniard was deadly serious: 'Call him a Utrillo,' he offered.[26]

Within a few weeks, the remark many had dismissed as a playful quip made in a moment of high-spirited revelry was being drawn up into a formal act of recognition.

Early in 1891, Miguel Utrillo arrived at the *mairie* of the 18th arrondissement and duly penned his signature on the Act of Recognition of Maurice Valadon-Utrillo. The document finally gave Maurice a father while enabling him to retain his French citizenship (Miguel had been careful to verify this point before signing).[27]

The act seemed to provide the ultimate resolution to the question of Maurice's paternity. People had already noticed how alike the Valadon boy and the Spaniard were. The resemblance was growing more striking the older Maurice got. Suzanne's drawings of both men – with their dark, slightly sunken eyes, fine-boned features and heavy lids – seemed to offer silent confirmation of the theory. Even similar gestures and mannerisms were starting to become apparent. But other people remained suspicious; Miguel was too obvious an answer. And why would he acknowledge the child now, after all this time? Might it not be the ultimate in selfless and chivalrous gestures, made for a best friend and soulmate who found herself in an impossible predicament of which there seemed no way out? A kindly sacrifice to save a child who was the blameless victim of the whole sorry situation? An apology for whatever disagreement no doubt caused him to flee France when Suzanne fell pregnant?

Suzanne had confounded Montmartre's gossips once again, and in so doing, had given Maurice a clearer sense of his own identity, which she believed might alleviate his suffering. Now she could only hope that life at home would become calmer as she returned to her own chaotic routine.

In Montmartre's dizzying social cocktail of people, parties and places, one acquaintance led to another, and it was seldom possible to recall who had introduced whom, or when. Some seemed to think Suzanne met Miguel's friend Paul Mousis at the Auberge du Clou, others at one of Lautrec's parties, and a few swore it happened at the Lapin Agile.[28] Either way, by the early 1890s the well-built businessman with a magnificent moustache was often seen in her company, and was quite clearly pursuing her.

The pairing struck many as odd; two years older than Suzanne, Mousis came from a strict Catholic family and seemed the very essence of bourgeois propriety.[29] He was wealthy, had a good, stable career with the firm Bel et Sainbénat and a respectable family who owned a house on the Rue de Clignancourt. He was the very antithesis of Suzanne's wild bohemianism, the embodiment of the stability she lacked.

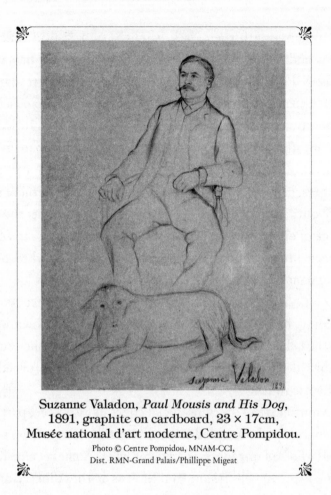

Suzanne Valadon, *Paul Mousis and His Dog*,
1891, graphite on cardboard, 23 × 17cm,
Musée national d'art moderne, Centre Pompidou.
Photo © Centre Pompidou, MNAM-CCI,
Dist. RMN-Grand Palais/Phillippe Migeat

However, her existing career as a model and her burgeoning one
as an artist both demanded attention. She had no desire to dedicate herself entirely to one man if she could enjoy the benefits of
Mousis's acquaintance without commitment. Through Degas particularly, she was making more contacts in the art world, and she
was equally determined not to let existing friendships slip or kind
gestures go un-thanked. 'Dear Mademoiselle, Why do you always
thank me?' Bartholomé enquired in response to one of her letters.
'One day, you brought me the joy of meeting a real artist; it is I
who am indebted to you.'[30]

But Suzanne was under no illusion: for a woman to even hope for an artistic career was, at best, wildly ambitious. Many would declare it impossible. It certainly would not happen overnight. As a single mother, she had to continue modelling to put food on the table.

A young student named Suzay Leudet, herself an aspiring female artist, was particularly struck by the model she and her classmates were asked to draw during a session in the studio of Hector Leroux one summer in 1891.[31] It was Suzanne. The students were impressed by her grace, professionalism and most of all, her stamina; for the fortnight for which she was hired, Suzanne demonstrated that she could hold a pose for four hours at a time with only a ten-minute break and without appearing to tire. But it was the conversation, after Suzanne's departure, between Leroux and their mentor Henner, who had come to inspect the students' work, that stayed with Leudet.

'You know, she's painting now,' Henner informed Leroux, referring to Suzanne.

'What's the painting like?' Leroux asked.

'Bad!' Henner proclaimed. 'But all the same, it's quite something to think that it's our influence that has given her the notion to paint.'

With a temperament like Suzanne's, it was fortunate for Henner and Leroux that their model did not overhear them.

Suzanne was ploughing her own furrow, pursuing her own creative vision, absorbing those influences she deemed useful, discarding the criticism and gender-based prejudice she did not. When it came to her artwork, she needed to stay focused if, as Degas maintained, she truly stood to make a serious profession of art. There was much to distract her if she allowed it.

Despite Miguel's presence in Paris and his formal recognition of Maurice as his son, the little boy's disquiet showed no signs of abating. The study of mental health and learning disabilities was in its infancy, but anyone could tell that something was amiss.

Suzanne decided that it might prove a long-term economy to seek specialist input. Therefore in 1891, she took Maurice, not yet eight, to consult a paediatric specialist at the Hôpital du Kremlin-Bicêtre.[32] They believed they could give a diagnosis: mental debility. Mme Valadon would do well to place her son in the nearby care home for children with mental handicaps, Suzanne was told. Appalled at the assessment, and never receptive to being 'told', Suzanne brought Maurice straight home and resolved that, in the long tradition of Limousin peasant families, the Valadons would deal with the 'problem' themselves.

Meanwhile, Miguel's role and purpose remained unclear. He was far from assuming responsibilities of *chef de famille*, and he did not live with the Valadons. But his commitment was such that he did not conceal it from his own family. 'Dearest mother,' Miguel wrote on Maurice's birthday that year, after the little boy had written a note to Señora Utrillo, '[Maurice] is well but remains fragile, his mother is still in a delicate state of health.'[33]

Still, if the relationship between Maurice and Miguel remained distant, scarcely more than the cold formality of a paper agreement, the Spaniard's profound and complicated bond with the child's mother was tangibly evidenced through drawings. In 1891, Miguel began a drawing of Suzanne, a delicate study in red chalk and coloured pencils. That same year, Miguel sat for Suzanne on numerous occasions, and allowed her sure hand to trace those features she knew so well, to study closely the subject who had assumed a new significance in her eyes. Her line caressed his elegant, aquiline profile, with his dark features and his straight nose. It was a familiar face – few observers would deny that besides the moustache, it was the very image of Maurice.

Suzanne's art was starting to attract notice. In 1892, Degas arranged for her to have some of her studies of Maurice sent to Le Barc de Boutteville's shop in the Rue Pelletier at the time of the exhibition 'Impressionistes et Symbolistes'. It was a small venue, but acceptance there carried immense prestige. Originally a dealer in old paintings, by the 1890s, Le Barc de Boutteville had become one of the foremost exhibitors of avant-garde art and a tireless promoter of previously unknown talent.[34] There, Suzanne, a woman, would have her work considered alongside canvases by Lautrec, Camille Pissarro and one of the leaders of the Nabis movement, Paul Sérusier.

The young art student Françis Jourdain was helping hang the exhibition, when Le Barc pointed out the work of one artist in particular.[35] He held up one of Suzanne's drawings of Maurice.

'Not bad, eh?' Le Barc mused. 'It's by a little model ... She never had any training ... Seeing one of the artists she was posing for at work, she thought she would have a go too ... Seriously talented, don't you think? ... You'd never guess that a woman had done that ...'

For the *Mercure de France*, Le Barc de Boutteville's exhibition of 'Impressionistes et Symbolistes' confirmed 'that real art can only be found outside the schools and official institutions'.[36] To the reviewer's mind, it was one of 'the true exhibitions of the year, the only ones that we should speak about'.

For Suzanne, having her work handled by Le Barc de Boutteville was a spectacular achievement, at once personally reaffirming and publicly demonstrating that she should be taken seriously. And as her confidence grew, so her artwork became braver. That year, she produced her first female nude. She also faced her trepidation about painting in oils, producing *Young Girl Crocheting* and *Portrait of a Young Girl*.

When she drew or painted, Suzanne dedicated herself fully to the task. It was intense work, so novel entertainments were always welcome when she set down her pencil or brush. And it just so happened that a new leisure activity was taking Montmartre by storm. By the 1890s, Miguel and his friends had become fascinated by the art of Chinese shadow theatre.

Shadow puppetry as a means of storytelling had a long history in Asia, but it was particularly the Chinese form of the art that found its way back to France via missionaries in the second half of the 18th century. The art took hold and it saw a resurgence in the 19th century. At a time when flat screens typically presented a static image, the animation of shadow theatre was unparalleled. With its movement, sound, effects, and the intimate contact it encouraged between performers and audiences, shadow theatre was perfectly attuned to fin-de-siècle tastes.

Always on the lookout for lucrative business ventures, Rodolphe Salis smelled an opportunity. He decided to try staging shadow shows at Le Chat Noir. The first show, *The Epic*, a retelling of Napoleon's war in Spain in 1808, was performed on 27 December 1886.[37] Audiences sat transfixed before the huge screen as the two-act pantomime unfolded. In the wings, machinists slid in some 50 plates cut out of zinc (which ensured a rigid form and a crisp outline) mounted on light pine chassis. And when lamps were directed on the action and Charles de Sivry's stirring score began to play, spectators were transported to a magical world. Gliding panels in at different angles created the illusion of depth, while well-timed effects with smoke and puffs of air added to the effect. Salis improvised a commentary, and the throng of audience members (some squeezed in perching on upturned barrels) felt so immersed in the action that they gasped and called out in response as the show unfolded. In moments, full-grown adults were returned to childlike wonder and the success of the cabaret's shadow theatre was confirmed. The performances became the venue's calling card, and showcased the talents of such artists as Henri Rivière, Caran d'Ache, Louis Morin and Fernand Fau, with *The Epic* and *The Walk by Starlight* (performed in January 1890) becoming its flagship shows.[38]

Miguel was among those Montmartrois captivated by the evocative power of shadow theatre. But watching from the audience was not enough; he wanted to be involved. Miguel began to study the art of shadow performance seriously. With his technical training and artistic skill, he was just the kind of multitalented individual who could excel at shadow theatre.

Since Le Chat Noir's venture, the craze for shadow theatre had spread. The proprietor of Le Chat Noir's great rival, the Auberge du Clou, calculated that staging shadow shows could boost their average customer spend too. And it was there that Miguel was booked to stage his first public show. Miguel's stage skills made him a big hit with the public. 'Completely new and highly original,' *Gil Blas* raved about one of the first productions Miguel was involved with, declaring it 'a well-deserved artistic success.'[39] Suzanne was among Miguel's loyal supporters, and she often arrived with Mousis following not far behind.

In 1892, Miguel was entrusted with directing and designing the end of year show at the Auberge du Clou. The text for *Noël* would be provided by the writer, composer and actor Vincent Hyspa.[40] And the music was to be composed by a friend of Miguel's, a bizarre young pianist by the name of Erik Satie.

With his frock coat, goatee beard and top hat perched on a crop of wild brown hair, the bespectacled, Normandy-born Satie looked the quintessential Montmartre bohemian. Brought to Paris aged four, he had become acquainted with heartbreak early; between the ages of five and six, he lost his baby sister and then his mother in quick succession, and found himself being sent back to Honfleur with his younger brother Conrad to live with his paternal grandparents.[41] A strict boarding-school education followed, where the only subjects in which Satie truly excelled were music and Latin.

Happily, his grandmother also arranged for him to have music lessons with a local organist. But then tragedy visited Satie again in 1878 when his grandmother drowned swimming, and he and his brother were returned to their father in Paris. After a brief period of casual home-schooling from his father, Satie was enrolled at the prestigious Conservatoire of music on the initiative of his father's new, musically orientated wife. The rigour and archaism suited him ill. He was declared 'gifted but indolent', the 'laziest student in the Conservatoire', and in 1882, Satie was dismissed.[42] He was readmitted in 1883, but by then his attention was elsewhere; Satie had begun composing and had acquired a taste for Montmartre's famous avant-garde art scene, with its smoky bars, its cabarets and its simmering cauldron of creativity. He left the Conservatoire in 1886 to begin military service, which he despised, and infected himself with bronchitis to hasten his release. By the end of the 1880s, Satie had rented a small apartment in Montmartre, the capital of the bohemian life with which he had fallen in love, and was dividing his time between composing and mingling with the artists, writers and musicians who haunted the area's cafés.

Satie was delighted to discover Le Chat Noir, which became his second home. Shortly after his first visit, he was hired as second pianist. So comfortable did Satie feel that the shy, reserved young man he had appeared to some quickly gave way to an outgoing and humorous, if eccentric, bohemian. However, with Rodolphe Salis's doubtful managerial skills and Satie's inherently free spirit, it was not long before the pair argued. He left Le Chat Noir. Moving to an even tinier flat at 6, Rue Cortot (a spot high enough to evade his creditors, he was fond of informing people), he also found new employment, becoming the pianist at the Auberge du Clou, hired to accompany Miguel's shadow shows.

Along with *Noël*, Satie was composing another piece intended for the Auberge du Clou, a 'Christian ballet', *Uspud*, for which the libretto would be provided by his friend, the poet J.P. Contamine de Latour.[43] By November 1892, *Uspud* was complete and ready for performance. Satie was excited. *Uspud* told the tale of a pagan's conversion, and the composer had incorporated a number of interludes for harp, strings and flute. He had put his heart and soul into this production, not to mention considerable time. *Uspud* was expected to create an unprecedented stir, to astound and astonish. It did – though not in the way Satie had hoped. As Latour remembered, initial feedback to the work encompassed 'wild approbation and violent reprobation'.[44] Satie was outraged.

Suzanne had watched the activity at Miguel's shadow theatre that Christmas with great curiosity. During that time, she came to know the odd figure of Satie a little better. The unusual fascinated her – and Satie was nothing if not unusual.

'I breathe with caution, a little at a time and I dance very rarely,' he warned.[45]

Where *Uspud* was concerned, Satie had the courage of his convictions. His work should – and would – be performed on the world's greatest stages, he declared. And there were few greater than the Opéra.

Satie proposed *Uspud* to the Opéra's director, Eugène Bertrand, and when, after persistent approaches, no response came, he challenged Bertrand to a duel.[46] Terrified into submission, Bertrand hastily agreed to look at the work and arranged to meet with the composer on 17 December. Ultimately, Satie's insistence that the project be overseen by a committee of musicians of his choosing scuppered any chance of the director yielding.[47] But the meeting alone was cause for celebration.

Satie arranged to have a deluxe edition of *Uspud* printed in honour of his achievement and Suzanne, he decided, would design the cover. Suzanne presented her profile studies of the production's authors in the form of a medallion. The work demanded a period of close contact, and in Satie's case, that time was extended; Suzanne also judged the composer's curious face sufficient motivation to gain mastery over her misgivings about working in oils. She began a portrait of Satie dressed in his uniform hat and frock coat, in which she captured his dark eyebrows, unkempt hair and pince-nez. So often, Suzanne found drawing to enrich her relationships. As they sat together, Satie holding his pose, Suzanne watching him closely, she began to understand the man behind the image of stud-ied eccentricity. And Satie fell deeply in love.

One 14 January 1893 (a Saturday, Satie remembered), Suzanne and the musician began an intense affair. Two days later, Satie brought her back to visit his dingy, cramped apartment, with its drawings peeling off the walls, its rickety, wrought-iron bed and its spartan furnishings.[48] They had barely got to know each other when he proposed. Suzanne quickly turned him down. 'She had too many things on her mind to get married,' Satie rationalised afterwards, 'so we never brought up the subject again.'[49]

For Suzanne, the circumstances of this new liaison were hardly glamorous. Nor did the affair offer the stability and security she could have in a moment if she accepted Mousis's advances. But it was exciting, intriguing, unpredictable. A person could never know what an afternoon with Satie might entail. There were trips to the Luxembourg Gardens to sail toy boats; gifts, including a necklace of sausages and a paper bag filled, Satie explained, with all the wonderful smells of the world.[50] There were long, passionate love letters in which Satie poured out his heart. She was his love, his darling, his 'Biqui'.

And then there was music, 'man's greatest invention', Suzanne enthused after her time in Satie's company.[51] Music said what all the letters in the world could not. Rusiñol captured Suzanne's bewitch-ing effect on Satie and his smothering affection for her in his *Una Romanza* (1894), a painting for which, in a poignant reversal of roles, Suzanne became the maestro playing the piano and Satie the reverent audience. The claustrophobia was palpable, the casting perceptive; musically erudite though Satie was, in his journey to become a man of the world, he was but an infant, an uninitiated boy to Suzanne's woman of worldly wisdom. He knew the emotive force of music, but he was unprepared to experience such surges of feeling from another human being.

Friends remembered that in addition to her portrait of Satie, Suzanne good-naturedly gave him a line drawing of herself.[52]

But with two such unique and passionate characters, each at a very different stage of life, the affair was always destined to be a fleeting interlude, not the protracted symphony Satie had desired. Satie was diverting but he was no serious match for Suzanne's tempestuous nature and could not provide the support she needed, either to counterbalance her own temperament, or in practical terms for her mother and Maurice. Before long, storm clouds were gathering over their transitory paradise.

The dawning realisation that he could never have and hold Suzanne lay behind a letter Satie penned on 11 March 1893. In the top left-hand corner was the crest of the 'Society of Old Hens', on which was inscribed the motto: 'Eagle I cannot be, turkey I deign not to be, chicken I am'. The letter read:

Dear little Biqui,

Impossible to stop thinking about your whole being; you are inside me completely; everywhere I see only your exquisite eyes, your gentle hands and your little child's feet.

You are happy; my poor thoughts will not wrinkle your untroubled brow; nor will you worry about not seeing me at all.

For me there is only icy solitude that makes my head feel empty and fills my heart with sadness.

Do not forget that your poor friend hopes to see you at at least one of these three rendezvous:

1. This evening at my place at eight forty-five
2. Tomorrow morning again at my place
3. Tomorrow evening at Dédé's (Maison Olivier)

I should add, darling Biqui, that I shall on no account get angry if you cannot come to any of these rendezvous; now I have become terribly reasonable, and that in spite of the great happiness that it gives me to see you.

I am beginning to understand that Biqui can't always do what she wants.

You see, little Biqui, there is a beginning to everything.

I send your heart the sweetest kisses.

Erik Satie[53]

The letter's close betrayed a recent history of disputes over Suzanne's limited availability. Satie's nine-part *Danses Gothiques*, composed not long after that letter, captured his mood. 'On the Occasion of a Great Suffering', he titled one piece, 'Concerning a Pardon for Insults Received' another, and the final dance: 'Having Been Granted Mitigation for One's Errors'.[54] Besides the suffocating nature of Satie's love and his possessiveness, the breakup was due at least in part to Suzanne's realisation of how much she would have to compromise if she remained with Satie. There were dreams she would never realise, demands she could not fulfil. The far more dependable presence of Mousis was hovering in the wings to remind her of the alternative. Meanwhile, Maurice now understood that he only had a father in name, and he was growing more fractious. The difficulties were only magnified when Miguel took up the offer of a role with the shadow theatre group Les Ombres Parisiennes in March 1893 and was invited to go to Chicago for the World Fair. He left France.[55]

People reasoned that Miguel was jealous of Satie. Initially, however, Suzanne was not unduly concerned. 'I thought he would come back as he had done so many times before,' she reflected years later. But she soon realised that she was wrong. Miguel was not going to return.[56]

Satie's *Bonjour Biqui, Bonjour!* was one of his last attempts to express the intensity of his affection. He composed the simple, four-bar song with just three chords and five notes on 2 April 1893, intending it to be an Easter Sunday gift for Suzanne. For the cover, he produced a pen and ink drawing of his beloved. But the plaintive tone bespoke a man who already knew that he had lost her. The affair was doomed. By the summer, it had ended acrimoniously, Satie having channelled his torment and anguish as the relationship deteriorated into the longer and repetitive piano piece *Vexations*. There was no agreement on how the affair finally ended, but Satie was broken. 'My love affair with Suzanne Valadon ended on Tuesday 20th of June,' he scrawled in blue and red ink, pinning a lock of her hair to the paper.[57] Lashing out, he issued all sorts of accusations. Sometimes, he would declare that he had pushed Suzanne out of a window, at others, he boasted that he had called the police to come and arrest her.[58] Just eight days after the breakup, he wrote to his brother, Conrad:

> I have just broken finally with Suzanne.
>
> I shall have great difficulty in regaining possession of myself, loving this little person as I have loved her ever since you left: she was able to take all of me.
>
> Time will do what at this moment I cannot do.[59]

Half-crazed, Satie threw himself into his art and religion. He had already been involved with the Rosicrucian cult of Joséphin Péladan in the early 1890s, where he served as house composer to

Péladan's sect.[60] The sect was an art-focused organisation which gave more than a passing nod to Catholicism, mysticism and the occult. The year he split with Suzanne, Satie branched out on his own and formed the 'Metropolitan Church of the Art of Jesus the Conductor', making himself 'Parcier' (Parcener) and Master of the Chapel.[61] He dressed in flowing robes, kept his hair long and his beard pointed, and began issuing all manner of religious pamphlets and writings from his little apartment. Music and poetry, he preached, would redeem souls. Then he tried to gain election to the Académie des Beaux-Arts. His nomination caused great amusement. 'Musicians, be afraid!' joked *Le Gaulois* when his candidature was announced.[62] Composer Maurice Ravel was less generous. Erik Satie, Ravel declared, was 'a complete lunatic'.[63]

Years later it emerged that the distraught Satie had written letter upon letter to Suzanne, which he never sent. When *Uspud* was republished, he erased Suzanne's signature from her cover drawing.[64] He eventually died in squalor and poverty in a disordered apartment in Arcueil, a suburb outside Paris. Suzanne's portrait of him was found hanging on the wall. He was alone; no one ever knew him to have another romantic relationship.

While Suzanne's role as a femme fatale and Satie's perceived decline into lunacy kept Montmartre's idle tongues busy, Suzanne now rebounded into the ready arms of Paul Mousis. Technically, Mousis still lived in his parents' home at 13, Rue de Clignancourt, but in practice, he and Suzanne spent more and more time together.[65]

Suzanne, Maurice and Madeleine had moved several times since the mother and daughter first arrived in Montmartre. For a time at the turn of the decade, Suzanne gave her address as 34, Rue de Laval, where she sublet living space on the fifth floor from a Mme Marguerite Gérard.[66] Then, in the early 1890s, Suzanne considered home to be 2, Rue Mont-Cenis, and not long after, she was living at 11, Rue Girardon.[67] But for Suzanne, her street name and number were of little consequence; home was Maurice and Madeleine, with her inexhaustible store of Limousin customs, tales and wisdom, reaffirming luggage which travelled with them wherever they went. Only Marie-Alix was missing, and Suzanne kept in regular contact with her half-sister, writing to enquire after her children. Meanwhile, Marie-Alix always sent a hamper of treats at Christmas time, and Suzanne never failed to write back in thanks, addressing her elder sibling affectionately as 'dear sister', 'kind sister', assuring her that the goose or the butter or the sausages were feasted upon and scolding Marie-Alix for the expense; Suzanne knew the cost of indulgence.[68]

Despite Maurice's continuing delinquency, with Satie gone and Mousis by her side, by 1894, Suzanne's life was taking on a less chaotic shape. Her portrait of herself in her late 20s reflected the confidence of both sitter and painter. Each seemed comfortable in their role, while the warm hues of orange and yellow oil paint were dexterously handled. Compared to her self-portrait at eighteen, she now appeared less defiant, more self-assured, at peace. And exquisitely beautiful. At times now, she could almost believe herself a bourgeois lady.

But then early in 1894, Degas made an unexpected and radical suggestion. Her work had become truly exceptional – one might almost say good enough to appear at the Salon de la Société Nationale des Beaux-Arts, he mused tantalisingly.

The notion was outrageous. Appearing at the Salon de la Société Nationale des Beaux-Arts was one of the highest markers of professional attainment to which a painter could aspire. For an untrained, lower-class woman artist to have her work accepted – it was outlandish, unthinkable, impossible. But Degas had sparked the flame of desire. Suzanne decided that she would do it.

CHAPTER 9

Picture Perfect

Fau naisser per èsser gente, se maridar per
èsser riche e crebar per èsser brave.
(You should be born to be sweet, marry
to be rich and die to be brave.)
OLD LIMOUSIN PROVERB[1]

What?' Puvis de Chavannes erupted. 'Never! Whose pupil are you? What will people say?'[2] Suzanne should have guessed that her request would be rebuffed. It had been Degas's idea to seek the support of 'the peacock', her former employer, in a bid to see her work hung in the Nationale. It was not a foolhardy approach; Puvis was one of the founders of the Salon de la Société Nationale des Beaux-Arts. The society had existed in embryonic form in the 1860s, but it was not until 1890 that it became the fully fledged, prestigious exhibition forum that Suzanne now hoped to penetrate. The rebirth had come about when dissatisfaction with the authoritarian approach of the official Salon (yet again) spurred a group of artists to seek an alternative place to exhibit, a salon which was more receptive to new ideas. The group was initially presided over by the renowned painter of battle scenes, Ernest Meissonier, and its committee included other acclaimed artists, not least Puvis, who was made vice-president (and subsequently president), and the sculptor Auguste Rodin. The organisation soon won the respect of critics and erudite amateurs. But however open-minded the society professed itself to be, exhibitors still had to have earned their stripes and the membership hierarchy was strictly codified. Those at the top, the founding members or *fondateurs*, invited fellow members to become *sociétaires*, the next class of member. *Sociétaires* would also serve in turn as jury. Beneath this group came *associés*, members who had already been admitted and exhibited at the group's exhibitions and were voted on by the *sociétaires*. Everyone else had to have all their work subjected to the scrutiny of the jury. A potential exhibitor's training was given close consideration. Without being formally enrolled in an atelier or school, Suzanne would need a champion on the inside – ideally, a member of the jury.[3]

Clearly, Degas's careful selection of his protégé's drawings had been in vain. Still, however well-regarded he was as president, Puvis was just one artist. His was not the only opinion which could decide an artist's fate. There was another tack they could try if he refused to be swayed, not as direct a contact perhaps, but a figure no less influential. Bartholomé, who was by now a regular exhibitor at the Nationale and a *sociétaire*, happened to know the sought-after painter of portraits, Paul Helleu, another *sociétaire*, who was much admired by the committee. The sculptor was delighted to be of service and wasted no time in writing to his colleague.[4]

'My dear Helleu,' he began:

four or five days ago, a poor woman arrived on my doorstep carrying an enormous folder of drawings, having been sent by a friend. She wanted to exhibit at the Champ de Mars and was seeking a sponsor. I do not recommend her to you, I ask only that you look at the drawings signed Valadon when they pass before the jury. You will see serious flaws, but also, I believe, such curious qualities that you will almost certainly be pleased to receive them.[5]

This time, the benefactors' tactic paid off; the salon committee agreed to take five of Suzanne's drawings.

The acceptance was an extraordinary coup. It was not so much her status as woman that jeopardised her chances of admission; American painter Elizabeth Nourse had actually been invited to join the Société Nationale des Beaux-Arts, and by the mid-1890s had become a regular participant at the group's annual salons, where she had earned herself a prodigious reputation.[6] But Nourse had been born into a highly respectable Catholic family from Cincinnati. She was extensively trained and had already established a reputation in the official Salon before she was approached to join the Nationale. Suzanne was resolutely working-class and had never set foot in an art school or atelier in any other capacity than as a model. Degas and Bartholomé could feel rightly proud.

On 25 April 1894, the doors of the Champ de Mars swung open. And there on the wall, among canvases by such prestigious names as Eugène Boudin and Carolus-Duran (and listed in the catalogue opposite Bartholomé's works) were Suzanne's drawings. She had submitted three studies of children, and two of a subject which formed an intrinsic part of her daily routine: *The Grandson's Toilette* and *Grandmother and Grandson*.[7]

What visitors saw when they stopped in front of Suzanne's exhibition space was revolutionary. 'The forms are always vague,' Gustave Geoffroy had written of Berthe Morisot's art in 1881. No such thing could be said of Suzanne's pieces.[8]

Suzanne had perfected drawings which were characterised by sharp, almost crude contours. Her profiles were executed with a pure, single line. To achieve such a crisp silhouette in what appeared to be a single stroke demanded confidence, courage and hours of practice. So determined was Suzanne that the figures look just so, that she sometimes used tracing to achieve the effect. But perhaps even more striking than her style was the handling of her subject matter, her compositions subverting the iconographic conventions familiar to the late 19th-century viewer.

Suzanne presented her drawings of children at a time when conceptions of the family were changing. Starting at the end of the 18th century, the family began to be characterised – or idealised – by more intimate relationships, while the child was increasingly treated not dispassionately as simply a means of securing property and continuing the family name (as in the past) but as an individual worthy of affection. Now, children should be cosseted, nurtured and adored by their parents, who were encouraged to take a more hands-on role in their care. In short, paternity and maternity had become deeply fashionable among the bourgeoisie, that same class who were, coincidentally, the main consumers of art.[9]

The Salon walls were obligingly filled with genre paintings in which, in a convenient recasting of the traditional Madonna and child theme, happy mothers cuddled contented, rosy-cheeked infants. Though less formal in style, Impressionists' canvases – like Mary Cassatt's *Baby's First Caress* (*c.* 1890) – were also inclined to support the vision of tender intimacy that was felt to characterise the parent–child bond.[10] Even Naturalist paintings of working-class children showed their subjects delighting in hard, physical labour. Art tended to reaffirm popular perceptions: children were good, happy and lovable and families were united.

Suzanne's pictures of children flew in the face of those idealised images of social harmony. Her youngsters were not nude, but unashamedly naked. They were not posed, but awkward, their scrawny limbs contracted into clumsy postures, ungainly, unaesthetic, but utterly natural. Self-aware but not self-conscious,

Suzanne Valadon, *Nude Girl Sitting*, 1894, black pencil and white chalk, 22 × 28cm, Musée national d'art moderne, Centre Pompidou.
Photo © Centre Pompidou, MNAM-CCI, Dist. RMN-Grand Palais/Phillippe Migeat

oblivious to the viewer's intrusive gaze, Suzanne's children looked introspective, isolated – and lonely, so incredibly lonely. The only carer to be found was the grandmother. The mother was nowhere to be seen.[11]

Other artists showed what viewers wanted to see. Suzanne showed them what was true.

But something else marked Suzanne out as different: in the catalogue to the exhibition, she was listed not as 'Mme' or 'Mlle' like other women exhibitors, but simply: 'Valadon, S.'. When viewers looked from the catalogue in their hands to the drawings in front of them, they had no way of knowing that the artist they were contemplating was a woman. Indeed, in the absence of such a title, convention would lead viewers to presume it was the work of a man. Suzanne spurned the notion of the *femme artiste* – she was an artist, pure and simple.[12]

It was perhaps that lack of clarity that led the paper *L'Argus* to forward a laudatory press cutting intended for Suzanne to the minor painter Jules Valadon, who specialised in pictures of young Neapolitans and had exhibited two canvases at the official Salon that year. The offended painter penned Suzanne a haughty letter requesting that she kindly sign her name in full in future to avoid further confusion, and he ended his missive 'Jules Valadon, Chevalier de la Légion d'Honneur'. Her temper fired, Suzanne had only one response for her rival: 'P★★★ off!'[13]

Suzanne was kicking down the restrictive walls of the art establishment, and no one could be more triumphant than Degas. 'You must have removed your drawings from the Champ de Mars, illustrious Valadon,' he wrote to her one Sunday in July at the end of the show. 'Come along tomorrow and bring me mine,' he instructed, for he had been sure to reserve one of her pictures for himself at the earliest possible opportunity. 'Bartholomé will have written to you about a drawing that he was burning to own,' Degas went on. 'Tell me, has his desire been satisfied?'[14]

Now that she was a proper artist, it was fitting that the bulk of her time be spent working in a studio. Accordingly, by November that year, Degas knew to address his letters to 2–4, Rue Cortot, where Paul Mousis had rented his lover a studio, next door to Erik Satie's apartment. One such read:

> Terrible Maria, yesterday at the Lebarc de Bouteville's [*sic*], I wanted to buy your excellent drawing, but he did not know the price. Come along tomorrow morning at 9.30 if you can with your portfolio; let's see if you haven't got something even better.[15]

Now, Degas was promoting Suzanne widely. Besides Le Barc de Boutteville, Degas saw to it that her work was known to enlightened amateurs and other dealers, including Ernest Stanislas Le Véel, Arsène Portier, Paul Durand-Ruel (the Impressionists' main dealer) and the inimitable Ambroise Vollard. The portly dealer from La Réunion had established his gallery in the Rue Lafitte in 1893 and had already made a name for himself as a tireless purveyor of avant-garde art. Rumour had it that Vollard took quite a shine to Suzanne when she was first presented to him in the mid-1890s, and that he had been fixed on marrying her. It was said to have taken all Degas's ingenuity to dissuade the dealer and spare his protégé.[16]

In any case, by 1895, everyone could see that Paul Mousis had become a firm fixture in Suzanne's life. He had stepped effortlessly into the role of *chef de famille* in the Valadon household and was making his presence felt.

While Mousis campaigned to persuade his strict Catholic family of Suzanne's virtues and her eligibility as a potential spouse, Suzanne enjoyed all the benefits of a bourgeois wife with few of the inconveniences – and none of the ties. People smiled knowingly when it was observed that Suzanne had been able to afford a maid, a buxom Breton girl named Catherine, who was seen walking Maurice to school. Then, Suzanne gave up modelling and began painting full-time.

Mousis did not boast the sparkling good humour of Lautrec, the multitalented, Mediterranean charm of Miguel, nor the thrilling eccentricity of Satie. But he was undeniably good-looking, manly – and secure. With Mousis providing a stable home life, one weight at least was lifted. Suzanne could now immerse herself in her art and continue in her role as the livewire who helped animate Montmartre's social scene.

For an inherently restless spirit like Suzanne, 1890s Paris was abuzz with excitement and change. The daily routine of modern Parisians would have been unrecognisable to her forbears back in Bessines. Technological advances were transforming everyday life. The city's familiar old buildings were gradually being demolished and gleaming new constructions were springing up in their wake, triumphant edifices beckoning towards the future. Already by the 1880s, telephones had begun to appear in upper-class households, and in the 1890s the motor car burst on to the market. All at once, distance became less critical and time telescoped down. Parisians were being tempted out of the shadows by progress, with freedom offered as their reward.

But not all change was auspicious. A man of business, Paul Mousis understood that better than anyone. If Paris was the locus of progress, it was simultaneously the centre of dramatic socio-political shifts and momentous public disputes. In 1892, the Panama Scandal had hit the headlines, shaming a number of Republican deputies when their corruption in the activity of the floundering Panama Canal Company was exposed.[17] Then, bewildered Parisians were plunged into terror, as a wave of merciless attacks by anarchists swept through the city. Bombs were planted in the homes of notable figures, public buildings were targeted (including a café in the busy Gare Saint-Lazare), and in June 1894, President Carnot was assassinated.[18] Finally, at the end of that year, just after Suzanne had removed her work from the Nationale, the alleged treason of the Jewish army captain Alfred Dreyfus exploded on to the front pages of the papers, turning daily life on its head and becoming one of the most sensational legal cases France had ever seen. Dreyfus was accused of passing top-secret information to the German attaché in Paris, Max von Schwartzkoppen.[19] His trial unfolded, with each unmissable daily instalment stirring up yet more anti-Semitic feeling. The affair divided families, turned neighbours into enemies and friends into foes. Dreyfus's name was on everybody's lips, and

Pierre-Auguste Renoir, *Dance at Bougival*, 1883, oil on canvas, 181.9 × 98.1cm,
Museum of Fine Arts, Boston, Picture Fund, 37.375.

Pierre-Auguste Renoir,
Dance in the City, 1883,
oil on canvas, 180 × 90cm,
Musée d'Orsay, Paris.

Pierre-Auguste Renoir,
Dance in the Country, 1883,
oil on canvas, 180 × 90 cm,
Musée d'Orsay, Paris.

Suzanne Valadon, *Self Portrait*, 1883, pastel on paper, 43.5 × 30.5cm, Musée national d'art moderne, Centre Georges Pompidou, Paris.

Suzanne Valadon, *e Grandmother*, 1883, red chalk, white chalk and pencil on paper, 35.2 × 29.5cm, Musée national d'art oderne, Centre Georges Pompidou, Paris.

Marcelin Gilbert Desboutin,
Portrait of Pierre Puvis de Chavann
1895, oil on canvas, 120 × 80cm
Musée de Picardie, Amiens,
France.

Pierre C. Puvis de Chavannes, *The Sacred Grove of the Arts and Muses*, 1884,
oil on canvas, 460 × 1040cm, Musée des Beaux-Arts de Lyon.

Pierre-Auguste Renoir, *The Large Bathers*, 1884–1887, oil on canvas, 117.8 × 170.8cm, Philadelphia Museum of Art.

Pierre-Auguste Renoir,
La Natte (*The Plait*),
86–1887, oil on canvas,
57 × 47cm,
Museum Langmatt.

ftung Langmatt Sidney und Jenny
Brown, Baden, Switzerland

Santiago Rusiñol, *Portrait of Miguel Utrillo*, 1890–1891, oil on canvas, 222.5 × 151cm, Museu Nacional d'Art de Catalunya, Barcelona.

Suzanne Valadon,
Maurice Utrillo, 1886, red chalk
on paper, 34.5 × 29cm,
Musée national d'art moderne,
Centre Georges Pompidou, Paris.

Henri de Toulouse-Lautrec, *The Hangover*, 1887–1889, oil on canvas, 47 × 55.3cm,
arvard Art Museums/Fogg Museum, Bequest from the Collection of Maurice Wertheim,
Class of 1906, 1951.63.

Suzanne Valadon, *Portrait of Erik Satie*, 1892–1893, oil on canvas, 41 × 22cm, Musée national d'art moderne, Centre Georges Pompidou, Paris.

Santiago Ruisiñol, *Una Romanza*, 18
oil on canvas, 89.5 × 111
Collection Museu Nacional d'
de Catalunya, Barcelo

his conviction and banishment to Devil's Island at the end of the year left a simmering trail of bitterness and social destruction in its wake.

Paris was in disarray. And with a mistress whose rampant sociability threatened to delay even further his very bourgeois goal of a happy marriage, Paul Mousis was growing disenchanted with the activity of the capital.

He concluded that a country retreat would be beneficial for his whole 'family'. But Suzanne was a creature of Montmartre; her very soul beat in time with its electric pulse. Making the case for a town in the suburbs was not going to be easy. Besides, Suzanne had too many other preoccupations for the time being to give thought to the idea.

Early in March 1895, the art world learned of the tragic death of Berthe Morisot, who expired at her home in Passy. Despite the social chasm between them, Suzanne could not help but be affected. Morisot had left an indelible mark on the history of women's art and a magnificent creative oeuvre. But just as poignant was her human legacy. The grief occasioned by her demise was something Suzanne witnessed first-hand, since Morisot's close friends like Degas and Bartholomé were deeply distressed.

'It seems that I must go to Passy tomorrow Terrible Maria,' Degas wrote, shortly after the news broke. 'Do make sure you come next Sunday if you can with new drawings. Now that you are well, work hard.'[20]

Morisot had left behind a daughter, sixteen-year-old Julie, about whom Degas felt almost paternally protective. The case of Morisot merely reiterated the complex negotiation process a woman artist was forced to undertake when pulled between love and art. It raised questions about a woman painter's priorities – but offered no answers.

Between illness, grief and the compelling call to support Julie,

Degas was again obliged to content himself with only written contact with Suzanne later in the month.

'You see, my poor Maria, I still cannot climb the hill to see you. Zandomeneghi and Portier have passed on your news. I would like to hear it directly. Have courage and take care.'[21]

When Suzanne finally did resume contact with her mentor, a new, practical focus relieved the need for uncomfortable talk of recent events. Degas wanted Suzanne to try soft ground etching, a technique whereby the artist executed a pencil drawing on a sheet of paper placed over a copper or zinc plate coated with a soft sticky ground.[22] The pencil pressure would lift the ground where it had passed, so that when the paper was removed, the plate would show the marks of the drawing. Next, the plate was immersed in acid, which would eat into the exposed metal. The plate could then be inked up, wiped so that only the lines would retain the ink, and finally printed from. The technique was thought to have originated in Italy in the 17th century, but it had been used frequently by late 18th and early 19th-century English landscape artists. Degas had become a master of the procedure, and other artists would sometimes come to him for advice.[23]

With Suzanne's command of line, soft ground etching was a fitting progression. It was the first formal art teaching she had ever received. Suzanne produced a series of nudes on Degas's press, several of her maid, Catherine, drying herself by the side of a tub. The shapes and contours of the human form tending to itself fascinated her. However, one of the first pieces she produced betrayed her noviciate; when she signed her name, she failed to take into account the mirrored effect of printing, and on the finished piece, her signature came out back to front.

The sheer all-consuming physicality of the technique had Suzanne thoroughly absorbed. When she first started, she pressed far harder than was necessary. It was, one critic later said of her early etching, 'almost as if a sculptor had defined the planes' and 'given so much weight to each form, in particular to the nudes which, although produced on white paper, have the gloss and the hardness of marble.'[24]

The act of creation obliged Suzanne to immerse herself fully in the present moment. It was a welcome release, a form of therapy. But no amount of creativity could ease the loss of a very personal kind which came later in the year. That May, word reached Suzanne that her half-sister, Marie-Alix, had passed away at Ancenis near Nantes, where she lived. It was a devastating blow. Though latterly the sisters had led very separate lives, they had been marked by poignant moments of shared history. Besides Madeleine, Marie-Alix was one of Suzanne's last surviving connections to her Limousin roots. The sisters had shared the flight to Paris and the anxiety of arriving in a strange city. Suzanne had stayed with Marie-Alix as she tried to find her feet in Nantes, and since they had lived apart, regular letters between the sisters had made the geographical distance seem less divisive.[25]

For Madeleine, the trauma was of a different kind. She had now outlived two of her children. It merely consolidated the importance of Suzanne and Maurice.

If ever there was a time for a change of horizon, it was now. In his quest to establish a secure family home, Paul Mousis settled on the picturesque suburban town of Pierrefitte, which lay just under 13km north of Paris. There was now plenty to recommend the idea to the rest of the family. Maurice's performance in school might have been improving, but he was approaching that notoriously difficult age where less distraction and more discipline were critical. Madeleine would come too of course. And with Paris so close, Suzanne could still work in her studio during the week if she liked and travel the short distance to Pierrefitte at weekends and during the holidays. Madeleine was more than capable of supervising Maurice, and in the country doing so would be even easier. Meanwhile, like a true bourgeois couple, Mousis and Suzanne could enjoy time alone together in the Rue Cortot and then rejoin the other two at the weekends. Besides, country air was said to work wonders for a person's health; Suzanne's annual winter malady would be a thing of the past. And surely Suzanne, so liberal in her views, must occasionally feel a pang of yearning to distance herself from the virulent anti-Semitic remarks of acquaintances like Degas? Then, with all that light and air and inspiration – what more could an artist desire? The move was decided.

Compared to Paris, Pierrefitte was claustrophobically small. With a population of just under 2,500, the inhabitants largely comprised members of the farming community. It had just one *tabac* and no market, and was decidedly quieter than the neighbourhood the Valadons had been used to in Montmartre. But there were trains running into Gare du Nord throughout the day and at only seventeen minutes each way, it did not take long to reach the capital. Added to which, there was a good boarding school for boys, the Institution Molin, where Mousis felt sure that Maurice's academic potential would be realised, even if he were only enrolled as a day pupil.[26]

Maurice would later recall the rainy September day when removal vehicles arrived in Montmartre to collect the family's belongings and transport them to their new home. After a short but symbolically significant journey, the convoy drew up outside 18, Avenue de Saint-Denis, Pierrefitte. It was a pretty country house close to the village of Montmagny, and situated next door to a bakery.[27]

From the very first, Maurice was deeply unhappy. His fragile frame, pristine white beret and city accent immediately turned him into an object of ridicule among the rural community. To their ears, he sounded like a show-off. Trying to get him to speak so that they could laugh at his pronunciation became a popular pastime.[28]

Suzanne Valadon and Maurice Utrillo, c. 1894.

But there was a silver lining to the dark clouds obscuring Maurice's horizon. The Limousin sense of family solidarity had not left Suzanne, and with her sister's passing, she felt compelled to reach out to the brood Marie-Alix had left behind. Suzanne was desperately fond of her late sister's eldest daughter, Marie-Lucienne, and she always loved receiving her niece's amusing letters. It was no hardship to welcome the young woman of twenty to come and stay with the Mousis-Valadon family towards the end of the year. The age gap between Maurice and his cousin was significant, but the presence of such a bright young woman in the house was a welcome distraction which made home life more interesting and justified his withdrawal from the hostile world outside.[29]

However, by the New Year, Marie-Lucienne had returned home, taking with her the sense of hope and energy she had temporarily injected into the household, even in her grief. By January, Madeleine and Maurice were feeling the chill of the season in a house in which, for much of the week, they rattled around alone. Madeleine was not inclined to dissuade Maurice when he decided that the time had come to write to Miguel.

Dearest Michel,

I don't want to start the year without telling you that I love you and think of you constantly. I hope everything you could wish for comes to you quickly, but I beg you, I would so like to see you. Why don't you come to the house? Why don't you think of me? I am so miserable, because Maman tells me all the time that you will never come back to us and I cry as I write this to you on New Year's Day, I am alone with Grandmother, my cousin Marie no longer living with us, and Maman has gone to work in Paris today. Maman is very unhappy and always sick, you wouldn't recognise her, she's aged so much, it's Grandmother who told me to write to you. Monsieur Paul came to put me in a boarding school in Pierrefitte and since we've lived here he hasn't come back and it's been three months since we've seen anyone. I'm bored and unhappy and so is Grandmother. I've wanted to write to you for a long time but Maman didn't want to give me your address because she said you didn't want to see me anymore. But I begged so hard that this morning, before she left for Paris, she gave it to me, but she didn't want to know what I was writing to you. Dearest Michel, I'm not writing because I want you to send me New Year's gifts. Anyway, I'm too old now and I think New Year's presents are for sissies. I only want one thing and that is to see you soon, because it hurts me not to. If you are angry with Maman, Grandmother says that you should address your letter to her, that way I will at least have some news from you. Grandmother sends you a kiss and I love you with all my heart and hug you as hard as I can.

Your son, who would very much like to come and find you.

Grandmother is sending you a little picture of Maman when she was 14 years old that she found in some packages. She wants you to see how much it looks like me. But because Maman knows that Grandmother found the picture, send it back to us as soon as you have looked at it, so that Maman doesn't find out that we sent it to you. I send you another kiss, dear daddy. Write to me very soon.

Maurice Utrillo

Here is the address:
Madeleine Valadon, 18 Avenue de Saint-Denis,
Pierrefitte (Seine).[30]

The letter failed to bring the deliverance the youngster craved. And as 1896 unfolded, his experience at his new school merely compounded his misery.

The Institution Molin ('Pension Pluminard', he nicknamed it) was, even Maurice had to concede, 'a superb building with a large orchard and lawn, a vast playing field and a playground of adequate proportions'. It was situated in the Rue de Paris and had 45 boys at the time the Valadon-Mousis family moved to Pierrefitte.

The headmaster welcomed Maurice warmly, and at first glance his fellow pupils, all dressed in the same uniform as him, seemed affable enough. But once the bell rang to announce break time, those hopeful first impressions evaporated. Maurice was a quiet, introspective child, and his reluctance to participate in the other boys' physically boisterous games immediately signalled his difference. He was picked on, jostled, teased and goaded, and his attempts to buy friends with sweets failed miserably. The weakling city boy was branded a dope and merciless teasing became a regular part of his daily routine.[31]

There seemed little chance of Maurice's bleak country existence changing, either. That year, Suzanne reconciled herself to the idea of forming a tie with a man, and Mousis's parents finally agreed to approve the match. The union was announced and the banns read on 26 July and 2 August. Then at midday on 5 August 1896, Mousis's family demonstrated their ultimate consent, as they stood in the town hall of the 18th arrondissement to witness Paul Mousis's marriage to Marie-Clémentine Valadon. The Mousis family's approval was dependent on things being done properly and, accordingly, Mousis gave his address as 13, Rue de Clignancourt, the family home, while Suzanne gave hers as 2, Rue Cortot. She also took two years off her age, giving her year of birth as 1867. Had it been true, Suzanne would only have been sixteen when she gave birth to Maurice, and he would represent not the error of an adult woman who should have known better, but an accident which had befallen a girl, a no doubt innocent minor.[32]

But on one point, Suzanne refused to conform to expectation. Less than eighteen months earlier, Berthe Morisot's death certificate had declared her to have 'no profession'.[33] Suzanne's wedding certificate described her proudly as an 'artist'.

Suzanne's marriage to Paul Mousis marked the start of a new chapter in her life. She was now the wife of a bourgeois gentleman, the mistress of a fine country house, whose material comfort was guaranteed. She had two maids, Catherine and another help named Louise, who ensured that her domestic surroundings were to her taste, and who obligingly served as models whenever Mme Valadon-Mousis (as Degas delighted in calling her) felt inspired to draw them.

That year, Paul Mousis also rented his wife a new studio with living accommodation at 10–12, Rue Cortot, the same street as her previous atelier. The bright, airy studio was located in a grand 17th-century building which had once been home to the actor 'Rosimonde' from Molière's troupe. The building had since been divided into ateliers. Indeed, Renoir had rented two rooms there in the mid-1870s in the left wing of the old stables, where he worked on a number of canvases, not least his important *Ball at the Moulin de la Galette* (1876).[34] Perched high above Montmartre, spectacular views were just a few steps away, and a leafy orchard garden provided a tranquil rural idyll in the heart of the city. Paul Mousis even bought Suzanne her own tilbury and mule so that she could travel between the studio and Pierrefitte whenever she desired. The sound of hooves and cartwheels rattling over the cobbles alerted people to her arrival and departure, and heads would turn as the tiny figure of Suzanne sped up or down the hill clasping the reins, her hair windswept and her cape flowing out behind her.[35]

Suzanne loved animals, and now that she had two stable homes, she could at last surround herself with pets. She kept five wolf-hounds, which she adored, as well as goats and even, for a time, a deer. It satisfied a deep yearning for the country – until she fully assimilated the practical demands of keeping such an agile, unhousetrained creature in a town and reluctantly conceded to give it to a zoo.

She also now had a pretty cottage garden to dig, plant and study. All at once, she was consumed by the earthy scent of freshly dug flowerbeds, the elation as fresh green shoots pushed through, the grateful jubilation at the smell of rain on sun-parched soil. Nature fulfilled her at a deep, spiritual level. 'Nature has a total hold of me,' she enthused. 'The trees, the sky, the water and living beings charm me passionately, deeply.'[36]

With a home of her own and domestic worries lifted, Suzanne also discovered previously unexplored channels for her creativity. Fallen timber and abundant woodland turned her mind to carpentry. With practice, she became handy with a saw and hammer, a chisel and a plane, and produced rugged carved seats and other furniture in oak. She was complimented on several pieces and certain of the neighbours even asked if they might purchase an item.[37]

Paul Mousis made every effort to ensure that his new wife was blissfully happy. Indeed, surrounded by animals and with a garden to tend, Suzanne edged closer to that sense of equilibrium that she always told people she craved. Peace of mind, that quality which had proved so elusive, at last seemed within reach. Suzanne began to work prolifically, creating studies of nudes and a poignant oil painting, *Grandmother and Little Rosalie* (1896).

But if her husband had lifted the pressure of money worries and the need to fret over domestic comfort, Suzanne was expected to fulfil her part of the tacit, bourgeois bargain. When it was first performed in Europe in 1877, Henrik Ibsen's play *A Doll's House* caused a public outrage by ending with a wife rejecting her role as the pretty, obedient actress on her husband's domestic stage.

At the turn of the century, the angel of the hearth was still held as the ideal figure of womanhood, and bourgeois society proved themselves reverent disciples. Accordingly, a model bourgeois wife was considered personally responsible for her husband's contentment. She was expected to manage the household efficiently, oversee the servants, entertain her husband's guests, speak intelligently, charm visitors and present herself immaculately. The pressure on women was immense. The more highly regarded a man was, socially and professionally, the more was expected of his wife. Paul Mousis did not remain in the same job throughout his career, and people remembered him working variously for Bel et Sainbénat; the fabric company A. Founeude et Cie; and later, for the Banque de France.[38] But at that level, the roles blended indistinguishably into one another and each new group of colleagues or clients Suzanne was expected to impress set another challenge in her path. It demanded that she rally herself whether she felt like it or not, speak politely and smile sweetly. She had become a sociable creature, but on her own terms. And she always spoke her mind. The task now demanded of her drew her into unfamiliar territory – but it was a role, and Suzanne excelled at playing roles.

However, in addition to her wifely duties, Suzanne had another concern: Maurice. His school grades were not especially poor, but his behaviour was alarming his teachers. His unpredictable temper would transform him from a timid and self-contained child to a wild and furious feral creature in a moment. He seemed to have no close friends and took little interest in the pastimes boys his age usually enjoyed. Suzanne was his idol. He pined for her when she left, worshipped her when she returned and pleased her in what he had learned to be the best way to win her attention: posing.

It was hoped that he would respond favourably to a move to the Collège Rollin in Paris at the end of 1897, when he was due to start 5ème (the year group for twelve- to thirteen-year-olds). And indeed, for a time it did seem to have eased the problem. Although he declared the building 'austere', Maurice appeared to enjoy his train ride back to Paris, and his grades were good.[39] But before long, bad behaviour and truanting marred what had been a promising start. Although it was hard to pinpoint what, something was seriously amiss.

The weight of marital and parental responsibilities started to take its toll. Suzanne's artistic output dried to a trickle.

Nonetheless, with Suzanne's extant work as ammunition, Degas continued his crusade to promote her. Her work was now regular currency with dealers like Vollard and Portier.[40]

Suzanne was determined that her art should be consumed and evaluated for what it was, and not through the distorting lens of gender. But for a financially disadvantaged female painter like herself, it was, ironically, only through marriage to a man like Paul Mousis that she could enjoy the luxury of painting full-time and developing her art free of monetary concerns. Having witnessed Suzanne's early struggles, and seen the very different opportunities afforded to Berthe Morisot and Mary Cassatt as a consequence of inherited wealth and status, Degas understood more than most men of his class what a blessing Suzanne's marriage was.

Degas wrote to Suzanne after her wedding, following another of her seasonal afflictions. 'I wish to remind you that once you are feeling better, you must – since your livelihood is now assured – think only of working, of using the singular talent that I am proud to see in you, those wicked drawings that I want to see again. You should have more pride.'[41]

But family demands were making Suzanne's visits to her mentor fewer and further between. Degas's letters rang with the hollow emptiness of the growing distance between them. 'Will this thank you for your kind wishes and remembrance even reach you?' he asked one January.[42] 'Are you still in the Rue Cortot?' Never reluctant to voice his displeasure, Degas let her feel the full weight of it. 'You must, despite your son's illness, get back into the habit of bringing me your wicked, supple drawings,' another New Year's greeting instructed her.[43] By the New Year of 1898, there was a supplicating tone to his request:

> I found your good wishes, Terrible Maria, when I got back from Bartholomé's, who read us yours to him at the table where they were brought up to him. [...] It would be a great pleasure and you would not be disturbing me in the slightest, as you fear, if you came by one day at the end of the afternoon, particularly if you bring along a folder of your fine drawings.[44]

In fact, Degas's letter arrived at a moment of intense preoccupation. Paul Mousis had proposed another move, and early in the year, the whole family were uprooted and obliged to settle into the even smarter 'Villa Hochard', at number 3, Rue de Paris. Their new home sat on the same, comparatively peopled street as Maurice's former school, near the Demi Lune Café and, conveniently, just opposite the tramway stop.[45]

But if Suzanne's hands were full acclimatising and ironing out the creases in her family life, Degas continued to refine her professional persona. In 1898, Suzanne was accepted to The Exhibition of the International Society of Sculptors, Painters and Gravers in London, where her work would be shown alongside what the *Pall Mall Gazette* commended as 'some eminent foreign masters of our day', artists such as Puvis, Manet, Degas, Lautrec and Fantin-Latour.[46] Set up with the expressed aim of 'the non-recognition of nationality in Art', the society's president was James Abbott McNeill Whistler – coincidentally, a great friend of Degas.[47] The ISSPG did not disdain, but rather welcomed women artists.

Here, a lady did not require a title which defined her in terms of male property; her name alone would earn her respect if it were due. Hence from May, for one shilling, English viewers could contemplate the work of 'Suzanne Valadon' and assess her etching in *Studies of the Nude*.[48]

With her international profile taking flight, by the summer of 1898, Suzanne had reason to feel optimistic. She was settled in a new home, and if his performance during the year had been far from exemplary, Maurice surprised everybody when he was awarded prizes for Mathematics and for French language at the end-of-term awards ceremony at the Collège Rollin.[49]

But that September, things started to unravel. Once Maurice entered the 4ème, his grades plummeted. His reports were full of telling collocations: 'insufficient effort', 'homework incomplete', 'could do better'. By the second term, it had become harder to judge his performance; he was seldom in class. Truanting had become his natural reflex. And there was another problem, too. It gradually dawned on Madeleine, on Paul Mousis, on the teachers at the Collège Rollin, and on Suzanne, with horror, that Maurice's odd behaviour, his mood swings and his frequent incoherence could be explained: the boy had discovered alcohol. He was not using it as a social lubricant to be enjoyed now and then in company, but as a solitary and vital means of evasion. The walk along the café-lined streets between the Collège Rollin and the Gare du Nord clutching his pocket money had become an irresistible window to the melancholy schoolboy. In fact, it had already reached the stage where he could barely get from breakfast through till bedtime without drink. He was not yet sixteen.[50]

Despite his poor performance during the academic year 1898–99, Maurice was provisionally allowed to progress to the next class. But by January, he was issued an ultimatum: either he repeat the previous year, or leave the school.[51]

Mousis advised Suzanne that they take advantage of the situation to start Maurice in a career, and with his wife's consent, he began to scour his contacts for possible positions. A post was eventually found working as an office boy for an English employer.[52]

It could have been a bright start to a prosperous future in business. But in Maurice's expulsion from the Collège Rollin, Suzanne could sense ominous overtones. All at once, subtle fault lines in the smooth veneer of her bourgeois life had become sizeable cracks. Her meticulously balanced composition had begun to fall apart.

CHAPTER 10

Deviants or Delinquents

Lou chiei ei per chassà, lo lèbre per fugi.
(The dog is made to hunt, the hare to flee.)
OLD LIMOUSIN PROVERB[1]

The 20th century was welcomed with a buzz of expectation. Spoken, its very sound had a novel, optimistic ring. In the last part of the 19th century, France had witnessed remarkable progress in areas as diverse as education, the arts, science and technology. Industry was booming, culture rich and prospering, and living conditions for the average Frenchman were better than ever before. 1900 was the dawn of a new age, and it was hoped that recent achievements would form the basis for even further French advancement.

Paris saw no better way to mark such a pivotal moment in history and declare national prowess than by hosting a world fair. Hence that April, what was tipped to be the most magnificent Exposition Universelle to date opened its doors to the triumphant peals of *La Marseillaise*, and for seven months, Paris was transformed into a carnivalesque spectacle such as had never been seen.

There were remarkable wonders to behold: the Palais d'Électricité dazzled hypnotically like an incandescent temple; the *trottoir roulant* or moving pavement transported visitors around the Champ de Mars; while the first underground line, the Métropolitan, was nearing completion, and potential passengers were promised that by July, they would be able to speed along beneath the surface of the Earth. There was already an additional railway station, the Gare d'Orsay, and one of the most talked-about new landmarks was the Pont Alexandre III, named after the late tsar and constructed across the Seine as a monument to the recent alliance between France and Russia. And in addition to over 200 temporary buildings and pavilions, there were two new permanent art palaces, the Petit Palais and the Grand Palais. 'To our childish eyes,' remarked visitor P. Morand, 'it was a marvel, a coloured picture book, a cave filled by strangers with treasure.'[2]

While everyone was welcome, Paris was reluctant to share the limelight. French exhibitors far outnumbered those of visiting countries. In the Exposition Décennale, France boasted over 1,000 exhibitors, the USA 251 and Great Britain only 223.[3] There was something of a competitive edge to the whole Exposition, which left a sour note in the mouths of certain foreign participants and even many French. Indeed, with so many visitors, France inevitably opened its doors to critics as well as supporters. Eulogies of France's glory were matched by criticism targeting misjudged expressions of self-importance and commercialism. 'What sort of fair is this odious bazaar,' Camille Pissarro exclaimed in a letter to his son Lucien, echoing a common view.[4] Moreover, the Exposition was far from complete when its doors opened in April, meaning that inaugural ceremonies had to take place in a state of constructional mayhem and mud.

Presenting such a far-ranging amalgam of styles and schools served up a spread many found indigestible and sickly. The organisers' decision-making process was loaded with controversy, too. The Impressionists were excluded from the Décennale; in the galleries where they were exhibited, conservative painter Jean-Léon Gérôme swept in front of President Émile Loubet when he attempted to visit the show, barring the entrance with the warning: 'the shame of French painting is in there'.[5]

Gérôme's melodramatic gesture encapsulated the tension at the heart of the Exposition. France was poised on a knife-edge, torn between old and new, permanence and change, regret and hope. Something of that ambience was reflected in Suzanne's life and mood as she entered her 35th year. The past was familiar yet flawed, the future loaded with uncertainty, fear and anticipation.

Maurice's employment with his stepfather's English colleague had been short-lived. After only a few months serving as a general dogsbody, delivering post, cleaning offices and answering the phone, Maurice found himself again at home, unemployed and melancholy. But then, to everyone's delight, another of Paul Mousis's enquiries on his stepson's part bore fruit. The *chef de famille* returned home one day to announce that Maurice had been found a job with the esteemed bank Crédit Lyonnais. It was an exciting prospect. With Maurice's mathematical skill, he was bound to excel in the role.[6]

One hot morning in June while swarms of Parisians flocked to the Exposition grounds, Suzanne and Madeleine ushered a carefully washed and dressed Maurice out of the house to begin his first day working for the biggest bank in France.

The mother and grandmother were heartened when the sixteen-year-old appeared keen as he set off towards the Boulevard des Italiens. But had anyone questioned him, they would have found his pleasure to be due not to his new post but to the smart bowler hat it entitled him to wear. He near-worshipped the accessory, it was his pride and joy – but also his downfall. Socially awkward by nature and accustomed to abuse, Maurice pre-empted his co-workers' antipathy and insulted them first. One evening as he came to leave the office, he found that one of his victims had sought revenge by beating in his precious hat. His upset quickly turning to anger, he seized his umbrella and brought it smashing down on the offender's head. Maurice stormed out of the offices and his banking career was over.[7]

Subsequent attempts to reset him on a career path failed miserably. He worked for a French sales representative, a German businessman, and several other companies. None of the positions lasted long, often only a few weeks. Somehow, Maurice always managed to put his employer's back up, either by failing to complete his duties efficiently or by simply being rude. Each time, there came a day when he had to return home and report to Suzanne and Madeleine that he had again been asked to leave. With his negative self-image, Maurice resigned himself to the conclusion that his character was fundamentally flawed. He was simply not cut out for business.

By the autumn, the Exposition Universelle was drawing to a close, and Maurice was again at home, where he moped around aimlessly, seeking comfort in the soothing embrace of liquor. He no longer made any attempt to conceal his shameful vice, helping himself to drink from Mousis's cellar and demanding more *rouge* from his grandmother whenever his glass ran dry. His mood oscillated precariously between bitter rage at his lot and deep, tearful remorse. Painfully insecure, whenever he felt hunted, his response was to lash out in defence. Some evenings, he would trip into town, and many a night saw him stumble home bruised and bloody having riled one or other of the locals. Curiously, he became deeply agitated whenever he encountered a pregnant woman, and any female with a swollen belly was subject to a torrent of abuse if she passed him in the street. Then on one occasion, he stepped out in front of a tram, his arms folded across his chest, and refused to move.[8]

Maurice's eccentric, antisocial behaviour became a feature of Pierrefitte. In town, residents whispered about the Mousis-Valadon family and their half-crazed son, while behind the closed doors of

Villa Hochard, fiery scenes became a fixed part of the weekly ritual. And the roles were always the same: Maurice throwing a tantrum, breaking glass and china if denied wine, or else sobbing remorsefully like a bereaved child; Madeleine at a loss but attempting to calm her 'Maumau' with grandmotherly love and reassurance; Paul Mousis, tired after a long day at the office, exasperated and hurt if Suzanne did not take his side; and then Suzanne, torn between the man she had married and who had sacrificed so much for them all, and the son she had carried inside her for nine months and who found life so cruelly weighted against him.

Art could no longer be Suzanne's priority.

Meanwhile, the art scene in the capital was flourishing. While Suzanne's career continued to stagnate, all around her, creativity was simmering. A new generation of young avant-garde painters had firmly grasped France's creative legacy and were carrying art into the new century with optimism and gusto.

In October, a twenty-year-old Spaniard with olive skin, eyes like obsidian and a penetrating stare, stepped off a train with his friend and fellow painter, Carles Casagemas.[9] The young Pablo Picasso had come to see a painting he had had accepted to the Exposition Universelle, *Last Moments* (1899), fittingly, just as the Exposition was closing. Born in Malaga in 1881, the youngster had paint and charcoal near coursing through his veins; his father was an artist and it was he who had given the boy his first lessons while enrolled at the Escuela Provincial de Bellas Artes. As a teenager, the Spaniard moved to Barcelona, where he was accepted into the academy aged fourteen, and later, to the Real Academia San Fernando in Madrid. After a summer at Horta de Ebro in 1898, he returned to Barcelona re-energised and eager to share ideas with other exponents of contemporary Spanish art. By 1899, he had become a regular at the quirky new café-cum-cabaret, El Quat Gats, which had established itself as a hub of literary and artistic expression. The venture was

modelled on Le Chat Noir, and with its Chinese shadow shows, literary evenings and exhibitions, it paid overt homage to its Parisian
forbear, itself no more after Rodolphe Salis's death in 1897. In the
spring of 1900, the young artist from Malaga mounted an exhibition
of portraits at the venue, which led to the foreman, Père Romeu,
commissioning him to produce a drawing for the establishment's
menu. Now in its third year, El Quat Gats had become a magnet for
avant-garde artists, writers and intellectuals in search of sympathetic confrères. And it just so happened that one of the founders
of the young Picasso's favourite haunt was a man Suzanne knew
well: Miguel Utrillo.

Picasso and Miguel were both part of a shifting group of young
Spanish artists who patronised El Quat Gats. In 1899, Picasso
had created a portrait of Miguel in pen and sepia ink wash. And
now arriving in Paris, Picasso could understand Miguel's affinity
with the French capital. Forward-thinking French painters like
Toulouse-Lautrec won his deep admiration. Picasso was eager to
discover the true origins of Spanish art, and to his delight, he found
that he did not have to do so alone. The Exposition attracted a
swarm of the Spanish artists who had made friends in Barcelona,
among them Ramon Pichot, Carles Casagemas, Germaine Gargallo
– and Miguel.

Accepting the hospitality of fellow painter Isidro Nonell in
Montmartre, Picasso quickly settled into the rhythm of life in the
capital.[10] He was enraptured to discover all Miguel and Suzanne's
old haunts. The Lapin Agile and the Moulin de la Galette became
favourite watering holes. The conversation, the stimulus, the creative freedom – it was as though oppressive walls had crumbled
and at last, he had a clear view of his surroundings. With Miguel
and the little colony of Spanish friends, Picasso smoked, drank and
talked, wandering around the Exposition in awe by day, stumbling
home sated with alcohol and inspiration at night. Picasso even did

a drawing of the group, Miguel among them, staggering out of the Exposition in a raucous fashion.[11]

Miguel did not use his return to Paris as an opportunity to forge any stronger connection with Suzanne or Maurice. Meanwhile, his friend was embarking on the kind of life Suzanne had just started to taste before she got married, an existence driven by creative purpose where the possibility of an exhibition was always just around the corner.

Picasso's early works had been naturalistic in style, and often depicted close family or those on the margins of society. As a teenager, he had also contributed satirical illustrations for local papers. Now, he started to fuse the palette of El Greco with the evocative imagery characteristic of the Symbolist movement.[12] Picasso used his time in Paris to introduce himself to dealers. Enlightened artists and collectors could see that his was a singular and original talent, and before long, one of these contacts, Pedro Mañach, offered him a contract. Soon after, another dealer – a sign of the times, a woman – Berthe Weill, also agreed to buy some drawings.[13]

By the end of 1900, Picasso was at the forefront of Parisian avant-garde art and looked set on an auspicious career path. Conversely, Suzanne's life seemed to have taken an altogether different course. With matters at home so chaotic, she had all but stopped producing the bold figure studies with confident lines that Degas so admired.

But Suzanne had not ceased working entirely; that year, she created two works, both of them uncharacteristic. The first was a still life, *Apples and Pear* (1900).[14] It was exceptional in her oeuvre to date. As a model, Suzanne had through default only ever seen artists working on the figure. With no formal training, she had gravitated towards what she knew. And the movement of the human form fascinated her; to her mind, capturing the fleeting moment and freezing it forever was what art was all about. She had always painted people as a way of understanding them, using her figure studies as a form of dialogue. Now, she felt compelled to choose subjects that demanded nothing of her in return. The composition was simple, naive even, the forms crudely drawn, the palette limited. With her personal life fraught, complex and demanding, Suzanne sought simplicity in her art. She took ownership of the work, signing it confidently with a sure and steady hand.

The other piece she produced that year was just as atypical. *Maternity* (1900) was the first mother and child scene she had ever drawn. And yet it was a subject she knew. The composition was tender, gentle, balanced – quite unlike her studies of older children and nudes. The baby and carer were engaged in an intimate and private act; they asked nothing of her. But if that was what Suzanne wanted at the time, she did not pursue the idea; she left the study as an experimental sketch rather than a finished piece and never again returned to the theme.[15]

Her withdrawal from creative life did not go unnoticed.

'Every year, Terrible Maria, I see arrive this firm, chiselled writing,' Degas observed, 'but I never see the author appear with a folder under her arm. And yet I am growing old. Happy New Year.'[16]

Then, in another letter:

My dear Maria. Your letter always arrives punctually with its handwriting, as firm as though it were carved. It is your drawings that I see no more. From time to time, I look at your study in red chalk, which is still hanging in my dining room; and I always say to myself: 'that she-devil Maria could draw like a little daemon'. Why don't you show me your work anymore? I am nearing 67.[17]

Degas was right; time was marching on. But the disorder into which Maurice's behaviour had thrown the family showed no signs of abating, and nor did the shame it brought. Eventually, the situation became so intolerable that, as Maurice remembered it, the Mousis-Valadons were obliged to move to the nearby town of Sannois temporarily until local ill-feeling had dissipated.[18]

Suzanne was still striving to steer Maurice towards a more salubrious way of life in early September 1901, when a shattering piece of news reached her: Henri de Toulouse-Lautrec was dead.

Lautrec had been on a steady path to self-destruction ever since he and Suzanne last spoke. Years of excessive living had eventually taken their toll, and alcohol and syphilis had combined to hasten his decline. Following a breakdown, he had been admitted to an asylum at Neuilly, where he stayed for some months. During a brief return to Paris, friends were horrified by his appearance. His body was emaciated; his eyes were sunken and the flickering light that always made them dance when he chuckled had all but gone out. He appeared 'finished, hollow, sick'.[19] He fought to give a credible performance of his jovial old self, but nobody was fooled. He returned to his family home to spend his last few days. It was a drawn-out and torturous process. 'Dying's damned hard,' he was heard to whisper to his mother just before he passed.[20] He was 37 years old.

Suzanne later admitted that she cried solidly for a week on hearing the news.[21]

All the while, Maurice continued to drink.

Having invested in land on the Butte Pinson in the commune of Montmagny, Paul Mousis proposed that he build the family a new house. They could have a high fenced garden and no immediate neighbours; it would be far less awkward whenever Maurice had one of his 'turns'. Thick stone walls would muffle raised voices; shutters could be snapped closed to avert prying eyes; and the tall, imposing structure would present a facade of stability and authority. They could still travel to and from Paris. And indeed, early in 1903, it became clear that for the time being, it would be most practical for the family to make their base the apartment in the Rue Cortot.[22]

Home to Montmartre, to the Rue Cortot, its buildings with dirty grey walls, crusts of saltpetre, and laundry drying in the windows; home, through the huge coach entranceway with its heavy door, to the garden overlooking Montmartre's famous vine; home to the twisted maze of dark, narrow corridors, opening out on to light and airy ateliers; and throughout the building, those little windows which offered a breathtaking panoramic view of the city, always changing according to the hour and the season – Maurice remembered the decision as one of the happiest ever made on his behalf.[23] For Suzanne, it was as though she had been reborn.

One of her few works of 1902 was a self-portrait in red chalk, Suzanne having once again felt drawn to introspection. Gazing wistfully out of the frame at an uncertain point, Suzanne appeared younger than her 37 years, beautiful, fresh, but quizzical. It was as though, for once, she did not have all the answers. But with that return to Montmartre, her self-assurance came flooding back. Suzanne began to work prolifically. She took familiar subjects: nudes, her maid Catherine, her dogs, and flowers – the beauty of which she had now come to appreciate. She also began work on a large canvas, *The Moon and the Sun and the Brunette and the Blonde* (1903).[24] Her painting reflected her altered state of mind.

Returning to Montmartre, Suzanne was like a wilted plant revived. People knew her, too, even if only by sight. Among young art students and amateur painters, her glittering backlist of employers like Puvis, Renoir and Lautrec had turned her into a minor celebrity. Renoir's interest in a woman immediately recommended her in the eyes of budding male artists. One morning, two such aspiring young painters had set up their easels in the Rue Saint-Vincent when Suzanne passed with her dogs. Their heads turned as the pretty, petite woman passed them. One of the men was stocky with a big nose, cheerful if unremarkable. But the other was angelically beautiful, slim with golden blond hair and smiling blue eyes. Suzanne glanced over their shoulders to see their creations as she passed. 'You can't paint the sky the same way you paint the ground!' she laughed as she went on her way.[25] They watched her go. The blond man in particular never forgot the encounter.

Just a few weeks after the Mousis-Valadon family arrived in Montmartre that February, Maurice's first, English employer was persuaded to give the lad a second chance. But within a short time, and following a series of blunders on Maurice's part, the boss was forced to return to his original conclusion. Then followed a job in a factory, making lampshades; that lasted only a few weeks before Maurice got into a fight.[26] And the more positions he was dismissed from, the more angry, self-critical and despondent he became. The fallout led to alcoholic binges of increasing severity and duration.

It was agreed that returning to the countryside for the summer months and removing Maurice from the temptations of Montmartre would be best. And Suzanne had another project in mind, too. Their family friend Dr Ettlinger, who had stood as witness at the couple's wedding, had urged Suzanne to teach Maurice to paint. Doing something creative with his hands would at the very least distract him and channel that unspent energy, Dr Ettlinger had reasoned. It might even prove the miracle cure to his malady. Suzanne was ready to pounce on any new idea which offered a potential remedy, however speculative the results. And painting was what she knew. She agreed: the countryside often proved a source of inspiration to new painters. It seemed worth a try.[27]

At first, Maurice begrudged being forced to acquire a new skill. But slowly his defences fell. Suzanne, who disdained formal education, became a teacher. And Maurice, who had always run up against authority, began to learn.

Collapsible tubes of paint had been available since the 1840s, and were developed primarily as a means of prolonging the life of premixed paint following the rapid expansion of mechanical colour grinding.[28] Tubes offered the advantage that paint could be easily transported, too, a blessing for landscape artists. However, by not mixing the dry ground colour and the binder (usually poppy oil) themselves, artists found that they lost the subtle distinctions in paint texture. Suzanne disliked using tubes of paint. She preferred the control of pigments that hand mixing allowed, and scoffed at the disdain in which certain painters held the business of mixing paints themselves (on the basis that it turned them into artisans rather than artists). Suzanne always mixed her own colours. Likewise, she prepared Maurice's palette for him with a limited range of colours: just five. Suzanne preferred to keep her own palette simple so that she would not have to think about it.[29] Similarly, for Maurice, she selected just two kinds of yellow, plus vermillion, Turkey red and zinc white, to see how he would fare.[30] Maurice later described his earliest attempts at painting as 'quite detestable'.[31] But after a time completing the daily exercises Suzanne set him, something startling became apparent. Suzanne could hardly believe it: Maurice's pictures were actually good – very good. And they were nothing like hers. He had a style which was entirely his own. 'You need to learn to draw,' his mother told him firmly once she had assimilated what she was observing.[32] The student and teacher had their next programme of study.

But Maurice's new hobby was not enough to silence the call of a more powerful master. When the family returned to Montmartre for the end-of-year festivities, Maurice went out on one of his most serious and prolonged drinking episodes yet. Disappearing in the New Year for some days, the twenty-year-old eventually returned, wild. He burst into the house, furniture was thrown and split, china smashed, glass shattered. There were screams and bellowing, and

Mousis grabbed his stepson firmly. There was a struggle, shouting; the men edged closer to an open window. Suzanne and Madeleine were terrified; Maurice was threatening violence. There was no time to think. Suzanne sent for the police, and once he had broken free from his stepson's grasp, Paul Mousis had the doctor fetched.[33]

Calm was eventually restored and Maurice subdued. But that day, everything changed.

The authorities ordered that Maurice be admitted to an institution to receive professional care. On 12 January 1904, he left his home with Suzanne, Madeleine and the man he still called 'M. Paul', and was escorted to Sainte-Anne's psychiatric hospital in Paris.[34]

The foreboding building had been operating as a psychiatric unit since the 1860s. With its specialists and healthcare, it offered the very best treatment available at the time. But psychoanalysis was still in its infancy, Freud having only coined the term in 1896.[35] Diagnosis and treatment remained primitive. Maurice later conceded that the establishment was 'discreet'; but in reality, the building was a fearful concretion of walls and bars, and visits were strictly limited to allocated days and times and closely supervised.[36] Suzanne could not bring Maurice any liquids, sharp instruments, string, food or other object which might incur injury or be used to make an escape.[37]

Maurice was placed in the care of Dr Vallon, and within 48 hours, an initial diagnosis had been made. Suzanne learned that her son was suffering from mental degeneration. It was thought to be due primarily to the heredity of his alcoholic father (assumed to be Adrien Boissy), though a second psychiatrist suggested that Suzanne's excitable nature should also be taken into account. Nobody spoke of alcoholism.[38]

While Dr Vallon set about his task of making Maurice fit to rejoin society, Suzanne could only wait, her mood fluctuating between relief, humiliation and debilitating worry. The weeks rolled by, then a month had passed, then two. The silence in the Rue Cortot was deafening.

Finally, in May 1904, it was agreed that the patient was ready to be released. On his return home to Montmagny, 'Maumau' was duly welcomed, fussed over, cosseted and cared for. Suzanne and Madeleine were relieved to see him calmer, quieter perhaps, but looking healthier. In fact, he was quite changed. More introverted than ever, he hardly spoke, never smiled, and would just sit gazing at an undefined spot on the wall or absent-mindedly stroking the cat. The only distraction which held his interest were scientific and technical journals that he could not possibly understand.[39] He sat studying them intently for hours, and it took all Suzanne and Madeleine's powers of persuasion to get him to set them aside to eat a meal.

Sainte-Anne had restored Maurice's body and Suzanne's peace of mind. But it had kept a part of his soul.

Maurice's nervous energy had been repressed and he had been reduced to a near-vegetative state. But inactivity did not suit his nervous disposition.[40] Slowly, eventually, he was persuaded to resume his painting and to go outside and capture what he could see. Soon, Suzanne was astonished and delighted to see that his work was developing. It was getting better. And his rate of production was staggering; in little more than a year, Maurice completed nearly 150 canvases.[41] Fascinatingly, he was not attracted to the figures that caught his mother's attention. Maurice shied away from human exchanges. Rather, he was drawn to buildings and walls, and he executed his studies with the exactness of an architect, using the same mathematical precision he had brought to his scrutiny of scientific manuals.

Maurice knew no more about the legacy of French art than Suzanne when she first started painting. He drank in whatever she told him. Once or twice, Suzanne happened to mention the work of the recently deceased Alfred Sisley, and henceforward, the painter became Maurice's obsession and his idol. He had seen nothing of Sisley's work but it was enough that he had heard his mother speak of him. It was true that the work Maurice was producing called to mind the Impressionist's views of buildings and roads. The painter became a yardstick against which Maurice measured his success.[42]

Now, Maurice spent all his spare hours painting, studying his canvas and whatever scene he wished to freeze on to it with intensity. On days when he felt unable to face the outside world, he copied comic strips and postcards.[43] Painting had finally brought Maurice what he had always craved: Suzanne's attention and an intimate mother–son bond. At last, they shared a closeness and an understanding unique to themselves, from which M. Paul was firmly excluded.

But little by little, Maurice's other master crept back into his life. To Suzanne's despair, her son's art progressed in tandem with his drinking. In fact, alcohol actually seemed necessary to his creative process. It did not mar his skill; on the contrary, it sustained Maurice's spirit and put him in a psychological place where he was able to work.

On one occasion, Maurice had gone out to paint in the fields around Montmagny. However, by the end of his sortie, he found himself intoxicated to the point that he was quite unable to stand, let alone navigate himself home.[44] By chance, a man a little younger than himself had also come out with his easel in search of interesting vistas, and when he spotted Maurice, he could immediately see his dilemma. The man's light blue eyes smiled with warmth and friendship. He had a lean physique and he was crowned with a halo of golden blond hair. A slurred exchange established the two men's common profession. The young man was struck by the strange-looking painter before him. His face was gaunt, his dark hair dishevelled and every so often, he jerked or twitched nervously and shouted his replies.[45] Both fascinated and concerned, the man good-naturedly offered to accompany Maurice home. Putting his arm around the drunkard, he attempted to hold Maurice upright as he weaved his way back to the house.

Whenever a knock at the door signalled the return of the drunken son, it was usually the police who Suzanne found standing opposite her. But this time, on the doorstep was instead the angelic-looking painter she had counselled on his landscape back in Montmartre.

Maurice did not have friends. The thought that he had made an acquaintance was as incredible as it was cheering. The young man introduced himself: he was André Utter. He painted too – or rather, he was training become an electrician; but painting, and Montmartre, were his true passions.[46]

Utter had been born into a family of modest artisans whose roots lay in Alsace. His father was a plumber in Montmartre, and as the only son of a couple whose other offspring were girls, the boy was doted on. Great things were expected of him.

He was a social lad who made friends easily and knew all the right words and gestures to keep them. He was also devilishly charming and the girls in Montmartre loved his easy manner and his smooth repartee. But his good friend Edmond Heuzé, the companion Utter had been painting with when the boys spied Suzanne in Montmartre, always held that Utter was of a serious and studious nature.[47]

On reaching puberty, Utter had thrown himself into Montmartre's art and social scene, enjoying drunken studio parties, experimenting with drugs like hashish and revelling in all the subversive and animated debates to which they gave rise. However, Utter was not merely a shallow dilettante drawn towards the nearest party, but was a shrewd and informed connoisseur of avant-garde art. He studied and read assiduously and could legitimise any new or controversial idea he might espouse with a back catalogue of theoretical and historical knowledge.

Still, Montmartre's social scene had taken its toll, and not long after Maurice had returned from his own rehabilitation in Sainte-Anne's, Utter's parents had arranged for him to spend some time away from the temptations of Montmartre staying with his grandparents, who owned a house on the Butte Pinson. For an amateur painter, the picturesque countryside softened the blow of leaving Montmartre. And it was in these circumstances that he came across Maurice.[48]

Henceforward, Utter became a regular visitor to the Villa Hochard, conversing with Mousis, making polite small talk with Madeleine, painting alongside Maurice, marvelling at his talent when sober, humouring him when he was drunk; and talking with Suzanne – passionately and at length, about art and life and Montmartre.

André Utter.
Collection Société le Vieux Montmartre/Musée de Montmartre

Utter was charming to many, but he in turn was particularly struck by Suzanne. She was stunning for a woman around 40, both 'Amazon and fairy', he told friends later, with a smooth, immaculate complexion, a tiny waist and intense blue eyes.[49] She crackled with energy and when she laughed, she did so heartily, fully, as though she did not know the meaning of restraint. Nor had she been spoilt by her time modelling for renowned artists; she looked as fresh as ever. And she was extraordinarily kind. She made little of the time when, one cold winter afternoon at the end of 1906, she noticed a man about Maurice's age working at an easel on the corner of the Place du Tertre, shivering with cold. 'You are mad to stay here in this weather,' she told him. 'You are purple! Come on, stop this instant and come with me.'[50] She led the man to the nearby restaurant and café of her friend, local landlady Mère Adèle (a former dancer from the Moulin Rouge who had previously run the Lapin Agile), and thought nothing of buying him a steaming glass of fruity, alcoholic grog. She had no idea that the man, an Italian newcomer to Montmartre, would soon make a name for himself as the legendary Futurist painter Gino Severini.

Utter was sensitive to such gestures. From then on, he and the Mousis-Valadons enjoyed each other's mutual acquaintance and respect.

Within a few years of his stay in Sainte-Anne's, Maurice was producing handsomely, and, benefiting from Suzanne's experience and contacts, was starting to sell work to dealers like Clovis Sagot, a former clown, and the picture framer Anzoli.[51] He had begun by painting the places he knew – the streets of Montmartre, a square in Montmagny, the colour merchant's shop in Saint Ouen. Then he turned to cathedrals and churches: Notre Dame, Reims, the church of Villiers le Bel. Enriching his paint with moss, plaster and cement, Maurice's surface was thickly painted and rich in texture. André Utter suspected the material additions to have been inspired by one

of the odd jobs Maurice undertook working for a construction company.[52] The happy result was some exquisite, atmospheric pieces,
which transported the viewer to the very spot depicted, bringing
the city and suburbia to life, with the smells of baking and soapy
water, the sounds of traffic and bells ringing as shop doors opened,
and the sensations of paint-flaked walls and plaster. Maurice's work
was utterly original – and he seemed completely unaware. 'Is it
ugly?' he enquired anxiously to Suzanne when he had completed his
painting of Notre Dame. To Suzanne's mind, ugliness was synonymous with truth and honesty; there could be nothing more noble.
'It can never be ugly enough,' she answered with a smile.[53]

Maurice was still drinking, of course, but by his mid-twenties,
Suzanne had come to accept this as an inconvenient foible that
needed supervising, rather than an evil that could be quashed.
Every time Maurice came home drunk, she would nurse him back
to sobriety – always short lived – and then the whole cycle would
start again.

One day, Suzanne was in her studio in the Rue Cortot when, out
of the window, she spotted Utter in the street below working on a
painting. She called down to him cheerfully and asked how the piece
was progressing. He returned the greeting. She continued, saying
that she would love to see what he was working on, and he was flat-
tered – why didn't he come up with his canvas for a moment? In
fact, she also had in mind a painting for which she needed a male
model. Maurice would not do for this piece, but Utter would be
perfect. Would he do it? Utter agreed.[54]

But somewhere between the talking and the critiquing and the
posing, there was a kiss – a first kiss. And then another. And no one
ever quite established how things progressed after that, but the kiss
was such that nothing would ever be the same again.

CHAPTER 11

❦

The Name of the Father

Foudrio no bèlo làto per so prenei en lou diàble.
(You need a hefty plank if you want to take on the Devil.)
OLD LIMOUSIN PROVERB[1]

We want to glorify war – the sole hygiene in the world –
militarism, patriotism, the destructive gesture of the
anarchists, the beautiful ideas that kill, and a contempt
for women.'[2] Readers of *Le Figaro* were horrified by the lines printed
on the paper's front page on 20 February 1909.

Poet and painter Filippo Tommaso Marinetti's *Futurist Manifesto*
seemed designed expressly to antagonise. 'The essential elements of our poetry will be courage, daring and revolt,' the Italian
declared. 'What good is there looking back as long as we have to
break down the mysterious doors of the impossible [...] We want
to demolish the museums, libraries, fight moralism, feminism and
all opportunistic and utilitarian weaknesses,' the author continued.[3]
The manifesto extolled the beauty of speed and the supremacy of
the machine. The future, Marinetti affirmed, was movement and
technology.

Within hours, *Le Figaro*'s offices were flooded with complaints.

Marinetti's proclamation was extreme, but it was symptomatic
of a more generalised urge to look forwards and view the world

afresh, free from the trappings of nostalgia. New takes were in vogue and that encompassed novel interpretations of themes previously considered sacrosanct – including religion.

Although religiosity had declined during the 19th century, by 1900 a more widespread yearning for spirituality in the face of mass consumerism had found an outlet in contemporary slants on the practice of religion and the significance of faith. Alongside the archetypal religious paintings expected at the Exposition Universelle in 1900 – exemplified by William-Adolphe Bouguereau's grandiose *Regina Angelorum* (1900) – there had been a notable influx of works which offered an original twist on the ancient Scriptures. Eugène Carrière's *Crucifixion* (1897) took a familiar theme from Christian iconography and veiled it with that mist so characteristic of late 19th-century Symbolism. A humble, contemporary setting gave religion greater poignancy in Léon Lhermitte's *Supper at Emmaus* (1892), which showed a Christ-like figure appearing, not in a village on the outskirts of Jerusalem, but in a recognisable French peasants' kitchen. Then there were countless contemporary mother-and-child pictures, providing a modern spin on the traditional Madonna and child theme.[4]

Suzanne had the pioneering ventures of a number of naturalist and avant-garde painters behind her when she was inspired to produce her own monumental reworking of a religious theme in 1909. Since the doors of the convent of Saint Vincent de Paul had closed firmly behind her as a girl, Suzanne had shied away from the church. Any religious picture she produced was bound to make a statement. And Suzanne felt so compelled by the idea she now had in mind that she decided to use oils.

Though Suzanne worked in paint, she did so only sporadically, always gravitating instinctively towards drawing. Historically, academic teaching drilled students to acquire a mastery of line before they progressed to using colour, so in process if not in style,

Suzanne's natural inclination reflected the rigour of the traditional teaching methods used to mould male art students. It bespoke her serious approach to her work.

Building on her previous year's drawings of bathers, that spring she executed a study of the poet Adrienne Farge, reclining nude. The piece was reminiscent of Ingres in the fine handling of line to bring out the contours and features of the face. There were also several drawings of nudes, including *Nude at Her Toilette* (1909) and *Three Nudes* (1909). But the current piece called for something bold.

From everyday scenes of children or bathers at their washtubs, aided by maids and grandmothers, often in an implied interior setting, Suzanne now chose to transport her nudes outside and to formally pose them. But not only that: she planned to depict a man and a woman to give her own interpretation of the iconic tale from Genesis 3, the Temptation. She would paint Adam and Eve, as yet unashamedly naked, with Eve contemplating the fateful fruit of knowledge. For a woman to paint a nude heterosexual couple showed extraordinary daring; it was simply not done. But the piece was audacious on a personal level, too. The figures poised on the precipice of sin, their naked bodies already entwined, were not just models – they were Suzanne and Utter.

Holding herself elegantly, her hair flowing down beneath her waist, Suzanne reached for an apple on the tree next to her, while Utter gently took her wrist in an ambiguous gesture – was he controlling or protecting, encouraging or dissuading? Would she yield to temptation? Seeming to float on air, their bodies moved together, onwards, upwards, outwards, their legs and feet mirroring each other, their hands interlocking behind their backs – hidden from view, Suzanne and Utter were already exploring each other's bodies. In the balanced composition and the classical proportions in a landscape setting, Suzanne's painting drew on what she had learned watching Puvis when she posed for his *The Sacred Grove of the Arts and Muses* (1884). Furthermore, the contrast between the luminosity of the sky and the dark, twisted branches of the tree were not without reference to earlier versions of the theme. Copies of Lucas Cranach the Elder's *Adam and Eve* (1531) were readily available in a culturally active capital like Paris.[5] But there was no serpent to be seen in Suzanne's painting – the couple, Suzanne confessed, were caught in a timeless paradise and they were both responsible for their sin.[6]

Suzanne's painting of Eve reflected the rush of freedom she felt in Utter's presence, while the close attention she gave his face betrayed her fascination and infatuation. Utter was 23; that year, Suzanne turned 44. She had never been more blissfully happy. Utter was young, attractive and kind; he was creative, energised and inspiring. And above all, he loved that she painted, and eulogised her work. His enthusiasm gave her confidence. Suddenly, nothing else mattered. So urgent was her need for this man that she even stole herself away from the rest of the family on her birthday to write him a hasty note.

'Monsieur,' she scribbled, 'I forgot yesterday that I have my model on Friday and Saturday, so I shall have to postpone our visit to the museum until next Tuesday. If that is possible for you, come and pick me up as planned. Fond wishes, Suzanne Valadon.'[7]

Suzanne and Utter had arranged a trip to the Musée Gustave Moreau. The late painter had bequeathed his stately townhouse and its contents to the city of Paris after his death in 1898, on the condition that the building be used to perpetuate his work. The museum had opened in 1903, drawing its exhibits from the vast collection of over 1,000 oils and 7,000 drawings that Moreau had left behind.[8] The Symbolist painter's work took inspiration from mythology, so it was natural that Suzanne and Utter's conversation should turn to Moreau as she perfected her contemporary reworking of the Temptation and equally fitting that the idea to visit the gallery should take form. But, swept up in lust and excitement, Suzanne was forgetting her existing commitments and responsibilities. Mousis's financial support meant that she had no longer had to rely on just her mother, Maurice and the goodwill of her maids whenever she needed someone to pose; now, she was in a position to pay professional models, just as artists used to hire her. She had a trusted handful of girls on whom she called regularly, such as Ketty, a shapely young woman with a glorious mane of lustrous long hair. It was a luxurious position in which to find herself, and Suzanne was acutely conscious of the dramatic trajectory her life had undergone. It would take something significant to make her overlook her assets or disrespect a girl plying her former trade.

Utter's physical presence was irresistible, his creative support and encouragement addictive. He was also a direct channel to the contemporary art scene. Utter was intimate with key proponents of avant-garde art and he moved in the same social circles as the Fauves and the Cubists. These were the people at the forefront of Paris's art scene. In the early 1900s, Fauves like Henri Matisse and Raoul Dufy were exploding paint on to canvases to produce flat patterns in blazing colours. Soon after, Cubists Georges Braque and Pablo Picasso were overturning conventional systems of perspective. The handful of friends who saw *Les Demoiselles d'Avignon* (1907), the canvas Picasso had been working on in his pokey studio at the unlikely crucible of avant-garde art that was the Bateau Lavoir, were left in no doubt that major artistic shifts were under way.[9] Utter had also made friends with an eccentric Jewish painter, newly arrived from Italy, named Amedeo Modigliani, whose work, good looks and drunken binges were already raising eyebrows, even in Montmartre. Then, besides the artists, Utter knew all sorts of influential critics (including Francis Carco, André Salmon and Gustave Coquiot) and dealers, as well as writers and poets, like Guillaume Apollinaire and Max Jacob. With such a cast, evenings in the Lapin Agile were as creatively charged and vibrant as the gatherings when Manet and his disciples had congregated at the Café Guerbois nearly 50 years earlier. The dramatis personae and the setting might have changed, but the talk was as passionate and revolutionary as ever.

On Utter's arm, all this was accessible to Suzanne. Suddenly, a door had been opened on to a thrilling new world, where anything and everything seemed possible. All at once, her creative life became exciting again and inspiration flowed. It was as if her art had received a shot of adrenaline and her soul had been reborn.

'One of fate's unexpected twists caused her life to be renewed,' Suzanne explained of herself, writing in the third person years later in reference to her meeting with Utter.[10] That was as much due to his connections as it was to his love and support.

Painting now became Suzanne's raison d'être. 'From the day she met me,' Utter boasted, 'she gave up drawing and engraving almost entirely in order to paint.'[11] 'It was only then that she began painting,' he insisted on a separate occasion. 'All her painted work dates from 1909.'[12] The claim was somewhat inflated, but even Suzanne had to admit that a shift in focus had taken place. The year she fell in love with Utter, her painting took flight. Besides *Adam and Eve* (1909), she felt drawn to the themes of self-reflection and femininity in *Nude at the Mirror* (1909) and *Little Girl at the Mirror* (1909). Then there was the bold *Neither Black nor White*, or *After the Bath* (1909), and, in particular, *Summer* (1909). With her lover as model, Suzanne produced sketch after sketch of André nude, but drawing was now primarily just a means to a painted end.

However, Suzanne's painting was more than just an outpouring of unbridled passion on to canvas. With Utter's encouragement and contacts, Suzanne began to conceive more seriously of her art as a career which could buy her independence. Painting would always be an emotive exercise, but she now developed a more businesslike approach to its marketing and its management. Encouraged by her lover, Suzanne decided to exhibit at the Salon d'Automne, which ran from 1 October to 8 November.

The Salon d'Automne was born in 1903, when the conservative policies of the official Salon prompted yet another group of artists to seek a more liberal exhibition forum. Georges Rouault, André Derain, Henri Matisse and Albert Marquet were instrumental in the Salon d'Automne's formation and their creative originality reflected something of its ethos. It owed its uniqueness to its role as a showcase for experimental art and, particularly, for its inclusiveness of drawing, sculpture and decorative arts, as well as painting. Bolstered by the endorsement of several respected names (notably Renoir), the Salon d'Automne quickly established itself as one of the foremost spaces of relevant contemporary art.[13]

Suzanne was jubilant: she was already basking in Utter's love and inspiration when her painting *Summer* was accepted for the Salon d'Automne. Her canvas made the front page of *Gil Blas*. 'Seven ladies!' trumpeted Louis Vauxcelles when he reviewed room 12 of the exhibition.[14] 'The fairer sex has triumphed' – though he admitted that the works on show clearly set these women apart from the exhibitors at the Salon des Femmes Peintres. Suzanne's canvas was commended as being 'quite well painted'. But for Suzanne, the crowning glory was that, with some persuasion, Maurice had also agreed to enter two canvases, and to everyone's delight, one (a bridge of Notre Dame) was accepted.[15] Mother and son were now exhibiting together, and as Suzanne's most adoring admirer, Maurice signed his canvases 'Maurice Utrillo V' (having been grudgingly persuaded that Maurice Valadon or M U Valadon would cause viewers too much confusion). For Suzanne, the year finished with a surge of pride. This was true happiness.

Meandering hand-in-hand beneath the turning leaves in Montmagny, drawing close and laughing like children between abandoned palettes and easels in the studio of the Rue Cortot, or stealing time in a discreet corner of a dimly lit bar in Montmartre; to Suzanne and Utter, it was as though they truly inhabited the Eden of Suzanne's picture. When they were together, nothing else mattered. Suzanne felt like an adolescent again.

Still, she could never fully dismiss the niggling awareness of how much she risked by continuing the affair with Utter. When she was with him, she was indescribably happy. But she was compromising the whole family's security and the duplicity was exhausting.

Edmond Heuzé recalled an occasion when he joined Utter on one of his visits to the Rue Cortot. The pair and Suzanne had been joking together when heavy footsteps were heard mounting the stairs to the apartment. From their pace and weight, they could only belong to one person. 'Hide!' Suzanne hissed, 'It's Degas!' Suzanne hurried the men into a cupboard. Her affair must not become public knowledge; it was better to avoid all encounters which might arouse suspicion. No sooner had Utter and Heuzé scrambled out of view than Degas entered – just as Utter was overcome with the irrepressible urge to sneeze. An explosion erupted from inside the cupboard, and Degas flung open the door to reveal the giggling youths. 'You need two of them now, do you?' he muttered darkly to Suzanne.[16]

The episode roused snorts of laughter once Degas had left. But Suzanne knew that she was playing a dangerous game. Finally, one day, Suzanne and Utter were surprised by a far less objective party: Maurice.

In his autobiography, Maurice said nothing about how he had caught his mother and his best friend in each other's arms. But all those who knew him reported how deeply it shook him. In fact, as far as Heuzé was concerned, it was the sight of the mother he idolised and the friend three years his junior in a passionate embrace that tipped Maurice into the realm of confirmed alcoholism.[17]

Tossed between the senses of betrayal, jealousy and confusion, Maurice's whole world was upended. The discovery was sufficient to upset the fragile equilibrium of his delicate psychological state.

But while Maurice wrestled with his tumultuous emotions, there was a more consequential showdown in store. Eventually, Paul Mousis heard of his wife's affair, and when he confronted Suzanne, only to become convinced of the adultery, he flew into a furious rage.

Latterly, their relationship had hardly been idyllic; Mousis offered safety and stability, but he could never comprehend the finer points of Suzanne's artistic concerns. For his part, Mousis had begun to resent his wife's escalating demands for money. He considered taking on Suzanne's entourage of Madeleine and Maurice, with all his problems, to be nothing short of heroic. After all he had suffered, Mousis fumed, this was how Suzanne repaid him. It was outrageous. The unspoken truth was that for a bourgeois male, it was also deeply humiliating. In the class to which Mousis belonged, to be made a cuckold was the ultimate disgrace. That Utter was practically a boy, and a painter, merely compounded the shame and magnified Mousis's anger. Seizing paintings, sketches, brushes and palettes, Mousis shooed Suzanne towards the door, forcing her to dodge the tools of her trade as they were flung out after her.[18] In the tsunami of artist's equipment, fine canvases were ripped and slashed, delicate sketches torn. But Suzanne did not care. As one door slammed behind her, another opened. It led to freedom and more happiness than she had ever dreamed possible.

Breaking free from the claustrophobic confines of bourgeois marriage, Suzanne flew into the open arms of her liberator, André Utter. Now, everything moved quickly; Madeleine and Maurice were made to ready themselves for another move. From the carefully measured order of a dignified bourgeois home, Suzanne, her new family and their dogs moved to a chaotic little artist's apartment at 5, Impasse de Guelma in Montmartre. It was a small, brand-new building with a huge courtyard, the whole space having been designed to offer moderately priced lettings for artists. Two studios on the second floor had been taken by Georges Braque. The artist Raoul Dufy had rented space on the first floor; as, coincidentally, had another painter Suzanne had met before – the Italian Gino Severini. The rooms were basic and cramped and residents were constantly aware of the comings and goings of their neighbours. Suzanne was in her element.[19]

Living in the heart of Montmartre, surrounded by fellow artists and each sharing a home with two other painters with whom they could express themselves freely, Suzanne, Utter and Maurice were deeply content. And with a new home to keep and her family around her, Madeleine accepted the arrangement. Since Suzanne and Utter were both sociable creatures, many of the neighbours became friends too. Besides the pleasure that brought, establishing a widespread network of allies gave Suzanne peace of mind. It was reassuring to know that there were others looking out for Maurice. Her son often staggered out to the Moulin de la Galette in the evening and on many occasions it was only thanks to Severini's intervention, and assurance that he would escort his neighbour home, that Maurice escaped arrest for being drunk and disorderly.[20]

For their part, Suzanne and Utter favoured the Lapin Agile, which had undergone a transformation since the eccentric potter Frédé took ownership of the establishment at the turn of the century.

With his long beard, felt hat and boots, the former fish merchant looked something of a cross between Robinson Crusoe and Santa Claus. As a cabaret owner, Frédé had cut his teeth on the popular Zut in the Rue de Ravignan before moving to the Lapin Agile. Installing himself with his ark of animals – not least his beloved old donkey, Lolo – Frédé set out to expand the venue's clientele and give it a more literary flavour. He wanted to, as he put it, 'create art', and so along with painters and musicians, writers and poets received a warm welcome. A ceramicist by day, at dusk Frédé transformed into a compère extraordinaire, bursting with bonhomie and addressing customers in the familiar 'tu'. *Veillées* at the Lapin Agile brought together drinkers from across Montmartre, and they would gather around Frédé and the roaring log fire to hear him croon timeless songs as he strummed his guitar. With the crackle of logs and the low lighting, the wafts of pipe smoke and the hum of friendly voices intermingling with the sound of Frédé's guitar or poetry being recited, the olde worlde ambience offered the perfect environment for creative types to unwind and share ideas. Writers and poets such as Léon-Paul Fargue, Max Jacob and Pierre Mac Orlan, and artists including Georges Braque, André Derain, Amedeo Modigliani and Pablo Picasso became regulars. Some poets spoke derisively about the quality of the literature shared and consumed at the cabaret, but the warmth and sense of good cheer usually turned doubters into converts.[21]

Though at the start of his career Picasso's attendance was restricted by his self-imposed 10pm curfew (he worked best at night), he and the patron were deeply fond of each other. To compliment the mishmash of pictures, paintings and photographs already adorning the walls, Frédé commissioned Picasso to create a painting to decorate the cabaret and from 1905, the artist's *At the Lapin Agile* took pride of place. It depicted Picasso dressed as a harlequin and his current lover Germaine, the downfall of his late friend Casagemas, who committed suicide in 1901. The canvas was bold and bright and highly original. But Picasso did not abandon convention altogether: in the long-standing tradition of painting commissions, Picasso showed the work's patron in the background, playing his guitar.[22]

Suzanne relished her evenings with André at the Lapin Agile. The generation of artists who had ruled Montmartre when she was an eighteen-year-old aspirant had almost all moved on. Manet, Toulouse-Lautrec and Puvis were dead. Miguel had returned to Spain; Renoir had relocated to the sun-drenched climes of Cagnes. Having always been the flighty youngster among seasoned painters, Suzanne was now the veteran with stores of colourful anecdotes to delight her juniors. As a result, she was invariably flanked by a swarm of friends and admirers.

Life was good. But for all the buzz of creativity, living with four adults and their dogs squeezed into the tiny apartment in the Impasse de Guelma quickly became unworkable. Paul Mousis was loath to give up the studio at the Rue Cortot, but he consented to Suzanne having the family house in Montmagny. It made living conditions infinitely more comfortable and the charms of the countryside were not lost on the family, provided Paris was still within easy reach. Even Maurice spoke fondly of the 'charming orchards, enchanting vineyards', the simple way of life and the healthy country air.[23]

But relinquishing the family home was just the first in a series of gestures on Mousis's part to disentangle himself from the Valadon family and reclaim his honour. Next, he wanted a divorce.

When the estranged husband and wife were summoned on 3 March 1910, Mousis and his lawyer arrived at the court pepped and determined to triumph. But as the hearing commenced, Suzanne was nowhere to be seen.

Mousis's first witness said that his behaviour towards his wife had been exemplary and that despite that, Suzanne had constantly hassled him for money. The court heard how she treated her husband like a pig, and had been heard to accuse him of harming her career. 'What will it take to get rid of this man?' someone remembered overhearing her ask. In addition, she was said to have stayed out all night on several occasions, been repeatedly rude without provocation and her behaviour was unpredictable.[24]

Suzanne never appeared to defend herself. The divorce had been called by Mousis and whatever accusations were fired at her, she had no intention of hampering the process. Mousis's request was granted.

The couple's property was divided up, with Suzanne keeping the house in Montmagny. Then her new life began.

After her divorce, Suzanne began painting furiously. Having spent months struggling to comprehend the perplexing shades of human character, she was seized by a renewed interest in portraiture. She produced many studies of herself and of the members of her reconfigured family, as though seeking to establish in her own mind who and what were now her priorities. She drew a portrait of Maurice on which she inscribed possessively 'my son'. Madeleine had always been the generic grandmother, but now Suzanne reclaimed her by association, when she painted the dark and intense *Maurice Utrillo, His Grandmother and His Dog* (1910). In this simplified but severe canvas, Suzanne employed a traditional pyramid-like structure, giving the piece a semi-biblical feel, while simultaneously drawing on contemporary influences from artists like Gauguin and cropping the scene in a style that recalled the work of Japanese woodcut artists. However, traditional rules of perspective were blatantly ignored, with Maurice in the background huge and overbearing, looming over Madeleine, who Suzanne sat with her hands folded in her lap in passive acceptance. The dark background drew attention to the faces, Madeleine tired, haggard and wrinkled, Maurice preoccupied and brooding. It was a disjointed family group, individuals brought together in body, but distinct in spirit, and only the dog, Pierrot, reached across the personal boundaries for affection as he held his paw up to Madeleine. All the social complexities of the preceding months were replayed on Suzanne's canvas.[25]

Freed from the constraints of marriage, Suzanne now lifted her vision and began to see things differently. Prompted by Utter, she turned to landscape, producing *Tree at Montmagny Quarry* (1910) and expanding her palette from five to fourteen colours. She added yellow ochre, raw sienna, light crimson lake, Venetian red, cobalt blue, deep ultramarine, and English and emerald green.[26] Over time, she also replaced black with ultramarine blue mixed with vermillion and English green or reddish-brown. Her landscape was rich and full-blooded, warm and gutsy, and she used expressive, confident sweeps of the brush in a manner reminiscent of Cézanne. Nothing in Suzanne's balanced and bright composition identified the Montmagny quarries as the site of an aggressive strike the previous September.[27]

The whole, unorthodox family loved Montmagny, but the draw of Montmartre was magnetic. Professionally and spiritually, Suzanne, Maurice and Utter were constantly called back to Paris. Now an arthritic and short-sighted old lady of 79, Madeleine fell into line with the trio, going wherever they deemed fit. With three such intense and passionate characters, there was hardly room for another tempestuous personality. Madeleine resigned herself to her role as a passive adjunct in her daughter's chaotic life. The household crackled with nervous energy which, when not channelled into painting, triggered explosive rows and passionate make-ups. The trio were soon baptised 'The Unholy Trinity'. They became the main protagonists in a long-running domestic drama and even when they retired to Montmagny, Montmartre was still their stage.

As avant-garde art marched forwards, Montparnasse was beginning to rival Montmartre as Paris's artistic mecca.[28] It attracted a number of the art scene's newest recruits like Modigliani, as well as some more established names including Picasso. Its appeal stemmed from its moderate prices and lively atmosphere, and it was also less tainted by tourism than Montmartre. Nonetheless, Montmartre still had its staunch loyalists, many of whom scorned the crass work now passing for contemporary 'art'. In the year of Suzanne's divorce, a group of regulars from the Lapin Agile, headed up by the novelist, journalist and enemy of the avant-garde, Roland Dorgelès, concocted what they considered to be a hilarious hoax.[29] Attaching a paintbrush to the tail of Frédé's much-cherished Lolo, they stood the bewildered creature with its rear pressed up against a blank canvas. Dipping its tail-paintbrush in brightly coloured pigments, they busied the donkey with oats, so that as he swished his tail back and forwards between mouthfuls, the canvas filled with sweeps of bright colour. Onlookers grew hysterical and applauded joyfully when they realised that Lolo's brushwork could be accelerated by offering him more treats. Delighted, the group published the humorous manifesto of the so-called 'Excessivists' to accompany the jest in the paper *Le Matin*. 'Let us smash the palettes of our ancestors,' it declared, 'make a bonfire of false masterpieces and establish grand principles which should govern the art of tomorrow. Our formula can be reduced to a single word: excessivism [...] Long live excess!'[30] The document was signed Joachim-Raphaël Boronali (an anagram of Aliboron, the name of a donkey in La Fontaine's *Fables*) – the same name attached to the much-hyped *Sunset over the Adriatic* which was shown at the Salon des Indépendants that spring. People flocked to the Salon to see the canvas everyone was talking about. Lolo was a star. When the painter's genus was revealed, some (mostly artists) were angry, others amused. But everyone conceded that the exhibition of Lolo's canvas was a sign of the times. The *Journal du Dimanche* said what many were thinking: the work was 'less ridiculous than many others' on show.[31] In 20th-century Paris, taste was increasingly subjective.

For Suzanne and Maurice, that mattered. Without Mousis's financial support, they depended on the public's approval of their work to survive. That meant first placating a powerful and notoriously fickle middleman: the dealer.

One busy afternoon at the dealer Druet's in the Rue Royale, Maurice burst into the gallery, emboldened by alcohol and swaying unsteadily, a folder of paintings under his arm. People whispered and laughed as he weaved his way over to the manager. Art critic Francis Jourdain was visiting the gallery at the time and he watched as Maurice displayed his wares. There were some inspired pieces. Jourdain tried to persuade Druet to give Maurice a chance, but the gallery owner refused. Druet's accountant also happened to be there, and he agreed to take a canvas. But it was hardly a substantial deal. Irritated by the rejection, and desperate, Maurice staggered back outside and began approaching passers-by, attempting to palm off his paintings as a market seller would surplus fruit.[32]

Just a few days later, Jourdain was perusing the offerings of another dealer, Louis Libaude, with his colleague, the critic and art historian Dr Élie Faure, when he spotted some works by the same hand he had admired at Druet's. Libaude was a crafty miser who suffered no fools. Formerly the editor of the publication *Art Littéraire*, he had subsequently worked as an auctioneer of horses before returning to the art world as a picture dealer, where he had already earned himself a reputation as an unscrupulous cut-throat. Even Jourdain, who knew him well, conceded that he was rapacious, though probably no more of a scoundrel than any other businessman trying to make a living from art. Libaude had first come across Maurice's paintings at Clovis Sagot's gallery, where a handsome study of Notre Dame persuaded him to take a chance on the young painter. Bypassing Sagot, Libaude slyly approached Suzanne to negotiate a deal – on the strict understanding that the price he paid remained confidential. However, the work he now had on show was not selling. Nonetheless, Jourdain was enraptured, and told the dealer so. He purchased two pictures of Montmagny for himself, and was so satisfied that he returned to the gallery with some friends – influential friends. They included the writer Octave Mirbeau, the publisher Paul Gallimard, and the Kapferer brothers, who were art enthusiasts. All bought pictures. Word spread. Suddenly, everyone wanted Utrillos. In a world where donkeys produced art for salons, Utrillo offered perspectivally coherent pictures of familiar streets in muted colours, unspoiled by pedestrians and in a form the viewer could recognise. His canvases made contemporary realism palatable. Unwittingly, Maurice had given the public just the visual reassurance they craved. Libaude was delighted, and agreed to negotiate with Maurice directly. He quickly calculated that he could acquire the canvases for little and sell them with a hefty mark-up. A deal was struck. Maurice would earn a pittance, but provided he painted, he would be assured of a regular monthly retainer.[33]

Suzanne was ecstatic. Maurice had lately learned that his application to study at the École des Beaux-Arts had been rejected, a rebuff he later described as 'one of the saddest things'.[34] This was the break Suzanne had dreamed of for her son. She hurried to thank Jourdain in person for what he had done. It was not for its own sake that the money pleased her. Suzanne truly believed that if only they could afford the best rehabilitation clinics, Maurice could be cured. In her eyes, Libaude was a lifeline who could give her back her son.

For Montmartre's struggling artists, canvases were like currency whose value was determined by the viewer. Paintings could be exchanged with dealers for cash, or, more often than not, traded with cabaret owners for a hearty meal – or for wine. For the first time in his life, Maurice was the master of his own, ready capital. He took full advantage. The profits from his paintings seldom found their way back to the family pot. Maurice became a well-known character on the Butte's cast list of local eccentrics. He was nicknamed l'Itrillo, and laughed at by children when they saw him mumbling to himself as he staggered through the streets. He was often seen ricocheting precariously from building to building, or else collapsed in a drunken heap, where he became a punch-bag for merciless louts. On nights when the police hauled him in, the treatment was little better. 'I am not mad,' became his frantic *cri de coeur*.[35] Many a time, Suzanne was summoned to come and collect her son from the station and pay whatever the fine amounted to this time.[36]

But Suzanne had not lost hope. Maurice had work and he had an income. Meanwhile, her own personal and professional life were full of contentment and promise. Her relationship with Utter was unfolding into one extended and glorious honeymoon period. They posed for each other and painted, talked and made love. And the more each discovered about the other, the deeper in love they fell. Suzanne's art prospered.

Her name was now getting known beyond Paris. By the time Suzanne came to exhibit three pieces in the 1910 Salon d'Automne, word had reached the Limousin that one of their number was achieving great things. The correspondent for *Limoges illustré* reported: 'We noticed various enamels by M.L. Jouhaud, a painting by M. Alluaud and several subjects by Mlle Valadon, all three artists originating from Limoges.'[37]

The following year, Suzanne was offered a solo exhibition by the dealer who first spotted Maurice's work, Clovis Sagot, in his gallery on the Rue Lafitte. Sales were disappointing, and Sagot grumbled that a series of recent skirmishes in the area no doubt deterred potential visitors.[38] Nonetheless, her first one-woman show marked a pivotal moment in Suzanne's career. And her submission to the Salon des Indépendants that spring received a more cheering response. *Limoges illustré* was again proud to claim Suzanne as one of their own and commended her work.[39] For *La Vie Artistique*, 'submissions of a distinguished quality' were rare in rooms 36–42, but the author singled Suzanne out for praise as an artist whose drawing was 'crisp, intelligent and innate'.[40]

But Suzanne's success at the Salon des Indépendants was clouded by a disturbing incident. Just after the show opened, Maurice was arrested, and this time, the charge was not only for drunkenness, but for indecent exposure. Suzanne learned how he had terrified passers-by in the Place du Tertre by stripping off his clothes. This time, the situation was beyond Suzanne's intervention. Maurice was sent to see out a month's prison sentence.[41]

Suzanne had often worried that Maurice never displayed any of the hallmarks of a typical young lad with a nascent libido. But the same year as his arrest, he finally had his first sexual encounter (which he later recounted that he did not enjoy). It should have brought Suzanne relief. But in Maurice's arrest, she saw the harbinger of a more concerning fate.

André Utter adored Suzanne, but his tolerance with his 'stepson' was waning. Utter himself was not an especially talented artist. His paintings were mediocre, not exceptional. But what he lacked in painterly skill, he made up for in business acumen. As soon as he moved in with Suzanne, he began guiding her career choices and he attempted to steer Maurice in what he considered to be the best professional direction. Utter was acutely sensitive to the skill and talent of both mother and son, but he also had a profound understanding of the complex market in which they were operating, and he had the interpersonal skills and smooth talk to earn dealers' trust. Together, the trio had a winning combination.

When she could dismiss her anxieties about Maurice's drinking, Suzanne had to admit that life was extraordinarily good. Her determination to focus on her blessings was reflected in the monumental *Joy of Life* (1911) that she submitted to the Salon d'Automne in October 1911. The conceptually complex work showed four nude or semi-clad women stretching, bending and crouching in various poses in a shady grove, while a naked young man stood to one side watching them, his arms folded. The human figure in a landscape setting had been a popular subject with painters since the second half of the 19th century, and Suzanne's work gave a nod to Manet's great *Déjeuner sur l'herbe* (1863). The picture was deeply informed by art of the past, and it also contained hints of Puvis, Gauguin and Matisse's work. But in many respects, the painting was a profoundly personal piece, and a clear reflection of Suzanne's current situation. With the mature, shapely women and the slender young man, physically, Suzanne could only be drawing on herself and Utter. But while he was cast in the role of voyeur, the female presences, three with their backs turned, another facing him but concealing her eyes in a melodramatic pose, appeared oblivious or untroubled by his stare. In a defiant visual statement, divorcee Suzanne dismissed society's judicial scrutiny and refuted the notion of the male gaze defining woman.[42]

Suzanne's work and relationship brought her deep fulfilment. But as the year drew to a close, Maurice's dependence on drink was becoming more pronounced. The apartment they had occupied in Montmartre had proved cramped and uncomfortable, but their spacious country dwelling felt isolated and remote from the city they all loved so dearly. Nobody was completely satisfied. Something had to change.

It did – and it came in an unexpected form. In 1910, Émile Bernard, the devout painter Suzanne had first met through Lautrec, had decided to vacate his studio apartment in the building Suzanne used to occupy in the Rue Cortot. Now, the proprietor was looking for a new tenant. The prospect of living back in Montmartre, not squeezed into a box at its foothills, but high above Paris in the place where she had been the happiest, was thrilling. Maurice would have to be supervised of course, but he had always been more at ease in Montmartre and his psychological state played a key part in his problems. Both relieved and excited, Suzanne eagerly agreed to the move.[43]

When the family arrived at their new home with their belongings, their eyes alighted on a notice that the previous tenant had fixed above the door:

> He who believes not in God,
> Raphael or Titian may not enter.[44]

This was the start of a new chapter for the family. Disregarding the warning, the Unholy Trinity opened the door and stepped inside.

CHAPTER 12

New Horizons

Vau mielhs tener un lapin que segre una lebre.
(It is better to hold a rabbit than to chase a hare.)
OLD LIMOUSIN PROVERB[1]

Number 12, Rue Cortot comprised a sprawling warren of dimly lit passageways and bright ateliers. Émile Bernard's former studio was in the opposite wing from the apartment where Suzanne and Paul Mousis had begun married life and it had valuable advantages. Arriving in front of the huge arched doorway, Suzanne could find the concierge in the tower-like structure on the left, and on the right, the wooden staircase which led to her new home. Mounting the creaking steps to the first floor, the muffled sound of a dog barking urgently could be heard on the other side of a nearby wall, while a heap of coal on the landing signalled occupancy. From the landing, the door on the left opened into the family's hallway, where approaching the window, Suzanne could gaze down at a spectacular panoramic view over the rooftops of northern Paris. There was a dining room, a cosy little bedroom of three metres squared, perfect for Maurice – and all the other living space the family could desire. Then from the hallway, two further rooms and a short corridor led to the engine room of the apartment: Suzanne's atelier.[2]

With its huge skylight, wooden slatted floor and rectangular windows looking out over the treetops, the whole studio felt as though it were a ship coasting through the air. Light flooded the room and the view across Paris was breathtaking. All around, a jumble of wood and canvas completed the furnishings: there were easels; part-finished paintings stood up against sturdy cupboards; and here and there, a chair or coffee table served as a temporary resting place for jars of turpentine, tubes of paint, brushes and palettes.

With Madeleine shuffling around keeping house, Suzanne settled into her new surroundings and quickly became as relaxed and comfortable as if she had been born there. Once the dogs had been walked in the morning, the working day saw Suzanne, Utter and Maurice busily engrossed in their own corners of the apartment. Every so often, a misplaced tube of paint or a borrowed brush triggered an explosive row, with abuse being hurled unrestrainedly at one artist by the other. When the equipment had been returned, peace was restored and industry resumed. Evenings were regularly interrupted by Maurice's ungainly reappearance after one of his drinking binges, either alone or in the custody of a police officer from the station in the Rue Lambert. When the blood and vomit had been mopped up, the revelation that he had yet again drunk the proceeds of a sale provoked more fiery disputes. But another masterpiece was never far away and it invariably redeemed him in his mother's eyes. It was a tumultuous existence, but for the most part, everyone was content. In her old age, Madeleine had her home and her family around her. Maurice got to be with the mother he adored and Montmartre was on his doorstep, while Utter had Suzanne and the bohemian existence he craved. And Suzanne had art and love and freedom.[3]

She celebrated the household with a *Family Portrait* (1912), a piece she had been planning for some time. The sombre picture depicted the four of them. Maurice was seated in the front, his head resting on his hands, his gaze lost and melancholy. Behind him, Madeleine looked a hunched, wrinkled and sullen secondary character, while at the far side, Utter appeared the tall and dignified adjunct to a family group centred on mother and son, and he looked out of the picture frame optimistically. And at the centre of them all was Suzanne, her hair centre-parted, her hand clasped to her chest, fixing her viewer in the eye in knowing complicity.

Madeleine was ageing. The new family arrangement prompted Suzanne to look at her mother afresh. She produced several studies of her that year, one seated outside with a stone wall and foliage behind her, a cloth in her hand indicating a pause from some domestic task; another showed her sitting indoors, a cup and saucer by her side, her gnarled hands clutching her glasses, her eyes still a striking shade of clear blue, but now watery and framed by pink lids and wrinkles.

Suzanne's respect for Madeleine had grown more profound as she matured. With Maurice's precarious oscillation between intense productivity and incoherent drunkenness, her mother's presence was a comfort. There were other supportive figures in Maurice's life: for instance the kindly César Gay, a former officer who had served in the corps of the *guardiens de la paix* and who now owned the restaurant the Casse-Croûte in the Rue Paul-Féval where Maurice was a regular.[4] 'M. Gay always gave me a warm welcome,' Maurice remembered, 'and made it easier for me to create my art.'[5] There was also Marie Vizier, the buxom blonde who ran the cabaret adjoining Père Gay's, À la Belle Gabrielle, and with whom Maurice even enjoyed a brief and casual romantic liaison. In Maurice's eyes, Marie was like 'a mother, always there whatever the circumstance'.[6] Both Père Gay and Marie Vizier were happy to let Maurice paint on their premises, and occasionally Marie agreed to let him stay the night. But she was not a woman to trifle with; she had no hesitation in beating Maurice and kicking him out whenever he drank too much.

Though Père Gay and Marie Vizier offered support, Suzanne was conscious that, having known Maurice from birth, Madeleine was the only other person who truly understood him and could share the load. And by early 1912, there was an additional grievance as far as Maurice was concerned: the arrangement with Libaude.

Libaude had craftily assured himself exclusivity on Maurice's work. But with Maurice seeing canvases as coupons for drink, the more liquor he needed, the more he was forced to produce. Before long, Libaude was inundated. 'Since the beginning of April,' the dealer complained, 'you have been bringing me a painting every other day. It is far too much and I fear that this hasty production will be detrimental to your career. I believe one can only build a serious reputation for oneself with careful work.'[7]

It was Suzanne and not Maurice who replied to the reprimand, irritated by the dealer's tone and rejection. By way of a threat, she proposed to reveal what her son was being paid.

Libaude did not deem her letter worthy of reply. He condescended to write to Maurice instead: 'I have received a threatening letter from Mme Valadon [...] So she speaks of divulging what I pay you? [...] I feel I must tell you that should this threat be carried through, I would cease buying paintings from you.'[8]

Concerned about her son's livelihood, and about the lengths to which his need for alcohol would drive him, Suzanne had wisely kept a stash of Maurice's early paintings hidden in the apartment. However, now, when there were no new canvases to trade, Maurice had taken to riffling through the house and stealing his own works. Realising that her strategy was no longer effective, Suzanne resigned herself to Libaude taking the paintings. Gathering up the last of the portfolio, she grudgingly offered them to the dealer. He took the lot for a pitiful 100 francs, leaving Maurice with little more than 50 sous (approximately 2 francs 50) for each canvas.[9] At the time, that money would not even buy *Le Figaro* for a month.[10]

Maurice Utrillo as a young man.
Martinie/Roger Viollet/Getty Images

By now, Maurice's most extreme and manic episodes of drunkenness were becoming more regular. Suzanne decided that something had to be done. She simply must seek help from outside.

After one particularly frightening and aggressive alcohol-induced outburst, Suzanne turned to her friend, the art critic Adolphe Tabarant, and begged him to intervene; Libaude must be persuaded to pay for Maurice's condition to be treated, in return for some canvases. But when he was approached, the dealer only grew more annoyed. He argued that there had never been a formal agreement between himself and Maurice, merely a moral obligation, and in any case, Maurice's continual breaching of their understanding hardly inspired in him the confidence to reach into his own pocket. Shortly after the confrontation, Libaude wrote to Maurice, enquiring maliciously: 'I am surprised not to have heard from you, are you unwell?'.[11]

Anxious that his name should not be tarnished by his declining assistance, Libaude spread the rumour that it was Suzanne who was opposed to the idea of Maurice being admitted for treatment. When word reached Suzanne, she was livid. Not wasting a moment, Suzanne, Utter and Maurice jumped in a taxi and raced to confront Libaude. The dealer's reception was farcical; he treated the whole interview as a joke, clearly relishing the power he wielded over the family. His refusal to help was determined. But eventually, Libaude grumbled that Dr Élie Faure – whose medical and artistic authority he could hardly dispute – had urged that it would be for everyone's benefit that Maurice be admitted to the care of the Dr Revertegat at his clinic in Sannois. At last, Libaude grudgingly agreed to pay the 300 francs-a-month fees. Maurice was admitted to the clinic.[12]

As she had when Maurice was sent to Sainte-Anne's, Suzanne had to relinquish control and was left to wonder how her son was spending his days. But this time she did so knowing that Maurice was in the best possible hands. Suzanne could now turn her attention back to her own career and to her friends.

Degas was in particular need of assistance. Ageing, increasingly cantankerous and plagued by failing eyesight and deteriorating health, his lot only became more burdensome to him when he learned that his home and atelier on the Rue Victor-Massé were to be demolished. At 77, Degas was an esteemed master of French painting – and he was homeless.

Suzanne saw less and less of her mentor these days, but she knew him better than many of his friends, several of whom tried to convince him to move to the serene and leafy area of Passy, where Berthe Morisot had lived. When Suzanne learned of the project, she was aghast. 'He would have died of boredom!' she exclaimed.[13]

Degas might have been old and set in his ways, but around him he needed movement and life – and Montmartre. Suzanne took matters into her own hands. She found Degas a studio on the Boulevard de Clichy, for which he was profoundly grateful.

The demolition of Degas's atelier was symptomatic of a broader shift under way in the capital. 'It is a bit of historic and artistic Paris which is disappearing,' lamented *L'Intransigeant* when the painter's home had been demolished that May.[14] The Paris Suzanne had come to know and love was changing, and Montmartre with it. But Suzanne could not allow nostalgia to divert her attention. To make a living, her career also demanded ongoing maintenance.

As a professional artist, Suzanne's year was now structured around the key exhibitions. Little happened in the summer, but the Salon d'Automne inaugurated the season in October, the Salon des Indépendants took place in the spring and around that there existed all manner of exhibition possibilities if an artist were shrewd and proactive. That May, Maurice's admission to the clinic at Sannois coincided with Suzanne's participation in a group show, Graphik, at the Galerie Der Sturm in Berlin. Exhibiting abroad was a sure sign of success and a cause for self-congratulation. But separated from Maurice, it was difficult to remain solely focused on work.[15]

At least her son's reports assured her that he was comfortable and well looked after. The leafy suburb of Sannois was already known to Maurice and Dr Revertegat's clinic was a well-managed establishment, familial in its welcome and attentive in its care. The doctor, Maurice said, was 'of the elite' and friendly.[16] He went on: 'excellent food, still, sterilised water to drink, very comfortable bedroom'.[17] Patients were allowed to smoke; coffee was served after lunch and at four o'clock in the afternoon. Maurice was even given permission to leave the grounds so that he could paint in the roads and countryside around the clinic. In one study, the straight, tree-lined Avenue Rozée where the clinic was located, with its blue-grey iron fence, appeared sunny and serene. The environment seemed to suit him, he responded well to the treatment and there was talk of him being released as early as July. But there was no telling if Dr Revertegat's sterling efforts would withstand Maurice's return to Montmartre society. Arriving at a crossroads, it was impossible for Suzanne not to speculate as to what the future might hold.

Something of her angst found an outlet in the huge *The Future Unveiled* (1912) which she produced that year. Stretched out naked on a divan in a richly coloured interior, Suzanne painted a curvaceous blonde looking down to inspect a set of cards that a crouching brunette in a blue dress had laid out in a circle on the floor. Fortune-telling had been practised for thousands of years when Suzanne executed her composition, but cartomancy (using playing cards to make predictions) became popular in the 18th century. Typically employed in a less serious context than the traditional Tarot, standard playing cards were nevertheless said to offer remarkably accurate forecasts. As interest in the occult and spiritualism mounted in the second half of the 19th century, playing cards lent themselves to the more informal and bohemian social gatherings which drew Montmartre's artists and writers. According to the traditional interpretations of cards, the future anticipated by Suzanne's spread was loaded with meaning. In the centre was the ace of hearts, signifying both the enquirer's emotional foundations and their physical base or home. The cards surrounding it highlighted wealth, prosperity and material success, though not, the seven of clubs warned, without challenges or indulging in frivolous luxuries, while the ace of diamonds foretold of splendid but erratic good fortune. The ace of spades hinted at exciting new adventures whose outcome was yet unknown. Significantly, the abundance of kings in the middle reflected different strains of male energy. And in her hand, the reader held up the queen of diamonds: a mature and forceful woman, though at times a bossy one.[18]

That July, Maurice was released and returned to Suzanne's care. Suzanne left nothing to chance. She did everything she could to choreograph her son's seamless reinsertion into everyday life. It was agreed that the family, along with Maurice's melancholy chemist friend, Richmond Chaudois, and all their dogs, should take a holiday. If Maurice were literally given a change of perspective, Suzanne reasoned, it would surely set him on a more favourable path when he returned to Paris. So it was that one summer evening in 1912, the party made their way to the Gare de l'Ouest and boarded the express train to Brittany via Conquet, where they planned to take a boat to the remote island of Ushant.[19]

The northern French coastline of Normandy and Brittany had soared in popularity during the second half of the 19th century, when it became increasingly attractive to holidaymakers. The English had first started the vogue for sea bathing in the early 19th century, and from the mid-1840s, a rapidly expanding rail network helped spread the trend and facilitate access to the coast. France's northern coast became so popular that by 1866, travel writer Adolphe Joanne could say of the Normandy seaside town of Trouville: 'It's the rendez-vous of sick people who are well, it is Paris, with its qualities, its foibles, and its vices, transported for two or three months to the edge of the ocean.'[20]

Brittany had much to offer the Parisian in search of distraction. 'Around the mountainous massif,' one 1911 guide to Brittany proclaimed, 'unfold, now desolate heath, now fertile plains, down to the magnificently jagged coastlines so revered by tourists.'[21] But even before the seasonal tourist industry rose up, artists and writers had been haunted by the rugged coastline, the dramatic scenery, the picturesque regional costumes and the mystical folklore in Brittany. For many painters, the rocky landscape at the mercy of the elements was beautiful in its weathered honesty. James Abbott McNeill Whistler had been drawn there in the autumn months of 1867. Jules Breton, the academic painter admired by Vincent van Gogh, had fallen in love with the region in the mid-1860s. And John Singer Sargent had braved the inclement summer of 1877 to create his celebrated *Oyster Gatherers of Cancale* (1878). By the time Suzanne travelled there, the trip to Brittany had become something of an obligatory pilgrimage for any self-respecting artist.

But Brittany was an especially poignant holiday destination for the Valadon family. Its granite terrain called to mind the landscape of the Limousin, while the thriving rural customs recalled Madeleine's heritage. Furthermore, Suzanne's maid Catherine was one of the many Breton girls who had migrated to Paris to find work in domestic service, subsequently introducing the Valadon house to her stock of regional traditions, customs and tales. Brittany was a natural place for Suzanne and Maurice to take a holiday.

After a train journey of several hours, the four adults with their suitcases, dogs and easels, stepped out on to the platform at Conquet in a cloud of steam and a spirit of expectation. 'The trip to Ushant was epic,' André Utter recalled later.[22] Upon arriving at Conquet, the party were obliged to travel by boat the eighteen miles to the isolated little island which marked the north-westernmost point of France.[23] At under six square miles, the rocky landmass had a population of less than 3,000 when Suzanne and her family took their holiday there. Ushant was the home of a thriving fishing community, as well as its particular breed of small black and brown sheep. But it was predominantly for its treacherous seafaring conditions that it was known. With its fast moving tidal streams and razor-sharp rocks, Ushant was the eerie graveyard of unknown sailors and lost vessels – the land of shipwrecks and terror, Maurice mused.[24] Observing the jagged rocks, perilous cliff faces and barren fauna, secretly Maurice could not help wishing himself home in Montmartre. True, it had its unsavoury characteristics, but at least they were familiar. However, the plan had been made to stay for several months, and it was unlikely to change. And a letter addressed to Maurice forwarded from Paris was sufficient reminder of the capital's less appealing traits.[25]

'I learned that you were going to leave Sannois to travel to Brittany,' Libaude wrote accusingly. 'May I remind you before you go, that from now on, I would like to receive exclusively canvases with dimensions of 25 [...] It is understood that you will deliver six canvases a month and that you will produce nothing for anyone else. I think we see eye to eye, I hope that we will continue to do so for a long time; it will be profitable for you as well as for myself.'[26]

Maurice, Suzanne and Utter spent the summer erecting their easels on the clifftops or looking out over the heathland, and they worked – as best they could – from nature. Maurice produced a series of melancholy landscapes, reflections of his mood as much as his surroundings. Suzanne, who was less experienced where landscape was concerned, found the trip to Brittany a valuable opportunity to focus on the genre while discovering new country-side. She produced studies which bore the imprint of Gauguin's influence. But with the dogs needing constant supervision, and removed from their well-equipped and familiar working environment, the trio's productivity diminished. 'It was a circus,' Utter remembered candidly, 'how were we supposed to work in such con-ditions?'[27] By October, the family were relieved to board the train which would carry them back to Montmartre.

Arriving home in time for the Salon d'Automne gave an imme-diate focus. Suzanne submitted *The Future Unveiled*, which was remarked upon, and Maurice also exhibited some work. In the same month as the Salon d'Automne opened, Suzanne and Maurice both participated in the group show organised by Clovis Sagot in Munich at the Galerie Hans Goltz, where pieces by Van Gogh and Picasso were also on show. If the seasonal festivities were more spartan than Suzanne might have liked, the Salon des Indépendants the following spring gave cause for hope. But by the time the New Year came around, Suzanne was feeling the financial strain of living by her art. Her work was admired by fellow artists, but it was not commercial in the same way as Maurice's. And he was at the mercy of Libaude's avarice.

Maurice had been made to pay for his Breton jaunt with some extra paintings inspired by his trip as part of his existing 'contract'. He had no choice but to consent. Libaude also insisted that Suzanne sign the canvases for her son, since her writing was much neater. Then in March, came a critical letter demanding that Maurice take more care to ensure the consistently high quality of his paintings. Libaude was constantly at pains to remind Maurice which of them wielded the power. 'You know that it would serve neither of us to deviate from the gold-paved route on which I have set your painting,' Libaude warned. 'That would certainly happen if you sold your canvases to dealers who could not keep them and who had to move them on as quickly as possible in order to survive.'[28]

Ironically, the member of the family with the highest earning potential was caught in an impossible stalemate. Utter did his best to smooth the fractious relations between Maurice and his dealer, but Libaude would only be pushed so far. Suzanne came to a sobering realisation: the family urgently needed more money. The house in Montmagny would have to be sold.

The loss of her only asset might have been distressing were it not for the anaesthetising effect of daily life as an artist and her relationship with Utter. Reconnecting with her niece, Marie-Lucienne Merlet, also offered a pleasant distraction that year. Marie-Lucienne now signed herself Marie Coca, for she had married, and had become a mother. Suzanne had always been fond of her half-sister's daughter, and she produced a portrait of Marie Coca with her daughter Gilberte, which she finished in time for the 1913 Salon des Indépendants that spring. Seated erect in a high-backed armchair, Marie Coca was shown looking out of the picture frame at an undefined point, while paintings on the wall behind her made a 'picture within a picture' – a device borrowed from Degas. At Marie Coca's feet, Gilberte presented a diminutive version of her mother. Having bribed her great-niece to keep still with sweets, Suzanne seated the little girl on a cushion, her right hand mirroring her mother's, her left possessively gripping the head of a doll which she nursed in her lap. The child fixed the viewer in the eye so as to drive home the artist's point – life, Suzanne demonstrated, was cyclical.[29]

That May, Suzanne had further cause to feel optimistic. Libaude, convinced that Maurice's work represented a still little-known gold mine, put all his energy – and his funds – into hiring Eugène Blot's gallery on the Rue Richepanse for two weeks. Filling the exhibition space with over 30 canvases, he was certain he would make a fortune. He was wrong – only two of Maurice's pieces sold. The silence in the press was deafening.

But that same year, Suzanne was more fortunate in her professional contacts. She was welcomed to participate in a group show at Berthe Weill's tiny shop on the Rue Victor-Massé.

The bespectacled, round-faced manager of the Galerie B. Weill was the same age as Suzanne and she shared the artist's fierce determination.[30] Weill had been born to a lower middle-class Jewish couple whose modest means obliged her to become apprenticed at a young age at the antique dealer Salvator Mayor's shop. Once the patron died in 1897, Weill moved into the fine arts trade and started a gallery, initially with one of her six siblings. However, Weill was an incorrigible risk-taker; from her partnership with her brother, in the early 20th century, she channelled all her resources into opening her own gallery. By the time she met Suzanne, she had become one of the foremost champions of the avant-garde and a particularly ardent defender of Fauvism and Cubism. She was one of the first dealers to spot Picasso's talent. His canvases immediately excited her, and she promptly filled her gallery with his work. As an enterprising woman with Jewish heritage, Weill, Suzanne knew, possessed all the qualities to antagonise Degas. But the dealer was intelligent and discerning, single-minded when she sensed she had happened upon new talent, and shrewder than many of her male counterparts. As a single woman operating – and succeeding – in a man's world, she had much in common with Suzanne. Suzanne's introduction to Berthe Weill marked the start of a deep friendship based on honesty and mutual respect.

With the dizzying course of professional peaks and troughs, and with the financial pressure eased by the sale of the house in Montmagny, the family decided that they sorely needed another, more uplifting break. They longed for somewhere warm, more exotic but without the additional complication of a linguistic hurdle to overcome. So that summer, when the art market experienced its annual slump, Suzanne, Maurice and Utter boarded an express train to Marseille where they took a steamboat to the Corsican capital of Ajaccio.

With its Mediterranean climate and relatively easy access from mainland France, Corsica had long been a popular travel destination with the more anthropologically curious Frenchman.[31] Once French became the official language in the mid-19th century and the introduction of steamboats facilitated travel, the cultural bond between the island and mainland France grew even stronger. The 'natural beauty of Corsica and its incomparable climate' made it a favoured destination among travel writers.[32] With its mountainous, granite terrain and cuisine enriched by an abundance of chestnuts, there was much to remind Suzanne of her early years in the Limousin.

But it was primarily the island's difference to anywhere she had yet experienced that struck her.

Corsica was a revelation. The vivid colour, the light and, particularly, the sun, so intense and all-consuming ('a sun unlike any other,' Suzanne enthused), bewitched her.[33] As the family travelled north from Ajaccio, Suzanne gradually discovered more of the island.

She was overcome by the scenery and the vistas, 'a jumble of houses, walls, gardens,' she observed.[34] Corsica nurtured her nascent affection for landscape. Once they arrived in Corte and the Unholy Trinity began working alongside each other, marvelling at the scenery from behind their easels, Suzanne felt inspired to paint 'a true, objective view of a town'.[35] In an unprecedented work, she captured the entire city of Corte in a sweeping panorama. Taking a high vantage point, her canvas showed the viewer down over the city. Not a detail was missed; Suzanne carefully painted each individual stone, every window in all the little buildings, in a meticulous style reminiscent of the luminescent religious paintings produced by Albrecht Dürer in the 16th century. From the intense sunlight which gave the outlines of rocks and mountains clearer definition, to the bold colours, with the bright green trees, the clear blue sky and the potent yellow and orange of the landscape – everything about Corsica conformed to Suzanne's aesthetic preferences. As subject matter, it allowed her to capitalise on her skills as a draughtsman. Besides the epic *View of Corte* (1913), she painted several Corsican landscapes, including a scene depicting the church at Belgodère. The visual elegance of fishermen manipulating their nets on the beach particularly struck her. It was as though everyday work had given rise to a sort of elaborate dance. The bodily contortions brought about by domestic tasks had always fascinated Suzanne, and she began a series of rapid sketches which she felt certain she could work up into a breathtaking canvas once she returned to Paris.[36]

Suzanne was not alone in her appreciation of the island. Even Maurice seemed to cheer. 'Picturesque and pleasant to explore,' he commented.[37] He found the food spicy (not a common complaint of the herb-infused Corsican cuisine, save of the spiced tomato purée used in many dishes).[38] But he nevertheless thought the meals decent, and certainly superior to many he had tasted in Paris. That Ajaccio and Calvi were also revered wine-growing areas, known for their full-bodied and aromatic wines, only made the dining experience more palatable. His enthusiasm was buoyed even further when, quite by chance, the trio bumped into Maurice's painter friend Augustin Grass-Mick at their hotel. Formerly an enthusiastic participant in Paris's bohemian life, the decoratively trained Grass-Mick had received a commission to embellish a local château near Belgodère. Though he and Maurice had enjoyed many a drunken sortie together in Montmartre, Grass-Mick had left Paris with his wife for the South of France earlier that year, so it was a fortuitous and pleasant encounter.[39]

The whole family felt fulfilled by their holiday. Each was disappointed when it came to an end. But as Suzanne, Utter and Maurice boarded the boat at l'Ile Rousse one rainy September day, which would ferry them to Toulon so that they could catch the train back to Paris, all three felt refreshed, revitalised and ready to showcase their talents as the capital's exhibition season resumed. With the Salon d'Automne approaching in November, there was much to do.

As soon as they were home, Maurice fell upon Montmartre's café culture like a starved man. He was often found at the Casse-Croûte or À la Belle Gabrielle. Père Gay, who was paternally fond of Maurice, allowed him to let a room with him and his wife for the inevitable nights when he became dangerously intoxicated and was unable to stagger home. Aware of his talent and his self-destructive tendencies, Père Gay and Marie Vizier conspired in

Maurice's interest, keeping him restrained on their premises and denying him wine until he produced a painting that could then be discreetly sold to amateur art enthusiasts for Maurice's profit. He also painted some decorative pieces for Marie's establishment, and on one occasion, became so taken with the idea of surprising her that he redecorated the walls of the toilet with a floral landscape. The landlady was furious and promptly ordered Maurice to restore the walls to their former glory.[40]

Gay also hung Maurice's canvases on his walls. One day, a dealer named Henri Delloue happened to drop in and spotted Maurice's work. Enchanted, Delloue showed Maurice's paintings to a fellow dealer and friend, M. Lepoutre, who was equally enthusiastic and took three canvases. Still, a handful of canvases hardly placed Maurice in a strong enough position to revolt against Libaude, who had again written to remind Maurice of his obligations towards him shortly before his Corsica trip. But that autumn, Maurice received interest from a dealer who made Libaude uneasy, and with good reason. M. Marseille could guarantee a 400 franc monthly retainer in exchange for a regular supply of canvases. Finally, Maurice did not have to pander to Libaude's whims. Thanks to Marie Vizier, César Gay, Delloue, Lepoutre and Marseille, Maurice's work was becoming better known and his reputation mounting.[41]

It was no surprise to Suzanne that her son's alcohol consumption increased in direct proportion to his success. And he would not be found a wife, no matter how hard Suzanne tried to nudge him towards many of the inoffensive young models she hired. But professionally, Maurice was prospering – and nobody was more surprised or bewildered by the interest than himself.

Suzanne's submission of *Little Girl at the Mirror* (1909) to the Salon d'Automne in November was clouded by Maurice's readmission to Dr Revertegat's care, a move rendered imperative by his declining health. While the rest of Montmartre toasted the arrival of 1914, Maurice remained in detoxification. Not a drop of alcohol passed his lips that New Year's Eve.[42]

Dr Revertegat was a skilled practitioner who rekindled the hope that Maurice might yet be cured. It was an optimistic backdrop as Suzanne put the finishing touches to the monumental *The Casting of the Nets* (1913) worked up from the studies she had produced in Corsica. She intended to submit the piece to the Salon des Indépendants that spring. Suzanne again took Utter as her model, depicting his nude figure in three different positions as he manhandled a net against a mountainous backdrop with sea and rocks at its base. As the three versions of Utter worked the prop, every muscle could be seen, each flexion detected, as Suzanne lingered over the dramatic bodily contortions and subtle spasms engendered by the task. The attempt to conceal Utter's genitalia with the rope of the net merely drew the viewer's eye more insistently to the censorable area. It was a magnificent and innovative work; links could be found with Gauguin, Henri Matisse – whose *The Dance* (1910) had caused a sensation at the 1910 Salon d'Automne – and Frédéric Bazille's *Fishermen with a Net* (1868), which was exhibited posthumously at the same show. Although the large-scale striving towards classicism gave a nod to art of the past, the vibrant colours and scrutiny of a male nude by a female painter were daringly contemporary.[43] Within the static, two-dimensional space of a flat canvas, Suzanne expanded time, evoked movement and celebrated the physical dexterity of the human form. The piece paid silent homage to Degas, who had been affected by the photographic studies of movement made by scientist Etienne-Jules Marey and photographer Eadweard Muybridge.[44] The press took notice, and Suzanne found herself singled out in *Lemouzi* and *La Presse*, and she was mentioned on the front page of *L'Aurore*.[45]

While Utter cast his lover's net across the walls of the Salon d'Automne, the battle with Libaude ground on. The dealer wrote to Utter that spring, flexing his muscles and stating that Maurice could be relied on neither to produce work consistently nor to be granted freedom from specialist supervision. In March, however, more trust was placed in Maurice, when the business tycoon-cum-art critic and collector André Level, from the Compagnie des Docks et Entrepôts de Marseilles, headed the first big sale of his work.[46] In 1904, Level had launched La Peau de l'Ours, a speculative business venture that invested in the work of modern and contemporary artists. His backing was auspicious and the sale proved an extraordinary success. But Libaude's threatening missives continued into the summer, when Maurice had to resign himself to another spell at Dr Revertegat's. A second sale organised at Delloue's initiative at the Hôtel Drouot in June was a bitter disappointment compared with the first. But one blessing came that July, when Libaude, due to family pressures, was finally forced to released Maurice from his 'contract'. The break, which in the past would have filled Suzanne with dread, was wonderfully liberating. They now had the reassurance that Maurice's work could sell, and well, and they no longer needed Libaude's assistance to achieve that.[47]

By the end of the summer, there was every reason to feel cheered. Suzanne's mood mirrored that of many Parisians still drunk on the heady narcotic of the Belle Époque. Rumblings of unease concerning international relations could still be heard; every now and then, someone mentioned the German threat, or the fight for control in Morocco, or the tension in the Balkans. But by and large, the reassuring rhythm of everyday life carried Parisian men and women along more or less contentedly.[48]

'Germany, who beat us and who abused her victory, has allied herself against us with Austria and Italy,' a 1912 school history textbook briefed the younger generation. 'But supported by solid friendships like that of Russia, our country has nothing to fear from its enemies, it has only justice and can look to the future with an un-furrowed brow.'[49]

It was an empty reassurance. On 3 August 1914, Germany declared war on France. The consequences were devastating. For Suzanne personally, the declaration of war was life-changing. In a few short weeks, her thinking altered, her priorities shifted and her very status as a woman changed forever.

CHAPTER 13

Till Death Do Us Part

Lou màù ve a chovàù, s'en torno d'ape.
(Evil arrives on a horse and returns on foot.)
OLD LIMOUSIN PROVERB[1]

'Calling all women of Paris,' *Le Figaro* entreated the day after war was declared. 'During the period on which we are now embarking, the solidarity of Parisian women can be put to good service.' By helping a neighbour in need, the paper specified, 'women of Paris will be accomplishing a sort of patriotic duty. We can count on them.'[2]

Suzanne was one of those to whom the rallying call was addressed. The city was not yet a battlefield, but overnight everything had changed.

When Suzanne stepped out into the street to walk the dogs in the morning, shops were closed, their shutters drawn, with merely a hastily erected sign by way of explication: Boss Away. Crudely pinned to buildings, tricolore flags flapped eerily in the breeze, while in the once-bustling streets, there reigned an unnatural quiet. Not an idle *flâneur* perused the boulevards; instead, men with solemn faces marched purposefully towards their chosen destination.[3]

By contrast, beneath the surface of the earth, the Metro stations – on the few lines still running – were packed with people;

people of all classes, from grand bourgeois to humble worker. Now, a common cause united them. Silken dresses brushed soiled rags, and nobody seemed to mind. Class had become irrelevant. Shared anxiety, that great social leveller, dissolved previously divisive social boundaries. And everywhere, on the trains, on the platforms and filling the Gare de l'Est, were uniformed men in their blue coats, blazing red kepis and trousers and creaking boots, preparing to leave their families and fight for France. National consciousness was stirring.[4]

All at once, artists with whom Suzanne had shared absinthe and ideas, men whose primary concern had always been their next great masterpiece, were setting art aside and enlisting to defend their country: Georges Braque, who had lived above Suzanne at the Impasse de Guelma, was posted to Sorgues; the dignified painter André Derain, a familiar face from the Lapin Agile, became a gunboat operator.[5] Only those prohibited by age (like Matisse), nationality (most notably the Spaniard Picasso) or those of weak constitution (such as Marcel Duchamp) remained. A willingness to fight became a measure of masculine virility. Suzanne could confidently predict that with his health devastated by alcoholism, Maurice would be rejected. But with sinking heart, she realised that her lover was among the most virile of France's young men. Soon after war was declared, André Utter enlisted as a soldier, along with his friend, Edmond Heuzé.

Faced with his departure, Suzanne agreed to a life-changing proposition: for the second time, she would become a wife. Her decision had a practical as well as a sentimental motivation; as Utter's wife, it would greatly facilitate his being granted leave to see her. She would also be entitled to the allowance the government paid to soldiers' spouses.

On 1 September 1914, just a few weeks before her 49th birthday, Suzanne made her way to the *mairie* of the 18th arrondissement to attend the utilitarian ceremony which would make her André Utter's wife. Wartime marriages were seldom extravagant shows of romantic decadence; Suzanne and Utter's wedding was designed primarily to gain public recognition of the union they already considered sacred. Neither Madeleine nor Maurice's names were recorded as witnesses, but Utter's parents attended and gave their consent. Some sense of the need to maintain a veneer of decorum remained; Utter gave his address as 76, Rue de Clignancourt, his family's home.[6]

When the couple stepped outside into the autumn sunlight after the ceremony, the sense of the shift they had undergone was overwhelming. They had accomplished a common rite of passage, but the mood in the capital was closer to that expected of a funeral than of a wedding. The Paris which met them was as a perishing flower whose petals were falling one by one. The day after the wedding the French government left the capital. And shortly after, so did André Utter.

Utter joined the 158th Infantry Division and at the end of September was posted to Belleville-sur-Saône in the Rhône department.[7]

Alone in Montmartre, Suzanne attempted to digest her new situation. On paper, she and Utter were more united than ever, yet the separation was an emotional torture on which neither party had reckoned. Every day, Suzanne woke to find an empty space in bed next to her, while each mealtime, the table had to be set with one less place. It was impossible to think of anything but Utter, his well-being and the agonising ache she felt for herself. And she could not escape the omnipresence of war. Her surroundings were a constant reminder that the notes of normal life were in discord.

Montmartre's café culture had wilted, with outdoor tables being hastily packed away. Many establishments had shut up shop entirely, while others now closed around 9pm. Even the lights in some *bureaux de tabac* had been extinguished. Where shops and markets remained open, all conversation between patrons and customers turned on the latest developments in the hostilities. Some shopkeepers were reluctant to let their products go at all, unless for exorbitant prices. Every now and then, a private car passed displaying a notice: 'Available to military personnel needing to transport luggage'.[8] Not even the Lapin Agile was immune to the influence of war; it now had a makeshift soup kitchen running alongside the cabaret, to provide affordable meals for abandoned wives and children.[9]

Tales of extraordinary courage filtered back to Paris from the front, rekindling optimism and buoying national spirit. The account of taxis ferrying soldiers to the front to reinforce the troops during the first battle of the Marne in early September was proudly repeated in the capital. In reality, the taxis played a comparatively minor role in France's victory at the Marne, only carrying 4,000 men to a base of secondary importance.[10] But the story was sufficiently stirring to be quickly woven into the romantic tapestry of the war. Such episodes were reaffirming, but they could scarcely alleviate Suzanne's longing for her husband and the gnawing anxiety that at any moment, she might receive word that he had been hurt.

Suzanne tried to work. That year, she produced several studies of nudes, and the psychologically challenging *The Dressmaker* (1914). The piece showed a well-to-do but unsmiling little girl in a sombre dress with lace collar standing in an interior while being fitted for a dress by the eponymous dressmaker. As the dressmaker busied herself with her task, the little girl was shown by a window, open, tantalisingly, just a crack and giving on to a colourful world beyond the interior's restricted confines. Only the blue bow and her vibrant red hair hinted at a natural ebullience being repressed. Suzanne's young girl stared straight out of the canvas at the viewer, implicating them in the scenario. The painting flirted with questions of freedom and confinement, desire and duty, claustrophobia and care, leaving them frustratingly unresolved.

Eventually, Suzanne decided that the separation from Utter had become so unbearable, and sales of her paintings in Paris so poor, that she risked nothing by going to be near him.[11] That way, she could at least be close by whenever he was granted a break from fighting. Imploring César Gay to watch over Maurice (whose unpredictable behaviour and drinking binges were now too much for the elderly Madeleine to deal with alone), Suzanne travelled to Belleville. The sense of relief was overwhelming and she even found some casual agricultural work to supplement her income while she was there.[12]

Meanwhile, back in Paris, deprived of the mother he loved and unfit to fight, Maurice sank into a deep depression. He felt helpless, a social outcast. Lodging at César Gay's, he channelled his melancholy musings into a muddled and digressive autobiography. Otherwise, he spent his time drinking and painting. In view of her own spiritual misgivings, Suzanne had never attempted to steer Maurice on to a religious path. However, in recent times, he had developed something of an obsession for the figure of Joan of Arc. He was consequently outraged when he learned of the destruction of Reims Cathedral, which he considered to be an 'admirable edifice, one of the most magnificent monuments of Gothic architecture in France and in the world'.[13] Reims had been the site of 25 coronations of French kings, including that of Charles VII, where Joan of Arc, with her 'pure, virtuous, candid and magnanimous heroic soul', was present, having first liberated the Cathedral.[14] At the outbreak of war, the edifice had served as a hospital and had then caught fire after shelling. Maurice, who was intensely patriotic, felt utterly powerless. Unlike other men, he could not fight back in response. And so he painted. He pictured the burning structure in a breathtaking outpouring of passion. He also painted scenes of the devastated villages around the Marne.

But ultimately, Maurice's art could not subdue his torment, nor rid him of the constant sense of being hunted. César Gay was unable to restrain him. Maurice was forever breaking out of his room when the alcohol he needed was denied, tearing down to the nearest bar, gasping for drink. On at least one occasion, Mme Gay was horrified to find that, in the absence of a more palatable beverage, her eau de Cologne had been greedily guzzled.[15]

The war had not been under way many months when, on one of his drunken breakouts in early December, Maurice attacked a woman in the street and vandalised a fire alarm. He was swiftly escorted into police custody, from where he penned a remorseful letter to Suzanne:

> I beg your forgiveness for the latest pain I am going to cause you, it is always that damned alcohol, that pernicious demon and maker of madness [...] I bitterly regret the miserable consequences of my execrable mistake, and I beg you once again to forgive me; please do, because, you are good and you have always taught me good.[16]

Suzanne had to return so as to plead with the authorities to release her son on the understanding that he would again receive professional help for his alcoholism.

All personal and circumstantial factors seemed to have conspired against Suzanne progressing in her career as an artist. The art scene in Paris had fallen silent. There was some talk of a new arrival in the capital: an Italian named Giorgio de Chirico, who had turned heads at the Salon des Indépendants in 1913 with his haunting vistas of buildings and architecture, with their crisp perspective and dreamlike ethereality.[17] But otherwise, the art schools felt abandoned and none of the big exhibitions were running.

Urgently needing to sell some paintings, in 1915, Suzanne implored Berthe Weill to mount an exhibition of her and Utter's work. Weill, now a friend and always empathetic towards struggling talent, was only too delighted. But sales from the show were disappointing. Perhaps, Weill reasoned, the Parisian public found avant-garde daring like Suzanne's just too much to stomach when it came from a woman.[18]

But Suzanne received some more promising boosts to her career that year. One came in the form of an important commission.

Writer, art critic and collector Gustave Coquiot was portly, with a double chin, flabby jowls, and eyes which were narrow and suspicious. Crucially for Suzanne, he wielded considerable influence in the art world.[19]

Just one day younger than Suzanne, but appearing several years her senior, Coquiot was a sharp and merciless critic. He had written at length about Maurice in his book *Cubistes, Futuristes, Passéistes* in 1914 (a volume Suzanne was to proudly include in a still life painted in 1915). Coquiot greatly admired both Maurice's and Suzanne's work. He had lately started purchasing artwork and had a nose for a potentially lucrative style of painting. Added to which, he was fascinated by female artists – the mother and son immediately caught Coquiot's attention. Before long, Suzanne and Maurice found themselves invited to Coquiot's and his wife Mauricia's home, which positively dripped with artwork. There they were wined and dined like royalty, and offered the finest port, liqueur and cigars.[20] It was a relief when, in the year of that disheartening exhibition at Berthe Weill's, Coquiot commissioned Suzanne to paint a portrait of himself and of his wife.

Suzanne treated the husband and wife as she did all her subjects: with brutal honesty.

Full-figured and formidable, Mauricia was shown in a revealing dress, her head tilted upwards dramatically, accentuating her impressive cleavage. With exotic flowers on one side and a richly patterned curtain on the other, the whole piece exuded theatricality and hinted at the preponderant role of artifice. For the husband's portrait, Suzanne focused in on the critic's head and neck as he looked out of the canvas to his right. She used dramatic tonal variation to bring out the relief of his facial features and to distil the essence of the larger-than-life character which had become Coquiot's trademark.

Protective of her friend and wise to the devious ways of collectors, Berthe Weill treated Coquiot with suspicion.[21] To her mind, the success of a man like Coquiot in the art world was an anomaly which could only be attributed to the distorting effect of war.[22] When Coquiot's demands did eventually strike Suzanne as unreasonable and a dispute erupted, Berthe Weill was one of the first to know. Few could deny Coquiot's cunning; but the association saved Suzanne that year and gave cause for optimism regarding the future.

However, as Suzanne's professional star was being realigned on its path to greatness, Maurice's mood continued to darken. In the first half of the year, the army called him up with the intention of reviewing his physical suitability to fight.[23] But Maurice was soon agreed quite incapable of defending himself, let alone his country. The rejection came as a cruel blow. It did nothing to lift him from his depression.

Then just a few weeks later, something unexpected turned Suzanne's and Maurice's worlds upside down, making all other preoccupations seem trivial: on 10 June 1915, Madeleine, whose health had been faltering for some time, passed away at home in the Rue Cortot.[24]

All at once, the stabilising constant in both Suzanne's and Maurice's lives, the final link to their Limousin roots, had gone. As age had gradually worn down Madeleine's resistance to the family's unconventional life, both the mother and son had come to take her presence for granted. The sounds of the old woman shuffling about the apartment muttering, of the clattering of pots and pans as she prepared her regional dishes, the soothing croon of traditional Limousin songs in her local dialect, and the long, repetitive country tales recounted by the hearthside – all those features which had felt such an intrinsic part of their everyday existence that at times they became positively irritating, suddenly seemed so precious that Suzanne and Maurice would have traded anything to have them back in an instant.

Both Suzanne and Maurice had spent all their lives with Madeleine. Her death left a gaping hole, the full magnitude of which Suzanne only realised at the funeral she arranged for her mother.

'I loved her so!' Suzanne sobbed afterwards. 'I knew how much I loved her on the day that, having made her a grave, I wanted to be there for the inhumation of what was left of her poor remains. I felt an unspeakable pain, something terrible that I could not even describe to you, because I could not see her hands, the remains of those dear little hands. Her little hands, where were they?'[25]

Suzanne was still mourning the loss of her mother when the following month, she learned that she had been awarded a subsidy from the Conseil Municipal de Paris, intended as 'encouragement' to artists in the extenuating times of war. It was at once a professional accolade and a practical lifeline. But it scarcely alleviated the melancholy permeating her personal life.[26]

It was consequently with delight that Suzanne received word that Utter would be granted leave for Christmas. But her elation at their first embrace as he stepped through the doorway of the apartment was short-lived; just after Christmas, Maurice went out on one of his wildest, most terrifying drunken episodes yet. The day after his 32nd birthday, Maurice was admitted to an asylum. On the visit he should have spent with his wife, André Utter instead found himself escorting his older stepson to a psychiatric unit.

The year 1916 started on a bleak note. In February, the biggest battle the French had yet fought commenced at Verdun. Soon, word was trickling back to Paris of horrific injuries, excruciating deaths, of an atrocious battle which could only ever be purely defensive. But it was hard to know how many of the rumours to believe; rigorous press censorship ensured that the truth remained an elusive concept.[27]

What was more certain was the degree of hardship Parisians were enduring on a daily basis. Though the citizens of Paris did not suffer as keenly as the inhabitants of some invaded regions, the cost of living had still risen by 20 per cent since the start of the war.[28] Meat and coal had become unaffordable to most. Sugar was virtually unattainable.[29] And as more and more sons, brothers and husbands were reported missing, or maimed, or worse, it was gradually dawning on Parisians that the hostilities might not be the swift precursor to the triumphant French glory so many had predicted.

In July, the Battle of the Somme tested the Allies' stamina still further. With heavy hearts, Parisians learned of the mass slaughter on an unprecedented scale of their English comrades. The reports provided a sobering backdrop to the gruelling reality of civilian life during the war.

Despite Utter's absence, Maurice's internment in Villejuif (the asylum for patients with pronounced psychiatric difficulties) and the still-recent loss of her mother, Suzanne continued to work. Under the circumstances, it was all she could do; total absorption was her greatest coping strategy. By focusing intensely on what was in front of her, she was able, if only for a short while, to take the edge off her pain.

That year, Suzanne produced several nudes, and still lifes with richly coloured flowers and landscapes. She drew pairs of dancers, girls trying on clothes, the Sacré-Coeur as seen from her window in the Rue Cortot; all unremarkable activities, frivolous even, or scenes she saw on a daily basis – all manageable in their mundanity.

To fill the void left by her disbanding family, Suzanne threw herself into her social life; she had spent enough time around Toulouse-Lautrec in days gone by for something of his modus vivendi to rub off. Stories of her increasingly outrageous behaviour began to circulate. She was reported to have been seen wearing a coat adorned with carrots and carrying a bouquet of lettuce leaves trimmed with snails.[30] Then she was spotted out with a menagerie of animals including a goat.[31] Neighbours complained of raucous parties being thrown at the Rue Cortot at all hours, with guests arriving with armfuls of food and wine, and a firm resolve to have fun. At 50, Suzanne had established herself as one of Montmartre's timeless eccentrics.

The social noise dulled the echo of solitude. But there were practical complications of living alone that simply could not be drowned out.

With her mother gone, Suzanne now had more to do to stay on top of the housework in addition to tending to her career. She was grateful when, from time to time, one of her young models named Gabby was willing to help out. Gabby was a plump and capable blonde, with an aquiline nose, an easy disposition and a kindly heart. As Suzanne came to know her better, it occurred to her that Gabby possessed all the qualities she would hope to find in a daughter-in-law should Maurice be persuaded to take a wife.

By the time Maurice was released in November, Suzanne had formulated what she considered to be an ingenious plan. By the end of the month, a wedding date had been set and Suzanne had started issuing invitations. Still to reacclimatise to life outside the clinic, where he had shared living quarters with inmates so deranged that they even ate his paints, Maurice seemed accepting of his mother's notion. However, Gabby proved more level-headed. The implications of a marriage to Maurice soon struck her and she pulled out of the union. If disappointed, Suzanne could hardly have been surprised. Nor could she stay cross with Gabby for long; her son was far from ideal husband material. There was not sufficient animosity for Gabby to stop modelling for Suzanne.[32]

In December, the bloody battle of Verdun finally concluded, before France was gripped by one of the coldest winters in living memory. On 24 January 1917, *Le Figaro* reported that the temperature had plummeted, with lows of −7° recorded in Dunkirk.[33] For the soldiers, the journalist sympathised, 'the terrible cold adds a mortal peril to those already being faced'.[34] The paper tried to remain optimistic; the sky was clear, after all, and civilians and soldiers would far rather 'the coldest of temperatures than the fog, rain and mud' they had been forced to endure for the last two months. But nobody could ignore the sharp edge the weather gave to already testing circumstances. With food and fuel in short supply, Parisians hunkered down with their mobilised loved ones in mind and survival their sole objective. Suzanne, however much she might be suffering, could not steer her thoughts from how much worse this bitter winter must be for Utter. She knew her friend the art critic Adolphe Tabarant to be both well-connected and persuasive. She wrote to him in February 1917, by which time the temperature had dropped still further, with many parts of France experiencing conditions of −20° or less.[35] Suzanne begged Tabarant to see if he could call in a favour or two to get Utter moved to where the environment was more humane.[36]

Suzanne had learned through Tabarant that the army were drafting in artists to paint camouflage sheets intended to be thrown over ship decks, tanks and aircraft to conceal them from enemy view. With Utter's proficiency as a painter, he would surely be an ideal candidate for such a post. But despite repeated appeals to

Tabarant (which she peppered with pleasantries in the form of updates on her own work), Suzanne seemed unable to sway fate in her husband's favour.[37]

Beyond a respite from the cold, the spring brought little to restore morale. The catastrophic offensive ordered by General Nivelle at the Chemin des Dames in the Aisne saw thousands of men meet premature deaths. Broken and weary, desertion and revolt were the soldiers' last resort. It was impossible for Suzanne to know at any given hour where Utter was, what he was doing, whether he was even now risking his life fighting the enemy, or if he was endangering himself becoming involved in the mutinies sweeping through the divisions. The uncertainty was torturous.[38]

Exhibiting work alongside Utter and Maurice at Berthe Weill's gallery that spring at least gave Suzanne a focus, and involvement in a group exhibition at the Galerie Bernheim-Jeune early in May gave a continued distraction with which to try and absorb herself.[39] The flourishing Galerie Bernheim-Jeune had been established in Paris in 1863 and had helped promote the Impressionists in 1874. Now, brothers Josse and Gaston Bernheim-Jeune had forged the gallery a prestigious reputation as an acclaimed forum of avant-garde art.[40] It was a valuable contact for Suzanne. 'In times of war,' *Le Carnet de la Semaine* noted, 'the support of the Rue Richepanse [the gallery's address] is invaluable to young artists.'[41] The author went on to praise Suzanne's 'crisp drawing', while in *Le Carnet des Artistes*, she was singled out, named and, significantly, not bracketed together with what the reporter dismissed as a 'whole batch of women's work'.[42]

But then just as Suzanne's career was gathering momentum, on 17 June she received some sickening news. It was the message she had most been dreading: André Utter had been shot.

Suzanne learned how her husband had received a bullet wound to his chest, so close to his heart that it was decided that it would be too dangerous to attempt to remove it. He would have to recover with it still in place.

Frantic, Suzanne immediately boarded a train to Meyzieu near Lyon, so that she could go to Utter at the military hospital to which he had been rushed.

As she sat anxiously by her husband's bedside, Suzanne consoled herself that César Gay would watch out for Maurice in her absence. The days passed, and gradually, to her relief, Utter began to recover. Soon, the convalescent was considered well enough for the couple to be able to go out and explore the surrounding countryside. Their shared discovery of the cherished homeland of Beaujolais wine growers reaffirmed their love for each other. Suzanne even found herself able to paint while she was there. Meanwhile, she wrote regularly to Maurice, keeping him informed and urging him not to drink.[43] 'André Utter is a brave man and I envy him,' Maurice admitted sorrowfully in a reply penned on 1 August 1917. 'Your place is in the Louvre; mine is in an asylum.'[44]

Suzanne returned to Paris briefly with Utter at the end of the summer, visiting Berthe Weill to negotiate the sale of some work while they were away from the capital.[45] Even when art did sell, it was seldom reaching high prices during the war. Finances were stretched, so much so that André Utter even attempted to resume contact with Maurice's roguish dealer, Louis Libaude.[46] Suzanne needed all the sales she could generate, for she planned to stay on in Belleville with Utter a little longer. The medical care was good and she found herself entranced by the region.

Once the couple had returned to Belleville, Suzanne continued her correspondence with Maurice, she always begging him to have pride and not to drink (at least not so much), Maurice insisting himself unworthy of her love and begging forgiveness for his behaviour. He claimed to have come to despise Montmartre and in many of his former friends he now saw only enemies.

But Maurice's tragic existence was not the only arm of suffering to reach out to Suzanne from Paris. On 28 September 1917, the attention of *Le Figaro*'s readers was arrested by one dramatic leading article on the front page:

M. Edgard [*sic*] Degas has just died. He enjoyed huge renown in the art world, and he leaves to posterity an oeuvre which justifies this success.[47]

An announcement made in two short sentences pulled the last stabilising support from under Suzanne.

The article went on to discuss Degas's work and success, and mention was made of his mordant wit. The author was particularly amused by Degas's response when a younger artist spoke enthusiastically about wanting to 'arrive': 'In my day, Sir, one did not "arrive".'

The piece concluded with recognition of Degas's unshakeable loyalty to a few, select friends. It mentioned Bartholomé, but not Suzanne. However, she did not need a journalist's acknowledgement to know that she was included in the group. Degas was her mentor, her tutor and her friend. But he was more than that: more brutally honest than a friend, more emotionally invested than a tutor, more patiently redressing than a father. Without Degas, Suzanne knew she would not be where she was, nor have achieved all she had. That so much energy, such life, talent and intellect could just suddenly disappear, was unfathomable.

As Degas was lowered into his final resting place at the Cimetière de Montmartre, the last of Suzanne's respected parental figures was lost to her forever.[48]

Whenever life became more turbulent than usual, Suzanne was inclined to self-reflect. To her, that meant self-exploration in paint. The events of 1917 prompted her to paint herself in a head and shoulder portrait, bare-breasted but desexualised, her frame and bone structure firm and well-defined, her features still exquisitely beautiful and radiating youth. For all the trauma she had experienced, Suzanne's self-portrait appeared blissfully serene. It was as though she had found an inner strength on which to draw, a tenacity which could withstand the crumbling world around her. The woman depicted was one who had made peace with herself and who now knew just what – and who – was important to her.

The New Year 1918 unfolded and Suzanne's upset was eased somewhat by spending as much time as possible in the countryside with her husband. In her absence, Maurice was becoming desperate. Added to which, January was again bitterly cold, with the northeastern town of Remiremont in the Vosges department recording a low of −23° on New Year's Day.[49] Food was in short supply and the dreadful hum of German bombers overhead had become a familiar feature of everyday life. Parisians were living in constant fear, their exhausted bodies fuelled only by adrenaline.

For Maurice, life had become too much. It was all he could do to write to the dealer Henri Delloue, begging for help. He attempted to channel his thoughts into a coherent letter:

> I am in an unhealthy nervous state, the victim of physical, intellectual and moral depression, the most alarming affliction. I absolutely must be cared for. I cannot really work. I have written to the woman who knows me best, asking her to write to you and explain the state of degeneration in which I find myself. I cannot speak highly enough of your goodness, but I must be treated in a clinic. That is the rigour required.[50]

At the time, Delloue had ample concerns of his own. He had two sons on the front and had just been mobilised himself. But Maurice's plea was heartbreaking. He agreed to help.

On 1 March 1918, Maurice was admitted to a clinic in Aulnay-sous-Bois in the department of Seine-Saint-Denis, north-east of Paris, to be treated by a Dr Vicq. His internment came just in time: on 23 March, the Germans unleashed Big Bertha on the capital.

The 420mm Big Bertha mortars had been developed in secret. They could shoot out a shell of more than a ton in weight and at a range of over 12km. So huge was this weapon that it would have taken 36 horses to move it. It wreaked devastation wherever it was aimed, giving Parisians a bitter taste of life on the front line. The end of Paris suddenly seemed a very real possibility.[51]

Elsewhere the war ground on. Every day, the papers reported more French losses at the front. In May, growing resentment triggered strikes across France.

However, in July, the Allies' victory at the second Battle of the Marne hinted that the tide might be turning. The people of France started to hope again. Still, for Suzanne, life remained frustratingly unsettled. All she wanted was to be peacefully back at home with Utter in the Rue Cortot. To add to her pains, at the end of August, Maurice escaped from the clinic and fled to César Gay's.[52] By the time an epidemic of Spanish flu swept through France in October, claiming an average of 350 Parisian lives a day, Suzanne, along with the rest of the French population, was at breaking point.[53]

On 11 November 1918, Parisians awoke to find the sky overcast, and there was a chill to the air. Citizens were poised in anticipation. For the last few days, word had it that the long-awaited announcement was imminent. But after four years of hostilities, people scarcely dared believe it was true. Now, a crowd such as had never been seen had gathered expectantly on the streets of Paris. Then, at 11am, something miraculous happened: the cannon of peace fired its first shot. All through the city, church bells began to chime and, slowly, the sun ventured out from behind the clouds. The war was over.[54]

Parisians exploded in a veritable frenzy. Citizens filled the streets, where impromptu singing and dancing began. *La Marseillaise* was sung out with gusto, *Madelon* was joyously rendered, while hastily formed bands struck up military marches. Houses, cars, windows – all were festooned in flags and bunting. Strangers embraced, women cried tears of joy and children waved tricolore flags with delight and indefatigable arms. Girls threw their arms around soldiers' necks and kissed them as they passed, taxis decked in flags rolled along with men still muddy from the trenches clinging to them, waving tricolores or swigging bottles of beer. Horns, drums and applause rang out. The whole of Paris buzzed feverishly with elation – like a school class surprised by a recess bell they had not been expecting, *Le Figaro* remarked.[55]

Suzanne too was ecstatic. Afterwards, people distinctly recalled having seen her among the throng in the Place du Tertre, singing, cheering and wearing nothing but a wrap of tricolore flags to hide her modesty.[56]

Before the end of the year, Suzanne could behold the cause of her celebration. She was alerted by whoops of delight from giggling girls as one of the finest-looking young soldiers strode into Montmartre: André Utter was back.[57]

And after several years away, Utter had returned to Paris determined. He had helped his country win the war. Now, he was going to ensure that the Unholy Trinity became the most successful artists in post-war Paris – and he was adamant that this time, nothing would stand in their way.

CHAPTER 14

What Money Can Buy

Gnio pà de feito sei lendemo.
(Every party has a morning after.)
OLD LIMOUSIN PROVERB[1]

ost-war France was a nation conflicted. On the one hand,
citizens had to assimilate the scale of devastation left by
the war and ponder the monumental task of reconstruction.
One point three million soldiers had lost their lives, 3 million had
been disabled and 200,000 civilians had died in the fighting.[2] Many
buildings were ruins, rotting corpses and shelling had rendered
much agricultural land unusable, while countless railways, roads
and bridges had been entirely destroyed.[3] When the value of the
franc plummeted, taxes could only go up. But at the same time,
the lingering aftertaste of winner's glory gave rise to an overriding
spirit of optimism. France basked in the euphoric glow of its long-
awaited freedom. Life had proved precarious – now, people were
determined to enjoy it while they could.

Where leisure and entertainment were concerned, escapism was
the order of the day. The arrival of African-American soldiers had
kindled a taste for the exotic.[4] These foreign guests introduced
Paris to jazz, whose lively rhythms and infectious melodies set
battle-scarred toes tapping. Jazz seemed the perfect antidote to

post-war malaise. People felt alive again, and an influx of Americans now acted as the perfect ambassadors for the music that was fast becoming a national phenomenon. Tempted to Paris by the promise of sexual liberation, gastronomic excess and cultural riches, fast-talking Yankees spilled out on to Montmartre's café terraces.[5] America was here to stay and its influence was far-reaching. Meanwhile, though many Frenchmen still clung to the notion of separate spheres, in defiance of traditional notions of femininity women now sported bobbed haircuts, short skirts and cloche hats, while flat chests were all the rage.[6] In Paris's bars and cabarets, carefree fun was clients' raison d'être. At last, anything seemed possible and aspiration led the way.

Before long, the art world had been swept up in the prevailing mood of good feeling and plenitude. Berthe Weill recorded heavy debts incurred during the hostilities. But soon, her diaries were filling up with dazzling new exhibitions which, while not always profitable in terms of sales, were nevertheless more numerous and diverse than they had been in years.[7] Paintings were a fashionable commodity once more. And while the fresh tranche of nouveaux riches were not sufficient to reconfigure France's social structure, their nascence did make a notable impact on the art world.[8] Foreigners proved particularly hungry for French art. It was just the aesthetic resurrection André Utter had been banking on.

The year 1919 was wonderfully productive for Suzanne. Utter's return and his keen encouragement of her work saw her creativity flourish. She bloomed in her husband's light. The result was an unprecedented outpouring of paintings. She produced considered still lifes with abundant dishes of fruit, loving studies of her cat Raminou, landscapes, and in keeping with the fashion for all things black, a series of paintings of a shapely mulatto woman, in which her brush seemed to relish the undulating curves of the model's silky skin. People on the Butte whispered that Suzanne's sultry

André Utter and Suzanne Valadon
at her easel in the studio, c. 1919.
Collection Société le Vieux Montmartre/Musée de Montmartre

temptress was sleeping with Maurice.[9] But Maurice's true passion lay elsewhere.

That year, Suzanne pictured him at his easel, brush in hand, a smart hat posed on his head.[10] Recognising him as a master of his craft showed extraordinary generosity on Suzanne's part. For all her dedication, Suzanne Valadon could not match the success of Maurice Utrillo. His paintings of *le vieux Paris*, apparently so effortlessly produced, were just the kind of visual reassurance the post-war public craved. But Maurice was unswayed by celebrity and, so long as there was money for drink, relaxed about the price his work commanded. Painting was as natural to him as eating and breathing; he did not consider his skill made him particularly special. What concerned him were the demands and expectations his career imposed. People worried him. He did not possess the social skills to woo and work them like Utter did. The inevitable public-relations engagements inflicted on him by Utter's management were deeply disturbing.

Suzanne could feel her son's tension. Her portrait showed him working, though boxed in by the sharp diagonal of his easel, oppressed by the weight of his own hat. He appeared confined, his facial expression troubled. As an artist, Suzanne saw success; as a mother, she sensed a cornered little boy in need of protection.

Utter was acutely sensitive to Maurice's commercial potential, but Suzanne's portfolio was more problematic. Her work was appreciated by fellow artists, less so by the public. Added to which, she often grew impatient when people requested a meeting, and her responses frequently left her viewers unsatisfied. Maurice was different. Whether he liked his stepson's style or not, Utter could not fail to see that in the post-war art world, Maurice Utrillo represented a goldmine – 'the best business prospect this century', the stepfather gloated.[11] Presented with such desirable merchandise, Utter proved himself a first-rate salesman. At the end of 1918, a buyer could expect to pay 30 francs for a Utrillo landscape; at a sale held at Durand-Ruel's on 24 February 1919, the artist's *La Maison Rose, rue de l'Abreuvoir* sold for 1,000 francs.[12]

But not even Utter could put a gloss on the nail-biting alcohol-induced plummets that ran parallel to Maurice's staggering artistic success. In July that year, Maurice again had to be admitted to an asylum, treatment for which Suzanne was grateful to secure funding through an agreement made with Amedeo Modigliani's Polish dealer, Leopold Zborowski.[13]

Having arrived in Paris as a literary student, 'Zbo' had subsequently sold books and prints on the banks of the Seine before turning his hand to art dealership. The Pole was a passionate supporter of modern unknowns, at once sensitive to Maurice's talent and sympathetic to his torment. He was the ideal benefactor and, with contributions from two other dealers, agreed to meet the costs of Maurice's treatment in return for instalments of canvases.[14]

The contact with Zbo was valuable in other ways, too. That August, Zbo conveyed a selection of French artwork to London to appear in the Mansard Gallery at Heals, and Suzanne and Maurice were among the exhibitors.[15]

Now, Suzanne's career was truly flourishing. She submitted *Black Venus* (1919) to the Salon d'Automne that year, where the work attracted notice and gained her a front page mention in *Comoedia*.[16] Then in November, she participated in a two-week long exhibition of drawings entitled *Noir et Blanc* at Berthe Weill's gallery: 'a great success,' Weill triumphed afterwards.[17]

But once again, Suzanne's glory was overshadowed that autumn when Maurice broke out of his asylum and headed straight to find Modigliani, who he and Suzanne had come to know through Utter, in Montparnasse. Delighted to reconnect, the companions set out on an impromptu jolly. The men meandered along to a favourite Italian restaurant of Modi's nearby, where the artist coaxed the landlady into supplying them with food and ample quantities of drink. Soon intoxicated, the pair weaved their way back to Modi's studio, with Maurice still wearing the slippers he had had on when he escaped.[18]

There, with a little prompting, Maurice painted two street scenes off-the-cuff, and Modi immediately bundled them up and carried them over to Zbo, who paid handsomely for the pair. With more cash in hand, the men continued their binge. When they could drink no more, they staggered back to Modi's studio, falling through the door, whereupon the artist's mistress, Jeanne Hébuterne, was obliged to put them to bed.

By the time Modi awoke the next day, his guest had gone – and so had his trousers. Maurice finally returned, minus the trousers – which he had pawned – but proudly clutching several bottles of wine, bought with the proceeds. The binge resumed. At last, Zbo discovered their antics, promptly gained back the trousers, and returned Modi to bed and Maurice to his mother. A few days later, a solemn Suzanne escorted Maurice back to the asylum. As fate would have it, the two friends never saw each other again.

To everyone's relief, Maurice's repeated spells in sanatoriums did not seem to dent his earning potential. That December, the dealer Lepoutre organised an exhibition at his gallery in the Rue La Boétie. Prefaced by a laudatory catalogue, the show was visited by flocks of enthusiastic viewers. The prices demanded were high and, for the family, the interest was thrilling.[19]

But for Suzanne, her son's first major exhibition coincided with another dramatic revelation. Just two days before Maurice's grand opening, national papers reported a death – that of Pierre-Auguste Renoir.

The news came as an unexpected yet decisive rupture with a past now so distant. Renoir had finished his days in Cagnes-sur-Mer in the South of France, having spent more than twenty years plagued by rheumatoid arthritis. To the end a dedicated practitioner of his craft, he had refused to succumb to his condition, and attempted to paint right into the latter stages of his illness, even when it meant seeking assistance to place his brush in his hand. Renoir was one of the last surviving significant artists for whom Suzanne had posed. With his passing, life ceased defining her as a painter's model; now, she was an artist.[20]

At the end of January, an even more horrific blow was delivered: at just 35 years old, Modigliani lost his life to tubercular meningitis. Devastated, his now-pregnant mistress Jeanne threw herself and her unborn child to their deaths from an upstairs window in her parents' apartment. Modi was a year younger than Maurice. He had still been visiting Suzanne, sometimes spending the night at the Rue Cortot, just weeks before. The news was apt to send shivers down the spine. Many artists considered the young Modi a genius. It was a tragic loss.[21]

Modi had looked up to Suzanne as a mother figure. Indeed, to many younger artists, she was something of a veteran. She had earned her stripes in the art world; the same month as Modi's death, it was announced that she had been elected on to the committee of members of the Salon d'Automne.[22] Her years of experience had fostered profound respect. But with those advancing years, Suzanne was also acutely aware of the more far-reaching changes taking place, of which Modi's death was merely symptomatic.

The transformation of her local area since the war was particularly perplexing. For the most part, the twisted streets she had scampered through as a child were still the same; it was just that now, pedestrians had to check for motor cars rumbling past before they crossed the street. The reasonably priced cafés where Suzanne and Miguel had sat with a single drink for an entire evening had grown wise to the remunerative potential of their quaintness. Prices soared, making them virtually unaffordable to all but tourists. Gradually, locals were seen out less and less.

In the eyes of long-serving Montmartrois, the cost of progress was too steep. This was the fatherland they knew and loved, part of their souls. Fired by nostalgia, Frédé from the Lapin Agile and a handful of other disgruntled Montmartre residents formed the Antigrattecielistes (anti-skyscraper party), a group concerned with local politics. The party's main political agenda encompassed the prevention of skyscrapers and the establishment of a Free Commune of Montmartre to run alongside the official town council; more outlandish proposals included placing the Butte on a turntable so that all sides would at some point face the sun, insisting that every window box be planted with vines and introducing a nine-month calendar so that winter would be eradicated. The party struck just the right balance between political gravity and jocular good cheer for Suzanne to grow impassioned. She was also popular, and soon found herself running as one of a small number of women candidates.[23]

Among the group's opponents were the Dadaists, who presented fierce competition. But the Antigrattecielistes were thrilled when votes were cast in April 1920 and they won. The Montmartrois were proud of their independence and their heritage, and the area was recast as a free town with its own administrative structure. The disadvantaged (particularly artists and children) were the group's chief charitable causes. The cartoonist Jules Dépaquit became the mayor and other activists included the artist Francisque Poulbot. With such an eccentric and bohemian administration, fundraisers invariably took on an absurd twist, including a mock bullfight and a race contested by the area's songwriters, women and children, while the work of artist friends was given keen support.[24]

The movement was just another of the idiosyncrasies that fuelled Suzanne's love of Montmartre. It was an amusing diversion with a laudable political incentive, and Suzanne always welcomed an opportunity to socialise. But she could not allow political activity to divert her from her career.

While the Antigrattecielistes were safeguarding Montmartre's heritage, Suzanne's work was on display at the Salon des Indépendants. She had decided to submit the canvas that encapsulated the start of her relationship with Utter, *Adam and Eve* (1909). 'A simple format,' reported *Floréal*; 'a solid canvas,' added *Le Populaire de Paris*, while *La Gerbe* esteemed it 'full of qualities', and for the *Chronique des arts*, Suzanne's 'confident drawing and charmless ugliness' reflected Degas's influence.[25] However, by the time the souvenir of the couple's love affair was revealed to the public, Suzanne had concealed Utter's genitalia with vine leaves. The threshold of sin had long been traversed; left only were the resultant anxieties.

As Suzanne reached her mid-50s, the age gap between herself and her lover impressed itself. Utter did not look out of place laughing and drinking among the new wave of fashionable young patrons populating Montmartre's bars and cafés. But in the same context, to strangers, Suzanne now appeared little more than an eccentric old bohemian.

Still, her everyday material existence and professional life were undeniably good. Living conditions were more comfortable than she could ever have dreamed possible when she left Paul Mousis, and food was never lacking. In the 1920s, she could afford an English housekeeper, Lily Walton, whose presence gave a flourish of refinement whenever there was a party to host.[26] Suzanne was also painting prodigiously and had her first sale at the prestigious Hôtel Drouot in 1920, as well as participating in the *Exposition de la jeune peinture française* at the Galerie Manzy Joyant.[27] Added to which, she boasted an enormous number of friends and acquaintances, many of whom subsequently became patrons. And as always, no matter how close a companion her sitter might be, Suzanne produced honest, unbiased portraits which penetrated to the darkest recesses of her subject's very soul. 'Her great merit,' Berthe Weill explained, 'is that she never makes a single concession, despite everything. A great artist!'[28]

But if busying herself helped numb the insecurities regarding her relationship and age, Maurice's ongoing fracases with the authorities were less easily ignored.

In April 1920, Suzanne was alerted that Maurice, who was currently undergoing another spell in an asylum, had become aggressive and violent when a jailer took two of his paintings. He was consequently locked in a cell. Rallying the most influential of her friends, Suzanne quickly launched a campaign for his release. '[My son] may be ill,' Suzanne conceded when she wrote to the Police Commissioner, 'but he has never been dangerous, either towards himself, or towards anyone else. This is why I beg you to return my son to me. I will care for him myself, and if needs be, place him in a private psychiatric clinic in the countryside.'[29]

Before her letter could yield results, Maurice had attempted to slash his wrists.

Suzanne secured a sponsor for Maurice's rehabilitation in the Picpus asylum that summer in the form of engineer and inventor Léon Levavasseur, who had developed aeroplane engines and who happened to be a generous art enthusiast.[30] Once again, finished canvases were offered as repayment. However, after some months, and following another attempted escape on Maurice's part, it was concluded that he was still unfit to be granted unmitigated freedom. As a transitional measure, the asylum agreed to release a strapping male nurse named Pierre to watch over Maurice at home.[31] The patient responded well to this arrangement. Pierre's presence gave Suzanne reassurance and before long, a new routine had established itself, which seemed to suit all parties. With her peace of mind restored, Suzanne could work fluidly.

Besides the Salon d'Automne, the last part of 1920 brought the *Exposition Internationale d'Art Moderne* in Geneva and a group exhibition at Berthe Weill's the following spring to prepare for. And about that time, another distraction presented itself for Suzanne, and for Maurice too. It came in the form of a colourful husband and wife whose friendship would radically alter both their lives.[32]

Robert Pauwels was a robust and erudite Belgian banker whose financial nous had enabled him to profit from the newly accessible post-war art market while indulging his penchant for modern painting. And wherever M. Pauwels went, his ebullient wife Lucie was invariably by his side.

An effervescence of prattle and perfume, plump and preened and studded with constellations of gaudy rings and jewellery, Lucie Pauwels was a former actress who had never fully accepted the break with her previous career that her marriage had demanded. 'I have always been extremely gifted,' she gushed. 'If I had stayed on the stage there is absolutely no question that I would have been the greatest actress in France.'[33]

Having abandoned her stage name of Valore, Lucie had quickly taken to her new role as Mme Pauwels. She and her husband claimed to 'adore' artists, and they attempted to surround themselves with painters at every possible opportunity. Nowadays, Lucie's 'stage' was the couple's comfortable apartment on the Boulevard Flandrin, which had been decorated with studied elegance, and where once a month they hosted a chic gathering.[34] At these events, tea and lemonade were served to a group of carefully selected guests, while music was played, verses recited and deals set in motion. For Berthe Weill, the polite small talk and forced refinement of these parties lacked warmth and intimacy, while the couple's approach to their art collection was decidedly snobbish.[35] But for Suzanne and Maurice, the Pauwelses' interest was at once flattering and financially transformative.

As Lucie remembered it, the couple had first come to Montmartre to look for the mother and son they had heard so much about the previous winter. By the beginning of 1921, the Utter family had become regular guests at the Pauwelses' teas. Lucie judged Utter 'a very attractive man, full of health, but despicable', and already in possession of a wandering eye.[36] But cultivating his acquaintance was a necessary rite of passage if a person wished to gain access to Suzanne and Maurice, both of whom Lucie instantly decided that she liked and admired immensely. For all her reservations about Suzanne's skills as a mother, Mme Pauwels decided that Mme Utter should become her dearest friend.[37] Before long,

Maurice's and Suzanne's canvases were adorning the walls of the Pauwelses' cherished abode.

'The memory that M. Utter and my son, M. Maurice Utrillo, as well as myself, retain of our charming hosts and your most interesting reception is as pleasant as it is vivid,' Suzanne wrote to thank Lucie on 21 February 1921 – a polite bourgeois response to a dignified bourgeois social gathering.[38] Suzanne's career now saw her moving in a very different social circle to the one into which she had been born. Drawings of her peasant mother or poor serving girls toiling to scrub clean a malnourished youngster had been superseded by prim society portraits of well-heeled ladies and powerful businessmen. When patrons like the Pauwelses called a tune, it was worth learning to dance.

Suzanne's social efforts paid off. That year, she participated in a record number of exhibitions and reviews began to accumulate. In the summer, Berthe Weill scheduled a joint exhibition of Suzanne's and Maurice's work. However, as so often before, professional glory was obscured by personal shame. As the opening approached, Maurice broke free from Pierre's supervision, and Suzanne was contacted with the news that he had been arrested in the Place de la Bourse for indecent exposure. He was subsequently moved to a *prison de la santé*, which was felt to be better placed to offer the care he required. From there, he was transferred once again to Sainte-Anne's.[39]

Conscious of the suffering he had occasioned, Maurice wrote a sheepish note to Berthe Weill expressing his regret that he had not come to the exhibition: 'I am truly sorry not to have been able to visit it, since my mother's canvases were on show and it is always an immense pleasure for me to see the admirable works that she paints with so much skill, because she is an artist of the first order, who paints with such sincerity.'[40]

After some weeks at Sainte-Anne's, Maurice was moved to a

clinic in Ivry-sur-Seine where he was assigned to a Dr Delmas.[41] Finally, at the end of the summer it was agreed that Maurice should be returned to Pierre's care, and, as an additional precaution, sent to spend time in the countryside away from the temptations of Montmartre until he readjusted to life outside the clinic. Arrangements were made for Maurice to stay with an acquaintance of Utter's named Marien Pré, and his family, in the commune of Anse in the Rhône department on the Saône river, not far from where Utter had convalesced when he was injured during the war. Suzanne was only too pleased to visit and to spend time and paint once again in the countryside with which she and Utter had both fallen in love during the war. While in Anse, Suzanne produced a series of landscapes, capturing the buildings and countryside she adored, with studies of orchards and stables. And during the course of the year, she worked prolifically, producing a number of portraits, including a study of Maurice, one of her great-niece Gilberte (both of which appeared at the Salon d'Automne), and, in particular, a portrait of her husband's family.

In *Portrait of the Utter Family* (1921), Suzanne showed Utter's closest relations sat tensely in a richly furnished, middle-class interior. Dark and solemn despite the evident material comfort, the lack of interaction between Suzanne's in-laws was unsettling.[42] The sense of discomfort and absence of visible family cohesion hinted at underlying tensions. Instead of the affirmation of unity expected in a family portrait, Suzanne's picture harked back to Degas's unsettling portrait of *The Bellelli Family* (1858–1867) and reflected a similarly remorseless treatment of family members.

Suzanne's genre painting *The Abandoned Doll* (1921) was still more challenging. Seated on a bed next to a mother or carer, a naked, pubescent girl with ripe breasts was shown regarding herself in a hand mirror. Suzanne depicted her subject having abandoned her doll, and by association, her childhood, a link the artist nudged her viewer to make by placing an identical bow in the hair of the toy and its owner. The older figure was shown attempting to towel dry the younger, but the latter turned away, rejecting the care which would fix her as a child. People who knew Suzanne insisted that the models were Marie Coca and her daughter Gilberte. But as the non-specificity of the title stressed, the identities of the sitters were irrelevant; only the message was of import. Just as the child discarded the doll, so the older woman had to release the child. The painting explored questions relating to age and transition, self-awareness and innocence. It was a poignant composition as Suzanne contemplated the autumn of her life. Painting enabled her to sift through the strands of multiple complex issues; seldom did it provide a neat resolution.

By the early 1920s, Suzanne was regularly attracting notice from the critics. Her 1921 Salon d'Automne entry earned her a front-page mention in *Le Gaulois*.[43] Then at the time her work was shown at the John Levy Gallery in Paris that December, plaudits began to flood in, many from committed allies.

'She excels [...] in the handling of charcoal and red conté,' Adolphe Tabarant wrote, 'this explains the lively admiration Degas held for her drawings of nudes, which, ironically he contrasted with those of Mary Cassatt.'[44] 'Suzanne Valadon's nudes,' André Warnod declared, 'painted in such a clear and radiant palette, enchant the viewer by virtue of the truth that emanates from them; powerful nudes, nudes in action, nudes stretched out on a divan.'[45] Robert Rey was even more laudatory: 'I cannot insist emphatically enough that in Suzanne Valadon, we have a great artist on a level at least equal to Berthe Morisot and whose talent we have not yet given due credit.'[46]

Though Morisot's class and style differed markedly from hers, and though Suzanne railed against the notion of the *femme artiste*, a comparison with such a renowned painter could only be reaffirming.

Professional recognition was indeed mounting. In February 1922, *Le Bulletin de la Vie Artistique* consulted Suzanne when seeking the opinions of seasoned exhibitors at the Salon des Indépendants on the renewed emphasis on easel painting at the expense of larger decorative works. 'Decorative painting never having lacked architecture, and our era being entirely without it, it is natural that this style of painting be abandoned,' Suzanne reasoned.[47]

As the critical responses to her work proliferated, so did her creative output. Portraits abounded in her oeuvre. In 1922, Suzanne painted her housekeeper, Lily Walton, seated in a chair in the Utters' comfortable interior, her legs crossed and Suzanne's cat perched on her lap. Miss Walton appeared dignified and demure, while comfortable in her own skin. The viewer was not presented with a deferential servant, but an individualised figure worthy of a portrait, one defined by her identity not her role; now, even Suzanne's employees had shifted social register. Another picture produced that year showed Mme Zamaron, the wife of the local police *secrétaire général*, whom Suzanne had encountered through Maurice's suite of escapades. Léon Zamaron was also an art enthusiast who purchased paintings and had used his influence to extricate Maurice from more than one scrape.[48] He and Suzanne had become great friends. She painted a portrait of M. Mori too, a respected curator. Then there were numerous landscapes, including a romantic and timeless study of the gardens at the Rue Cortot.

Suzanne's production was reaching its peak when her friend and admirer Robert Rey, the acquisitions adviser and conservationist at the Musée du Fontainebleau, started work on the first monograph of her painting. It was an important landmark. Then besides the Salon des Indépendants, Suzanne had two exhibitions at Berthe Weill's gallery that year, and acknowledgement from her *pays* in the form of an exhibition at the Galerie Dalpayrat in Limoges.

By the end of the summer, there was much to cheer the Unholy

Trinity. Maurice's work was selling well, and for magnificently high prices. Utter, with his business acumen and charm, and 'laughter bubbling up in his great clear eyes', was proving himself a shrewd manager.[49] And Suzanne was in her element, professionally and socially, with an ongoing stream of exhibitions and even more lively parties hosted at her home, which, to her delight, was now regularly filled with people.

But the exhilarating highs the trio enjoyed were matched by devastating lows. Maurice was virtually a prisoner under his own roof, since the cost of his freedom had repeatedly proved too terrifying to sanction. In fact, his continued release was only permitted on the understanding that he would be closely guarded, a condition to which Utter had been made to formally agree by signing a contract.[50] Moreover, living and working so closely told on Suzanne's and Utter's relationship.

Utter was constantly inspired by Suzanne's talent and passion, just as he was astounded by Maurice's unassuming production of masterpieces. But as the youngest of the three, he found the extremes visited by his companions tested him to the limits. Suzanne was a woman of dramatic contrasts; her tempers could be fierce and she was invariably the last person left dancing at a party, despite her age. Those bright blue eyes were always lively and quizzical, while from her petite frame she exuded a strangely masculine confidence and strength. At social functions, her extraordinary stories and excited, high-pitched laughter kept her audience gripped. Electricity seemed to crackle through her, and friends noticed that it was only growing more pronounced with age. Such energy and eccentricity made her an irresistible guest or host. But for Utter, living permanently on the edge was stressful. Besides, now that money was starting to flow into the household, Suzanne's generosity was being given free rein, and she showered her friends with gifts, sometimes offering paintings by either herself or Maurice.[51]

Such gestures flew in the face of Utter's project. Those were assets too valuable to simply squander. Meanwhile, Maurice had taken his stepfather on a hair-raising tour of Paris's most sinister institutions. Cells, sanatoriums, psychiatric units – places Utter never thought he would experience; now, he knew them all intimately.

He found that the occasional drink made the task of corralling such volatile characters more manageable. Still, he had less mastery over his reactions when softened by alcohol. Suzanne discovered that when pushed, her husband could more than match her tempers. When the fire of rage was ignited, Utter would shout, swear and seize whatever object was nearest, indiscriminately, on which to vent his anger. Often it was a piece of furniture which met its sorry end, sometimes a canvas – representing the source of his woes as well as his wins. Exquisite paintings were thus mercilessly slashed or torn.[52]

But when apologies were made and the air cleared, the ripples from such terrible outbursts soon dissipated. With Suzanne's infectious passion and impetuous nature, Utter came to see each of their arguments as the precursor to a heartfelt making-up.

A change of scene could often smooth family frictions too, and at the end of the summer 1922, the trio travelled to the little village of Genêts in Brittany, in the picturesque Baie du Mont-Saint-Michel, not far from Avranches.[53] It was a welcome break which allowed all three to concentrate on landscape studies. But once they had returned from their holiday and the Salon d'Automne was successfully complete, the sense of anticlimax began to grate. Suzanne decided that something must be done. What was called for was a party.

Arrangements were made, invitations issued, and then on the appointed night, the apartment at 12, Rue Cortot filled with festive merrymakers intent on partaking in the most frolicsome Christmas party imaginable. The buffet Suzanne and Utter laid on was magnificent, Berthe Weill recalled, the frenzied dancing and singing went on into the small hours.[54] And miraculously, nobody drank too excessively. Even Maurice kept his alcohol intake in check.

But the high-spirited revelry with which 1922 culminated merely provided a temporary respite; the New Year began eventfully. Not long after the opening of the Salon des Indépendants, Maurice was diagnosed with a double hernia and speedily admitted for surgery.[55] A joint exhibition of Maurice's and Suzanne's work at the Galerie Bernheim-Jeune in June gave the family a focus while he convalesced. Again, Maurice Utrillo far outshone Suzanne Valadon, who was now more than ever defined in terms of her relationship to the great painter of Montmartre. As the summer approached, the need for a break was again making itself felt. And it was then that a marvellous project began to take shape.

Two of Suzanne's and Utter's great friends were Georges and Nora Kars. Georges was a Czech painter, fine-boned and pallid, who had arrived in Paris not long before the war. By contrast, his wife was a dark-haired, round-faced woman with a double chin and a severe appearance. Notwithstanding, Suzanne had warmed to her, having painted her portrait the previous year; as she had got to know her subject better, the closer the two women had become.[56] The Karses were regular guests at the Pauwelses' little gatherings, and in conversation it emerged that they owned a property in Ségalas near Orthez, in what was then the Basses-Pyrénées.[57] When they invited the Utter family to stay with them in the summer of 1923, Suzanne was delighted. After recent upheavals, the prospect of a holiday was thrilling.

The two families, along with Suzanne's current maid-cum-cook and occasional model, Paulette, set out on what they anticipated would be a glorious adventure. Georges had hired a car; he had not driven before, but how hard could it be, everyone reasoned? The drive was terrifying; the party were bombarded by a hailstorm (nobody knew how to close the stylish open-top roof), brought to a screeching halt by a stray cow, and confronted with a serious mechanical setback when the car lost a wheel.[58]

When at last they arrived at the country retreat, the group were in greater need than ever of a relaxing break. With its cream paintwork and terracotta roof, the Karses' holiday house was grand and well maintained with a neat garden.[59] And as the guests settled in and began to discover their surroundings, Suzanne realised that there was much to admire on the mountainous French–Spanish border. The vivid colours of the landscape were just to her taste, and she began to paint.

As the days passed, close proximity encouraged more intimate acquaintances, while time to think gave rise to new ideas. It occurred to Suzanne that the union she had ultimately been unable to secure between Maurice and Gabby might be formed more successfully between her son and Paulette. Paulette was a sturdy and straightforward girl, who had formerly sold fish in the market at Les Batignolles. She was a simple soul who could cook a decent meal and keep a good home. It was just what Maurice needed. When presented with this idea, Paulette began to consider it. Suzanne was hopeful. Would she be able to wear a pretty dress in cerise-coloured satin, the girl enquired after a while? Suzanne promised she would. Then she would do it, she announced.[60]

Suzanne was ecstatic. Arrangements were made for an engagement party, the requisite cerise satin gown duly shopped for and the *mairie* notified. But before the vows could be made, Suzanne awoke one morning to find that Paulette had left, without so much as a goodbye or an explanation. It was a chastening disappointment to all but Maurice, who seemed unfazed.

But Suzanne had not given up on her son yet. And the stay in the Karses' holiday home had sown the seeds of an idea. What if they too had a country property to which they could retreat whenever life in Paris became too intense? Somewhere more rural, like the house they had owned in Montmagny, but deeper into the countryside, further from the capital. It would surely be beneficial to Maurice and a little novelty could only add spice to her relationship with Utter. And that was to say nothing of the artistic inspiration they might all glean. Suzanne knew how well they had liked the Beaujolais countryside around the area where Utter and then Maurice had convalesced. With preparations for the Salon d'Automne complete, Suzanne conducted her family on a reconnaissance trip to the Saône Valley in the Ain department.

As they scoured the area, the trio came across the little commune of Saint-Bernard. The area was familiar to Suzanne, for she had painted there on a previous trip. In one of her studies, she had been enchanted by a small and picturesque 18th-century château on the edge of the village.[61] It had its very own moat and drawbridge, and a stream could be heard bubbling close by. It was a timeless romantic wilderness – and by chance, to Suzanne's delight and disbelief, the family discovered that since their last visit, the château's owner M. Goujat had resolved to sell the property. It was a marvellous stroke of good fortune.[62]

Upon Suzanne and Utter making enquiries, a visit was arranged. And as soon as she stepped through the gates of the imposing structure, Suzanne fell deeply, hopelessly in love.

The whole property looked like a miniature fort. It comprised a main building and two towers, one round and one square, which overlooked a terrace garden with a rounded support wall. A staircase had been cut into one of the thick, 2.5m-high walls, and it gave access to a rampart walk which ran along beneath the roof. Inside, the suggestion of idyllic rural living continued. In the main reception room, Suzanne beheld an enormous fireplace – ideal for roaring log fires when the cold wind licked at the thick stone walls. The grand staircase led the party up to the first floor, where they found the room situated in the square tower to be especially narrow. Notwithstanding, it afforded a tremendous view out over the garden and the nearby church. With secure bars on the windows, it would be the perfect space for Maurice, who needed a safe environment in which to live and paint, and who seemed to thrive working in confined spaces. Nobody could deny that the dilapidated structure, with its flaking paint and crumbling stonework, demanded serious renovation. There was no electricity and no running water, merely a well from which heavy pails would have to be heaved up and transported back to the house. Winters would be glacial and living focused on survival. But instead of flaws, Suzanne saw only potential – both for the building and the life she now believed to be within reach. Saint-Bernard was a fairytale castle. Suzanne determined that it must be hers.[63]

That November, Suzanne's *The Blue Room* (1923) turned heads at the Salon d'Automne. In it, she depicted a rotund, brunette model reclining seductively in a richly patterned, blue interior. Hovering between a genre painting and a portrait, the subject's stance subverted traditional conceptions of femininity. The model lay back in an ungainly fashion, a cigarette dangling from her lips, at once sexually available, yet self-assured and confident in her own feminine prowess. Strength, Suzanne suggested, was compatible with and even complementary to the idea of 'woman'. The canvas was a triumphant homage to feminine fortitude, and Suzanne was commended for her 'fresh' and 'lively' style, while *Comoedia* picked her out as one of the exhibitors who proved that talent abounded at that year's Salon d'Automne.[64]

And just two weeks after those laudatory reviews, Suzanne acquired her own trophy of prowess: on 14 November 1923, André Utter signed for the château at Saint-Bernard. It was bought with proceeds of painting sales, including a picture by Maurice of the village of Maixe, sold to the Pauwelses.[65]

In the year before she turned 60, Suzanne Valadon's life bore little resemblance to that of the infant Marie-Clémentine, born in a rural backwater far away from the clamour and culture of the capital. From commoner to châtelaine, Suzanne now witnessed more and more money flowing into the house, much due to Maurice's talent and Utter's salesmanship, but a good proportion a consequence of her own increasing success. With the future bright, money in her pocket, and with a backdrop to suit, Suzanne stopped keeping track of her expenses. At last, she started to live.

That year she bought a gleaming Panhard car and hired a chauffeur to drive it, whom she dressed in white flannel livery.[66] If by chance she was inconvenienced by the car being serviced or repaired when seized by the whim to escape to Saint-Bernard, she simply took a taxi the 440 odd kilometres from Paris. More than once, she told the taxi driver to wait while she saw to this or that task, and then forgot all about him – and the mounting cab fare. Similarly, Suzanne had always regarded fashion with a disdainful eye, but now she purchased expensive hats and fur coats in all colours and shades from Paris's top designers, most of which she would never wear. In fact, when her mongrel dogs L'Arbi and La Misse showed a liking for an astrakhan coat she had just bought, it immediately became their bed.[67] Those dogs, housewives in Montmartre hissed, now dined on juicy sirloin steak which Suzanne had specially prepared by her favourite local restaurateurs. Meanwhile, her cats' palates had become accustomed to the sophisticated taste of caviar. The stories of Suzanne's largesse abounded: she had picked up 50 children from the local area and treated them to an evening at the circus; she had seen a young artist working in the street on a cheap canvas and replaced it with one made of linen; she noticed a cigarette burn on a friend's sofa and promptly ordered them another one. She remembered important personal dates too, so her generosity seldom lacked an outlet; she was sure to give the postman a card on his wedding anniversary, or a local laundress a bunch of flowers on her birthday. Taxi and train drivers were given eye-watering tips, while tramps found themselves able to dine like kings for a week when just the day before they had thought they might starve. Often, Suzanne left the tips anonymously and when questioned, denied any involvement. Her altruism and extravagance were such that it was hard to know which of the many stories to believe.

Friends distinctly remembered being interrupted every now and then by an unscheduled visit, whereupon they would open the door to find Suzanne beaming. Her hair was now greying and cut with a fringe, her still-clear skin creased with laughter lines, and in the winter she wore a cape pulled round her petite shoulders. She would thrust armfuls of gifts through the doorway towards her recipient.[68] Or else she would issue an invitation to a dinner or party, either in Montmartre or, if her guest could free their schedule, in Saint-Bernard. There were alfresco luncheons, dinners at expensive restaurants and once, friends recalled, even a midnight supper party in a cemetery. The food was invariably delicious and the wine of the very finest quality.

During the spring and summer of that pivotal year, professional ascent and personal anguish again ran parallel – but this time, both were sugared with fiscal abundance. Suzanne had fewer exhibitions scheduled than the previous year, when barely a month had passed without a show. However, the venues in which she now presented her work were chosen with care and her paintings were attracting more and more critical acclaim.

Maurice's ongoing troubles had a habit of dampening Suzanne's moments of professional glory. He spent much of the spring of 1924 in a sanatorium at Ivry-sur-Seine.[69] But there was good news too, for both him and Suzanne, in the form of a joint exhibition to be held at the Galerie Bernheim-Jeune in the summer. The novelty of a mother and son exhibiting together turned the show into a major piece of cultural gossip. Though Mme Valadon's handling was occasionally 'a bit heavy' *Comoedia* critiqued, she always remained true to her conception of beauty. Meanwhile, 'the painting of M. Utrillo is the triumph of instinct to the service of an imagination which only needs a street corner, a church, a patch of sky or a humble wall to work', the same journalist declared.[70] 'A certain melancholy pervades the work of both artists,' assessed *L'Intransigeant*, perceptively; 'in Valadon's case it is more bitter, in Utrillo's, more resigned.'[71] However, on the whole, reviews were favourable and the exhibition a resounding success.

The very notion of a working-class female living by her brush would have been unthinkable when Suzanne first went to Puvis seeking support. Now, she had truly arrived. The significance of her achievement was not lost on seasoned artists and critics. And in the year of that great exhibition at Bernheim-Jeune, her friend, the art critic Adolphe Tabarant, resolved that a banquet should be thrown to mark how far she had come.[72] Tabarant booked La Maison Rose, a rustic, salmon-coloured hillside tavern in Montmartre that Maurice had painted, and invitations were issued for what promised to be an unforgettable evening.

For centuries, banquets had been thrown as a way of uniting large numbers of people for ceremonial occasions, and in 1908, the banquet arranged by Pablo Picasso in honour of Henri Rousseau had firmly established such events in the art world as the most fashionable way to mark an important celebration.[73]

Suzanne's banquet was greeted with enthusiasm. The guests included the cream of Paris's artists, such as Georges Braque, as well as writers and critics like Florent Fels, Francis Carco, Gustave Coquiot and André Warnod. Staff at La Maison Rose knew just the touches to guarantee a sensational evening, with tables set with pristine white cloths and napkins, and vases of beautiful flowers – by now Suzanne's great weakness. The spread was as sumptuous, the company as engaging and the conversation as stimulating as could be found anywhere in the capital. It was, Utter remembered, 'a banquet worthy of comparison with that of Douanier Rousseau'.[74]

'The Parisians will never trade a throne for a banquet,' King Louis-Philippe famously proclaimed.[75] Suzanne, it seemed, did not have to choose. That night, she was the queen, the art world's most esteemed figures her loyal subjects. She was as the *Woman with White Stockings* (1924) that she painted that year, and in which many people believed she had depicted herself: a voluptuous female, mature in age but young in spirit, and dressed and posed provocatively. Heavily made up and confident in her sexual magnetism, she sat in the same regal chair in which Lily Walton had posed so primly, but unlike her predecessor, she sprawled over it erotically. Suzanne's 'queen' was a lower-class woman elevated to sovereignty at her very own banquet, and thus a woman of her time.[76]

But behind the veneer of flamboyance and success lay deep and dark cavities that it was becoming increasingly difficult to hide. Little did Suzanne know at the time, but as she left La Maison Rose that night and stepped out into the lamplit street, drunk on happiness, she edged just a little closer to the realisation of her worst fears. For in the months to come, Suzanne was about to see her relationship, her home and even her son's life compromised in the most appalling of ways – and this time, she would be powerless to countervail.

CHAPTER 15

In and Out

Vau mielhs rire a la chabana que purar au chasteu.
(It is better to laugh in a hut than to cry in a château.)
OLD LIMOUSIN PROVERB[1]

Suicide and self-harm were regular occurrences in the art world. In 1890, Vincent van Gogh had shot himself in the chest. Eleven years later, Picasso's heartbroken friend Carles Casagemas had shocked his companions by taking his own life. More recently, the tragic suicide of Jeanne Hébuterne when she learned of Modigliani's passing remained freshly imprinted in artists' minds. Many creative types flirted with death. Suzanne herself had been heard to threaten suicide when she stood to lose something she loved. But words were distinct from actions. Neither suicide nor serious instances of self-harm had ever struck in Suzanne's immediate circle – until now.

It had been hoped that keeping Maurice under close surveillance once he returned home to the Rue Cortot would be sufficient to ensure his safety. The hypothesis proved ill-judged.

One morning, Suzanne awoke to find her son's room empty. The sickening realisation hit her: he had escaped. Suzanne became frantic. Summoning Utter, she began to search everywhere she could think of. Maurice was nowhere to be found. Two interminable days passed, and then there was a knock at the door. The policeman who stood in the entranceway gripped Maurice by the arm. Beholding her son, Suzanne's initial relief quickly turned to horror – his head had been bandaged up and blood seeped through the dressing.[2]

Maurice, it transpired, had been found drunk and was taken to the police station. Thrown into a cell, he became frenzied at the thought of returning to an asylum. Like a cornered quarry, panicking, he hunted for a way out. Realising he was trapped, he resorted to repeatedly smashing his head against a wall. The injury was acute.

Suzanne hurried him inside and for the next few weeks, became his personal nurse, patiently caring for him, cleaning him and encouraging him to speak. Then as soon as he was considered fit, she arranged for him to be driven to Saint-Bernard to spend the rest of the summer recuperating.

Saint-Bernard held all the ingredients for an idyllic existence. There was a glorious garden to tend (even if it did take an hour to fill a watering can from the well), and it inspired Suzanne to paint numerous still lifes of flowers, her most cherished and patient models. There was the fast-flowing river to fish in and plenty of well-stocked land on which to hunt. Hares, pheasants, trout and all sorts of fresh produce found their way to the Utter family table. With fresh milk available locally, Suzanne experimented with making her own cheeses. In the springtime, the nearby meadows filled with a carpet of dandelions, attracting those local children brave enough to hazard the wrath of the resident geese. Maurice, who loved animals, adored the geese, calling them his 'yoyottes', and he spent hours tenderly stroking them. Then, when night fell, all would become still, with only the piercing cry of an owl or the distant chug of the night train passing to cut through the silence. That was when Maurice worked best; solitude was a familiar friend.[3]

During the day, there were usually people coming and going; it was how Suzanne preferred it. She liked to have the house amply staffed by domestics; they offered a comforting reminder of the trajectory her life had taken. With country walks all around and the atmospheric backdrop of the château, Saint-Bernard was the perfect venue in which to entertain guests, too. Suzanne and Utter urged friends from Paris to visit as often as possible. The Coquiots, the Karses, Utter's family; the corpulent, cardigan-wearing painter Maurice de Vlaminck, a former music hall violinist, writer and bicycle enthusiast beneath whose redoubtable physique and booming voice lay a gentle giant who abhorred alcohol – everyone was welcome at Suzanne's castle. Besides the Parisian guests, the painter Antonin Ponchon, who ran a gallery in Lyon and had a house nearby, often came to call on Maurice. And there was one particularly prominent visitor – Édouard Herriot, the Mayor of Lyon.[4]

Dark-haired with a smart moustache, the round and amiable radical politician had been mayor of Suzanne's nearest city since 1905. A former pupil of the École Normale Supérieure, Herriot was resolutely professional middle-class. Since graduating, he had taught and written, and felt strongly that secondary education should be democratised, a view which found a sympathetic ally in Suzanne, who was always riled by class-based discrimination. From local politics, Herriot had progressed to hold his first ministerial role during the war, and afterwards had been elected on to the Chamber of Deputies. By the 1920s, Herriot had risen to the forefront of national politics, and in June 1924 he had become prime minister, heading the Cartel des Gauches, a coalition of radicalists and socialists. Though many considered his grasp of economics to be wanting, his eloquent speeches and rich cultural knowledge won him ardent supporters. With his intellect, honesty and attention to local amenities, he had captured the hearts of the Lyonnais people. Passionate about the arts, and cultured, Herriot's meeting with

Suzanne Valadon painting.
Bettmann/Getty Images

Suzanne naturally blossomed into a close and mutually admiring friendship. 'This great, this very great and pure artist,' he once acclaimed her.[5] Herriot was a valuable addition to Suzanne's group of friends, and his presence at a dinner guaranteed an unforgettable evening animated with brilliant conversation. Herriot in turn adored Saint-Bernard, where he observed that the trio were really 'in their element'.[6] He became a regular guest.

On good days, life at Saint-Bernard could be paradise. Suzanne painted, Utter strode off to hunt, while Maurice could be found painting, writing (often letters, sometimes poetry), or else contemplating the animals. And the Utters' parties soon became legendary.

But when the guests had left, the same old grievances remained. The grand setting abetted epic dramas. Saint-Bernard was not a place of moderation.

In a tripartite relationship on which the financial and spiritual well-being of all parties depended, the strains triggered explosive arguments. Even Suzanne's friends conceded that she was inclined to become wildly jealous at the slightest friendly gesture Utter made towards another female. The sound of Mme Utter screaming abuse through the corridors, the master of the house swearing back in response, to an accompaniment of breaking china and slamming doors, became a familiar feature to passers-by. Sporadically, Utter would grow so incensed that he would throw the rest of the family out, declaring that it was 'his' castle. Or else he stormed off, and word now had it in Montmartre and Saint-Bernard that Suzanne's hunch was correct, that he was keeping lady friends. Then when Maurice managed to get his hands on drink, his breakouts quickly had him branded a madman among the locals. More alarmingly, he had a habit of firing shots with a small pistol wherever he saw movement in the bushes. The Utters were soon renowned for their eccentricity and feared for the threat their unruly son posed to neighbours.[7]

Still, even when times were good, none of the trio could release their yearning for the capital. Paris, with its noise and life and people, ever moving, always changing – the city was in their blood.

Paris was nightclubs like the trendy Boeuf sur le Toit, whose owner, Louis Moyses, Suzanne painted that year and where jazz now jollied the post-war spirits of poet Jean Cocteau, composer Darius Milhaud and their fellow *Samedistes*.[8] There were inspirational exhibitions, such as the retrospective at the Galerie Barbazanges-Hodebert in 1924 of the Russian painter Marc Chagall, that conjuror of technicolour dreams, whose creative oeuvre proudly defied classification. Even the more challenging art movements at least caught the attention, like Dada, that strange group born during the war who seemed set on revolt and had all of Paris talking with their nihilistic ideas; or Surrealism, whose leader André Breton had published a manifesto in October 1924, which insisted that the world was corrupt and should be reconsidered through the lens of childhood, madness and the subconscious – all were facets of the Paris that the Unholy Trinity still loved.[9]

Suzanne and Maurice were perhaps less comfortable with the changes now taking place than Utter; culture-hungry foreigners and literati, particularly Americans like Ernest Hemingway and F. Scott Fitzgerald, were taking advantage of the franc's weakness and had invaded the area around Montparnasse. Fellow American Sylvia Beach's English-language bookshop and lending library, Shakespeare and Co., was flourishing as a result. Fashionable café society of young artists, writers and socialites posed, cocktail in hand, to revel in the glamour and luxury previously the exclusive privilege of the aristocracy and the grande bourgeoisie. Ladies sported red lipstick, ostrich feather fans and evening dresses with daringly low backs, men laughed and joked in suits cut for ease of movement. New fashions, fast-paced living, jazz and the foxtrot, that supremely social, smooth and rhythmic dance so attuned to contemporary music tastes, had established a clear divide between those who conformed and those who were 'other'. In a city of cliques, age and introspection placed a person firmly on the margins.

More specifically, bohemian Montmartre was no more. 'The stranger who comes to see the place gets very often an indifferent meal for which he has to pay a ridiculous price and comes away with the wrong idea of Montmartre, confusing the Montmartre of Commerce with the Montmartre of Art,' lamented Jean Émile-Bayard in the mid-1920s.[10] 'Flats with every modern improvement rise above studios of plaster tiles [...] Crowds of visitors come in their motor-cars to see the famous "Lapin Agile".'[11] Though

Suzanne Valadon,
Adam and Eve, 1909,
oil on canvas, 162 × 131cm,
Musée national d'art moderne,
Centre Georges
Pompidou, Paris.

Photo © Centre Pompidou, MNAM-CCI,
Dist. RMN-Grand Palais/Jacqueline Hyde

Suzanne Valadon,
*Maurice Utrillo,
his Grandmother and his Dog*, 1910,
oil on cardboard,
70 × 50cm,
Musée des Beaux-Arts, Limoges.

Photo © Centre Pompidou, MNAM-CCI, Dist.
RMN-Grand Palais/Jacqueline Hyde

Suzanne Valadon, *Joy of Life*, 1911, oil on canvas, 122.9 × 205.8cm,
The Metropolitan Museum of Art, New York.

Suzanne Valadon,
Family Portrait, 191?
oil on canvas,
98 × 73.5cm, Musé?
national d'art mode?
Centre Georges
Pompidou, Paris.

nne Valadon,
Future Unveiled,
, oil on canvas,
× 163cm,
ection: Association
Amis du Musée du
Palais, Geneva.

Suzanne Valadon,
Portrait of the Artist's Mother,
12, oil on board, 80 × 64cm,
usée national d'art moderne,
re Georges Pompidou, Paris.

Suzanne Valadon, *Marie Coca and her Daughter Gilberte*, 1913,
oil on canvas, 162 × 129.5cm, Musée des Beaux-Arts, Lyon.

Image © Lyon MBA – Photo Alain Basset

Suzanne Valadon, *The Casting of the Nets*, 1914,
oil on canvas, 201 × 301cm, Musée des Beaux-Arts, Nancy.

Suzanne Valadon,
*e Sacré-Coeur seen from
the Garden of the Rue
Cortot*, 1916,
oil on canvas,
63 × 53cm, Musée
:ional d'art moderne,
Centre Pompidou.

Suzanne Valadon, *The Abandoned Doll*, 1921, oil on canvas, 130 × 81cm,
The National Museum of Women in the Arts, Washington, DC.

Courtesy of The National Museum of Women in the Arts, Washington, DC,
Gift of Wallace and Wilhelmina Holladay; Photo by Lee Stalsworth

Maurice Utrillo, *Bessines Church in the Snow*, 1927,
oil on canvas, 73 × 100cm, private collection.

Suzanne Valadon,
Bouquet of Flowers, 1930,
oil on canvas, 73 × 54.3cm,
Musée des Beaux-Arts, Limoges.

Suzanne Valadon,
André Utter and his Dogs,
1932, oil on canvas,
163.5 × 131cm,
Musée Municipal Paul Dini,
Villefranche-sur-Saône.

pockets of Montmartrois launched various schemes and societies to protect their heritage, progress was a persistent opponent. But both Suzanne and Maurice clung nostalgically to their memory of pre-war Paris. That was enough for the city to retain their loyalty. Paris always gave cause to hope.

Of all the trio, it was Maurice who most had cause to feel trapped in the infernal paradise of Saint-Bernard. Fortunately, his photographic memory allowed him to recall, whenever he chose, any one of his favourite corners of Montmartre. He would spend hours working on a canvas in the countryside, only for the finished work to represent an emotive scene of the Butte.

Edmond Heuzé remembered an occasion when he was painting at the foot of the Sacré-Coeur. Maurice sidled up and leant on a handrail to watch.[12]

'Are you not doing anything?' Heuzé enquired.

'No, I would rather watch,' came the reply.

For two or three hours, the men remained alongside each other in silence, Heuzé painting, Maurice observing. A few days later, Heuzé called in at the Rue Cortot. There on an easel in Maurice's bedroom was the exact scene Heuzé had been attempting to capture. It was painted entirely from memory – and it was magnificent: sensitive, true, subtle and perfectly proportioned with flawless perspective. Heuzé could see in an instant that it far surpassed his own attempt.

For a socially awkward man, Maurice was a great letter writer, too. In December 1924, he wrote a long New Year's greeting to the young medic, translator and art collector Robert Le Masle. With his dark brown hair, angular eyebrows and chiselled features, Suzanne's good friend was both beautiful and erudite. A man of letters, Le Masle exchanged correspondence with Maurice Ravel and moved in the same circles as Suzanne's former lover, Erik Satie. He had recently undergone an operation for a hernia, and Maurice felt compelled to write to offer his sympathy and understanding, and to send a gouache of the Moulin de la Galette, a vestige of when Montmartre was 'picturesque' and 'interesting', he explained.[13] Then there was Lucie Pauwels. His stepfather encouraged them to maintain good relations with buyers, and Mme Pauwels was always enthusiastic about his work. A card or note every now and then seemed a pleasant gesture to make.

Thanks to collectors like the Pauwelses, Maurice was earning well, and it was principally on his income that the family were surviving. 'You see that pair over there?' he was heard to say to people, gesturing towards Suzanne and Utter. 'I have to work all the time to support them.'[14] But in many respects, the arrangement was the lesser of two evils. Handing money to Maurice was as good as placing him in a sanatorium, and thanks to Utter's astute business sense, his stepson's skills were receiving the recognition they deserved. Meanwhile, Suzanne acted as the perfect mediator between her lover and her son, at once empathising with Maurice's sensitive disposition yet cognisant of the onerous demands of the profession.

But Suzanne acting as treasurer for the family budget was far from trouble-free. Not only did she give away paintings, but it seemed anyone presenting themselves at her door with a sorry tale to tell would leave with a handout

By 1925, the Galerie Bernheim-Jeune had cause to be concerned. Maurice Utrillo was a potential goldmine, which the gallery had no intention of passing by. But he could not be trusted with cash and his security was imperative if he were to produce the merchandise they desired. Furthermore, his mother and custodian spent recklessly, faster than he could earn. So early in the year, the gallery made a proposition which was felt to be in everyone's interest: they would buy a house in Maurice's name in the sparkling new Avenue Junot in order to secure his work.[15]

Maurice was accustomed to being told what to do, but Utter strongly opposed this manner of payment. Still, the gallery wielded power. Their terms had to be accepted. For Suzanne, uprooting herself from the Rue Cortot would be the most seismic shift she had yet endured. From that point, her production dwindled.

Fortunately, she still had a substantial body of work from which to draw exhibition pieces. The spring of 1925 brought the Salon des Indépendants, and there was a sale of her work at the Hôtel Drouot in March. But when the *Exposition internationale des Arts décoratifs et industriels modernes* opened in April and all the world's eyes turned to Paris, Suzanne received a body blow: Louis Vauxcelles, the organiser of the corollary exhibition *Cinquante ans de peinture française* at the Musée des Arts Décoratifs (now, significantly, located in the Louvre's Pavillon de Marsan), had systematically excluded Suzanne from the show.[16]

Few exhibitions heralded the blurring of art and fashion characteristic of *les Années Folles* as flagrantly as this world fair. It had been nearly fifteen years in the planning. The exposition was designed to showcase the decorative arts and trumpet Paris's supremacy in the fields of art and design. Fifteen thousand exhibitors established themselves across 57 acres in central Paris and around the Grand Palais. Though at least twenty countries were invited to join, two-thirds of the exhibition space was dominated by France; Germany received its invitation too late to organise an exhibit. With pavilions housing the capital's key manufacturers and department stores, including Galeries Lafayette and Le Bon Marché, the show was an unashamed celebration of consumerism, which announced Paris as an arbiter of taste and a centre for shopping. Exhibits lined the banks of the Seine, the entertainments included cafés, ballets, fashion shows and fireworks, while richly decorated barges enticed visitors to dance and dine on the river. With the professed criteria for entry being modernity, the exhibition was the big international event of the moment. Vauxcelles refusing Suzanne entry to the Louvre was as symbolic as it was offensive.[17]

Critics pounced on Vauxcelles's self-appointed role as curator of the history of French art. 'Of course an exhibition must have its limits,' Gustave Khan conceded, 'but why limit itself based on received ideas? [...] This is an exhibition which reflects the taste of the contemporary amateur. It is full of holes.'[18]

'They failed to invite Suzanne Valadon,' Berthe Weill exclaimed when she learned of the omission. 'I think she counts!' To which Vauxcelles had a simple retort: 'I do not like Valadon's painting.'[19]

If women were now grudgingly accepted in the art world, it was still felt that the form their work should take needed to meet strict criteria. The palette should be muted, the handling delicate and any feminine form depicted slim and fragile in appearance. Marie Laurencin, the tall, svelte and distinguished former muse of the late Guillaume Apollinaire with doe-like, almond-shaped eyes, had wisely calculated what the public craved from a woman artist. Her use of pastel pinks, greys and blues, and breathy female forms won favour with the critics. Intelligent and ambitious, it made no difference to her that her late lover's companions found her manner affected. Comfortable in the company of lesbian friends like American Natalie Clifford Barney, she exaggerated her prim mien and cultivated her femininity, as though it were a distinguishing quirk. Marie Laurencin was first and foremost a woman, who also painted; Suzanne Valadon was an artist.[20]

With her bold contours and plump, self-assured models, Suzanne's work flew in the face of popular conceptions of femininity and fine art. Added to which, her painting could not be neatly tied to a school. Not surprisingly, Vauxcelles also excluded her from the chapter on women's painting in the book he wrote on French art. Suzanne's style and its resistance to categorisation stood between her and the annals of French art history.[21]

Suzanne Valadon in 1925, her 60th year.
Collection Jean Fabris

'The history of women's art is determined by what the critic likes or deems to be acceptable,' Berthe Weill concluded, aghast. 'Painters he dislikes must be erased from the History of Art.'[22]

Weill need not have worried on Suzanne's account; anyone brave enough to slight Mme Valadon should expect a consequence. When Vauxcelles put himself forward as a candidate to become the next curator of the Musée du Luxembourg, Suzanne signed a petition raised to protest against his election.[23]

Meanwhile, Maurice's painting career was going from strength to strength. Early canvases from what critics now termed his 'Montmagny period' and his 'Impressionist period' were a great source of interest. Paintings from his 'White period' (from the time Suzanne met Utter to the outbreak of the war), were commanding astonishing prices. His current work, now with more colour and incorporating signs with lettering and even the occasional figure, was in constant demand in France and overseas.

If Maurice found it hard to conceptualise success abroad without visible evidence, admirers like the Pauwelses, with their soirées and purchases, were a more tangible part of the Utter family's life. In April that year, Maurice dedicated a poem to Lucie Pauwels by way of thanks.[24]

Not only was Maurice's income keeping the family, but something of his celebrity status reflected on Suzanne as well. In June, the Unholy Trinity showed their work together in an exhibition at the Galerie Bernheim-Jeune. Suzanne's friends were also a constant source of encouragement, and that year Gustave Coquiot threw another banquet in her honour.

Still, the responsibility of Maurice, who was now legally under her and Utter's control (the authorities having judged him not of sound mind), was an ongoing concern. Regular trips to Saint-Bernard were essential to help change Suzanne's perspective and revitalise her. That was where the family headed in the summer of 1925, with invitations urgently being extended to friends and family, including Marie Coca and André Utter's sister Germaine, to help break the intensity in the increasingly fraught family drama.

Germaine was a healthy-looking girl with a beautiful mane of golden hair. Both Utter and Suzanne had their different motives for hoping a romance might blossom between her and Maurice. But despite their best efforts, the summer drew to a close and the desired union was yet unformed. Suzanne and Utter resigned themselves to the likelihood that Maurice's unpredictable behaviour had startled Germaine.[25]

The company of family was diverting, but it could scarcely plaster over the widening cracks in Suzanne and Utter's marriage.

That summer, in between the couple's rows, Suzanne also learned of the death of Erik Satie. And so guttered another chapter of her life. The discovery of her portrait in the deceased's squalid apartment merely confirmed suspicions that she was the only love he had ever known.[26] For all the angst, Suzanne had enjoyed moments of true happiness and enormous fun with Satie. His death gave cause for reflection as the fights between her and her husband intensified. Those days had seemed so carefree. Now, the mere sight of Utter's freshly polished shoes – a sure sign that he was meeting someone he wished to impress – was devastating for its implications.[27]

Suzanne could at least console herself that she still exerted a powerful hold over her husband; letters begging her forgiveness after a quarrel, apologising for another loss of temper, attempting to coax her back to a more biddable humour, were common. 'I ask for the forgiveness of my Suzanne, my wife of whom I am so proud and whom I love,' read one letter written just two months after Satie's death. 'I beg her forgiveness for the harm I have done her by insulting her and for my tempers which prevent her living in peace.'[28] Family relations were now fraught with tension and bad faith. But in the stormy sea of life, there was too much at stake to release what they knew.

Music and dance were a theme that autumn, as mulatto Josephine Baker took Paris by storm with her erotic dance moves and a voice like velvet kisses, and Utter was approached by Paul Guillaume of the Barnes Foundation and asked if Maurice would design the decor and costumes for the Russian Serge de Diaghilev's forthcoming ballet *Barabu*.[29] It was due to take place at the Théâtre Sarah-Bernhardt the following year. The commission would publicise Maurice's work even more widely, and Utter had no qualms about accepting the proposal.

But before the show opened, the family had another cataclysm to endure: in January 1926, the door to the apartment in the Rue

Cortot closed behind Suzanne and she moved her son and her belongings to number 11, Avenue Junot.

As she left, Suzanne hoped rather than knew that the move would prove sagacious. One thing was certain: for better or worse, after more than fifteen years, 12, Rue Cortot had become part of her soul. Only the months to come would determine whether it was a part she truly wanted to discard – or whether she had just made the biggest mistake of her life.

CHAPTER 16

Behind Closed Doors

Li o toujours no meichanto lego de chemi a fà.
(There is always a mile of
rough terrain still to travel.)

OLD LIMOUSIN PROVERB[1]

Construction of the Avenue Junot had only begun in 1910, and had controversially involved building over the Maquis, a shambolic stretch of tumbledown shacks which housed many of Montmartre's poorer artists, rag-and-bone men and second-hand goods dealers. The grand road now taking its place was wide, and the new apartments on either side rose up tall, bourgeois and imposing. The whole street was built to form a curve, and it swept assuredly up the hill. Large, leafy and refined, the avenue was the very antithesis of the narrow, cobbled streets Suzanne had chased through as a child.[2]

The family's living quarters were spacious. From the main reception room, a staircase led up to the first floor and Maurice's disordered room. There was a studio for Suzanne and plenty of space for the parties and receptions she loved to host. In setting up Maurice's and the family's new home, the Galerie Bernheim-Jeune had anticipated every material comfort Suzanne could wish for. Only her heart had been neglected.[3]

Ties with the Rue Cortot had not been severed entirely; it was decided that the family should keep the apartment, which Utter would use himself, 'for work', he explained.[4] Already deeply suspicious of her husband's activity, Suzanne could hardly feel at ease with the arrangement. It was true that Utter always came back to her. But it soon became clear that, while the family's move had altered the setting, the characters and the drama being played out remained unchanged.

Suzanne and Utter's fights were now ferocious, typically triggered by one or the other's behaviour or a poor business decision, and invariably fuelled by alcohol. When a row was over and Utter had stormed back to the Rue Cortot, Suzanne collected up the pieces of broken furniture and quietly secreted them in a convenient cupboard under the stairs. Then daily life resumed and the pattern continued.[5]

As she settled into her new home, the spring at least brought some familiarity in the form of the Salon des Indépendants and a group show at the Galerie Bernheim-Jeune. But just as she was about to leave Paris for Saint-Bernard that summer, Suzanne received an unexpected letter. Its contents shook her to her very core.

The note was from Conrad Satie, Erik's brother. He advised her that he had found a bundle of letters his brother had written but never sent – all were addressed to her. Conrad wanted to meet to show her the letters. Suzanne hurriedly penned him a reply:

Cher ami, your very friendly letter arrived just as I about to leave Paris [*sic*] – an emergency forces me to put off your visit – if however you can – wait until the last week of August, for I should be back in Paris then.

The meeting will be a very moving one and so many memories are heart-rending indeed and yet very sweet to me.[6]

Suzanne Valadon, Maurice Utrillo and André Utter
sharing a drink in the studio of the Avenue Junot, c. 1926.
Martinie/Roger Viollet/Getty Images

Having assured Conrad of her friendship, in her haste, Suzanne signed her name twice. When a date was finally agreed for Satie's correspondence to be handed over, friends reported that Suzanne studied each of the letters closely, several times. Then she gathered them together and burned them.[7]

As ever, time with her extended family brought comfort that unsettling summer. Marie Coca sat to pose for a sober-looking portrait. The sitter had aged considerably, but Suzanne depicted her niece with kindly, smiling eyes in a more sympathetic handling than usual. She also painted Germaine seated by a window at the château in Saint-Bernard, her glorious golden hair falling down her back like a modern-day Rapunzel, her attention entirely absorbed by the view below. The young girl's gaze, like the diagonals of the open window, invited the viewer's eye outside to where an explosion of green and yellow foliage harmonised with the subject's hair. The summer concluded on an optimistic note, as Suzanne participated in her most far-flung exhibition yet, in Tokyo.

Over the following twelve months, her time was divided between the Avenue Junot and Saint-Bernard. In both locations, she painted, socialised and attempted to contain Maurice. Fiery arguments with her husband were followed by profound relief as they made up. There were exhibitions too, including a retrospective show of her work at Berthe Weill's gallery in January the following year and then a group exhibition with Bernheim-Jeune. She had four pieces on display at the Salon des Tuileries in the spring and she showed *The Blue Room* (1923) at the Salon du Musée du Luxembourg. She also sent work to the Galerie Max Bing. In May, Suzanne was asked to design a poster for a charity ball that was due to take place in Montmartre in aid of artists, and she executed an exquisite line drawing which showed a back view of a nude holding a palette and paintbrushes in her left hand, with a stream of tumbling coloured foliage falling from the brush she held aloft in her right. She produced many other nudes that year, as well as flower studies and landscapes, taking Saint-Bernard as her subject. In one of her pictures, she depicted the terrace, where she played with the unusual angles of the building glimpsed from the awkward position she had chosen. Certainly, she was working. However, her output was no longer what it used to be.

Suzanne was now in her 60s and all too conscious of her age. Despite that, she never attended closely to her appearance, and dressed in oversized clothes, with baggy cardigans and shapeless skirts; they were practical and comfy, and to her, that was all that mattered.[8] She captured her timeworn face in a harsh and angular self-portrait that year. The fabric, vase and apples around her figure demonstrated her mastery of gentle curves and flowing lines; the application of sharp, angular diagonals to her own face was intentional. Her head was tilted, twisted round to one side and scowling, while the oranges and reds and bold sweeps of the brush conveyed anger and defiance – but also unquestionable strength. And the frame of the mirror into which she looked was included, as though to put the viewer in her position and to ask: what did it feel like to see such a reflection staring back?[9]

Suzanne and Maurice were now together a great deal, Utter frequently finding an excuse to evade their company. Again and again, he returned to the Rue Cortot to paint, as though part of him could not release his nostalgia for how things used to be. More damaging was that Utter still nursed a debilitating jealousy of his stepson's celebrity. 'Utrillo's success annoyed me,' he confessed, 'I despised him.'[10] Maurice's unassuming approach to his work and innocent wonder at his fame only infuriated the younger man more. On one occasion, Antonin Ponchon called in at Saint-Bernard and enquired as to how Maurice's current exhibition in Paris was going. Maurice said he knew nothing about it. He was not kept informed of the exhibitions André Utter set up, he explained with acceptance.[11] Another time, Maurice dropped in to the Galerie Bernheim-Jeune and noticed an enthusiastic crowd swarming around a painting. Moving closer to investigate the cause of their excitement, he joyously agreed: 'Isn't it good? It really is very fine. You would have to be a painter to have done that.' He seemed completely unaware that he was the author of the masterpiece being admired.[12]

To compound Utter's resentment, Utrillo's 'masterpieces' were increasingly created from postcards. Maurice would carefully grid up picture postcards and turn them into scenes so vivid as to make the viewer feel they were right there on the spot. This way of working appealed to Maurice's exacting nature and keen eye for precision. It also had the advantage that, on bad days, he did not need to leave the house to continue working. His brush could travel across France to places he might never have visited but which spoke to his inner sensibilities – places like Bessines, his mother and grandmother's natal town, whose snow-covered church he captured in a haunting painting.

The crowning glory to Maurice's achievements that year came in the form of a contract from Bernheim-Jeune, who now felt more confident in his ability to satisfy such an agreement. A regular income in return for paintings – for any artist, it would have been a triumphant coup. For an unstable alcoholic with no formal training and a precarious home life, it bordered on miraculous.[13]

Suzanne never begrudged Maurice his success, but rather sang his praises openly. There were several books published on her son that year, including one by Francis Carco for which she provided illustrations. When she was interviewed by author Maximilian Ilyin for a work he was compiling, Suzanne spoke candidly about Maurice's gift:

> the first stage in the life of a painter is the response to a certain summons: the time when he is unaware of his power, the time of sincerity. The second stage begins with the moment when he discovers the conventional in art and the restraints of his profession, when he exerts himself to create the lie, his lie, which will henceforth be his reality. The third stage, which I shall undoubtedly never attain, is that in which the painter, liberated from the routine of his profession, learns to control even his feelings, and becomes a creator guided only by intuition. [...] Well, my son has reached that last stage in an exceptionally short time – a few years. [...] He is a genius.[14]

Nowadays, when Suzanne and Utter were together, arguments were the norm. 'You screamed at me,' Utter wrote that May. 'I was catching up with Warnod [...] That is all I have done wrong. I love you and you know it. You have to forgive me.'[15]

But for all her jealous outbursts, Suzanne still exerted a powerful hold over her husband who, like an addict, was unable to resist the stimulus she provided. Refusing to exhibit was one way Suzanne could claw back control. Utter had been trying to persuade her to show work in Lyon, and he was both delighted and grateful when in January 1928, he got his way and a selection of her pieces appeared at the Galerie des Archers.

Most of the exhibitions which followed that year were group shows, including the Salon des Tuileries and even an exhibition in Holland. But the usual schedule was punctuated dramatically in the summer when Maurice hit a particularly difficult period and was drinking more heavily than usual. The situation was not helped by the fact that Mme Thiériot, the primary school teacher who had been employed as an extra pair of eyes to watch over him, was the subject of malicious teasing on the part of the existing governess, 'Mère Thiret'. By May, Utter had had enough of the family drama, and he drew up a formal contract in which he gave Maurice eight days to leave Saint-Bernard for good.[16]

As usual, Utter's temper eventually subsided, and despite the ultimatum, Maurice was still at Saint-Bernard once the allotted time had elapsed. Before long, Annette Jacquinot had become his primary supervisor as well as a general help at the château. A local woman, she was dumbfounded by the way the Unholy Trinity lived and the fiery scenes that took place between Suzanne and her husband. She regularly found herself caught in the crossfire. Mme Jacquinot's responsibilities soon became clear: when Suzanne and Utter were obliged to return to Paris, she was to guard Maurice closely. He was not to be left alone, he was to receive no post or parcels and there were to be no visitors. He could go to Mass on Sundays provided he was accompanied. On more than one occasion, he broke free of Mme Jacquinot's custody, and she telephoned Suzanne in a panic. 'Don't worry,' was Suzanne's usual reaction.

'He'll come back.' And mostly, he did. Mme Jacquinot took to hiding keys.[17]

When Suzanne was away, Maurice wrote to her every day, and Utter had any paintings he created sent on to Paris. The letters were invariably full of affection and love, and he always sent his warm regards to his stepfather. Never once did he complain about being left at the château.[18]

Towards the end of that tumultuous summer, there was an unexpected cause for celebration: the Utter family learned that Maurice was to be awarded the Croix de la Légion d'Honneur for his contribution to French art. It transpired that Francis Carco had proposed Maurice as a worthy recipient, and Lyon's favourite political celebrity, Édouard Herriot, was thrilled to support the nomination and present the award. So it was that on 1 August 1928, Maurice, washed and looking dapper in a dark suit and tie, accompanied by Suzanne in an unusually smart, light summer skirt, blouse and hat, as well as Utter, looking typically dashing, stepped out into the sun at Saint-Bernard to witness the commendation.[19] Maurice seated himself on a low wall and played absent-mindedly with yellow leaves that fluttered down or fumbled with his hat.[20] He would rather the award had been a Palmes, he told Herriot, since he preferred purple to red. The recipient was gently reminded that the Légion d'Honneur was a far superior decoration.[21] The medal was ceremoniously bestowed, words of praise spoken and thanks duly muttered, before a lunch was given for all attending. When a toast was proposed and glasses raised, Maurice offered his audience a word of reassurance: 'Gentlemen,' he announced, 'mine is watered.'[22] With that, he drained the contents in one gulp.

The press could not resist the opportunity to make a jibe at the great artist's other famous passion. 'This extraordinary man' usually preferred a draught to a decoration, quipped Robert Destez in *L'Homme Libre*.[23] No doubt his reaction when told the happy news was 'shall we toast?' The journalist related Maurice's eventful past – including the popular view that Adrien Boissy was his father – and detailed his history of stays in clinics and sanatoriums. But Maurice was given full credit for his exceptional skill, and 'if he has paid dearly for his ribbon, Suzanne Valadon has as well,' the author conceded.[24] Those present at the ceremony remembered Suzanne shedding tears. The event was cause for mixed emotions.

Family was much on Suzanne's mind that year. Besides her usual studies of nudes and of her beloved Saint-Bernard, she painted two sisters. She sat a pair of girls side-by-side, both scowling, their bodies close but their legs crossed. One sister had her arms folded. Suzanne arranged the composition so that her viewer was prompted to examine the similarities and differences between the girls, and to attempt to deduce the nature of their sisterly relationship.

By the late 1920s, Suzanne's work could be found all over Paris. In January 1929, the Galerie Bernier mounted a retrospective of her work, which was well received. 'One gets the impression that the excellent artist makes drawing the very soul of her art,' raved one reviewer, before quoting Picasso's response when he made a visit to the Salon d'Automne: 'If I were to purchase something here, it would be the picture by Suzanne Valadon.'[25] Suzanne then exhibited two paintings of flowers at the Musée du Luxembourg in March and followed up her retrospective at the Galerie Bernier in July by participating in a group show at the venue. That same year, a monograph written by Adolphe Basler appeared. In September, Suzanne's work was praised for its durability by G. Charensol in an article he wrote for *Les Chroniques du jour*. The author cited Marie Laurencin as 'the artist best qualified to produce feminine painting', but added that 'while it is uncertain whether Marie Laurencin's painting will appear as seductive to viewers tomorrow, by contrast, one cannot doubt that the work of Suzanne Valadon will touch people in the future and even more so than it does those today.'[26] But as ever, the compliment came with a predictable conclusion: 'Because if we love Valadon, it is not only because she is a great painter, but also because she has given us this fantastic genius who, to pay daily homage to his mother, signs his canvases: *Maurice Utrillo V.*'

With Utter having commandeered the apartment at the Rue Cortot, Suzanne's most productive periods now took place at the château in Saint-Bernard. Her oeuvre abounded with the evidence of it, with numerous still lifes of produce and flowers from the grounds.

On a personal level though, Suzanne was pained to find Utter growing more and more distant. The Montmartre grapevine positively buzzed with tales of his affairs. There was talk of a girl named Madeleine whom, Utter claimed, it was impossible for him to stop seeing; there was a model called Eveline who expected a constant flow of presents; and still another mistress, a well-bred young lady referred to simply as 'Yvette' for reasons of discretion, whom people said had at one point been employed by the family as a secretary.[27] One titillating story even had the man now ironically branded 'the Pope of Montmartre' taking his lover back to Saint-Bernard, whereupon Suzanne, tipped off, raced to confront the pair. Finding them in each other's arms, people giggled that she had locked them in the bedroom and passed insipid meals of cabbage up to them through a window, using a bucket and pulley system. It was all they were given to eat for a week.[28]

At Saint-Bernard, Suzanne often found Utter preparing to go out somewhere, at pains over his appearance, and ordering Mme Jacquinot to shine his shoes or iron his shirt. Then the request would invariably come: could his dear Suzanne lend him the money for the Metro? Or to buy Warnod a drink?

'How much money do you want to stop seeing this woman?' Suzanne asked once.[29]

Utter's response was immediate: '30,000 francs and it is over, I promise you Suzanne!'

Suzanne Valadon, Maurice Utrillo and André Utter, c. 1930.
Martinie/Roger Viollet/Getty Images

She could only laugh.

Family tensions were hardly eased when, in May 1929, Maurice wrote a long and earnest letter to Germaine Utter, to clarify that their feelings for each other were the fondness of a brother and sister, not the love shared by a husband and a wife. Any impression he might have given to the contrary was, he insisted, a consequence of his psychological imbalance. The realisation that a new Utter–Valadon union was wishful thinking drove a further wedge between Suzanne and her husband.[30]

But love and time and necessity had forged a bond between Suzanne and Utter that was not easily severed. Professionally, too, Utter played an indispensable role in the maintenance of the Unholy Trinity's career. Maximilian Ilyin remembered a business lunch where, after polite small talk, Utter and a prominent New York art dealer desirous of Utrillos, turned their attention to money. The dealer named an elevated sum.

'That's what you propose for paintings which are steadily going up in price!' Utter fumed. 'After his death they'll bring absolutely fantastic amounts! Surely you're making fun! I have four mistresses, my dear sir, and for each one I need furs and diamonds. And Suzanne! She throws money out of the window; she gives taxi drivers five times what's marked on the meter ... And the Château Saint-Bernard where we keep Maurice! ... Waiter! The bill!'

Utter threw down some money and stormed out. The dealer was dumbfounded.

'What impertinence!' Ilyin offered sympathetically.

'But such a magnificent impertinence,' the dealer murmured in admiration.[31]

Utter's reputation was legendary, so the handsome, blue-eyed, olive skinned Cypriot Paul Pétridès was understandably anxious when the opportunity arose to take lunch with him that year. Pétridès was working as a tailor at M. Mazella's on the Boulevard Poissonnière and he had admired some Vlamincks and Utrillos on the wall of his employer's home. As an amateur collector, he wondered how he might acquire a Utrillo. By chance, sharing this desire with a fabric merchant named Roussel, Pétridès discovered that his business contact was friends with Utter; would Pétridès like to meet him for lunch? Pétridès could scarcely contain his enthusiasm.[32]

Roussel warned his colleague that Utter did not take kindly to people angling for an introduction to his wife and stepson. But when Utter discovered Pétridès's trade, such a request was unnecessary.

'Make me a suit, old man,' Utter instructed Pétridès, 'and I'll do your portrait.'

In a particularly good humour that day, Utter also proposed that they go and meet his wife and stepson straightaway. Pétridès was jubilant.

Suzanne received the tailor warmly. 'I like you,' she announced finally after they had been chatting for a while. 'I will introduce you to my son.'

Pétridès was led up to Maurice's room – and he was horrified: the artist's careless, grubby appearance was as squalid as his living space. Sensing Pétridès's unease, Suzanne broke the awkward silence.

'Make him a suit in exchange for something.'

A large gouache was offered. Pétridès agreed.

'Blue,' Maurice uttered mechanically.

The very next day, Pétridès arrived to take measurements. As he fashioned a suit more fitting of a great artist, Pétridès's work was punctuated by sittings with Utter at the Rue Cortot. He began to know the family better. At first, Utter's warm and amenable facade seemed at odds with the popular image of him as a cut-throat businessman. But as he grew more relaxed in the tailor's company, he began to vent his bitterness, which to Pétridès at least, seemed directed sweepingly 'at the world'.

The portrait complete, Utter took it to Suzanne for her approval. The critique resulted in her making some alterations.

'Look what I've done, Annette,' Utter triumphed proudly to Mme Jacquinot, who offered her compliments.

Once he had left, Suzanne exploded. Mme Jacquinot bitterly regretted her misplaced praise.[33]

One day, as Suzanne sat watching Pétridès make the final adjustments to Maurice's suit, she suddenly declared: 'I would like to do your portrait.'[34]

Pétridès having agreed, a date for the first sitting was set. She told him to arrive at 9am.

'Don't be late,' she warned.

As requested, Pétridès arrived on the appointed day at 9am. Suzanne asked him to sit down and then turned her attention to her palette, which she began cleaning assiduously. Pétridès waited for further instructions. The palette cleaned to her satisfaction, she started to pet her dogs and cats and to lay out food. Not until 11am did she begin painting. At midday, she set down her brushes; the session was over.

'Well then, see you tomorrow at 9am sharp,' she instructed.

Pétridès was bewildered. The pattern continued for the next two sittings. By the fourth, he had resolved to make better use of his time and arrived at 11am. Suzanne opened the door furious, her hands on her hips and a scowl across her forehead.

'That's what you call punctuality is it?' she spat. 'You are too late for today.'

'But I was giving you time to clean your palette and see to your cats and dogs,' Pétridès protested.

'What? But I have not had time to do anything, I was waiting for you.'

Pétridès was stunned.

'Come back tomorrow,' she instructed angrily, 'and make sure you are on time.'

The portrait was eventually completed to everyone's satisfaction.

From Pétridès's unconventional introduction to the family, he developed a fondness for all three members. Henceforward, he became an important figure in their lives and a reliable purchaser.

The year after the Unholy Trinity met Paul Pétridès marked the start of a new decade. The Wall Street crash in 1929 had set businessmen's hearts racing, but as the months passed, Frenchmen were relieved to observe the impact on their country to be minimal.[35] Optimism prevailed and Suzanne's curriculum vitae glittered. The year began with an exhibition of her drawings at the Galerie Bernheim-Jeune, and the same month, André Salmon wrote an article complimenting her style, while acknowledging the hazardous journey she had taken to get to the position she had reached.[36] Suzanne participated in the exhibition *L'Art Vivant* at the Théâtre Pigalle that year, as well as a group show at the Galerie Bernheim-Jeune from March to April. And throughout the year, the whole family were buoyed by the ongoing possibility of a sale, whether to Bernheim-Jeune, or the Pauwelses, or Paul Pétridès.

In 1930, Suzanne capitalised on the fruits of her surroundings. She painted Saint-Bernard and numerous still lifes of flowers, gathered at the property and arranged to spectacular effect. Ripe russet apples along with booty from Utter's hunts, whether a hare, duck or pheasant, were brought back to the house and transformed into rustic-looking still lifes which exuded rural plenitude.

However, to Suzanne's incomprehension, the greater her professional achievements, the more strained relations in her marriage became. Fights still prompted Utter to pen heartfelt apologies, in which he addressed her affectionately by her pet name as his 'You-You' and begged her to continue painting.[37] But with Utter now in his mid-40s and Suzanne in her mid-60s, neither possessed the energy they had once had to weather the marital storms.

In 1931, Suzanne explored her self-awareness in a devastating portrait. She showed herself at 66, nude to the waist, her breasts drooping, but painted surprisingly high on her chest nonetheless. Effort had clearly been made to prepare her appearance for the piece, but her jowls were now more capacious, her lips drawn and

Suzanne Valadon with her dogs
at the property in the Avenue Junot, c. 1930–1.
Collection Jean Fabris

pursed. Her eyes, though still a striking shade of blue, were sunken, while her whole expression appeared tired, timeworn and resigned. Viewed with her other self-portraits, this was the next instalment in what had become a near-scientific charting of the effects of time on the female body. The work reflected a kind of naturalistic objectivity. Indeed, despite the ageing process, her self-portraits were noteworthy for their continuity. All were the product of merciless self-scrutiny and each was characterised by its honesty. Together, they showed mounting confidence and pride.[38]

In that year, Suzanne's paintings received international attention. Between December 1930 and January 1931, her work was on show at the Demotte Gallery in New York. Then an exhibition at the Galerie Bernheim-Jeune in February was followed by the show

L'École de Paris in Prague. In May, Suzanne had an exhibition at the Galerie Le Portique, for which her friend Herriot good-naturedly wrote the preface. 'Valadon is wholeheartedly within each of her works,' commended René Barotte in *L'Homme Libre* when he saw the exhibition.[39] 'I do not know what will last of the visual art of our era,' concluded Barotte, 'but Valadon's work, elaborated in solitude, will remain outside time, like something at once sensitive, pure and strong.' Suzanne's work could also be seen at the Galerie Le Centaure later that year in November. However, she rebuffed the notion of involving herself with organisations like the Société des Femmes Artistes Modernes, founded by Marie-Anne Camax-Zoegger that year. Exhibiting abroad was one thing; marketing herself in gendered terms, quite another.

By the end of 1931, Suzanne's international profile was rising. But the increased publicity had arrived at an unfortunate time; as it turned out, the impact of the depression in France was not quite as negligible as people had hoped. It was merely delayed – and in 1931, it hit.[40]

All at once, France's overseas trade declined, while the balance of payments deficit increased. French goods – especially luxury goods – were considered overpriced on the international market and exports fell. Within the country itself, production diminished and profits and prices plummeted. The possessing classes had less ready cash available to fritter away on dispensable luxuries like paintings. Fear froze the purse strings of the art-loving bourgeoisie. Suzanne had never been able to boast the sales Maurice enjoyed. Her paintings were an acquired taste. In the current market, such work stood even less chance of securing buyers.

'The abrupt halt of all transactions which are not completely necessary to daily life has affected modern painting, like all luxury industries,' reported G. Charensol in *Formes* in May 1931.[41] More hopefully, Maurice's *Lapin Agile* had lately reached 10,000 francs, when it was only valued at 5,000. Perhaps, Charensol reasoned optimistically, the financial storm would 'purify the pictorial climate, bring about a reassessment of values and an elimination of those painters too weak to weather the storm'. Maurice was one of the lucky ones. But Suzanne could not be so certain that she would survive the tempest.

The very vocal succour of her influential friend Édouard Herriot certainly helped; support for the Cartel des Gauches was gathering momentum, and many of his devotees were convinced Herriot would again serve as prime minister. His was a powerful voice.

In the meantime, Suzanne tried to stay focused and to persist in her work. In the spring of 1932, she travelled with Utter, Maurice and Mme Jacquinot to attend the opening of an exhibition they had been offered with their friend the Lyonnais sculptor Georges Salendre at the Galerie Moos in Geneva.

The family planned to spend a few days in Switzerland. It had been some time since they had all taken such a trip together, but packing was an uncomplicated affair, particularly for Maurice and Suzanne, who gave little thought to clothes. Maurice had been given a brand-new marine blue suit and some beige summer trousers, and those were duly packed so that he might appear respectable; his stepfather was always mindful of the importance of appearances.[42]

Utter drove the car and every time they spotted a poor or destitute native en route, he was made to pull over so that the wretch could be given some money. To Suzanne's delight, for much of the trip Maurice seemed relatively content, absorbed in his new surroundings and happy to be fussed over.

It proved a pleasant interlude, and afterwards the trio returned to France and prepared to spend the summer at Saint-Bernard, where they would be visited by friends.

One of their closest acquaintances had exciting news to celebrate, too. In June, Édouard Herriot was re-elected prime minister.

His victory had obvious benefits for Suzanne: now, she could boast the support of France's head of government whenever she exhibited her work.

But nothing could remedy the fact that Suzanne's marriage was now in tatters. There was much tension and bad feeling to set aside when she painted Utter in a nostalgic portrait in the grounds of Saint-Bernard that summer. The picture was unique in Suzanne's oeuvre. Unusually, she showed her subject outside, seated on a fallen chestnut tree with his dogs by his side. Something of the composition recalled traditional 19th-century portraiture, where property owners were frequently depicted on their rolling estates. Suzanne's subject was dressed in loose-fitting summer clothes, and he filled his personal space. But for all that his bright blue eyes and dimpled chin offered a reminder of the man Suzanne had fallen in love with, Utter's hairline was now receding and his waistline insulated with a notable belly. He was still, by his own self-appointment, the Lord of the Manor, but Suzanne showed his youth fading and his expression pensive and solemn. It was as much a statement of their withering love as it was a snapshot of Utter in his 40s.[43]

Despite the grim financial climate and the degeneration of her marriage, Suzanne would not resign herself to taking a half-hearted approach to her career. She had another show at the Galerie Le Portique that year. Then, in October, there came an exciting opportunity: the Galerie Georges Petit agreed to mount a large retrospective of her work. It was to be organised by Mauricia Coquiot and it would be the most important exhibition of Suzanne's painting to date.

As the opening approached, Suzanne and Utter were full of hope and expectation. The show would display some of her major works, including *Adam and Eve* (1909), *Joy of Life* (1911) and *André Utter and his Dogs* (1932). Herriot had added a foreword to the catalogue, while the critic and art historian Claude Roger-Marx had published a book of her engravings, printed by the craftsman Daragnès, to complement the exhibition, copies of which Suzanne herself had made available for sale from the Avenue Junot since the summer.[44] People even whispered that Prime Minister Herriot might attend the grand opening. Everything was set for a show-stopping retrospective.

On the day of the vernissage, the press were there in force. And as people wandered around the gallery, one question played on everybody's minds: would the prime minister come?

Time ticked by, visitors came and went, and the likelihood of a ministerial visit seemed increasingly remote. After all, the prime minister was due to catch a train to London for a meeting later that afternoon. But then suddenly, at 4pm, the gallery door swung open and in walked Herriot, unannounced and unhurried, ready to savour the work of his favourite châtelaine-cum-artist.[45]

Approaching Suzanne, he took her warmly by the arm, his eyes sparkling with pleasure. Not a gesture was missed by the press. Suzanne proceeded to introduce him to her painter friend, Emilie Charmy. It was, one reporter commented, like a family reunion. Suzanne and Herriot were clearly old friends.

Before long, a Cabinet official approached. 'M. le Président? The train leaves in twelve minutes.'

'Coming,' Herriot muttered distractedly as he contemplated the canvas in front of him.

'What a great artist,' he murmured to himself.

People noticed Suzanne's eyes becoming watery behind the horn-rimmed spectacles she was now obliged to wear.

'M. le Président, eight minutes.'

Ignoring the prompt, Herriot turned to Suzanne. 'So,' he began playfully, 'when will you do my portrait?'

'M. le Président, the train!'

And with that, Herriot was gone.

Despite his presence, sales from the exhibition were disappointing and the book fared little better. But the publicity was like nothing Suzanne had ever experienced. That afternoon, time stood still and just for a moment, art and politics had shared the stage in perfect harmony.

'Her work reflects a mounting progression, a lightening of the palette, a simplification,' enthused René Barotte in *L'Homme Libre*. 'She knows that great art is about making something from nothing.' In years to come, the author continued, Valadon's drawings and painting would, 'in their pure truth, declare what a female painter was in our age of uncertainty, just one woman, it is true, but one worthy of being placed next to Lautrec and joining the great masters of yesteryear'.[46]

The exhibition offered a triumphant account of Suzanne's entire creative oeuvre. But that celebration of her life was framed by two unexpected deaths.

Just before the show opened in September 1932, Suzanne learned of the passing of her first husband, Paul Mousis. Then in February 1933, a shock hit the Unholy Trinity when it was reported that Robert Pauwels, one of their principal buyers, had died having been afflicted with uraemia following the stress provoked by the financial climate. Both deaths had a profound effect on the Utter family in general, and on Suzanne in particular. One loss concluded an important chapter in her past; the other was to bring her current existence to a shuddering halt and have a life changing-impact on her entire future.

CHAPTER 17

Empty Chairs and Empty Tables

Pisses pas dins lo potz, benleu ne'n beuràs l'aiga.
(Don't piss in the well, you might drink the water.)
OLD LIMOUSIN PROVERB[1]

Lucie Pauwels had always known her marriage to be one of real distinction. Robert Pauwels came from a well-regarded family of Belgian bankers. He was handsome, educated (he spoke several languages fluently), and enjoyed a pleasing array of hobbies, including motor cars, horses, botany and stuffed birds. Meanwhile, his social standing and keen appreciation of painting (specifically his purchasing power) had earned him a superlative reputation in the art world. M. Pauwels was Lucie's proudest accessory. When he died aged 52, she lost the validation for her persona. 'I didn't know what to do,' she admitted.[2]

Maurice was prompt in writing to express his heartfelt condolences. Lucie's late husband was both 'good' and 'intelligent', and would be much missed, Maurice assured her.[3]

Sentimental considerations aside, the departure of such a prominent buyer would have a profound impact on the Unholy Trinity. Maurice's fortune was now assured, his painting receiving substantial investment from sources in France and abroad. But with Suzanne's less commercial pictures, the loss of any single buyer was bound to hit her hard. Robert Pauwels's death merely tightened her dependence on Maurice.

Suzanne was also increasingly aware of a change in Maurice and it made her uncomfortable. He was showing a mounting hunger for religion. Maurice now clung greedily to any expression of faith his daily life led him to encounter: the daughter of the concierge at 12, Rue Cortot embarking on her catechism, discussions with Mme Jacquinot, the glimpse of the little church from his window at Saint-Bernard, or even simply meditating on his own long-held reverence for Joan of Arc.[4]

Such a craving for religion bewildered Suzanne. It was an area of life in which she possessed little wisdom to be able to guide her son, and too much suspicion to do so dispassionately. When Maurice was at Saint-Bernard, Suzanne let him attend Mass uninhibited. Mme Jacquinot was happy to escort him and she was struck by how Maurice would invariably approach the vicar after the service to offer a warm greeting. Once, she was amazed to see Maurice hand over a small gouache of the church as a gift. She supervised him round the clock, yet she had not even noticed him creating it.

Through discussion with her charge, Mme Jacquinot learned that Maurice had not been baptised. He believed himself inhabited by a demon, he said. If he were baptised, Mme Jacquinot counselled him gently as she walked him back to the château, his inner turmoil would be over.

'I don't know what it is I have up here,' he lamented, drumming his finger on his temple.[5]

It was after another of Maurice's escapades that things came to a head. Climbing through a skylight, he managed to access Suzanne's dressing table where he discovered a bottle of Dubonnet and drained the contents. When Mme Jacquinot found him, he was so intoxicated that she genuinely feared for his well-being. She took him back to his room and immediately telephoned Suzanne in Paris, urging that a doctor be sent. Suzanne replied that alerting an authority was neither desirable nor necessary. By the time she reached him, Maurice had indeed recovered. But now he had just one thing on his mind: 'Mme Jacquinot is right,' he told his mother, 'I must be baptised, I will not be tormented by this demon anymore.'

'Very well, my son,' Suzanne sighed. 'We will get you baptised.'

As Maurice prepared to take the holy sacrament and Utter found comfort in other women's arms, Suzanne sought solace in her painting. Her oeuvre was now primarily taken up with flower studies. Blossoms and blooms provided the colours and forms she craved, and demanded nothing in return. They also made economic models when funds were scarce. The 1930s saw her gradually simplifying her flower pieces, choosing less elaborate arrangements, reducing them to their essential qualities, always defining her elements with bold outlines.[6]

However, Suzanne's energy was now flagging and money increasingly hard-won (or too easily spent). Early in 1933, she finally conceded to exhibit with Mme Camax-Zoegger's Société des Femmes Artistes Modernes at the Maison de France. Though her absence at the group's show the previous year had been keenly felt by critics, Suzanne never enjoyed having to swallow her pride.[7] That women she respected such as Emilie Charmy and Mme Camax-Zoegger herself were participating sweetened a potentially bitter pill. Suzanne also exhibited at the Musée Galliera that spring and had work accepted to the Musée du Luxembourg.[8] But as ever, sales of her paintings were underwhelming. More alarmingly, she was finding she had less energy to create at the rate she once could.

Though the responsibility of Maurice and the torturous degradation of her marriage were weighty pressures, neither one was new. Still, for some reason, she now felt especially tired, so very tired, as though every last drop of energy had been drained, to the point where she could scarcely remember what it was to feel alive and invigorated. On many days, all she craved was a little rest.

The 8th of June 1933 would be remembered in the art world as the date 49-year-old Maurice Utrillo finally got baptised in a decorous ceremony in Lyon.[9] However, Montmartre gossip recounted another story, whereby Maurice had gone out on an alcohol-fuelled evening with the son of a Doctor Laforêt, into whose care Suzanne had entrusted him while she was away and there were no domestic staff at the château to supervise him. It was said that at first light of day, Maurice had stumbled into a little church in Bron, asking to be baptised. On both accounts of his alleged performance of the rite of passage, it was whispered that no formal proof existed and people speculated that Suzanne might be the cause of Maurice's uncertain religious status. Some even held that she had led him to believe that he was already baptised, making such a ceremony in his late 40s unnecessary.[10]

Suzanne certainly had little time for piety, but she had too many of her own concerns to sabotage her son's spiritual pilgrimage. She and Utter were now on the point of separation. Utter wanted to cease living as husband and wife. For Suzanne's part, however much she resented his affairs and the agonising demise of her marriage, she could not reconcile herself to thinking of Utter as anything other than her husband. And everywhere she went, there were memories of the man who no longer wished to be with her. Visits to Saint-Bernard were especially painful. The château was an edifice to a happiness that was no more, a home bought in the glorious springtime of love, now abandoned in a winter tainted by contempt. No longer able to bear the heartache, Suzanne decided she would not return to Saint-Bernard as usual that summer – in fact, she vowed she would never go there again. 'He [Utter] has poisoned the well,' she told friends.[11]

Financial pressures only made the emotional torture harder to endure. It was not that money had stopped flowing; Suzanne's own paintings still brought some profit and Maurice's sales provided a more reliable income. But with his repeated stays in clinics and need for round-the-clock supervision, Maurice's care was costly. Then after years of flamboyant living, Suzanne had lost her gauge on moderation. Her benevolence towards friends and acquaintances was another substantial outlay. On 10 July 1933, she was forced to borrow 20,000 francs from her contact M. Bellier, on the understanding that she would repay the loan in full after three months.[12] Of course, her benefactor would need some form of guarantee. Suzanne offered three of Maurice's paintings, all of churches. It was not the first time she had used the trio's artwork to secure funds in a hurry. But one of the pictures she now chose was an especially poignant canvas to compromise: the study of the little church in Bessines.

Suzanne was pushed to the limit; there was no place for sentimentality under such circumstances. She was grappling to stay afloat. Life's twists and turns had carried her to a miserable destination.

⁂

Fate should have known better than to try such a sleight of hand on a woman like Lucie Pauwels. Once the initial shock of her husband's death had passed, Lucie scheduled a serious council of war with fortune. Amid the upset of M. Pauwels's death, she had returned to the property she owned in her native Angoulême, 'La Doulce France', where she lived with a pair of friends, also widows. The situation was hardly ideal, but she could not yet bring herself to make her permanent home in Paris, where she had lived with her husband for so long. Most of all, Lucie was anxious about her future.[13]

'I was not old but I wasn't young,' she conceded candidly, 'and although I wasn't thinking about another husband I wondered what the future would bring.'[14]

Ever pragmatic, Lucie decided to take matters into her own hands. From a friend, she learned there to be a reputed clairvoyant working just across from where she had lived in Paris. Lucie had always regarded the occult with suspicion, but now she was desperate to claw back control. A reading was scheduled, during which the clairvoyant explained she would use palmistry and cards to provide Lucie with a forecast. The information was revelatory.[15]

Lucie was assured that in two years' time, she would be married again – and that her next marriage would be with 'one of the greatest men in all of France'. 'You will look after him as one would a child,' the clairvoyant continued.[16]

Lucie was incredulous but intrigued. She sought a second mystic's guidance and the forecast reiterated and supplemented the first: 'With this man, you will be in the public eye – one might even say famous.' Then came the climax: 'You already know him and he loves you in silence.'[17]

Lucie scoured her memory. The Pauwelses were a social couple, and Lucie could think of several eligible men in their acquaintance whom she suspected might harbour amorous feelings. But to no avail: she could not place her mysterious admirer.[18]

Meanwhile, Lucie remained in close and regular contact with the Unholy Trinity. She and Maurice continued to write to each other, sending either letters or a friendly postcard, like the one Maurice wrote from Saint-Bernard on 18 September 1933, to offer a warm greeting until he could see Lucie in person.[19] Word also had it in Montmartre that Utter was good-naturedly helping Lucie to get her affairs in order, M. Pauwels having left business matters unresolved.[20]

For all that the Butte gossiped about Utter's motivations

whenever he behaved kindly towards a woman, his interest lay elsewhere than with Lucie Pauwels. In fact, it was now Suzanne who was raising eyebrows, due to a new acquaintance she had formed. The man in question was an artist, of striking appearance and no more than half her age. But more scandalously, Suzanne's new companion was not just another bohemian from Montmartre – he was a prince.

Gazi Igna Ghirei originated from the Crimean peninsula, where it was said that his father was a prince descended from Genghis Khan. When the Bolshevik revolution took place in 1917, Gazi, like so many others, fled his home. He went to study art in Naples. Having gleaned a wealth of knowledge from the Neapolitan masters, he arrived in Paris in 1920 eager to immerse himself in French artistic life. He gravitated first towards the Latin Quarter, where he frequented the artistic haunts of Montparnasse. And through the network of painters, he encountered Suzanne.[21]

Stocky with square shoulders, dark features, bright eyes and a bushy moustache, Gazi was just the type of man Suzanne had always been drawn to in her youth. Peter de Polnay, who lived on the Butte, vividly remembered Gazi.[22] The 'prince' always wore a soft hat marked with grease stains, the rim of which he would touch lightly with his equally ubiquitous cane by way of salute whenever he greeted people. Gazi's repertoire of accessories was not complete without his shopping bag, which seemed to go with him wherever he went. He was an otherworldly creature, de Polnay recalled, an old soul with a sage's wisdom and an unsettling gift of prescience.

Suzanne and the prince made a curious pair, Gazi swarthy, taller than her (though not by much), Suzanne tiny in her thick stockings and horn-rimmed glasses, animated with nervous energy and increasingly given to dichotomous mood swings.

Gazi quickly developed a deep affection for Suzanne which bordered on idolisation. He near-worshipped her and was fiercely protective of the woman he viewed as his adoptive mother, his *mémère* (an affectionate infants' term for grandma). Suzanne talked and talked about painting, guiding Gazi as he created scenes of Montmartre not unlike those of Maurice, while Gazi showed his gratitude by helping her around the house with chores.

Though ensconced with his paramour 'Yvette' in the apartment at the Rue Cortot, Utter was not about to let another man step into his shoes so easily.[23] He could not be with Suzanne, but her character was so intense as to leave an uncomfortable chasm when they were apart. Utter asked his and Suzanne's mutual friend, the Swiss-born painter Robert Naly, to keep a watch on his estranged wife. She had been picking up tramps and taking them home with her, Utter told his friend. He was certain she was using them to appease her still-rampant libido now that he had left. Naly agreed that he would do what he could.[24]

It was on one of his unannounced visits to see Suzanne that Naly, accompanied by Utter, found Gazi perfectly at home. The men were quick to throw him out. However, it was not long before Naly regretted his prejudice.

'This Gazi was completely honest,' Naly admitted. 'He proved himself devoted to Valadon, so much so that Utter eventually accepted his presence, which was far preferable to that of tramps.'[25]

Gazi was a devout adherent of the Greek Catholic Church; Suzanne thought all religion superstitious nonsense.[26] He tried to engage her in conversations about faith; Suzanne would not be converted. But theirs was a strange and mystical bond. It was as though two kindred spirits had finally found each other and had tacitly resolved to be together regardless of circumstance, creed or credence. With Utter gone, Gazi filled an aching hole for companionship and understanding, while Suzanne gave the prince a parental figure to cosset in her old age. Suzanne needed him as much as he did her.

Suzanne produced little during 1934, but she exhibited once again with the Société des Femmes Artistes Modernes, where her portrait of her mother was declared a masterpiece.[27]

However, fatigue and lethargy were weighing her down. The news that Miguel Utrillo had died in Sitges in Spain that year did nothing to restore her peace of mind.[28] As 1934 progressed, she was growing noticeably weaker. Finally, in January 1935, the inner crisis reached a head: Suzanne's body gave its ultimate protest.

Friends were dismayed when news broke that the great artist, Suzanne Valadon, had been rushed to the American Hospital in Neuilly following a severe nasal haemorrhage.[29] It soon became clear that Suzanne was suffering with uraemia.[30] She was also diagnosed with diabetes. At last, the nausea, the profound tiredness and all the other niggling complaints she had tried to dismiss made sense. But the maladies were already advanced.

One of the first to arrive at her hospital bedside was Lucie Pauwels. Later, Lucie insisted that it was Suzanne who, in her panic, had sent her driver to fetch her. Suzanne energetically denied the tale. Either way, when Lucie arrived, Suzanne was in a desperate state. Naturally, when she felt her body withering, her first thought was of Maurice.[31]

Suzanne was fiercely proud of her son, but she entertained no illusions: he was intensely needy. He could be wonderfully loving but was equally given to wild, unpredictable tantrums. Only when he was utterly absorbed in his painting – or engrossed with the train set which had been put in place for him at the Avenue Junot – could Suzanne be certain that he was at peace.

Lucie was moved by Suzanne's upset. 'What will become of him if I die?' Suzanne asked frantically. 'He needs a support, a great soul, he's a child, Maurice is *un enfant terrible*.'[32]

It was at that moment, Lucie claimed, that she received her great awakening: Maurice Utrillo was the man she was meant to marry. When she received one of Maurice's affectionate letters later that day, enquiring if she was still her 'suave' self, Lucie took it as confirmation of her epiphany.[33]

In the hospital, Suzanne proved a frustrating patient. She bothered the nurses, questioned the medication, and when she was finally discharged the relief was unanimous.[34]

Those who knew the Unholy Trinity told different accounts of the order in which events happened next. But on one point, everyone agreed: when Suzanne returned from hospital, she was wracked with indecision.

On the one hand, Lucie Pauwels was a strong woman who, once she had set her feathered hat at a man, would protect and care for him to the death. It would take that unique kind of stamina to weather Maurice's alcoholism and his mood swings, and to nurture his gift. Then there was Utter. Suzanne knew that nothing would hurt him more than stemming the flow of money he still enjoyed from Maurice. How would he keep his mistress? Suzanne could think of no sweeter revenge.

But to be left entirely alone was unthinkable. It was frightening. To lose her only son – and to such a woman, in whom Suzanne could not help seeing a resemblance to the wide-hipped female figure who often appeared in Maurice's pictures – it was more than she could bear.[35] It would take little encouragement from Utter for her to withdraw her consent.

But it was too late: Suzanne's acquiescence, if only fleeting, was all the clearance Lucie required. As soon as Suzanne was discharged, Lucie was on hand to help. Once the invalid was safely reinstalled in her bed in the Avenue Junot, Lucie and Maurice took dinner together – and by the end of the meal, he had proposed.[36]

Now that she had established herself as Maurice Utrillo's fiancée, Lucie began to frequent the Avenue Junot on a regular basis, Maurice being unable to go out alone. However, when she discovered Suzanne's ambivalence regarding the union, and wisely reckoning on Utter's opposition, Lucie decided that there was no time to lose. She headed straight to the Avenue Junot with her nephew Robert in tow, determined to hasten a conclusion. But when the door opened, she had a shock: it was André Utter – and he was primed for a fight.[37]

Utter tried to bar her passage, but few people expelled Mme Lucie Pauwels successfully. A furious row ensued; names and accusations were hurled. Maurice was to be sent to Lyon to stay with friends, Utter declared, and there was nothing Lucie could do to stop it. As the shouts became louder and the gestures more frantic, Suzanne ran to an upstairs window: 'Help, murder, murder!' she screamed.[38]

Maurice was distraught. 'They want to take me far away from you,' he wailed to Lucie, 'but don't worry, I will be your husband; I love you, I love you Lucie!'[39]

Terrified, tearful and distraught, Lucie left the Avenue Junot shaken.

But she was not to be dissuaded so easily. Lucie vowed that she would have this man as her husband, and even Suzanne's friends assured her that, knowing the Unholy Trinity's temperaments, a little time would guarantee her a warmer reception at the Avenue Junot.[40]

In the meantime, Lucie was determined to confront André Utter. She found him in a restaurant, La Bonne Franquette, not far from the Rue Cortot – and there followed one of the most explosive showdowns the residents of Montmartre had ever witnessed.[41] Utter accused Lucie of pursuing Maurice for his money; Lucie retaliated that Utter had been living off his earnings for years. In the end, Lucie was the first to get up and leave. But she was not vanquished; whether secretly relieved at the lifting of his stepfatherly duties or too much in love to fight with his usual vigour, André Utter accepted that he had met his match. Once his opponent had stormed out, he turned to the audience of customers and offered a dramatic digest: 'The firm of Utrillo has changed hands.'[42]

When Lucie returned to the Avenue Junot, some said Suzanne reiterated her enthusiasm for the marriage, her anger having been rekindled once she learned that Utter had taken his mistress on a cruise.[43] Others maintained that she had again declared the union impossible and when Lucie told Maurice to leave with her, issued her son with an ultimatum: 'Her or me.'[44] Suzanne's feelings about the marriage oscillated so precariously that nobody, least of all Maurice and Lucie, could be certain what she thought. And that, explained the painter Jean Dufy, brother of the great Raoul and friend of the family, was the problem: when Suzanne supported the marriage, Maurice believed his mother no longer wanted him.[45] Then when she vacillated and turned on Lucie, she merely pushed Maurice (who hated confrontation) into the safe arms of the woman who just moments ago, she had praised to the skies. Leaving with this formidable, elegant and great lady who was offering him care and security was the most attractive option available.

Once the decision was made, Suzanne wanted the whole business resolved immediately. She complained to Lucie that Maurice had become complacent and rude towards her since their engagement, and that Lucie might as well take her prize and leave that instant. 'Long live liberty!' Lucie remembered her fiancé proclaiming as he followed her outside to a waiting car.[46] Passers-by said the departure was made so hastily that Maurice was still wearing his slippers.[47]

Between the couple's departure and their wedding, Lucie faced a ponderous task. She had already issued Maurice with a warning that his tendency towards excess must be addressed if their marriage were to be a happy one.[48] She urged him to call on his faith for support. But Maurice's alcoholism was a deep-rooted problem. Lucie realised that there were more immediate concerns to attend to.

For one thing, Maurice looked positively bedraggled. His clothes needed mending – or better still, replacing. Lucie also insisted on a church wedding, and that, she said, provided the motivation for Maurice to make his first Communion, since Lucie was given to understand that up until then, he had only been baptised.[49] He had to present his military card to get married, and in the confusion at the Avenue Junot, it could not be located. (Anyway, Suzanne informed Lucie, when one owned a Panhard, a military card was unnecessary.) Fortunately, Maurice's photographic memory and gift with numbers came to the fore; to Lucie's delight, her husband-to-be could remember every detail on the card, including the all-important reference number. A replacement was quickly issued.[50]

The couple travelled to Angoulême, intending to return to Paris for their civil wedding ceremony in the middle of April.

As soon as news of the forthcoming marriage broke, it became the celebrity scoop of the moment. Lucie basked in her new-found fame, and Maurice's profile soared. When the couple travelled to Chartres Cathedral shortly before their wedding to pray for marital harmony, a fleet of reporters followed them. René Barotte, who was writing a sensational article for the front page of *Paris-Soir*, was impressed when Maurice suggested to his fiancée that they light a candle in memory of her first husband. Lucie seized the opportunity of press attention to confide in Barotte, and insisted that she and Maurice had loved each other for a long time. When the appearance was over, a car drove the couple back to Paris. Maurice dozed, stirring only every now and then to mumble a demand for wine. Every time, Lucie gently calmed him and steered conversation on to another topic. Barotte claimed that Maurice returned that evening to spend the night with Suzanne.[51]

At least one falsehood could finally be dispelled after the trip: Barotte had watched in awe as Maurice sat down and sketched a magnificent landscape before his eyes, proof that his work was not executed by copyists as many people believed. But for the awkward alcoholic to marry such a formidable *dame de lettres* as Lucie Pauwels – could it really be true? Barotte was sceptical. 'I will believe it when I see it,' he concluded.[52]

He did not have long to wait. One bright spring morning less than a week after Barotte's article appeared in *Paris-Soir*, Maurice and Lucie were married at the *mairie* of the 16th arrondissement under the watchful eye of the public. Jean Bloch, an old school acquaintance of Maurice's from the Collège Rollin, performed the ceremony.[53] The crowd of admirers was not as large as Lucie had anticipated, but people distinctly remembered Suzanne and Utter being present among the attendees.[54]

The following month, Suzanne exhibited *The Casting of the Nets* (1914) at the Salon de la Société des Femmes Artistes Modernes. The *Petit Parisien* praised the original draughtsmanship and constructional skills of an artist the journalist considered to be an excellent *femme peintre*, 'one of the foremost of our time'.[55] And that same month, Maurice and Lucie Utrillo posed on the steps of the church of Saint-Ausone in Angoulême for an official photograph as husband and wife.

The occasion was just the show of pomp and circumstance Lucie had hoped for. There were flowers, fine tapestries, organ music and even the Bishop of Angoulême, Mgr Mégnin, whose services were enlisted to bless the couple. Maurice wore a smart suit and hat, while Lucie made her grand appearance in a dark, figure-hugging dress and matching hat perched on top of her brunette coiffure, with long white gloves and an enormous corsage pinned to her bosom.[56] In one hand she gripped a chic clutch bag, while her other arm was wrapped possessively around her new husband. The couple were

flanked by the Préfet de la Charente (ironically, given his authoritative status and the bridegroom's continued delinquency, Maurice's
witness), the sculptor Pajot (who acted as Lucie's), the priest Mgr
Gabriel Palmer and Lucie's elderly mother.

Suzanne did not attend the religious ceremony. 'I never believed
that he could leave me,' she said, falteringly, when friends called at
the unnaturally quiet house to check on her.[57] Suzanne had lived for
Maurice and for her painting. 'The umbilical cord between mother
and son had never been cut,' Lucie agreed, continuing proudly, 'and
I was the one destiny chose to sever this magnificent tie.'[58]

Suzanne had lost the person most dear to her. The question was:
how long could she live sustained by art alone?

CHAPTER 18

Flickering Shades

Tou ce que chàbo ne duro pà.
(Things with an ending do not last.)
OLD LIMOUSIN PROVERB[1]

arly in June 1935, Mme Lucie Utrillo was at home at 'La Doulce France' when she received a letter.

'Madame,' it began:

Suzanne Valadon still suffering and having been obliged to have her gravely sick dog operated on, she has been unable to acknowledge receipt of the canvas which was sent to her until now.

As stated in her previous letter, she asks that you refrain from sending further canvases, because they will be returned to you.

She wishes only to be kept informed of any change of address should you move.

She hopes you are both in good health and sends you her regards.

Mme S Valadon[2]

Having settled her husband into his new living quarters, Lucie had been eager to dissolve the lingering ill-feeling between her and her mother-in-law, so had sent one of Maurice's pictures as a peace offering. Suzanne had dictated her reply to a friend. The frosty rebuff in the third person could leave Lucie in no doubt as to the reception her gesture had been given. Fortunately for family equanimity, as Paul Pétridès observed, Lucie was of that curious breed 'who are oblivious to what other people truly think of them'.[3] She dismissed the rejection and began planning her next move.

It had been decided that M. and Mme Utrillo would make their home at La Doulce France. From there, Lucie could organise the sale of her apartment and take time to look for a more suitable home, somewhere closer to the commercial hub of the capital, yet sufficiently far from the temptation of Montmartre's cabarets. The new Mme Utrillo prided herself that in all things but proximity to Paris, her property in Angoulême provided the perfect environment for a great artist.

Situated on the edge of the Charente River, La Doulce France was an imposing exercise in studied bourgeois elegance.[4] The surrounding landscape comprised cattle-studded pastures, while the house itself was agreeable and decorated with an eye to first impressions. A fine collection of original paintings adorned the walls, while the house and garden were neat and maintained in regimented order. As a result, the outward appearance was perfectly in keeping with the image Lucie wished to project and the lifestyle to which she had grown accustomed. It was an empty vestige; in reality, besides a car and a little savings, La Doulce France was all that remained of the comfortable existence Lucie had enjoyed with her first husband.[5] Robert Pauwels's business dealings latterly had been far from lucrative, and nowadays Lucie's only luxuries were her treasured Pekinese dogs and her collection of hats.[6] She entertained no illusions: she urgently needed to review her assets and lay foundations which would safeguard her future.

Maurice Utrillo and his wife Lucie Valore.
Keystone–France/Gamma-Rapho/Getty Images

While her methods and manner could be faulted, Lucie's under-standing of Maurice's needs was unimpeachable.[7] As soon as they were married, she assumed the roles of matron, mother and man-ager, and excelled at all three.

Lucie saw that order, routine and calm were the conditions necessary to her great artist's production, and she made every effort to ensure that such an environment was maintained. A quiet studio was set up for Maurice, and henceforward his day was structured around a strict timetable; he could be in no doubt as to what he was expected to be doing and when. Social engagements, such as meetings with dealers, were occasional. But one unmovable commitment was Mass on Sunday, which nothing was allowed to interrupt.

If Lucie had to go out, she left a responsible adult in charge. She accepted that sobriety was a wishful – even detrimental – aspiration. But from now on, Maurice's wine was served watered and free access to alcohol denied. Moderation in all things, Lucie stipulated, was imperative.

With her charge corralled, Lucie could turn her attention to her managerial duties. She had only ever played a supporting role in her first husband's affairs, but now she was called on to become the leading lady in a glamorous new business venture.[8] Lucie performed her part as though she were born to it. She proved herself a shrewd and efficient businessperson, at least as effective as André Utter, and in many respects, more so.

Maurice's unquenchable thirst combined with Suzanne's profligate spending had led to him producing vast quantities of canvases and passing them off quickly, sometimes with the paint still wet. Lucie knew that in a saturated market, scarcity generated desire – and where there was demand, there was money. She scaled down Maurice's rate of production and was selective in her choice of sales. Dealers began to take notice. The price of Utrillos soared.[9]

With Maurice now a passive pawn, Lucie took a hands-on role in all his important business moves. That August, she travelled alone to Paris to attend to their affairs, and, ever subservient, Maurice wrote to assure his queen that he was behaving:

My dear Lucie,

I am writing to you on Saint Bernard's day to reassure you on
my account, I am well, as is your mother. I took lunch with her
yesterday, she is very content.

On Sunday, I worked on my Cathedral of Angoulême and I
have started another painting.

I hope that you have seen my mother and that she is in good
health. Send her my love, and to Utter as well. In any case, do
not worry about me. I think that Monseigneur Palmer is on
good form, last Sunday I was at Mass at the Saint-Ausone church
and everything went well, so you can feel reassured and have no
worries about me.

I look forward to seeing you my dear wife Lucie, I send you
lots of love.

Your dear husband,
Maurice Utrillo, V.[10]

As it happened, Suzanne was not in as good fettle as Maurice hoped.
For one thing, her beloved mongrel, La Misse, the loyal companion
who had been by her side through countless dramas with Maurice
and as many fights with Utter, was still unwell.[11] Added to the
loss of her son, Suzanne felt there could be no suffering more cruel
than the kind she was experiencing now. Furthermore, if her paintings did not sell (and sales were sporadic), her income was entirely
dependent on Lucie's inclination. To feel beholden was dispiriting
enough; that her benefactress should be 'that woman' was positively
humiliating. Every exchange with her daughter-in-law precipitated
a fresh surge of anger.

'You know,' Lucie mused when speaking to one of Maurice's
biographers, 'Suzanne Valadon, all the time I knew her, right up
until a few days before my marriage with Maurice, was one of my
best friends. But then she became very jealous of me.'[12] Lucie was

incredulous. Why, when discussion had turned to the property in the Avenue Junot, she had even been so altruistic as to tell Suzanne: 'And you may stay in my house until you die.'[13] Her mother-in-law's feral reaction surpassed ingratitude. Meanwhile, having retreated with his mistress to the Rue Cortot, André Utter received nothing.

Save for the odd visitor or her neighbours the Poulbots, who called regularly to check on her, Suzanne now rattled around at 11, Avenue Junot quite alone. Withdrawing, she moved her painting equipment from the studio she had latterly occupied outside into the main house, where she set her workspace up in Maurice's old 'cell'.[14] She scarcely painted though; in that first year without Maurice, she produced little besides a few etchings.

Maurice was anxious about his mother. He wrote to her in October enquiring as to how she was and asking whether La Misse was a little better, since he too was desperately fond of the animal.[15] He assured Suzanne that he was very happy, that the people in Angoulême were friendly and the weather decidedly clement. He asked after Utter, and at the end of his letter, earnestly implored her to come and stay and to share in his newfound joy. It was the express wish of his wife, he said.

But Suzanne would not leave Montmartre. That was her home.

In Suzanne's mind, Montmartre was still the hive of camaraderie and community it had always been. Blossoming window boxes and open doors welcomed you in summer; neighbours huddled together contentedly behind battened hatches in winter. Montmartre was yet the essence of the life Suzanne had known as a little girl – an existence which was, in many respects, akin to the one she had experienced in the Limousin. Besides, she was not alone for long.

Her uncertain relationship with Utter persisted. Half-married, not officially separated, they squabbled as they always had whenever he called in. Suzanne was a difficult woman to leave and impossible to forget. Utter continued to badger Naly to keep watch over his 'wife', and now, Suzanne was glad of the company.

For several months, Naly arrived each evening to sleep at the Avenue Junot. In practice, though, not much sleep was had. 'This little woman, a bundle of nerves, did not sleep,' Naly corrected. 'She kept me up all night talking about painting with an insatiable passion. She would take down an album of Venetian art and proceed to analyse the technique of Titian or Tintoretto with extraordinary intensity and lucidity. She taught me everything I know.'[16]

As a consequence of Suzanne's pride and her disgust at the prospect of accepting handouts from Lucie, money was now scarcer than ever. Suzanne started taking on the odd art student for coaching if she felt they showed particular promise. Her pupils satisfied her need for youthful companionship, though how much money changed hands remained an opaque matter.

'I need some cash,' Suzanne announced one day to Naly. 'Let's go and see Mettey [*sic*].'[17]

Jean Metthey was the dealer through whom both Maurice and Suzanne had sold work recently, and Suzanne had fallen into the pattern of heading straight to see him whenever she was short of money. She ushered Naly into a taxi, with just the fare to get to Metthey's in her pocket. When they arrived at the dealer's, Naly urged her to settle the cab fare immediately.

'No, we will keep it running,' Suzanne told him. 'We won't be long.'

The discussion with Metthey lasted two hours. Finally, the dealer grudgingly handed over 200 francs, and Suzanne and Naly got back into the taxi.

'Now I need some face powder,' Suzanne declared. The taxi driver was told to stop in front of several boutiques, where Suzanne repeatedly rejected the samples Naly was asked to go and fetch. None was sufficiently high quality – or costly enough. At last, she settled on a pot and they returned home. Once the taxi had been paid, only 60 francs of Metthey's payment remained. When they got to the door, Naly had a shock: there in the entranceway was a gift of a small box of face powder. It had been left by one of Suzanne's students. Smiling, Suzanne took the powder and squirrelled it away in a drawer with the one they had just purchased. Naly could scarcely believe his eyes: in the drawer were at least ten other packages of face powder. Suzanne never powdered her face.

Once Suzanne was known to be alone, Gazi also made himself a more regular presence, so much so that many maintained he had moved in with Suzanne that year.[18]

All the same, Maurice continued to fret about his mother. The death of La Misse before the end of the year, the pet he knew Suzanne loved so much, only sharpened his anxiety.[19] Lucie shuttling between Angoulême and the capital brought a degree of reassurance and the sense that he was somehow closer to his mother. And his wife was doing a magnificent job as his personal ambassadress. The Christmas holidays barely over, early in January 1936, Lucie was again in Paris promoting. She negotiated an exhibition at the Galerie Frappat in Grenoble that New Year. Time in Paris also gave her the opportunity to meet with Paul Pétridès, who was now working as an art dealer.

'If you have the chance, do come and see us in Angoulême,' she purred when she left her rendezvous with the dealer. 'It would bring my husband so much pleasure, he has such fond memories of you.'[20]

Maurice was sure to keep in touch with his wife while she was away (though he reminded her that, like his mother, he hated writing letters). He complained that the weather in Angoulême had turned unpleasant, but was nonetheless at pains to impress his gratitude: 'I thank you wholeheartedly for the good work and effort you are putting in to manage my painting,' he wrote sincerely, before urging his wife to pass on his warmest regards to everyone he held dear in Paris and assuring her that he had kissed her darling Pekinese dogs, Baba and Lolo, on her behalf.[21]

But Lucie was not the only one nurturing an artistic career that New Year. With her strength a little restored since her hospital stay, Suzanne began painting again in earnest. She produced several still lifes, including many flower studies (one with the triumphant battle cry 'Vive la Jeunesse' inscribed on the vase), and a portrait or two. One of these was a portrait of Geneviève Camax-Zoegger, the daughter of her indomitable friend and founder of the Société des Femmes Artistes Modernes, Marie-Anne Camax-Zoegger. Geneviève was a bright girl who was currently enrolled as a student at both the prestigious École du Louvre and the École des Beaux-Arts, testimony to her excellence in both the theory and the practice of art. Suzanne thought her distinguished and erudite sitter charming, and she called her Angelique on account of her golden hair and heavenly appearance. Geneviève recalled that she only posed for three, three-hour sessions at the Avenue Junot, and during that time, she noticed that the vigour and stamina for which Suzanne was famed seemed to be faltering. Geneviève suspected the end result to be unfinished. But the piece Suzanne produced in those sittings was as remarkable as ever, and featured her characteristic bold outlines. Suzanne showed a head-and-shoulders view of the young girl seated in a rose-coloured chair which brought out the healthy glow of her cheeks. Her dark clothing merely emphasised the light, ethereal tone of her décolletage, peachy skin and golden hair, while her sweet, rosebud lips betrayed the flicker of a smile as her dark eyes invited the viewer's gaze to meet hers.[22]

While she paid homage to the daughter, Suzanne also brought pleasure to the mother. She submitted *Adam and Eve* (1909) to the Salon de la Société des Femmes Artistes Modernes that year. The exhibition highlighted the extent to which the artistic climate in

Paris had changed since Suzanne first started showing her work publicly. 'Increasingly, women's art must be produced and judged according to the same criteria as are applied to men,' wrote the reviewer in *L'Art et les artistes*. Suzanne was one of the artists picked out for special praise. 'A painter of real distinction,' the reviewer mused, 'it is hard to know whether one prefers the energetic drawing or the deep harmonies she creates.'[23]

Suzanne's work appeared in several other shows that year. But despite his mother's renewed spasm of industry, Maurice was conscious that age and financial anguish threatened her well-being. The possibility of making their new home with Suzanne was something he and Lucie were seriously considering.[24]

'I hope you have been to see my mother,' was one of his first utterances when Paul Pétridès accepted Lucie's invitation to visit them early in the year.[25] The dealer had travelled to Angoulême sooner than expected in order to confirm the suspicion that one of the supposed Utrillos he had recently handled was a fake – an increasingly common problem.

Pétridès assured Maurice that he had visited Suzanne, and had even purchased several paintings from her. Maurice sat back in his chair and smiled, visibly relieved.

In fact, Suzanne was now gathering around her a swarm of loyal, mostly younger friends. Her students Germaine Eisenmann, Odette Dumaret and the devoted Pierre Noyelle rekindled her vitality and gave her purpose now that the responsibility of Maurice had been lifted. The young Robert Le Masle was a great source of companionship too, and paid her frequent visits. Suzanne, Lucie remembered, 'coddled this pretty boy', since she 'always held masculine beauty in higher regard than its feminine counterpart'.[26] In her letters, Suzanne scolded him with exaggerated displeasure if he failed to pay her a visit she had expected, and Le Masle teased her playfully and appealed to her pride with gushing hyperbole. On at least one occasion, Suzanne also wrote to Le Masle's mother to express her appreciation of her son's time and care.[27]

Male friends like Noyelle and Le Masle were youthful, vital and bursting with artistic stimulation. Like Gazi, they saw Suzanne as a mother figure. André Utter was irked. He made his dislike of Suzanne's new social circle abundantly clear.

Utter had at least come to accept that he was no longer the primary puppeteer in the Maurice Utrillo show. But little by little, it occurred to him that if he could overcome his anger, the marionette might still dance to his tune. All he had to do was charm its new operator.

'Dear daughter-in-law and friend,' Utter wrote to Lucie Utrillo on 8 October 1936.

> Yesterday, I received the 400 francs from Methey [*sic*] that you wrote asking him to give me [...] thank you, you have done me a great favour.
>
> The Indépendants de Bordeaux sent me an urgent telegram asking if I could get hold of one of Suzanne's canvases. I did what was required and then at the last moment, when the packagers came to collect the delivery, she refused the canvas she had promised. So she will not be exhibiting in Bordeaux. My own canvas has gone off [...]
>
> Suzanne grows more and more incomprehensible and is going through a proud and immeasurably pretentious phase. Modesty became her so well, but I believe that this modesty was merely superficial and that only pathological shyness disguised an obstinate pride. It's too bad.

Utter could not resist agitating the family cauldron by confiding in Lucie that he had heard Suzanne making snide comments about a letter she had sent. 'I see from your last letter that you are again considering your project of living with Suzanne and Maurice in the Avenue Junot,' Utter continued, before making his feelings clear:

> If you will permit me to say, I think that you are incorrigible and your optimism leads you to take on projects which will be impossible to bring to fruition. In this combination, there will certainly be a victim: You! Maybe Suzanne … or Maurice … perhaps all three. But victim there will be, whether morally, artistically or financially.
>
> Cohabitation, Suzanne–Maurice with you in the middle, is practically impossible. Besides, Maurice cannot be in Montmartre for any stay extending beyond two days. Believe me and don't attempt it. What Maurice needs to the end of his days is isolation. Have you not yet understood? If you have witnessed satisfaction and a semblance of calm in Maurice's life recently, it is due to the isolation in which you keep him and an organised life with routine. With Suzanne it will be anarchy. She lives by night, and is used to receiving 20 people a day and given her age and character, you won't be able to stop her.[28]

Utter's counselling issued, he turned his attention to pecuniary concerns: could Lucie send him two gouaches and two paintings as soon as possible? He could get a good price for them.

On one matter at least, Lucie's plans correlated with Utter's desires: M. and Mme Maurice Utrillo would not be returning to the Avenue Junot to live.

Le Vésinet was a well-to-do, leafy suburb twenty minutes west of Paris that boasted tree-lined avenues, tranquil lakes and neat bourgeois homes with occupants to match. Learning of the Utrillos' property hunt and search criteria, Lucie's contact, the novelist Jean Boulant, whom she and Maurice had met on their travels that summer, enthusiastically recommended the area. The clean air and quiet, and the respectable properties with their discreet residents who kept themselves to themselves, was just the environment Lucie had had in mind. That autumn, she leased a rental property on the Route de la Plaine so that they could verify that Le Vésinet would satisfy her requirements for a permanent move.[29]

In Montmartre, gossip was rife. Such an elegant corner of the globe was hardly the place for a savage alcoholic painter like Utrillo, people sneered. But Lucie was defiant: her Maurice, now washed and clean-shaven, dressed in smart suits and hats, took his meals in a civilised manner in a dining room whose walls were lined with beautiful paintings. He smoked a cigarette after supper, petted his pedigree dogs and attended Mass on a Sunday. Besides, Maurice Utrillo was a great artist: what home could be more befitting than the commune which had once been the residence of the poet and dandy Count Robert de Montesquiou, who attracted celebrated personalities and intellectuals like writers Marcel Proust and Anna de Noailles?[30]

By the end of the year, the Utrillos had settled in and they extended an invitation to Paul Pétridès and his wife Odette to join them for the Christmas festivities.

'Since you are selling my husband's work so well and you like what he produces,' Lucie had pushed Pétridès, 'why not offer him a contract?'[31]

On 1 January 1937, a contract was duly signed. Pétridès had a sales strategy in mind which he immediately set in motion. The Cypriot did the rounds of Paris dealers, explaining that he was in desperate search of Utrillos, because he had a contract with the artist but that he was producing less and less. Word spread. Maurice's paintings became even more sought-after and his prices rocketed.[32]

Meanwhile, Lucie had decided that she liked Le Vésinet very much indeed and that M. and Mme Utrillo should begin to look for a permanent home. She found a property which had formerly been owned by the sculptor Antoine Bourdelle. The house needed work, but the location was superb. And what was good enough for Antoine Bourdelle, Lucie reasoned, was good enough for Maurice Utrillo. With a loan from Pétridès, Lucie purchased the property, and set to work redesigning the house and gardens, employing the necessary tradespeople to carry out substantial renovations and landscaping.[33] The finished result was grand, imposing and immaculate. The house was a masterpiece of geometric symmetry. Windows brought light flooding into rooms which were finished with parquet flooring and rich rugs, while Maurice had a studio built specially, and was given his own private chapel; from now on, he could worship without exposing himself to the temptations which lay beyond the property's boundaries. Lucie staffed the home with plenty of servants, including a Polish valet named Valentin and a personal secretary, Mlle Marguerite Manbre. Meanwhile, the garden was clipped into a tidy display of carefully pruned bushes, gravel pathways and neat lawns, complete with Grecian statues and ornamental frogs. There was an aviary for birds and even a run for the Pekinese dogs with which Lucie loved to compete in shows.[34]

When the house was complete to Lucie's satisfaction, all that was lacking was a name. The solution was felt to be an inspired choice: from now on, all Maurice's correspondence would be addressed to 'La Bonne Lucie'.

Maurice Utrillo, people joked, had become positively bourgeois. Suzanne refused to visit.

Lucie suspected that Suzanne had thought her daughter-in-law would be unable to handle Maurice; but a blend of Charentais and Vendean blood coursed through her veins.[35] And when, as the couple were preparing to move, Lucie lost her own mother, one of the effects was that now, all her focus could be directed on Maurice.

Suzanne's behaviour betrayed increasing resentment of Lucie's authority and the couple's affluence. She continued to refuse their monetary gifts, yet her financial situation was now bleak.

On several occasions, Naly was shocked when he arrived at the Avenue Junot to discover a fundamental appliance like the boiler had broken and Suzanne was sitting in the kitchen shivering.[36] At one point, the gas company threatened to cut off her supply when her bill was left unpaid. Suzanne was incensed: they would not dare do such a thing to a loyal customer like herself.[37]

Still Suzanne would not go to Le Vésinet. The painter and Mme Utrillo – as Lucie signed their Christmas cards – would have to come to her.

Nonetheless, Suzanne's bond with Maurice was titanic. And there were still enough civilised exchanges with the Utrillos as a couple to maintain face-to-face contact. In 1937, Suzanne sought to understand the unfathomable creature her son had married in the way she had always done when faced with a disconcerting individual. At last, mother and daughter-in-law sat down together, Lucie eager to be glorified by Suzanne Valadon's famous hand, Suzanne ready to scrutinise with her merciless brush.

'To see Suzanne Valadon paint was enchanting,' Lucie recalled, 'like hearing some kind of soothing prayer that lifted you, because at that moment, calm washed over you and she herself was transformed; her face became angelic, her art had taken hold of her and turned her into another creature.'[38]

Lucie was endlessly reverent: 'What masterly art! What powerful drawing! What vigorous marks!' Lucie glowed with satisfaction whenever she told people that Suzanne Valadon was her mother-in-law, whom she delighted in calling *ma Grande*.[39]

But Suzanne left Lucie in no doubt as to her aesthetic ethos: 'None of those sweet, syrupy embellishments which women adore. The uglier they are,' Suzanne informed Lucie pointedly, 'the more I enjoy painting them.'[40]

Suzanne showed Lucie against a deep pink background, wearing a fur coat over a brown bodice with a bold white collar. Lucie sported one of her famous hats as she stared fixedly at her viewer – and, simultaneously, at the artist. The expression on her face spoke a thousand words. Her plump neck led down to an exposed décolletage, while her jowls appeared flabby, her jaw set and determined. Her cheeks were flushed with pink, her mouth unsmiling and her eyes hard and obstinate. The painted figure was bold, dramatic and uncompromising; it was a vision Suzanne knew only too well.

'For the excellent, for the best, I urge my reader to go straight to the back of the last room, where a canvas by Suzanne Valadon awaits,' advised G. Brunon Guardia when he reviewed the exhibition *Salon de portraits contemporains* where the portrait of Lucie was shown later that year. 'In this little canvas, I can see a "great portrait" in the traditional sense, insofar as it is the image not only of a face, but of a soul.'[41]

Suzanne's interpretation of Lucie's soul did nothing to mitigate the friction between the women. Suzanne still would not visit Le Vésinet, and in any case, she tired too easily to undertake much travel these days. From time to time, Lucie brought Maurice into Montmartre, where they would take lunch with Suzanne (usually at the Moulin Joyeux), often in the company of Paul Pétridès and his wife.[42]

Pétridès remembered Suzanne's disbelief when she witnessed the transformation her son had undergone. Under Lucie's sovereignty, he was pampered, cosseted, contained and, with some help from Pétridès, turned out in the finest suits Paris had to offer. Lucie smothered her husband with care and anticipated his every need.

But more than Maurice's incongruous *embourgeoisement*, it was his submission to this formidable female that most bewildered Suzanne. Perhaps, Pétridès surmised, she had simply grown too tired to fight the ongoing battle that shadowed Maurice. No doubt that was what had prompted her to give her son up. But, the transfer of power complete, it was unsettling to see the new authority excelling in Suzanne's former role. At worst, it seemed Suzanne was now redundant.[43]

Under the circumstances, professional recognition was more reaffirming than ever. It rekindled her vitality and her playful spirit. That spring, Suzanne showed work in the exhibition *Femmes artistes d'Europe* at the Musée du Jeu de Paume. Reviewing the show, *La Revue de l'Art* branded her a 'valiant survivor', while *Le Figaro* picked her out for special praise.[44] Suzanne had always held great pride in her art, maintaining that she did not seek celebrity, merely recognition for her work. Now, she was being exhibited alongside artists like Berthe Morisot and Mary Cassatt. When Suzanne visited the exhibition and studied the other women's pieces, friends remembered her reaction: 'You know, *chérie*, I often boasted about my art because I thought that was what people expected – for an artist to boast. After what we have seen this afternoon I am very humble. The women of France can paint too, *hein*? ... But do you know, *chérie*,' – Suzanne's eyes sparkled – 'I think perhaps God has made me France's greatest woman painter.'[45]

In May, the Galerie Lucy Krohg mounted a show of Suzanne's and her students' work. Suzanne was praised for the consistency of style in her paintings, which G. Brunon Guardia wrote 'show this frankness, with an almost virile temperament that is found in identical form in her very first canvases'. Meanwhile, her students Germaine Eisenmann, Odette Dumaret and Pierre Noyelle, though influenced by their teacher, were felt to have retained their individuality.[46]

And there were still more professional accolades that year. Suzanne's international profile was growing, with paintings being shown in Chicago, Prague and Berlin. Then the crowning glory in 1937 came in the form of a very special sale. This time, the buyer interested in her work was not a dealer or a plucky avant-garde connoisseur – it was the state.

Adam and Eve (1909), *The Casting of the Nets* (1914), *Maurice Utrillo, his Grandmother and his Dog* (1910) and several drawings, including one of Suzanne's earliest studies of her mother, were purchased and duly added to the state's collection. Suzanne Valadon had received the recognition she had always craved. In her 71st year, it was a spectacular achievement.

Throughout all her professional successes, Maurice would always be a source of anxiety. That summer, he became the unwitting subject of more probing public scrutiny than usual when the catalogue entry for a recent exhibition at the Tate Gallery in London declared that he had died in 1934 due to alcoholism, and an absurd court case ensued.[47] But on a day-to-day basis, Suzanne was no longer the first to be alerted if something were amiss.

Now that she had lost Maurice, young people and her painting kept her going. Gazi could often be found ensconced at the Avenue Junot, where he and Suzanne would talk for hours. Gazi had not abandoned his quest to turn her to religion, and on one occasion he showed her a small icon of the Virgin he kept by his bed. Suzanne scoffed at his veneration and an animated dispute erupted. The next day, Suzanne confessed sheepishly that their argument had reminded her of an experience she had had as a child. She had injured herself and was taken by a friend to meet the friend's grandmother who would tend to her wound. When a small fragment of stone which was on display in the house caught Suzanne's attention, the grandmother explained that it was a piece of the statue of Our Lady of Montmartre which was destroyed during the French Revolution. Gazi protested: both the statue and the idea of a cult of Notre-Dame-de-Montmartre were unheard of on the Butte, he explained. But Suzanne insisted that he investigate. When he did, Gazi was astounded: there had been such a statue in Montmartre and the cult associated with it had petered out after the Revolution.[48] The authentication of the childhood story unnerved even Suzanne. She never declared herself a believer, though as she felt herself weakening, it seemed reasonable to entertain the possibility of faith.

Meanwhile, Suzanne's complicated relationship with Utter continued. Officially, they were still married. Suzanne's friends reported that she sent him money when she could, while he surveyed her social activities with a critical eye. They fought like husband-and-wife when they were together. And when they were apart, Utter wrote her brooding letters steeped in nostalgia over how things once had been.[49]

Two days before Suzanne's 72nd birthday, Maurice sat down to write his mother a greeting in a small white card with a humble illustration of flowers on the front. It was a twee offering from a revered painter of international renown. The endearing simplicity masked the depth of their shared experience. In saying so little, it expressed so much.[50]

Early in 1938, Suzanne sent work to the Salon de la Société des Femmes Artistes Modernes. Critics welcomed her appearance, and now even her arch nemesis, Louis Vauxcelles, had positive words to say. 'Valadon is one of the very strong painters of our day,' Vauxcelles admitted when he reviewed the women's offerings.[51]

But Suzanne's work had grown stronger than its creator. Francis Carco paid her a visit at about that time and he was shocked by the woman he beheld. Suzanne, he recalled:

> had taken refuge in the downstairs room in the house in the Avenue Junot, where she had installed a divan among stretchers and frames that made the room look like a dusty and bizarre property room. My first impression was so vivid I was unable to dissimulate it; it was almost a year since I had seen Valadon and I had some difficulty in recognising her. One felt that she was at the end of her strength. Her worn-out shoes, grubby dressing

gown, the strands of white hair falling over her forehead, and
the deterioration in her shiny, wrinkled face made her look like
an old woman whose body appeared to have shrunk ...[52]

Carco was horrified by her apparent submission, so out of character.

'Why should I struggle?' she asked. 'For the sake of whom? As
long as I had Maurice to look after, my life had some meaning ...'

Was painting no longer enough, Carco wondered?

'My work? My work is finished, and the only satisfaction it
gives me is never to have betrayed or surrendered anything which
I believed. You will see that is true one day, perhaps, if anyone ever
takes the trouble to do me justice.'[53]

Justice was closer than Suzanne imagined. That spring, a magnificent retrospective of her work opened at the Galerie Bernier.
Reviews were laudatory.

'Of all the women painters, Suzanne Valadon is the most justifiably famous of our time and also the most personal,' commended
George Besson in *Ce Soir*.[54] 'Rarely has painting by a woman been
less feminine,' added the reviewer for *La Renaissance*.[55] He continued:
'Valadon's art is sure, cruelly realistic. However glittering her colours they never destroy the line. She follows the chromatic formulas
of Cezanne [*sic*] without imitating Cezanne in the least.' 'One of
the most virile painters of our time,' seconded the critic writing
for *Marianne*, 'her place in the history of 20th-century painting is
already assured.' He concluded with a familiar, double-edged compliment, describing Suzanne as 'this painter to whom the French
school is doubly indebted: firstly for her oeuvre, and secondly for
a gifted son, Maurice Utrillo.'[56]

The exhibition had not yet been dismantled when the sun
rose over Montmartre on 7 April 1938. Suzanne set up her easel
to paint.[57] She had felt particularly drawn to the theme of a nude
standing by a fig tree recently, and as her fellow Montmartrois

began their day Suzanne absorbed herself in the all-consuming world of her painting.

April was mild that year and Suzanne's studio window was open when her neighbour, Mme Poulbot, walked past and heard a cry. Alarmed, Mme Poulbot summoned her friend, Mme Kvapil. When no answer came at Suzanne's door, the two women forced their way in. Suzanne lay motionless on the floor in front of her easel.

A doctor was called and Suzanne's neighbours waited anxiously while he made his assessment. They soon learned that Suzanne had suffered a stroke.

Dr Gauthier telephoned for Lucie. When she arrived, Suzanne was unable to speak. She looked Lucie straight in the eye, took both her hands and squeezed them. Lucie understood.[58]

The doctor insisted that Suzanne be taken to hospital, so Lucie called an ambulance before going on ahead to see to the administrative necessities. Mme Kvapil travelled with Suzanne in the ambulance.[59]

As it sped towards the Clinique Piccini, the ambulance traced the streets and boulevards Suzanne knew so well. The capital's landscape had been her playground, her school – her life. It was *her* Paris. The vehicle turned a corner at the Arc de Triomphe – and it was at that moment, Mme Kvapil recalled, that Suzanne let out a long sigh. She was gone.[60]

The ambulance arrived at the Clinique Piccini too late. André Utter rushed to the hospital as soon as he heard, choked with emotion, and proceeded to receive the visitors who were not yet reconciled to the notion of 'Mme Utrillo'.

When he was brought to the clinic, Maurice broke down. Lucie decided that it would be best for him not to attend the funeral.

When Suzanne's death was made public, the art world of Montmartre was rocked. Writing in *Le Figaro*, André Warnod thought back to the show at the Galerie Bernier: 'Who would have thought on the day of the private view, that this was to be a truly retrospective exhibition?'[61]

At 3.30 p.m. on Saturday 9 April 1938, a stream of solemn-faced artists, friends and family began arriving at the church of Saint-Pierre in Montmartre to attend the funeral service of Suzanne Valadon. White lilacs blossomed on a wall in front of the church as mourners made their way to the ceremony. Édouard Herriot could not help but be struck by the poignancy, nor by the wreaths – one composed of purple lilacs – fitting tributes for the woman known for her love of flowers and colour. Besides Herriot, the gathering included the General Director of Beaux-Arts, Georges Huisman, as well as Lucie Utrillo, Francis Carco, André Warnod, André Derain, Raoul Dufy, Marc Chagall, Georges Kars, Emilie Charmy and André Salmon. André Utter could also be seen, sobbing uncontrollably. Several moving speeches were given.[62]

Afterwards, Suzanne's body was laid to rest with her mother Madeleine at Saint-Ouen.

Robert Le Masle received an overwhelming number of condolence letters after Suzanne's death. He was determined to keep her memory alive and instigated the issuing of a commemorative bronze coin. Its face bore the profile of Suzanne as she depicted herself in her 1883 self-portrait.[63] And on the reverse was a heart with a rose in its centre and around it, three words:

Give, Love, Paint

Suzanne Valadon's life had been an ode to all three. And she had done each as she did everything – with passion.

Epilogue

Finally, the curtain was drawn back and a murmur rippled through the crowd gathered in Bessines-sur-Gartempe:

In this house was born the great artist
Suzanne Valadon
1865–1938
Mother of the artist Maurice Utrillo

'It is a great honour for Bessines to welcome such a guest,' the mayor began solemnly.[1]

A small girl was summoned to the front to read a poem specially composed for the occasion. Mlle Meyrat gave a well-practised recital of *Suzanne and the Fairy*, which told how one of the Limousin's fairies had blessed Suzanne with her creative gift as a baby. It was a touching addition to the ceremony. But as she read, people could not divert their gaze from the gaunt-looking man at the front. Maurice's eyes had filled with tears.

Next, it was Lucie's turn to take the stage, and she did so with aplomb, giving a polished performance of Maurice's own poem to his mother. At the end, Maurice motioned the sign of the cross over his chest.

Then, Jean Vertex, president of the 'Amitiés de Montmartre', and Edmond Heuzé took it in turns to pay their respects. How hard it was for young artists, Heuzé's discourse concluded, when they did not receive the recognition they deserved.

The ceremony finished with a tour of the Guimbaud inn, before the illustrious guests were ushered across the town, past the church, to the Hôtel du Commerce for lunch. But as Maurice made his way, his path was repeatedly blocked by swarms of men, women and children, waving cards and pieces of paper in front of him, pressing for autographs. Though bewildered by the confrontation, Maurice started to gratify the requests. But soon he was overwhelmed.

'This is exhausting me,' he pleaded. He was swiftly led away.

The French table had suffered cruelly at the hands of the Nazis. Rations on bread had only been lifted that February. Coffee and sugar were still restricted. The spread at the Hôtel du Commerce seemed little short of miraculous. There was jellied York ham, chilled cantaloupe melon, celery remoulade, crayfish, fillet of beef with mushrooms, chicken with cress, and a selection of fine desserts. When the wine was served – a 1934 Châteauneuf-du-Pape – a quick exchange of glances established that the visitor's glass should be small and topped up with water. But Maurice was accustomed to such ploys. He grew angry and swept the adulterated drink aside. A fresh glass was hastily brought to him.

In the middle of the meal, one of Lucie's maids appeared with a request: might it be possible to have a little beef fillet for the two Pekinese dogs they had brought with them? They had been waiting so patiently in the car.

Lunch was rounded off with a champagne toast by the mayor and then Maurice and Lucie were treated to a guided tour of the area. In the small country town, the landmarks which had charted Madeleine's daily routine had become veritable tourist attractions.

But everyone was curious to know: what did the orphan think of his *région maternelle*?

Maurice gave a faint smile. 'This is a sin I will commit again,' he answered. 'It is so beautiful here, one of the most picturesque corners of the world I know.'

Bessines, the local paper reported, had honoured its child. And it had done so in true Limousin style – with frankness and spontaneity.

⸗⸙

Suzanne Valadon knew better than anyone: there is no mystery greater than the human self. Maurice shied away from it, but Suzanne tried to understand it – again and again, in all its forms. 'I have found myself,' Suzanne told Jean Vertex at the end of her life. 'I made myself what I am, and I think I have said what I had to say.' Having achieved that, 'what would be the good of going on?' Suzanne had asked.[2]

Never was provenance more pertinent. The self is shaped and perpetuated through lineage, and through those links, transcends time. That day, the *fille du peuple* returned to her roots. And so the legacy continues.

Appendix

TO MY MOTHER
by *Maurice Utrillo*

Suzanne Valadon, my mother is thus named.
She is a noble woman, as beautiful as she is good
In virtue, in beauty; and what's more, God of genius
Endowed her with His divine breath.

Then, of all the arts, the fine one of
painting was bestowed on her
So that she could reach
Unimaginable summits defying humans
Where enthroned are the masters, only the pure, a very few.

With a firm and sure brush, defying matter,
She enchants, she animates sky, flowers and stone.
Houses have a soul, amid their profound secrets
Which she embellishes in spite of what the Beaux-Arts decree.

Her personality both so great and so pure
And with her mastery of human form
The most complex face, the most enigmatic laugh,
Is instinctively interpreted onto her canvas in a single stroke.

In magic colours, blending natural tones,
Darker hues and pinks to paint Caucasians, sepia for blacks
(Black women to be precise), oh how many paintings!
So many fine subjects, titanic works!

In a word, and this to my modesty
From her breast giving me life and nectar
With her noble art, she anticipates and fulfils my wishes,
She whom I love, adore, with a pious love.

Maurice Utrillo, V.

Afterword

For Suzanne Valadon's admirers, in death, as in life, she did not receive the recognition she deserved.

With international tension mounting, Suzanne's passing inevitably jostled for press space among the fusillade of topical news items. Adolf Hitler was accruing power with ominous rapacity, and shortly before Suzanne died, Germany had annexed Austria. Meanwhile, the edition of *Regards* containing Suzanne's homage bore a half-shot of a Chinese fighter on its cover, one of those branded a hero as he and his fellow students marched to defend their country against the Japanese.[1]

Nevertheless, the art world was determined to honour the painter many now saw as the matriarch of creative rebellion and gutsy expressivity. Georges Kars was the first to do so when he produced a drawing of Suzanne's body as she lay in state. Louis Vauxcelles wrote a long and respectful article for *Le Monde illustré*. Though he guarded against excessive reverence, he now conceded that since the death of Berthe Morisot, Suzanne was 'the strongest [woman painter] of all', and 'the greatest contemporary "paintress"'.[2] Coming from Vauxcelles, that was praise indeed. Édouard Herriot, Adolphe Tabarant, Claude Roger-Marx and Adolphe Basler were among the artistic elite to join Vauxcelles and pay their respects in a full-page spread in *Beaux-Arts*.[3] But it was Yves-Bonnat who offered Suzanne the ultimate compliment in *Regards*, the kind of recognition for which she had always strived: Suzanne, he asserted, was not simply a great woman artist – she was *un grand peintre*.[4]

Suzanne's mark on the art world was reiterated just a few months later when Jean Boulant, the novelist who had recommended the suburb of Le Vésinet to Lucie and Maurice, decided to write *Maurice Utrillo's Love Story*. The tale took Maurice's relationship with Lucie as its subject, and threatened to divulge all manner of scintillating gossip on Suzanne, Maurice and Utter when it was printed in *Paris-Soir*. Angered by what they felt to be the exposure of one of their own, a committee of artists including Pablo Picasso, André Derain, Adolphe Basler, André Warnod, Maurice de Vlaminck and Jean Dufy wrote a formal protest to be printed in *Beaux-Arts*. Maurice was quick to respond with a letter, which he asked to appear alongside their opposition on 18 November 1938. He expressed his gratitude for their concern, but informed them politely yet firmly that he was in no need of their defence. He was aware of the author's project, and in any case, the book was far less objectionable than previous works which depicted him as fit only for a psychiatric ward.[5]

André Utter was apparently not consulted. Utter was haunted by the memory of his late wife for the rest of his days, obsessed with the cult of Valadon which he strove to perpetuate. Having sold the château in Saint-Bernard in 1943, Utter returned to the Rue Cortot where he painted still lifes, portraits and landscapes. He gave talks and lectures on Suzanne and Maurice, produced articles on the artists, and even planned to write a book, for which preparatory notes are held by the Musée Nationale d'Art Moderne at the Centre Georges Pompidou. The book was never finished; Utter died of pneumonia in 1948 in his early 60s. 'I can only reproach him for having abused my mother in words and actions,' was Maurice's single criticism in an otherwise considerate article he wrote on his stepfather's death. 'Let us not dwell on that.'[6]

Maurice Utrillo lived with Lucie at Le Vésinet for the rest of his life, his painting, his faith and his wife his sole preoccupations. He never attained sobriety. Thanks to Lucie's business acumen, the Utrillos became wealthy. They lived in comfort, took their holidays in Dax and on the Riviera, and when they did venture out from 'La Bonne Lucie' to socialise, they rubbed shoulders with the most elegant company. In the late 1940s, they became acquainted with Prince Aly Khan and Rita Hayworth, and to Lucie's gratification they were invited to attend the couple's wedding. But for all the glamour and the fame, Maurice was once asked, did he not miss Montmartre? No, he answered hastily, people there were idiots and all that mattered to him now was his wife and his painting. Then when Lucie had left the room: 'There's not an hour that I don't think of it.'[7]

In the early 1950s, Maurice appeared in Sacha Guitry's film *Si Paris nous était conté* (released in 1956), in which he played himself. Afterwards, he travelled with Lucie to Dax to take their annual spa treatment. While there, he fell ill. Three days later, on 5 November 1955, Maurice died at one o'clock in the afternoon – the same time as he was born. An incomplete gouache was found on his easel after he died; it was a study of 12, Rue Cortot.[8] Maurice Utrillo's paintings remain sought after and still command enormous sums whenever they appear at auction.

Lucie Utrillo dedicated the rest of her life to caring for Maurice, managing his career and, after his death, perpetuating his legacy. After Suzanne died, she fancied she too might be a painter, and started producing what a contemporary described as 'crudely drawn' compositions using 'bright, flat colours'.[9] Figures, flowers and her dogs were her subjects of choice. Lucie always venerated Suzanne, 'but of course,' she told one of Maurice's biographers, 'the future will tell how great I am going to be, and the future will choose'.[10] She took her role as a famous artist's wife with the utmost seriousness, and the couple's newfound prosperity meant that she could select the appropriate costumes to play the part. They were invariably sourced from Paris's top fashion houses: 'I must dress in keeping with my name as the wife of the greatest painter in France,' she reasoned.[11] When Maurice died, Lucie was devastated. She died in Paris in 1965.

Even after Maurice, Utter and Lucie had passed away, Robert Le Masle continued his admirable quest to safeguard Suzanne's memory. In 1961, the doctor orchestrated the dedication of a square in Suzanne's honour. The Place Suzanne-Valadon can be found in the 18th arrondissement in Paris between the Sacré-Coeur and the Boulevard de Rochechouart. Le Masle left his substantial collection of letters, photographs, documents and objects to the Musée Nationale d'Art Moderne. Collectively, they tell Suzanne's tale.

In 1960, 12, Rue Cortot became the Musée de Montmartre, with a mission to retell the history of Montmartre through artefacts, photographs, documents and drawings. The Musée Utrillo-Valadon at Sannois, the Association Maurice Utrillo (created by Lucie in 1963) and the Espace Valadon in Bessines also remain committed to preserving Suzanne's and Maurice's memory. In September 2015, La Poste issued a commemorative stamp to mark the 150th anniversary of Suzanne's birth. Fittingly, it showed the 1924 painting *Woman with White Stockings*, a piece created when Suzanne was at the pinnacle of her artistic career.

In her lifetime, Suzanne Valadon is known to have produced some 478 paintings, 273 drawings and 31 etchings. This takes no account of pieces which were given away or destroyed. Her surviving works hang proudly on the walls of permanent collections across the world, with many located in France and the USA. There have been numerous exhibitions dedicated to Suzanne's work since her death, including several coordinated by Lucie which showcased her own paintings alongside Suzanne's and Maurice's, such as the show at the Hammer Gallery in New York in 1958. Important Valadon retrospectives took place in Paris in 1939, 1947 and 1967. A large exhibition of her paintings and drawings was mounted at the

Fondation Pierre Gianadda in Switzerland in 1996, while the shows *Valadon Utrillo: Au tournant du siècle à Montmartre – de l'Impressionisme à l'École de Paris* at the Pinacothèque de Paris in 2009 and *Valadon, Utrillo & Utter à l'atelier de la rue Cortot: 1912–1926* at the Musée de Montmartre in 2015 have also provided valuable opportunities to enjoy her paintings and drawings. Meanwhile, Suzanne still greets viewers with her challenging stare as she gazes out of the compositions of Renoir, Toulouse-Lautrec and so many other great artists whose works now hang in museums around the world.

All too often, Suzanne Valadon has been relegated to a cursory footnote in the tomes of art history. A burgeoning library of scholarship on women's art has begun to rectify this oversight. However, for many, she remains Utrillo's mother, Renoir's model, Toulouse-Lautrec's muse. Illustrious names cast a long shadow; Suzanne was a victim of the company she kept. But besides her connections to some of France's greatest male artists, Suzanne's lack of prominence owes as much to the challenge her work presents and her rejection of the label 'woman artist'. She espoused no theory and adhered to no school. She simply painted what she saw with honesty and conviction. Suzanne employed bold outlines and strong colours, and pared subjects down to their bare essentials as she sought to understand the world around her. 'I can't flatter a subject,' she once warned an admirer.[12] And therein lies the challenge at the heart of her creative oeuvre: truth. Suzanne's viewers must prepare themselves for honesty and passion. Truth can be uncomfortable; it is not always pretty. There is nothing half-hearted about Suzanne Valadon's work. It is up to the viewer to decide whether they wish to turn their back on what the artist shows them – or whether, like Maurice and Utter, they are prepared to let Valadon take their hand and lead them on a journey so dramatic and so vivid that it is one they are likely never to forget.

Acknowledgements

When I first pushed open the heavy oak door to the derelict Limousin cottage that would become my second home, I had no suspicion that a great painter had been born just minutes away, still less that her life would become such an integral part of my own. It takes many viewpoints to show a subject in multiple dimensions; I am grateful to the individuals and organisations who have helped me bring Suzanne's story to life.

Sincere thanks are due to Duncan Heath, Andrew Furlow, Robert Sharman, Jasmin Singh and the publishing team at Icon Books, as well as to Ruth Killick. In addition, the dedication, support and sheer hard work of my agent, Andrew Lownie, never fail to impress me.

This book has been enriched by the first-hand accounts of people whose lives were personally touched by Suzanne and Maurice. The recollections of Jeanine Warnod, who remembers Suzanne's visits to her house when she was a little girl, brought colour to Suzanne's character for me. Similarly, Christiane Barny Duditlieu's vivid memories of Maurice's and Lucie's visit to Bessines-sur-Gartempe in 1949 formed the starting point of this book.

A number of experts, associations, museums and galleries have been of tremendous assistance. I am profoundly grateful to Jean Michel Buck at the Musée de Montmartre et Jardins Renoir for having been so generous with his time and assistance throughout this project. Isabelle Ducatez at the museum has also been a great source of knowledge. Hélène Bruneau at the Association Utrillo has been an invaluable point of contact in verifying the chronology and particulars of Maurice Utrillo's life, and Cédric Paillier has also been immensely helpful. I have also been fortunate to benefit from the assistance of staff at the Musée Utrillo-Valadon at Sannois. My research into daily life in the 19th-century Limousin has been greatly assisted by Pascale Marouseau at the Archives Départmentales de la Haute-Vienne and Hélène Jager at the Musée René Baubérot in Châteauponsac. I am equally indebted to Christine Papin, Emmanuel Soyer and Ludovic Guiral at the Centre d'Archives Historiques de la SNCF for the research into train times and travel costs from the Limousin to Paris in the 19th century. My understanding of Suzanne's time in other parts of France has been enhanced by Elisabeth Guillaume at the Archives de Nantes and Maureen Brugaro at the Office de Tourisme de Cancale. The Filles de la Charité de Saint Vincent de Paul were kind enough to share their archives with me; this proved indispensable when piecing together Suzanne's educational history. Thanks are also owed to Mme de la Rivière of the École de Saint-Jean de Montmartre. Isabelle Lawson and Michel King at the Société Nationale des Beaux-Arts were most generous in sharing their thoughts on Suzanne's involvement with the society. My immense gratitude also goes to Guy-Patrice Dauverville at Bernheim-Jeune & Cie for his diligent research into the gallery's archives which shed light on Suzanne's and Maurice's relationship with Bernheim-Jeune. In addition, I should like to thank Professor Tamar Garb at University College London for her time and thoughts regarding painting as a woman in 19th-century France.

I am grateful to all the museums, galleries and collections who have kindly allowed works to be reproduced in this book. Staff at the British Library in London, the Courtauld Institute of Art Book Library and the Witt Library at Somerset House have been of great assistance. In Paris, I am indebted to staff at the Musée d'Orsay, the Musée Carnavalet and the Bibliothèque Kandinsky (particularly

Brigitte Vincens and Dominique Liquois) at the Centre Georges Pompidou.

Professor John House has never been far from my thoughts while writing; I hope he would approve of the results. Mention should also be made of Suzanne Courdesses-Betout, whose legacy of research on Suzanne has made my own work so much easier.

Professor Colin Davis at Royal Holloway, University of London continues to be a valued point of reference, guidance and support. Once again, Sarah Sears's scrupulous attention to detail and the literary expertise of Harriet Reuter Hapgood have been greatly appreciated.

Special thanks must be extended to Professor David Russell Jones, Dr Michelle Conn, Joanne Wallis and Alison Little. All have ensured that the tools of the trade remain in optimum order.

Suzanne Valadon was a *fille du peuple*, and this book would not have been the same without her people – the people of Bessines, for whom it is written. From the outset, Cécile Bonnefoy Cudraz and Sylvie Dupic at the Office de Tourisme in Bessines have shown extraordinary support for both this project and its author, going out of their way to source documents and pursue contacts, at once facilitating and enriching the process of research – *mille fois merci les deux*. I am indebted to l'Association Racines à Bessines for allowing me to access the Valadons' birth, marriage and death records. I am grateful to Père Nicolas Sabléry for making the church records accessible and to Mme Blanche Brisset for taking time to study them with me. Monsieur and Mme Pierre Chastenet showed me extraordinary generosity and hospitality when I was researching the Auberge Guimbaud. It is thanks to the passion and dedication of Bessinauds like Didier and Dany Deroussen at the Café de la Place, Jean-Pierre and Gladys Faurie and their team at the Maison Faurie Boulangerie, and Pascal and Françoise Voisin at the Hôtel Bellevue, that Bessines remains the lively hub of community spirit which has long been its distinguishing quality. I feel especially privileged to have been the recipient of the kindness and friendship of all those in Les Petits Magneux, in particular Jacques Tanty, Irène Blondin, and Raymond and Yvonne Geay.

Lastly, my heartfelt gratitude goes to my family. As ever, John, Elaine and Sam Hewitt have been a constant source of love, support and friendship, as well as a welcome proofreading service.

And finally, thank you to Alex Forrest – for proving that when you wish upon a star, sometimes, dreams really do come true.

Selected Bibliography

(MNAM – Musée National d'Art Moderne)

Books

1900: Art at the Crossroads, exhib. cat. (London: Royal Academy of Arts, 2000)

Adler, Kathleen & Tamar Garb, eds, *The Correspondence of Berthe Morisot* (London: Camden Press Ltd, 1986)

Ariès, Philippe, *Centuries of Childhood* (Harmondsworth: Penguin Books, 1986)

— and George Duby, eds, *A History of Private Life*, trans. by Arthur Goldhammer, 5 vols (Cambridge, MA and London: Belknap Press of Harvard University Press, 1987–1991)

Arnold, Odile, *Le Corps et l'âme: La Vie des religieuses au XIXe siècle* (Paris: Éditions du Seuil, 1984)

L'Art en France sous le Second Empire, exhib. cat. (Paris: Éditions de la Réunion des musées nationaux, 1979)

Audoin-Rouzeau, Stéphane, and Annette Becker, *La Grande Guerre 1914–1918* (Paris: Gallimard, 1998)

Bailey, Colin B., *Renoir's Portraits* (New Haven and London: Yale University Press, 1997)

Banlin-Lacroix, Catherine, 'Miguel Utrillo i Morlius', in Jean Fabris, *Utrillo, sa vie, son oeuvre* (Paris: Éditions Frédéric Birr, 1982), pp. 13–16.

Barter, Judith A., 'Childhood and Maternity', in Judith A. Barter and others, *Mary Cassatt: Modern Woman* (Chicago: Art Institute of Chicago and Harry N. Abrams, Inc., 1998), pp. 69–81.

— and others, *Mary Cassatt: Modern Woman* (Chicago: Art Institute of Chicago and Harry N. Abrams, Inc., 1998)

Bazire, Edmond, *Manet* (Paris, 1884)

Beachboard, Robert, *La Trinité maudite* (Paris: Amiot-Dumont, 1952)

Brettell, Richard R. and Caroline B. Brettell, *Painters and Peasants in the Nineteenth Century* (Geneva: Skira, 1983)

Burke, David, *Writers in Paris: Literary Lives in the City of Light* (Counterpoint: Berkeley, CA, 2008)

Bury, J.P.T., *France 1814–1940* (London: Methuen & Co. Ltd, 1969)

Callen, Anthea, *Techniques of the Impressionists* (London: Tiger Books International, 1990)

Carco, Francis, *L'Ami des peintres* (Paris: Éditions Gallimard, 1953)

— *La Légende et la vie d'Utrillo* (Paris: Bernard Grasset, 1928)

Catalogue illustré des ouvrages de peinture, sculpture, dessins, gravure et objets d'art et architecture exposés au Champ-de-Mars, 25 April 1894 (reissued New York & London: Garland Publishing, Inc., 1981)

Catalogue of the Exhibition of International Art, Knightsbridge (London, 1898)

Cate, Phillip Dennis, 'L'esprit de Montmartre et l'art moderne, 1875–1910' in *L'Esprit de Montmartre et l'Art Moderne 1875–1910*, exhib. cat. (Paris: Musée de Montmartre, 2014), pp. 23–40.

Cerbelaud Salagnac, Georges, *Histoire du Limousin* (Paris: Éditions France-Empire, 1996)

Chalon, Jean, *Liane de Pougy: Courtisane, princesse et sainte* (Paris: Flammarion, 1994)

Clancier, Georges-Emmanuel, *La Vie quotidienne en Limousin au XIXe siècle* (Paris: Hachette, 1976)

Clayson, Hollis, *Paris in Despair: Art and Everyday Life under Siege (1870–71)* (Chicago and London: University of Chicago Press, 2002)

de Conty, H.A., *Paris en poche – Guide pratique Conty*, 6th edn (Paris, 1875)

Cope, Susan, and others, eds, *Larousse Gastronomique* (London: Mandarin, 1990)

Copley, Esther, *The Young Servant's Friendly Instructor or A Summary of the Duties of Domestic Servants* (London, 1827)

Coquiot, Gustave, *Des Peintres maudits* (Paris: André Delpeuch, 1924)

— *Renoir* (Paris: Albin Michel, 1925)

Coughlan, Robert, *The Wine of Genius: A Life of Maurice Utrillo* (London: Gollancz, 1952)

Courdesses-Betout, Suzanne, *Bessines au fil des siècles* (Limoges: [n. pub.], 1990)

—'Le Panthéon de Bessines – les origines de Suzanne Valadon' in *Suzanne Valadon 1865–1938*, exhib. cat. (Martigny: Fondation Pierre Gianadda, 1996), pp. 65–9.

Crespelle, Jean-Paul, *Le Monde de Degas* (Paris, 1974), cited in June Rose, *Mistress of Montmartre: A Life of Suzanne Valadon* (London: Richard Cohen Books, 1998)

— *Montmartre vivant* (Paris: Hachette, 1964)

Cumming, Robert, *Art* (London, New York, Munich, Melbourne & Delhi: Dorling Kindersley, 2005)

Dabot, Henri, *Souvenirs et impressions d'un bourgeois du Quartier Latin mai 1854 à mai 1869* (Quentin: Péronne, 1895), cited in Richardson, p. 75.

Daniel, Howard, and John Berger, *Encyclopaedia of Themes and Subjects in Painting* (London: Thames and Hudson, 1971)

Davis, Mary E., *Erik Satie* (London: Reaktion Books Ltd, 2007)

Delvau, Alfred, *Histoire anecdotique des cafés et des cabarets de Paris* (Paris, 1862)

Deroyer, Michelle, *Quelques souvenirs autour de Suzanne Valadon* (Paris: Fayard, 1947)

Dortu, M.G., and Ph. Huisman, 'Introduction', in Henri de Toulouse-Lautrec and Maurice Joyant, *The Art of Cuisine*, trans. by Margery Weiner (New York, Chicago and San Francisco: Holt, Rinehart and Winston, 1966), pp. 11–12.

Dupanloup, Mgr, *La Femme studieuse*, 7th edn (Paris, 1900)

Ehrlich White, Barbara, *Renoir: His Life, Art, and Letters* (New York: Harry N. Abrams, 1984)

Émile-Bayard, Jean, *Montmartre Past and Present*, trans. by Ralph Anningson and Tudor Davies (London: T. Fisher Unwin Ltd, 1926)

L'Esprit de Montmartre et l'art moderne, 1875–1910, exhib. cat. (Paris: Musée de Montmartre, 2014)

État des communes à la fin du XIXe siècle – Pierrefitte (Montévrain, 1896)

Fabris, Jean, *Maurice Utrillo, – folie?* (Paris: Galerie Pétridès, 1992)

— *Utrillo, sa vie, son oeuvre* (Paris: Éditions Frédéric Birr, 1982)

Ferrier, Jean-Louis, ed., *Art of Our Century*, trans. by Walter D. Glanze (Harlow, Essex: Longman Group UK Ltd, 1990)

Frank, Nino, *Montmartre ou les enfants de la folie* (Paris: Calmann-Levy, 1956)

Frascina, Francis, and others, *Modernity and Modernism: French Painting in the Nineteenth Century* (New Haven and London: Yale University Press, 1993)

Fuchs, Rachel, *Abandoned Children: Foundlings and Child Welfare in 19th-Century France* (Albany: State University of New York Press, 1984)

Galbally, Ann, *Charles Conder: The Last Bohemian* (Melbourne: Melbourne University Press, 2003)

Garb, Tamar, 'Gender and Representation' in Francis Frascina and others, *Modernity and Modernism: French Painting in the Nineteenth Century* (New Haven and London: Yale University Press, 1993), pp. 219–89.

Gauzi, François, *My Friend Toulouse-Lautrec*, trans. by Paul Dinnage (London: Neville Spearman, 1957)

Gendron, Bernard, *Between Montmartre and the Mudd Club: Popular Music and the Avant-Garde* (Chicago: University of Chicago Press, 2002)

Goldschmidt, Lucien and Herbert Schimmel, eds, *Unpublished Correspondence of Henri de Toulouse-Lautrec*, (London: Phaidon, 1969)

de Goncourt, Edmond, *Paris under Siege, 1870–1871: From the Goncourt Journal*, ed. and trans. by George J. Becker (Ithaca and London: Cornell University Press, 1969)

The Green Guide Dordogne, Berry, Limousin (Herts: Michelin Apa Publications Ltd, 2007)

Groom, Gloria, and others, *L'Impressionisme et la mode*, exhib. cat. Musée d'Orsay (Paris: Skira/Flammarion, 2013)

Gruitrooy, Gerhard, *Mary Cassatt – An American Impressionist* (New York: Todtri, 1996)

Guerin, Marcel, ed., *Degas – Lettres* (Paris: Bernard Grasset, 2011)

Guilbaud-Rabiller, Bérangère, *Le Grand Almanach du Limousin 2016* (La Crèche: Geste éditions, 2015)

Hargrove, J., and N. McWilliam, eds, *Nationalism and French Visual Culture* (New Haven and London: Yale University Press, 2005)

Hautecoeur, Louis, *Les Peintres de la vie familiale* (Paris: Galerie Charpentier, 1945)

Heekin Burke, Mary Alice, *Elizabeth Nourse, 1859–1938 – A Salon Career* (Washington, DC: National Museum of American Art and the Cincinnati Art Museum, 1983)

Herbert, Robert L., *Impressionism: Art, Leisure, and Parisian Society* (New Haven and London: Yale University Press, 1988)

Higonnet, Anne, *Berthe Morisot* (Berkeley and Los Angeles: University of California Press, 1995)

Horne, Alistair, *Seven Ages of Paris* (London: Pan Macmillan, 2003)

House, John, *Impressionism: Paint and Politics* (New Haven and London: Yale University Press, 2004)

— *Impressionists by the Sea*, exhib. cat. (London: Royal Academy of Arts, 2007)

— *Renoir in Guernsey* (Guernsey: Guernsey Museum & Art Gallery, 1988)

— and Anne Distel, *Renoir*, exhib. cat. (London: Hayward Gallery, 1985)

Hunt, Lynn, 'The Unstable Boundaries of the French Revolution' in *A History of Private Life*, ed. by Philippe Ariès and George Duby, trans. by Arthur Goldhammer, 5 vols (Cambridge, MA, and London: Belknap Press of Harvard University Press, 1987–1991), vol. 4: *From the Fires of Revolution to the Great War*, ed. by Michelle Perrot (1990), pp. 13–45.

Ilyin, Maximilian, *Utrillo* (London: A. Zwemmer; Paris: Fernand Hazan, 1953)

Impressionists in Winter: Effets de Neige, exhib. cat. (Washington DC: The Phillips Collection, 1999)

Janet, Paul, *La Famille*, 17th edn (Paris, 1900)

Joanne, Adolphe, *Itinéraire général de la France: Normandie* (Paris, 1866)

— *Paris Illustré, Nouveau guide de l'étranger et du parisien* (Paris, 1867)

Jones, Colin, *Cambridge Illustrated History of France* (Cambridge: Cambridge University Press, 1994)

Jourdain, Francis, *Utrillo* (Paris: Braun et Cie, 1948)

Kendall, Richard, and Jill DeVonyar, *Degas and the ballet: Picturing Movement*, exhib. cat. (London: Royal Academy of Arts, 2011)

King, Francis X., *The Encyclopedia of Fortune Telling* (London: Octopus Books Ltd, 1988)

King, Graham, *Garden of Zola: Émile Zola and his Novels for English Readers* (London: Barrie and Jenkins Ltd, 1978)

Krebs, Sophie, 'Montmartre, colline inspirée?' in *Valadon Utrillo: Au tournant du siècle à Montmartre – de l'Impressionisme à l'École de Paris*, exhib. cat. (Paris: Pinacothèque de Paris, 2009), pp. 37–47.

Lacan, Claude, *Histoire du chemin de fer en Limousin* (Limoges: René Dessagne, 1984)

Larousse, Grand dictionnaire du XIX siècle (Paris, 1900)

Lassaigne, Jacques, *Impressionism*, trans. by Paul Eve (London: Heron Books, 1966)

Lavisse, Ernest, *La Première année d'histoire de France, cours moyen* (Paris: Armand Colin, 1912)

de Leeuw, Ronald, ed., *The Letters of Vincent van Gogh*, trans. by Arnold Pomerans (London: Penguin Books, 1996)

Leighton, John, Richard Thomson and others, *Seurat and The Bathers* (London: National Gallery Publications Limited, 1997)

Lelarge, J., and E. Bourdon, *Petite Histoire de la Bretagne* (Paris: Libraire Félix Juven, 1911)

Leroy-Beaulieu, Paul, *Le Travail des femmes* (Paris, 1873)

Lethève, Jacques, *La Vie quotidienne des artistes français au XIXe siècle* (Paris: Hachette, 1968)

Loyrette, Henri, *Degas: Passion and Intellect*, trans. by Mark Paris (London: Thames and Hudson, 1993)

Manuel de la piété à l'usage de la jeune pensionnaire (144), 1865.

Martin-Fugier, Anne, 'Bourgeois Rituals' in *A History of Private Life*, ed. by Philippe Ariès and George Duby, trans. by Arthur Goldhammer, 5 vols (Cambridge, MA and London: Belknap Press of Harvard University Press, 1987–1991), vol. 4: *From the Fires of Revolution to the Great War*, ed. by Michelle Perrot (1990), pp. 261–337.

du Maurier, George, *Trilby* (Hertfordshire: Wordsworth Editions Ltd, 1995)

McMillan, James F., *Twentieth-Century France: Politics and Society 1898–1991* (London, New York, Sydney and Auckland: Arnold, 1992)

Michel, André, *Puvis de Chavannes* (London: William Heinemann, 1912)

Mme Millet, *Journal de l'agriculture pratique*, 5 December 1859, cited in Mme Marie-Sincère Romieu, *Des Paysans et de l'agriculture en France au XIXe siècle* (Paris, 1865), p. 383.

Millman, Ian, *Georges de Feure: maître du symbolisme et de l'art nouveau* (Paris: ACR, 1992)

Moore, George, *Confessions of a Young Man* (Middlesex: Penguin Books, 1939)

Munck, Jacqueline, 'La Peinture de Suzanne Valadon: 1909–1914, une passion décisive' in *Valadon, Utrillo & Utter à l'atelier de la rue Cortot: 1912–1926*, exhib. cat. (Paris: Musée de Montmartre, 2015), pp. 29–37.

Ooms, Saskia, 'Les Artistes-Résidents du 12–14, rue Cortot' in *L'Esprit de Montmartre et l'art moderne, 1875–1910*, exhib. cat. (Paris: Musée de Montmartre, 2014), pp. 19–20.

Orledge, Robert, *Satie the Composer* (Cambridge: Cambridge University Press, 1990)

— *Satie Remembered* (London: Faber and Faber, 1995)

Osborne, Richard, *Freud for Beginners* (New York & London: Writers and Readers, 1993)

Perrot, Michelle, 'Roles and Characters' in *A History of Private Life*, ed. by Philippe Ariès and George Duby, trans. by Arthur Goldhammer, 5 vols (Cambridge, MA, London: Belknap Press of Harvard University Press, 1987–1991), vol. 4: *From the Fires of Revolution to the Great War*, ed. by Michelle Perrot (1990), pp. 167–259.

Perruchot, Henri, *Toulouse-Lautrec*, trans. by Humphrey Hare (London: Constable and Company Ltd, 1958)

Pétridès, Paul, *Ma Chance et ma réussite* (Paris: Plon, 1978)

— ed., *L'Oeuvre complète de Suzanne Valadon* (Paris: Compagnie française des arts graphiques, 1971)

Pickles, Sheila, ed., *The Grand Tour* (London: Pavilion Books Limited, 1991)

Pickvance, Ronald, '*Terrible Maria*: Degas and Suzanne Valadon' in *Suzanne Valadon – 1865–1938*, exhib. cat. (Martigny, Switzerland: Fondation Pierre Gianadda, 1996), pp. 23–8.

de Polnay, Peter, *The World of Maurice Utrillo* (London: Heinemann, 1967)

Post-Impressionism: Cross Currents in European Painting, exhib. cat. (London: Royal Academy of Arts, 1979)

Potter, Caroline, ed., *Erik Satie: Music, Art and Literature* (Oxon: Routledge, 2016)

Price, Roger, *A Social History of Nineteenth-Century France* (London: Hutchinson, 1987)

Ravel, L., *La Corse, resources de son sol et de son climat* (Paris: Charles Amat, 1911)

Recueil Cirque Molier 1884–1933, Bibliothèque nationale de France

Renoir in the 20th Century, exhib. cat. (Los Angeles: Los Angeles County Museum of Art, 2009)

Renoir, Jean, *Renoir, My Father*, trans. by Randolph and Dorothy Weaver (London: The Reprint Society Ltd, 1962)

Rewald, John, *The History of Impressionism*, 4th edn (New York: Museum of Modern Art and London: Secker & Warburg, 1973)

— *Seurat* (London: Thames and Hudson, 1990)

Rey, Robert, *Suzanne Valadon* (Paris: Gallimard, 1922)

Richardson, Joanna, *La Vie Parisienne 1852–1870* (London: Hamish Hamilton, 1971)

Robb, Graham, *The Discovery of France* (London: Picador, 2008)

— *Parisians: An Adventure History of Paris* (London: Picador, 2010)

Robert, Maurice, *La Maison, le village, le paysan en Limousin*, 4th edn, 2 vols (Pageas: Société d'Ethnographie et de Sauvegarde des Patrimoines en Limousin, 2007), vol. 2.

Romieu, Mme Marie-Sincère, *Des Paysans et de l'agriculture en France au XIXe siècle* (Paris, 1865)

Rose, June, *Mistress of Montmartre: A Life of Suzanne Valadon* (London: Richard Cohen Books, 1998)

— *Modigliani: The Pure Bohemian* (London: Constable, 1990)

Rosenblum, Robert, 'Art in 1900: Twilight or Dawn?' in *1900: Art at the Crossroads*, exhib. cat. (London: Royal Academy of Arts, 2000), pp. 26–53.

Rosinsky, Thérèse Diamand, 'Les multiples identités de Suzanne Valadon: Marie-Clémentine, "Biqui", ou "Terrible Maria"?' in *Suzanne Valadon – 1865–1938*, exhib. cat. (Martigny, Switzerland: Fondation Pierre Gianadda, 1996), pp. 31–53.

— *Suzanne Valadon* (New York: Universe Publishing, 1994)

Rounding, Virginia, *Grandes Horizontales: The Lives and Legends of Four 19th-Century Courtesans* (London: Bloomsbury, 2003)

Satie, Erik, letter to Suzanne Valadon, MNAM.

Sée, *Aujourd'hui Paris* in Clayson, p. 86.

Shaw, J.L., 'Frenchness, Memory and Abstraction: The Case of Pierre Puvis de Chavannes' in *Nationalism and French Visual Culture*, ed. by J. Hargrove and N. McWilliam (New Haven and London: Yale University Press, 2005), p. 153.

Shaw-Miller, Simon, 'The Only Musician with Eyes – Erik Satie and Visual Art', in *Erik Satie: Music, Art and Literature*, ed. by Caroline Potter (Oxon: Routledge, 2016), pp. 85–114.

Simon, Jules and Gustave, *La Femme au XXe siècle* (Paris, 1892)

Simon, Linda, *The Greatest Show on Earth: A History of the Circus* (London: Reaktion Books Ltd, 2014). Google ebook.

Stevens, Maryanne, 'The Exposition Universelle: "This vast competition of effort, realisation and victories"' in *1900: Art at the Crossroads*, exhib. cat. (London: Royal Academy of Arts, 2000), pp. 55–71.

Storm, John, *The Valadon Drama: The Life of Suzanne Valadon* (New York: E.P. Dutton & Co., Inc., 1959)

Suzanne Valadon, exhib. cat. (Paris: Musée national d'art moderne, 1967)

Suzanne Valadon – 1865–1938, exhib. cat. (Martigny, Switzerland: Fondation Pierre Gianadda, 1996)

Tabarant, Adolphe, *Utrillo* (Paris: Bernheim-Jeune, 1926)

Tillier, Alan, *Paris* (London, New York, Stuttgart & Moscow: Dorling Kindersley, 1999)

Tindall, Gillian, *The Journey of Martin Nadaud: A Life and Turbulent Times* (London: Chatto & Windus, 1999)

Todd, Pamela, *The Impressionists' Table* (London: Pavilion Books, 1997)

de Toulouse-Lautrec, Henri, and Maurice Joyant, *The Art of Cuisine*, trans. by Margery Weiner (New York, Chicago and San Francisco: Holt, Rinehart and Winston, 1966)

Utrillo, Maurice, *Histoire de ma jeunesse jusqu'à ce jour*, published in *Valadon Utrillo: Au tournant du siècle à Montmartre – de l'Impressionisme à l'École de Paris*, exhib. Cat. (Paris: Pinacothèque de Paris, 2009), pp. 65–131.

Utter, André, *Entre Peintres*, MNAM, cited in Thérèse Diamand Rosinsky, 'Les multiples identités de Suzanne Valadon: Marie-Clémentine, "Biqui", ou "Terrible Maria"?' in *Suzanne Valadon – 1865–1938*, exhib. cat. (Martigny, Switzerland: Fondation Pierre Gianadda, 1996), pp. 31–53.

Valadon, Suzanne, 'Suzanne Valadon ou l'absolu', n.d., MNAM.

Valadon Utrillo: Au tournant du siècle à Montmartre – de l'Impressionisme à l'École de Paris, exhib. cat. (Paris: Pinacothèque de Paris, 2009)

Valadon, Utrillo & Utter à l'atelier de la rue Cortot: 1912–1926, exhib. cat. (Paris: Musée de Montmartre, 2015)

Valéry, Paul, *Degas Danse Dessin* (Paris: Gallimard, 1936), cited in Henri Loyrette, *Degas: Passion and Intellect*, trans. by Mark Paris (London: Thames and Hudson, 1993), pp. 155–7.

Valore, Lucie, *Maurice Utrillo, mon mari* (Paris: Joseph Foret, 1956)

Visitor guide, *Musée René Baubérot – Archéologie & Ethnographie – Châteauponsac, Haute-Vienne.*

Vollard, Ambroise, *Degas* (Paris: les Editions G. Crès et cie, 1924)

Volta, Ornella, *Satie Seen Through his Letters*, trans. by Michael Bullock (London: Marion Boyars, 1989)

Waller, Susan S., *The Invention of the Model – Artists and Models in Paris, 1830–1870* (Aldershot: Ashgate Publishing Ltd, 2006)

Walther, Ingo F., *Pablo Picasso 1881–1973: Genius of the Century* (Greven: Taschen, 1993)

— and Rainer Metzger, *Vincent van Gogh: The Complete Paintings*, trans. by Michael Hulse, 2 vols (Los Angeles: Taschen, 2010)

Warnod, Jeanine, *L'École de Paris* (Paris: Arcadia Éditions, 2004)

— *Suzanne Valadon*, trans. by Shirley Jennings (Naefels, Switzerland: Bonfini Press, 1981)

Weill, Berthe, *Pan! … dans l'Oeil* (Paris: L'Échelle de Jacob, 2009)

Wiart, Claude, 'Utrillo Le Simple' in Jean Fabris, *Utrillo, sa vie, son oeuvre* (Paris: Éditions Frédéric Birr, 1982), pp. 121–46.

Zeldin, Theodore, *France 1848–1945: Ambition and Love* (Oxford, New York, Toronto and Melbourne: Oxford University Press, 1988)

Zola, Émile, *The Drinking Den*, trans. by Robin Buss (London: Penguin Books, 2003)

Articles

'L'Actualité – Les Expositions', *L'Art et les artistes*, March 1936–July 1936, p. 249.

'L'Actualité Artistique – Expositions', *Mobilier & décoration*, 1934, p. 301.

Alexandre, Arsène, 'Edgard Degas', *Le Figaro*, 28 September 1917, p. 1.

'Appel aux Parisiennes', *Le Figaro*, 4 August 1914, p. 2.

Barotte, René, 'A la Cathédrale de Chartres quand Maurice Utrillo peintre génial de la Butte et maniaque de la solitude, prie avec sa fiancée', *Paris-Soir*, 12 April 1935, pp. 1, 7.

— 'Chez Georges Petit – Suzanne Valadon', *L'Homme Libre*, 20 October 1932, p. 2.

— 'Au Portique – Suzanne Valadon', *L'Homme Libre*, 11 May 1931, pp. 1–2.

Besson, George, 'Le marchand de couleurs – Suzanne Valadon', *Ce Soir*, 20 March 1938, p. 8.

'Boronali – Aliboron', *Fantasio*, 1910, pp. 599–600.

Brunon Guardia, G., 'Les arts – Portraits', *L'Intransigeant*, 16 November 1937, p. 2.

— 'Les Arts – Suzanne Valadon et ses satellites,' *L'Intransigeant*, 15 May 1937, p. 2.

Cahors, Béatrice, 'Le vieux Montmartre et le théâtre d'ombres du Chat Noir: Napoléon et la Butte', *Le Vieux Montmartre*, 85 (January 2016), pp. 16–23.

'Les Carriers de Montmagny', *L'Aurore*, 27 September 1909, p. 3.

Castaing, M., 'Le Salon des Indépendants', *Floréal*, 14 February 1920, p. 160.

Charensol, G., 'Les Grandes Ventes', *Formes*, May 1931, pp. 89–90.

— 'Suzanne Valadon', *Les Chroniques du jour*, September 1929, pp. 22–5.

Claretie, Jules, *Le Temps*, 16 May 1884, p. 3.

'Cour d'assises de la Haute-Vienne', *Le 20 Décembre – Courrier de Limoges*, 1–2 March 1857, p. 3.

Destez, Robert, 'Heur et Malheur de Maurice Utrillo, Chevalier de la Légion d'honneur', *L'Homme Libre*, 21 September 1928, p. 1.

F.H.L., 'Suzanne Valadon (Galerie Bernier)', *Marianne*, 16 March 1938, p. 11.

Flamant, Albert, 'Jours de Guerre', *Le Monde illustré*, 20 October 1917, p. 212.

'Le Froid et le charbon', *Le Figaro*, 1 February 1917, p. 2.

Geoffroy, Gustave, *La Justice*, 19 April 1881.

Imbourg, Pierre, '12, rue Cortot', *Beaux-Arts*, 6 January 1939, p. 3.

Jeanniot, Georges, 'Souvenirs sur Degas', *La Revue universelle*, 15 October and 1 November 1933.

'La Joie de Paris', *Le Figaro*, 12 November 1918, p. 2.

'La Journée – Quelques impressions de Paris', *Le Figaro*, 4 August 1914, p. 2.

Kahn, Gustave, 'Art', *Mercure de France*, 15 July 1925, pp. 494–8.

Léon-Martin, Louis, 'Les femmes artistes modernes', *Paris-Soir*, 17 February 1932, p. 6.

Lécuyer, Raymond, 'Les Femmes Artistes d'Europe exposent au Musée du Jeu de Paume', *Le Figaro*, 14 February 1937, p. 2.

Leudet, Suzay, 'Suzanne Valadon chez les pompiers', *Beaux-Arts*, Paris, May 1938.

M.R., 'Exposition Suzanne Valadon', *L'Intransigeant*, 29 January 1929, p. 5.

'Le Maire de Montmartre', *La Presse*, 12 April 1920, p. 2.

Manier, Stéphane, 'Quelques minutes avant de partir pour Londres M. Édouard Herriot nous a parlé du peintre Suzanne Valadon', *Paris-Soir*, 14 October 1932, p. 3.

Misme, Clotilde, 'Les Salons du Grand Palais', *La Chronique des arts*, 15 February 1920, pp. 18–19.

Morin-Jean, 'Au Salon des Indépendants', *La Gerbe*, March 1920, pp. 172–3.

'Musée du Luxembourg', *Bulletin des musées de France*, July 1933, pp. 104–5.

'Nouvelles Diverses – La Température', *Le Figaro*, 24 January 1917, p. 4.

'Nouvelles Diverses – Le Froid', *Le Figaro*, 1 January 1918, p. 4.

'La Peinture et la sculpture au Salon d'Automne', *Comoedia*, 4 November 1919, p. 1.

Peyrat, Marie-Louise, 'Suzanne de Bessines', *Limousin Magazine*, March 1965, pp. 16–19.

'Pour les futurs biographes de Suzanne Valadon et d'Utrillo', *Cahiers de France*, October 1938, p. 86.

R.A.M.S., 'The International Society of Sculptors, Painters, and Gravers', *Pall Mall Gazette*, Monday 16 May 1898, p. 1.

R.G., 'Autres et derniers salons', *Mercure de France*, June 1892, pp. 166–9.

Rey, Robert, *L'Opinion*, 25 December 1921, cited in Robert Rey, *Suzanne Valadon* (Paris: Gallimard, 1922), p. 15.

Roger-Marx, Claude, and Waldemar George, 'Suzanne Valadon' *La Renaissance*, April 1938, p. 48.

Le Roux, Hugues, 'Les Modèles', in *L'Enfer parisien* (Paris, 1888)

Salmon, André, in *Revue de France*, January 1930, cited in June Rose, *Mistress of Montmartre: A Life of Suzanne Valadon* (London: Richard Cohen Books, 1998), p. 221.

'Le Salon de 1884', *Le Figaro*, 30 April 1884, p. 1.

'Au Salon des Indépendants', *La Vie artistique*, April 1911, p. 59.

'Le Salon des Indépendants', *Le Populaire de Paris*, 29 January 1920, p. 1.

'Le Salon des Indépendants 25e exposition', *Le Matin*, 19 March 1910, p. 4.

Soulier, A.R., 'D'une manière simple et touchante Bessines a honoré Suzanne Valadon', *Le Populaire du centre*, October 1949.

— 'Après l'hommage rendu à Suzanne Valadon', *Le Populaire du centre*, October 1949.

'Suzanne Valadon', *Beaux-Arts*, 15 April 1938, p. 3.

'Suzanne Valadon', *Le Vieux Montmartre*, March–April 1938, p. 4.

Tabarant, Adolphe, 'Suzanne Valadon et ses souvenirs de modèle', *Bulletin de la vie artistique*, Paris, December 1921, pp. 626–9.

— in *L'Oeuvre*, December 1921, cited in Robert Rey, *Suzanne Valadon* (Paris: Gallimard, 1922), pp. 14–15.

'Le Tableau de l'âne', *Le Journal du dimanche*, 26 June 1910, p. 402.

'Tableaux de chevalet, ou peinture décorative?', *Bulletin de la vie artistique*, 15 February 1922, p. 78.

'Transactions Immobilières', *Le Gaulois*, 29 September 1924, p. 3.

Utter, André, 'La Carrière de Maurice Utrillo', *Beaux-Arts*, 28 October 1938, p. 2.

V., 'Les "Femmes artistes" et "Les Universitaires"', *Le Petit Parisien*, 30 May 1935, p. 4.

Valadon, Suzanne, 'Suzanne Valadon par elle-même', *Prométhée* (Paris: Editions littéraires de France, March 1939), pp. 53–4.

Vauxcelles, Louis, 'A travers les expositions', *Le Carnet des Artistes*, 15 March 1917, p. 19.

— 'Les Femmes Artistes Modernes', *Le Monde illustré*, 2 April 1938, p. 16.

— 'Le Salon d'Automne', *Gil Blas*, 1 October 1909, pp. 1–2.

— 'Suzanne Valadon', *Le Monde illustré*, 16 April 1938, p. 14.

Warnod, André, in *L'Avenir*, 19 December 1921, cited in Robert Rey, *Suzanne Valadon* (Paris: Gallimard, 1922), p. 15.

— 'L'hommage des artistes à Suzanne Valadon', *Beaux-Arts*, 15 April 1938, p. 1.

— 'Suzanne Valadon est morte', *Le Figaro*, 8 April 1938, p. 2.

Yves-Bonnat, 'Suzanne Valadon – Un Grand peintre', *Regards*, 21 April 1938, p. 14.

Newspapers and Journals

L'Aurore, 1 March 1914, p. 1.

Le Bulletin de la vie artistique, 15 January 1920, p. 101.

Le Bulletin de la vie artistique, 15 June 1925, pp. 265–6.

Bulletin municipal official de la ville de Paris, 30 July 1915, p. 1631.

Comoedia, 30 October 1923, p. 4.

Comoedia, 1 June 1924, p. 4.

Le Figaro, 22 May 1882, p. 3.

Le Figaro, 30 August 1882, p. 7.

Le Figaro, 6 May 1883, p. 2.

Le Figaro, 23 September 1886, p. 1.

Le Figaro, 20 February 1909, p. 1.

Le Gaulois, 28 March 1880, p. 2.

Le Gaulois, 9 October 1882, p. 1.

Le Gaulois, 17 December 1893, p. 4.

Le Gaulois, 1 November 1921, p. 1.

Gil Blas, 14 February 1892, p. 4.

L'Intransigeant, 18 May 1912, p. 2.

L'Intransigeant, 31 October 1923, p. 2.

L'Intransigeant, 2 June 1924, p. 2.

La Justice, 21 June 1881, p. 2.

Limoges Illustré, 15 October 1910, p. 1.

Limoges Illustré, 15 May 1911, p. 3942.

Lemouzi, April 1914, p. 190.

Le Monde artiste, 30 June 1877, p. 7.

Les Nouvelles littéraires, 2 July 1932, p. 9.

Paris-Soir, 4 May 1935, p. 14.

Le Passant, 1 June 1882, p. 6.

La Presse, 4 March 1914, p. 2.

La Revue de l'Art, April 1937, p. 70.

Websites and online articles

www.artistes-independantes.fr

http://www.artist-info.com/users/publicpagegallery/19404 [accessed 1 December 2016] http://augustingrass-mick.pagesperso-orange.fr/ [accessed 7 December 2016]

http://www.bernheim-jeune.com/story/ [accessed 10 January 2017]

http://www.boeufsurletoit.com [accessed 23 February 2017]

http://www.brittanytourism.com/discover-our-destinations/ brest-terres-oceanes/unmissable-sites/ushant-and-the-iroise-islands [accessed 2 December 2016]

http://www.elysee-montmartre.com/historique [accessed 14 February 2016]

http://www.au-lapin-agile.com/ [accessed 20 April 2016]

http://www.metmuseum.org/art/collection/search/486162 [accessed 8 November 2016]

http://www.metmuseum.org/art/libraries-and-research-centers/ leonard-lauder-research-center/programs-and-resources/ index-of-cubist-art-collectors/level [accessed 15 December 2016]

http://www.metmuseum.org/art/libraries-and-research-centers/ leonard-lauder-research-center/programs-and-resources/ index-of-cubist-art-collectors/weill [accessed 5 December 2016]

http://montmartre-secret.com/article-frede-le-lapin-agile-et-l-ane-92424120.html [accessed 8 November 2016]

http://www.patrimoine-histoire.fr/Patrimoine/Paris/ Paris-Saint-Pierre-de-Montmartre.htm [accessed 9 February 2016]

http://www.salonautomne.com/en [accessed 4 November 2016]

http://www.salondesbeauxarts.com/snba/histoire-de-la-snba/ [accessed 4 September 2016]

http://www.sothebys.com/en/auctions/ecatalogue/2014/ impressionist-modern-art-evening-sale-n09139/lot.17.html [accessed 10 October 2016]

Les Amis de Paul-César Helleu http://www.helleu.org.biographie.htm [accessed 9 September 2016]

Angier, Natalie, 'What Ailed Toulouse-Lautrec? Scientists Zero In on a Key Gene', *New York Times* (6 June 1995), http://www.nytimes. com/1995/06/06/science/what-ailed-toulouse-lautrec-scientists-zero-in-on-a-key-gene.html [accessed 23 June 2016]

'Art Deco: The 1925 Paris Exhibition – Victoria and Albert Museum' http://www.vam.ac.uk/content/articles/a/the-1925-paris-exhibition/ [accessed 24 February 2017]

Association Maurice Utrillo http://www.utrillo.com/fr/node/44 [accessed 15 October 2016]

The Biography.US http://thebiography.us/en/bartholome-paul-albert [accessed 22 July 2016]

Christies, Lot notes, sale 2888, Lot 19, 5 November 2014 http://www.christies.com/lotfinder/paintings/pierre-auguste-renoir-la-jeune-fille-au-5840862-details.aspx [accessed 4/7/2016]

Encyclopaedia Britannica – Albert Bartholomé https://www.britannica.com/biography/Albert-Bartholome [accessed 22/7/2016]

Encyclopaedia Britannica – Édouard Herriot https://www.britannica.com/biography/Edouard-Herriot [accessed 21 February 2017]

Encyclopaedia Britannica – Reims Cathedral https://www.britannica.com/topic/Reims-Cathedral [accessed 29 December 2016]

Encyclopédie Larousse en ligne – Édouard Herriot http://www.larousse.fr/encyclopedie/personnage/%C3%89douard_Herriot/123780 [accessed 20 February 2017]

Encyclopedia of Printmaking Art http://www.visual-arts-cork.com/printmaking/etching.htm [accessed 4 September 2016]

Fiederer, Luke, 'AD Classics: Exposition Internationale des Arts Décoratifs et Industriels Modernes', *Arch Daily* http://www.archdaily.com/793367/ad-classics-exposition-internationale-des-arts-decoratifs-et-industriels-modernes [accessed 24 February 2017]

'Gazi Le Tatar' http://genealogie.lelong.pagesperso-orange.fr/curiosites/gazi_le_tatar2.htm [accessed 22 March 2017]

Jones, Jonathan, 'When Henri met Pablo', *Guardian*, 29 October 2005 https://www.theguardian.com/artanddesign/2005/oct/29/art [accessed 9 February 2017]

Leroi, Armand Marie, 'Noble Figure', *Guardian*, Saturday 20 November 2004 https://www.theguardian.com/books/2004/nov/20/featuresreviews.guardianreview33 [accessed 23 June 2016]

Lestz, Margo 'History of Jazz in France', *The Good Life France* http://www.thegoodlifefrance.com/history-jazz-france/ [accessed 24 January 2017]

'*La Marche à l'Étoile*, by the Chat Noir (Black Cat) shadow theatre', Gadagne Musées http://www.gadagne.musees.lyon.fr/index.../zoom_marche_etoile.pdf [accessed 18 August 2016]

Meacock, Joanna, 'Introductory Essay: The Exhibition Society' http://www.exhibitionculture.arts.gla.ac.uk/essays.php?eid=02 [accessed 22 September 2016]

Montmartre – Paris's Secret Vineyard http://www.cooknwithclass.com/montmartre-paris-s-secret-vineyard-_ar133.html [accessed 11 February 2016]

'Montmartre Village – Place Tertre History', travelfranceonline.com (5 June 2015) http://www.travelfranceonline.com/montmartre-village-place-tertre-history/ [accessed 12 February 2016]

Rosa, Frederico, 'Tracing the Legends of Bohemian Paris and Magical Montmartre', *The Culture Trip*, (25 January 2016) http://theculturetrip.com/europe/france/paris/articles/tracing-the-legends-of-bohemian-paris-and-magical-montmartre/ [accessed 11 February 2016]

Rudorff, Raymond, *The Belle Epoque; Paris in the Nineties (1) – The World of Montmartre – The Pleasure Capital* http://www.iub.edu/~paris10/ParisOSS/D14Montmartre/Rudorff1Montmartre.html [accessed 12 February 2016]

Museums, galleries and archives consulted

André Utter archives, MNAM, Paris

Archives Départmentales de la Haute-Vienne

Archives de Nantes

L'Association Racines à Bessines, Haute-Vienne

Bibliothèque Kandinsky, Paris

British Library, London

Centre d'Archives Historiques de la SNCF

Centre d'Art et de Culture Georges Pompidou, Paris

Collection Robert Le Masle, MNAM, Paris

Espace Valadon, Office de Tourisme, Bessines-sur-Gartempe, Haute-Vienne

Musée des Beaux-Arts Palais de l'Evêché, Limoges

Musée Carnavalet, Paris

Musée de Montmartre et Jardins Renoir, Paris

Musée d'Orsay, Paris

Musée René Baubérot – Archéologie & Ethnographie – Châteauponsac, Haute-Vienne

Musée Utrillo-Valadon, Sannois

Office de tourisme de Cancale

Service des archives et de la documentation de Pierrefitte-sur-Seine

The Witt Library, Somerset House, London

Notes

PROLOGUE

1. The following is drawn from the local paper's report of this event in Bessines in 1949. A.R. Soulier, 'D'une manière simple et touchante Bessines a honoré Suzanne Valadon', *Le Populaire du centre*, October 1949. See also A.R. Soulier, 'Après l'hommage rendu à Suzanne Valadon', *Le Populaire du centre*, October 1949. Marie-Louise Peyrat, 'Suzanne de Bessines', *Limousin Magazine*, March 1965, pp. 16–19.

2. Suzanne Courdesses-Betout, *Bessines au fil des siècles* (Limoges: [n. Pub.], 1990), p. 272.

3. Maurice Utrillo, *Histoire de ma jeunesse jusqu'à ce jour*, published in *Valadon Utrillo: Au tournant du siècle à Montmartre – de l'Impressionisme à l'École de Paris*, exhib. cat. (Paris: Pinacothèque de Paris, 2009), pp. 65–131 (p. 68).

CHAPTER 1

1. Local dialect or patois was still the main form of social communication in the rural Limousin in the mid-19th century.

2. Georges Cerbelaud Salagnac, *Histoire du Limousin* (Paris: Éditions France-Empire, 1996), p. 271.

3. *The Green Guide Dordogne, Berry, Limousin* (Herts: Michelin Apa Publications Ltd, 2007), p. 20.

4. On traditional costume, see *Musée René Baubérot – Archéologie & Ethnographie – Châteauponsac, Haute-Vienne*, visitor guide, pp. 16–17. Bérangère Guilbaud-Rabiller, *Le Grand Almanach du Limousin 2016* (La Crèche: Geste éditions, 2015), semaine 23. Maurice Robert, *La Maison, Le Village, Le Paysan en Limousin*, 4th edn, 2 vols (Pageas: Société d'Ethnographie et de Sauvegarde des Patrimoines en Limousin, 2007), vol. II, pp. 159–60.

5. Georges-Emmanuel Clancier, *La Vie quotidienne en Limousin au XIXe siècle* (Paris: Hachette, 1976), p. 91.

6. Robert, p. 129.

7. Clancier, p. 159.

8. On the Limousin's climate and traditional dwellings, see Clancier, pp. 29–31.

9. Clancier, pp. 85–6.

10. I am indebted to l'Association Racines à Bessines for allowing me to access all the Valadons' birth, marriage and death records and particularly for helping locate the original plans of Mathieu-Alexandre Valadon's estate.

11. On marriage in rural society during the 19th century, see Roger Price, *A Social History of Nineteenth-Century France* (London: Hutchinson, 1987), pp. 165–70. Clancier, p. 78.

12. On Limousin superstition and traditions regarding engagement, see Clancier, pp. 78–9.

13. Suzanne Courdesses-Betout, *Bessines au fil des siècles* (Limoges: [n. Pub.], 1990), pp. 287–91.

14. Clancier, pp. 53–75.

15. Clancier, p. 33.

16. Guilbaud-Rabiller, semaine 7.

17. Robert, p. 185.

18. On Limousin household size, see Robert, pp. 181–4.

19. Clancier, p. 44.

20. Birth, marriage and death records reveal that women tended to use their maiden name rather than that of their husband on all official documents.

21. Courdesses-Betout, p. 258.

22. Esther Copley, *The Young Servant's Friendly Instructor or A Summary of the Duties of Domestic Servants* (London, 1827), pp. 75–82.

23. Price, p. 169.

24. Courdesses-Betout, p. 212.

25. Courdesses-Betout, p. 212

26. Clancier, p. 80. Salagnac, p. 270.

27. Robert, p. 185. I am grateful to Père Nicolas Sabléry for making the church records accessible to me and to Mme Blanche Brisset for taking time to study them with me.

28. On Limousin weddings, see Salagnac, pp. 271–2.

29. On Limousin wedding rituals, see Robert, pp. 213–15.

30. Clancier, p. 81.

31. Courdesses-Betout, p. 281.

32. Robert, p. 184.

33. Anne Martin-Fugier, 'Bourgeois Rituals' in *A History of Private Life*, ed. by Philippe Ariès and George Duby, trans. by Arthur Goldhammer, 5 vols

(Cambridge, MA, London: Belknap Press of Harvard University Press, 1987–1991), vol. 4: *From the Fires of Revolution to the Great War*, ed. by Michelle Perrot (1990), pp. 261–337 (p. 305).

34. Price, p. 81.
35. On birth and superstition in the Limousin, see Clancier, pp. 76–7.
36. Evidenced by Marie-Alix Coulaud's birth certificate.
37. 'Cour d'assises de la Haute-Vienne', *Le 20 Décembre – Courrier de Limoges*, 1–2 March 1857, p. 3.
38. Salagnac, p. 253.
39. Salagnac, p. 254.
40. Courdesses-Betout, p. 132.
41. Alistair Horne, *Seven Ages of Paris* (London: Pan Macmillan, 2003), pp. 262–3.
42. Courdesses-Betout, p. 132.
43. Salagnac, p. 256.
44. June Rose, *Mistress of Montmartre: A Life of Suzanne Valadon* (London: Richard Cohen Books, 1998), pp. 12–13.
45. 'Cour d'assises de la Haute-Vienne', *Le 20 Décembre – Courrier de Limoges*, 1–2 March 1857, p. 3.
46. The trial was reported in full in 'Cour d'assises de la Haute-Vienne', *Le 20 Décembre – Courrier de Limoges*, 1–2 March 1857, p. 3.
47. Courdesses-Betout, p. 258.
48. Courdesses-Betout, pp. 258–9.
49. Courdesses-Betout, p. 259.
50. John Storm, *The Valadon Drama: The Life of Suzanne Valadon* (New York: E.P. Dutton & Co., Inc., 1959), p. 19.
51. Courdesses-Betout, p. 258.
52. Guilbaud-Rabiller, semaine 38.
53. Clancier, p. 292.
54. Courdesses-Betout, p. 259.
55. Courdesses-Betout, p. 259.
56. *Impressionists in Winter: Effets de Neige*, exhib. cat., (Washington DC: The Phillips Collection, 1999), p. 221.
57. Courdesses-Betout, p. 259.
58. Storm, p. 19.
59. Maximilian Ilyin, *Utrillo* (London: A. Zwemmer; Paris: Fernand Hazan, 1953), p. 4.
60. Courdesses-Betout, p. 259.

61. There is no evidence in the village archives to suggest that Marie-Céline Coulaud was a relative of Léger Coulaud. Coulaud was a common surname.

62. Robert, p. 213. Clancier, pp. 77–8.

CHAPTER 2

1. Georges-Emmanuel Clancier, *La Vie quotidienne en Limousin au XIXe siècle* (Paris: Hachette, 1976), p. 145.

2. Georges-Emmanuel Clancier, *La Vie quotidienne en Limousin au XIXe siècle* (Paris: Hachette, 1976), pp. 29–30.

3. Marie Dony's death certificate is dated 25 March 1867.

4. Maurice Robert, *La Maison, Le Village, Le Paysan en Limousin*, 4th edn, 2 vols (Pageas: Société d'Ethnographie et de Sauvegarde des Patrimoines en Limousin, 2007), vol. II, p. 185.

5. Roger Price, *A Social History of Nineteenth-Century France* (London: Hutchinson, 1987), p. 73.

6. Suzanne Courdesses-Betout, *Bessines au fil des siècles* (Limoges: [n. Pub.], 1990), p. 285.

7. On Limousin children's games, see Clancier, pp. 94–9.

8. Courdesses-Betout, p. 234.

9. Courdesses-Betout, p. 234.

10. Courdesses-Betout, p. 235.

11. Claude Lacan, *Histoire du chemin de fer en Limousin* (Limoges: René Dessagne, 1984), pp. 7, 41.

12. Alistair Horne, *Seven Ages of Paris* (London: Pan Macmillan, 2003), p. 244.

13. Lacan, p. 21.

14. See Gillian Tindall's excellent biography. Gillian Tindall, *The Journey of Martin Nadaud: A Life and Turbulent Times* (London: Chatto & Windus, 1999).

15. Courdesses-Betout, p. 235.

16. Courdesses-Betout, p. 260.

17. This information was revealed in Suzanne Courdesses-Betout's updated article 'Le Panthéon de Bessines – les origines de Suzanne Valadon' in *Suzanne Valadon 1865–1938*, exhib. cat. (Martigny: Fondation Pierre Gianadda, 1996), pp. 65–9. Bessines holds no records of this relative, but there are two records for a Marie-Anne Valadon, one indicating a year of birth of 1830, held by the Hôtel de Ville de Paris.

18. *Larousse, Grand dictionnaire du XIX siècle* (Paris, 1900), p. 537. Paul Leroy-Beaulieu, *Le Travail des femmes* (Paris, 1873), p. 114.

19. An adult's single, third-class ticket from Limoges to Paris cost 24 francs 64 in 1870. I am indebted to the Centre d'Archives Historiques de la SNCF and to the Archives Départmentales de la Haute-Vienne for this information.

20. I am indebted to the Centre d'Archives Historiques de la SNCF and to the Archives Départmentales de la Haute-Vienne for this information.

21. *The Grand Tour*, ed. by Sheila Pickles (London Pavilion Books Limited, 1991), p. 22.

22. Horne, p. 243.

23. Horne, p. 111.

24. Graham Robb, *Parisians: An Adventure History of Paris* (London: Picador, 2010), pp. 387–8.

25. On Paris in 1870, see Alistair Horne, *Seven Ages of Paris* (London: Pan Macmillan, 2003), pp. 282–313.

26. On Paris in 1870, see Horne, pp. 282–313.

27. Edmond de Goncourt, 8 December 1870, cited in Hollis Clayson, *Paris in Despair: Art and Everyday Life under Siege (1870–71)* (Chicago and London: University of Chicago Press, 2002), p. 164.

28. Sée, *Aujourd'hui Paris*, pp. 267–269, cited in Clayson, p. 86.

29. Clayson, p. 174.

30. Edmond de Goncourt, cited in Horne, p. 294.

31. Clayson, p. 67.

32. Ethnologist Maurice Robert particularly makes this observation of Limousin migrants in the 19th century. See Robert, pp. 131, 180.

33. There exists a wealth of literature on Montmartre and its history. Particularly informative are: Adolphe Joanne, *Paris Illustré, Nouveau guide de l'étranger et du parisien* (Paris, 1867), pp. 289–92. June Rose, *Mistress of Montmartre: A Life of Suzanne Valadon* (London: Richard Cohen Books, 1998), pp. 14–30. John Storm, *The Valadon Drama: The Life of Suzanne Valadon* (New York: E.P. Dutton & Co., Inc., 1959), pp. 17–40. Alan Tillier, *Paris* (London: Dorling Kindersley, 1999), pp. 291–7. http://www.patrimoine-histoire.fr/Patrimoine/Paris/Paris-Saint-Pierre-de-Montmartre.htm [accessed 9 February 2016].

34. Frederico Rosa, 'Tracing the Legends of Bohemian Paris and Magical Montmartre', *The Culture Trip* (25 January 2016), http://theculturetrip.com/europe/france/paris/articles/tracing-the-legends-of-bohemian-paris-and-magical-montmartre/ [accessed 11 February 2016]. Raymond Rudorff, *The Belle Epoque; Paris in the Nineties (1) – The World of Montmartre – The Pleasure Capital* http://www.iub.edu/~paris10/ParisOSS/D14Montmartre/

RudorfflMontmartre.html [accessed 12 February 2016]. *Montmartre – Paris's Secret Vineyard* http://www.cooknwithclass.com/montmartre-paris-s-secret-vineyard-_ar133.html [accessed 11 February 2016].

35. Horne, p. 232.

36. Ann Galbally, *Charles Conder: The Last Bohemian* (Melbourne: Melbourne University Press, 2003), pp. 72–3. David Burke, *Writers in Paris: Literary Lives in the City of Light* (Counterpoint: Berkley, CA, 2008), p. 410.

37. Sophie Krebs, 'Montmartre, colline inspirée?' in *Valadon Utrillo: Au tournant du siècle à Montmartre – de l'Impressionisme à l'École de Paris*, exhib. cat. (Paris: Pinacothèque de Paris, 2009), pp. 37–47 (p. 38). Joanne, p. 291. 'Montmartre Village – Place Tertre History', *travelfranceonline.com* (5 June 2015) http://www.travelfranceonline.com/montmartre-village-place-tertre-history/ [accessed 12 February 2016].

38. John Rewald, *The History of Impressionism*, 4th edn (New York: Museum of Modern Art and London: Secker & Warburg, 1973), pp. 197–8.

39. Edmond Bazire, *Manet* (Paris, 1884), p. 30.

40. Rewald, p. 197.

41. Galbally, pp. 72–5.

42. H.A. de Conty, *Paris en poche – Guide pratique Conty*, 6th edn (Paris, 1875), p. 264.

43. http://www.elysee-montmartre.com/historique [accessed 14 February 2016]

44. Clayson, p. 331.

45. Juliette Lamber Adam, 1–2 October 1870, cited in Clayson, p. 330.

46. Edmond de Goncourt, 30 October 1870, cited in Clayson, p. 330.

47. Cited in Storm, p. 31.

48. Storm, p. 36.

49. On Paris during the siege and the Commune, see Alistair Horne, *Seven Ages of Paris* (London: Pan Macmillan, 2003), pp. 282–313.

50. J.P.T. Bury, *France 1814–1940* (London: Methuen & Co. Ltd, 1969), pp. 133–4.

51. Horne, pp. 301–2.

52. Horne, p. 308. Phillip Dennis Cate, 'L'esprit de Montmartre et l'art moderne, 1875–1910' in *L'Esprit de Montmartre et l'Art Moderne 1875–1910*, exhib. cat. (Paris: Musée de Montmartre, 2014), pp. 23–40 (p. 30).

53. Edmond de Goncourt, *Paris under Siege, 1870–1871: From the Goncourt Journal*, ed. and trans. by George J. Becker (Ithaca and London: Cornell University Press, 1969), p. 312.

54. Edmond de Goncourt, *Paris under Siege, 1870–1871: From the Goncourt Journal*, ed. and trans. by George J. Becker (Ithaca and London: Cornell University Press, 1969), pp. 311–14.

55. Clayson, p. 174.

56. Marie-Alix Coulaud and Georges Camille Merlet married in Paris on 1 February 1874.

57. On gossip and rumours Madeleine inspired, see Storm, pp. 32–3.

58. On Madeleine's character, see Robert Beachboard, *La Trinité maudite* (Paris, 1952), p. 23.

59. On Madeleine's appearance, see Storm, p. 33

60. Storm, p. 39. Beachboard, p. 23.

CHAPTER 3

1. Georges-Emmanuel Clancier, *La Vie quotidienne en Limousin au XIXe siècle* (Paris: Hachette, 1976), p. 143.

2. M. de Maistre, cited in Mgr Dupanloup, *La Femme studieuse*, 7th edn (Paris, 1900), pp. 122–3.

3. Jules and Gustave Simon, *La Femme au XXe siècle* (Paris, 1892), p. 67.

4. Paul Janet, *La Famille*, 17th edn (Paris, 1900), pp. 203, 204, 209.

5. Philippe Ariès, *Centuries of Childhood* (Harmondsworth: Penguin Books, 1986), p. 285.

6. Ariès, p. 358.

7. Theodore Zeldin, *France 1848–1945: Ambition and Love* (Oxford, New York, Toronto and Melbourne: Oxford University Press, 1988), p. 344.

8. Zeldin, p. 344.

9. Dupanloup, p. 131.

10. Janet, pp. 216–17.

11. Mme Millet, *Journal de l'agriculture pratique*, 5 December 1859, cited in Mme Marie-Sincère Romieu, *Des Paysans et de l'agriculture en France au XIXe siècle* (Paris, 1865), p. 383.

12. Clancier, p. 145.

13. Clancier, p. 145.

14. Suzanne Courdesses-Betout, *Bessines au fil des siècles* (Limoges: [n. Pub.], 1990), p. 215.

15. Lynn Hunt, 'The Unstable Boundaries of the French Revolution' in *A History of Private Life*, ed. by Philippe Ariès and George Duby, trans. by Arthur Goldhammer, 5 vols (Cambridge, MA, London: Belknap Press of Harvard

University Press, 1987–1991), vol. 4: *From the Fires of Revolution to the Great War*, ed. by Michelle Perrot (1990), pp. 13–45 (pp. 22–23). Clancier, pp. 136–7.

16. Maurice Robert, *La Maison, Le Village, Le Paysan en Limousin*, 4th edn, 2 vols (Pageas: Société d'Ethnographie et de Sauvegarde des Patrimoines en Limousin, 2007), vol. II, p. 180.

17. Martin Nadaud, cited in Robert, p. 180.

18. Ariès, p. 292.

19. Ariès, p. 292. Odile Arnold, *Le Corps et l'Âme: La Vie des religieuses au XIXe siècle* (Paris: Éditions du Seuil, 1984), p. 178.

20. Roger Price, *A Social History of Nineteenth-Century France* (London: Hutchinson, 1987), p. 319.

21. Ariès, p. 293.

22. Michelle Perrot, 'Roles and Characters' in *A History of Private Life*, ed. by Philippe Ariès and George Duby, trans. by Arthur Goldhammer, 5 vols (Cambridge, MA, London: Belknap Press of Harvard University Press, 1987–1991), vol. 4: *From the Fires of Revolution to the Great War*, ed. by Michelle Perrot (1990), pp. 167–259 (p. 210).

23. Perrot, pp. 243–4.

24. Arnold, p. 195.

25. Stendhal, cited in Perrot, p. 243.

26. Arnold, p. 185.

27. Arnold, p. 185.

28. Arnold, p. 180.

29. *Manuel de la piété à l'usage de la jeune pensionnaire* (144), 1865, p. 20. Cited in Arnold, p. 191.

30. Arnold, pp. 190–1.

31. Jean Chalon, *Liane de Pougy: Courtisane, princesse et sainte* (Paris: Flammarion, 1994), p. 25.

32. John Storm, *The Valadon Drama: The Life of Suzanne Valadon* (New York: E.P. Dutton & Co., Inc.,1959), p. 34.

33. Storm, p. 35.

34. Suzanne Valadon, 'Suzanne Valadon ou l'absolu', n.d., MNAM.

35. Storm, p. 35.

36. Arnold, p. 186.

37. Chalon, p. 23.

38. Chalon, p. 23.

39. Storm, p. 35.

40. Suzanne Valadon, 'Suzanne Valadon ou l'absolu', n.d., MNAM.

41. Suzanne Valadon, 'Suzanne Valadon ou l'absolu', n.d., MNAM.

42. On Marie-Clémentine's childhood antics, see Storm, pp. 34–40.

43. Suzanne Valadon, 'Suzanne Valadon ou l'absolu', n.d., MNAM.

44. On Marie-Clémentine's first artistic attempts, see Storm, pp. 41–2.

45. Suzanne Valadon, 'Suzanne Valadon ou l'absolu', n.d., MNAM.

46. Robert Rey, *Suzanne Valadon* (Paris: Gallimard, 1922), pp. 4–5.

47. Rey, p. 5.

48. Georges Merlet first appears on electoral registers in Nantes in 1875. I am indebted to the Archives de Nantes for this information.

49. Price, p. 158.

50. On her jobs, see Rey, p. 5. Jeanine Warnod, *Suzanne Valadon*, trans. by Shirley Jennings (Naefels, Switzerland: Bonfini Press, 1981), p. 13. Storm, pp. 48–9.

51. Storm, p. 48.

52. On Paris in the 1880s, see Colin Jones, *Cambridge Illustrated History of France* (Cambridge: Cambridge University Press, 1994), pp. 226–31. Alistair Horne, *Seven Ages of Paris* (London: Pan Macmillan, 2003), p. 331.

53. Horne, p. 331.

54. Joanna Richardson, *La Vie Parisienne 1852–1870* (London: Hamish Hamilton, 1971), p. 75.

55. Henri Dabot, *Souvenirs et Impressions d'un bourgeois du Quartier Latin mai 1854 à mai 1869* (Quentin: Péronne, 1895), cited in Richardson, p. 75.

56. *Le Gaulois*, 9 October 1882, p. 1.

57. On the Cirque Fernando, see Henri Perruchot, *Toulouse-Lautrec*, trans. by Humphrey Hare (London: Constable and Company Ltd, 1958), p. 59.

58. *Le Monde Artiste*, 30 June 1877, p. 7.

59. On Molier and his circus, see *Recueil Cirque Molier 1884–1933*, Bibliothèque nationale de France. Linda Simon, *The Greatest Show on Earth: A History of the Circus* (London: Reaktion Books Ltd, 2014). Google ebook.

60. *Le Gaulois*, 28 March 1880, p. 2.

61. *Le Gaulois*, 28 March 1880, p. 2. In the original text, the pun is 'lapins sautés'/'lapins sauteurs': 'Nous connaissions les lapins sautés. M. Molier a inauguré les lapins sauteurs. C'est bien la chose la plus folle du monde.'

62. *Le Figaro*, 6 May 1883, p. 2.

63. *La Justice*, 21 June 1881, p. 2. *Le Passant*, 1 June 1882, p. 6.

64. André Utter, MNAM.

65. *Recueil Cirque Molier 1884–1933*, Bibliothèque nationale de France

66. So Marie-Clémentine recounted to François Gauzi. See François Gauzi, *My Friend Toulouse-Lautrec*, trans. by Paul Dinnage (London: Neville Spearman, 1957), p. 70.

67. *Le Figaro*, 22 May 1882, p. 3. Originally referring to the 18th–19th-century circus performer Anselme-Pierre Loyal, the name became a general reference term for any circus manager.

68. Rey, p. 5.

69. Storm, p. 51.

CHAPTER 4

1. Georges-Emmanuel Clancier, *La Vie quotidienne en Limousin au XIXe siècle* (Paris: Hachette, 1976), p. 143.

2. Suzanne Valadon, 'Suzanne Valadon ou l'absolu', n.d., MNAM.

3. Tamar Garb, 'Gender and Representation' in Francis Frascina and others, *Modernity and Modernism: French Painting in the Nineteenth Century* (New Haven and London: Yale University Press, 1993), pp. 219–89 (p. 285).

4. Suzanne Valadon, 'Suzanne Valadon ou l'absolu', n.d., MNAM.

5. Anne Higonnet, *Berthe Morisot* (Berkeley and Los Angeles: University of California Press, 1995), p. 100.

6. Gerhard Gruitrooy, *Mary Cassatt – An American Impressionist* (New York: Todtri, 1996), p. 13.

7. Cited in Higonnet, p. 19.

8. J.K. Huysmans, cited in Judith A. Barter, 'Childhood and Maternity', in Judith A. Barter and others, *Mary Cassatt: Modern Woman* (Chicago: Art Institute of Chicago and Harry N. Abrams, Inc., 1998), pp. 69–81 (p. 69).

9. André Utter, MNAM.

10. Jacques Lethève, *La Vie quotidienne des artistes français au XIXe siècle* (Paris: Hachette, 1968), p. 80.

11. Susan S. Waller, *The Invention of the Model – Artists and Models in Paris, 1830–1870* (Aldershot: Ashgate Publishing Ltd, 2006), p. 51.

12. On the Italians, modelling and wages, see Hugues Le Roux, 'Les Modèles', in *L'Enfer parisien* (Paris, 1888), pp. 68–82.

13. Le Roux, p. 74. Lethève, p. 79.

14. Lethève, p. 80.

15. On the market, see Lethève, p. 80.

16. Richard R. Brettell and Caroline B. Brettell, *Painters and Peasants in the Nineteenth Century* (Geneva: Skira, 1983), pp. 75–76.

17. On these stories, see John Storm, *The Valadon Drama: The Life of Suzanne Valadon* (New York: E.P. Dutton & Co., Inc., 1959), p. 56. June Rose, *Mistress of Montmartre: A Life of Suzanne Valadon* (London: Richard Cohen Books, 1998), pp. 41–2.

18. Rose, p. 41.

19. André Michel, *Puvis de Chavannes* (London: William Heinemann, 1912), p. vii.

20. *The Correspondence of Berthe Morisot*, ed. by Kathleen Adler and Tamar Garb (London: Camden Press Ltd, 1986), p. 141.

21. *The Correspondence of Berthe Morisot*, ed. by Kathleen Adler and Tamar Garb (London: Camden Press Ltd, 1986), p. 40. André Utter archives, MNAM.

22. *The Correspondence of Berthe Morisot*, ed. by Kathleen Adler and Tamar Garb (London: Camden Press Ltd, 1986), p. 171.

23. For a brief biography of Puvis de Chavannes, see *L'Art en France sous le Second Empire*, exhib. cat. (Paris: Éditions de la Réunion des musées nationaux, 1979), p. 400.

24. *The Correspondence of Berthe Morisot*, ed. by Kathleen Adler and Tamar Garb (London: Camden Press Ltd, 1986), p. 180.

25. Cited in J.L. Shaw, 'Frenchness, Memory and Abstraction: The Case of Pierre Puvis de Chavannes' in *Nationalism and French Visual Culture*, ed. by J. Hargrove and N. McWilliam (New Haven and London: Yale University Press, 2005), p. 153.

26. Adolphe Tabarant, 'Suzanne Valadon et ses souvenirs de modèle', *Bulletin de La Vie Artistique*, Paris, December 1921, p. 628.

27. On a model's day, see Le Roux, pp. 73–5.

28. Tabarant, p. 628. In a letter to Berthe Morisot, Puvis complains about the heat of the studio in the summer. See *The Correspondence of Berthe Morisot*, ed. by Kathleen Adler and Tamar Garb (London: Camden Press Ltd, 1986), p. 87.

29. Lethève, pp. 79–80.

30. Waller, p. 58.

31. George du Maurier, *Trilby* (Hertfordshire: Wordsworth Editions Ltd, 1995), p. 97.

32. On this work, see Michel, pp. 67–8.

33. Tabarant, p. 628.

34. *The Correspondence of Berthe Morisot*, ed. by Kathleen Adler and Tamar Garb (London: Camden Press Ltd, 1986), p. 133.

35. In 1898, she became his wife. Both Puvis and the Princesse then died the same year.

36. Michel, pp. 65–6.

37. Waller, p. 47.

38. On the gossip, see Storm, pp. 56–61.

39. Tabarant, p. 628.

40. Cited in Lethève, p. 78.

41. Jeanine Warnod, *Suzanne Valadon*, trans. by Shirley Jennings (Naefels, Switzerland: Bonfini Press, 1981), p. 30.

42. Jean-Jacques Henner, *Melancholy*, date unknown. Warnod, p. 30. On the painters Marie-Clémentine posed for, see Rose, p. 46.

43. Gustav Wertheimer produced several paintings on this theme during the 1880s. It is unknown how many of these Maria posed for.

CHAPTER 5

1. Michel Chadeuil, *Expressions et dictons Périgord Limousin* (Chamalières: Christine Bonneton, 2015), p. 99.

2. http://www.elysee-montmartre.com/historique [accessed 14 February 2016]

3. François Gauzi, *My Friend Toulouse-Lautrec*, trans. by Paul Dinnage (London: Neville Spearman, 1957), p. 34.

4. H.A. de Conty, *Paris en poche – Guide pratique Conty*, 6th edn (Paris, 1875), p. 264.

5. John House, *Impressionism: Paint and Politics* (New Haven and London: Yale University Press, 2004), p. 142.

6. On the Moulin de la Galette, see Robert L. Herbert, *Impressionism: Art, Leisure, and Parisian Society* (New Haven and London: Yale University Press, 1988), pp. 133–9.

7. John House, *Impressionism: Paint and Politics* (New Haven and London: Yale University Press, 2004), p. 141.

8. Conty, p. 28.

9. On cafés, see Herbert, pp. 59–76.

10. Conty, pp. 28–9.

11. Conty, pp. 28–9.

12. On absinthe, see Susan Cope and others, eds, *Larousse Gastronomique* (London: Mandarin, 1990), p. 3. See also Herbert, pp. 74–5.

13. Alfred Delvau, *Histoire anecdotique des café et des cabarets de Paris* (Paris, 1862), cited in Herbert, p. 74.

14. On the Lapin Agile, see http://www.au-lapin-agile.com/ [accessed 20 April 2016]. See also June Rose, *Mistress of Montmartre: A Life of Suzanne Valadon* (London: Richard Cohen Books, 1998), p. 45.

15. Interview with Christiane Barny Duditlieu who attended the Lapin Agile in her youth.

16. On the café and the regular patrons, see Pamela Todd, *The Impressionists' Table* (London: Pavilion Books Limited, 1997), pp. 52–7.

17. George Moore, *Confessions of a Young Man* (Middlesex: Penguin Books, 1939), pp. 90–1.

18. Todd, pp. 52–7.

19. On café-concerts and these restrictions, see Herbert, pp. 66–82.

20. Conty, p. 30.

21. On Salis, see François Gauzi, *My Friend Toulouse-Lautrec*, trans. by Paul Dinnage (London: Neville Spearman, 1957), pp. 45–51. See also Henri Perruchot, *Toulouse-Lautrec*, trans. by Humphrey Hare (London: Constable and Company Ltd, 1958), p. 87.

22. Perruchot, p. 87.

23. Bernard Gendron, *Between Montmartre and the Mudd Club: Popular Music and the Avant-Garde* (Chicago: University of Chicago Press, 2002), pp. 37–9. Perruchot, p. 87.

24. Gendron, pp. 37–9.

25. On Le Chat Noir, see John Storm, *The Valadon Drama: The Life of Suzanne Valadon* (New York: E.P. Dutton & Co., Inc., 1959), p. 63. Rose, pp. 46–7. Perruchot, p. 87.

26. Cited in Phillip Dennis Cate, 'L'Esprit de Montmartre et l'art moderne, 1875–1910' in *L'Esprit de Montmartre et l'Art Moderne 1875–1910*, exhib. cat. (Paris: Musée de Montmartre, 2014), pp. 23–40 (p. 25).

27. Gauzi, p. 46.

28. Gauzi, pp. 45–6.

29. On Le Chat Noir's clientele, see Perruchot, p. 87. Rose, pp. 47–50.

30. Gauzi, p. 47.

31. Perruchot, p. 87.

32. On Bruant, see Gauzi, pp. 54–6. Perruchot, pp. 96–8.

33. Sophie Krebs, 'Montmartre, colline inspirée?' in *Valadon Utrillo: Au tournant du siècle à Montmartre – de l'Impressionisme à l'École de Paris*, exhib. cat. (Paris: Pinacothèque de Paris, 2009), pp. 37–47(p. 44).

34. On this prank, see Rose, p. 47.

35. Reported in *Le Figaro*, 30 August 1882, p. 7.

36. Rose, pp. 50–1. Jeanine Warnod, *Suzanne Valadon*, trans. by Shirley Jennings (Naefels, Switzerland: Bonfini Press, 1981), p. 13.

37. On Maria's lovers, see Storm, p. 55.

38. On Miguel, see: Catherine Banlin Lacroix, 'Miguel Utrillo i Morlius', in Jean Fabris, *Utrillo, sa vie, son oeuvre* (Paris: Éditions Frédéric Birr, 1982), pp. 13–16. Storm, pp. 64–5.

39. Storm, p. 64.

40. Storm, p. 64.

41. Cited in Banlin Lacroix, p. 13.

42. Cited in Banlin Lacroix, p. 13.

43. On Zando, see *Post-Impressionism: Cross Currents in European Painting*, exhib. cat. (London: Royal Academy of Arts, 1979), p. 251. Gauzi, p. 69. Perruchot, p. 93.

44. *Post-Impressionism: Cross Currents in European Painting*, exhib. cat. (London: Royal Academy of Arts, 1979), p. 251.

45. *L'Art en France sous le Second Empire*, exhib. cat. (Paris: Éditions de la Réunion des musées nationaux, 1979), p. 403.

46. Colin B. Bailey, *Renoir's Portraits* (New Haven and London: Yale University Press, 1997), p. 6.

47. Jean Renoir, *Renoir, My Father*, trans. by Randolph and Dorothy Weaver (London: The Reprint Society Ltd, 1962), p. 31.

48. House, p. 188.

49. Barbara Ehrlich White, *Renoir: His Life, Art, and Letters* (New York: Abrams, 1984), p. 105.

50. On Renoir's travels, see White, pp. 105–28.

51. Bailey, p. 200.

52. Warnod, p. 33.

53. Gustave Coquiot, *Renoir* (Paris: Albin Michel, 1925), p. 95.

54. Renoir, p. 80.

55. Renoir, pp. 83–4.

56. Gloria Groom, and others, *L'Impressionisme et la mode*, exhib. cat. Musée d'Orsay (Paris: Skira/Flammarion, 2013), p. 93.

57. Coquiot, p. 97.

58. Adolphe Tabarant, 'Suzanne Valadon et ses souvenirs de modèle', *Bulletin de La Vie Artistique*, Paris, December 1921, pp. 626–7. Coquiot, pp. 87–96.

59. *Post-Impressionism: Cross Currents in European Painting*, exhib. cat. (London: Royal Academy of Arts, 1979), p. 171.

60. Renoir, p. 79.

61. Rose, p. 60.

62. On Renoir's background, see Bailey, p. 104.

63. Mme Blanche to Dr Blanche, cited in White, p. 107.

64. Renoir, p. 87.

65. Coquiot, pp. 88, 96–7.

66. Bailey, p. 201.

67. Bailey, p. 201.

68. Coquiot, p. 96. Bailey, p. 201.

69. Tabarant, p. 627.

70. The sources of gossip are eloquently summarised by June Rose. Rose, p. 60.

71. Jean-Paul Crespelle, *Montmartre vivant* (Paris: Hachette, 1964), p. 163.

72. On the name changes, see: John House and Anne Distel, *Renoir*, exhib. cat. (London: Hayward Gallery, 1985), p. 236. Bailey, p. 200.

73. John House and Anne Distel, *Renoir*, exhib. cat. (London: Hayward Gallery, 1985), p. 236. Bailey, p. 200.

74. Tabarant, p. 627.

75. André Utter Archives, MNAM.

76. Jean-Paul Crespelle, *Montmartre vivant* (Paris: Hachette, 1964), p. 163.

77. Crespelle, p. 163.

78. On Renoir's views on women, see Renoir, pp. 78–91.

CHAPTER 6

1. Georges-Emmanuel Clancier, *La Vie quotidienne en Limousin au XIXe siècle* (Paris: Hachette, 1976), p. 143.

2. Rachel Fuchs, *Abandoned Children: Foundlings and Child Welfare in 19th-Century France* (Albany: State University of New York Press, 1984), p. 174.

3. Émile Zola, *The Drinking Den*, trans. by Robin Buss (London: Penguin Books, 2003), p. 18.

4. For a useful summary of 19th-century contraceptives, see Virginia Rounding, *Grandes Horizontales: The Lives and Legends of Four 19th-Century Courtesans* (London: Bloomsbury, 2003), pp. 21–2.

5. John Storm, *The Valadon Drama: The Life of Suzanne Valadon* (New York: E.P. Dutton & Co., Inc., 1959), p. 62.

6. Catherine Banlin Lacroix, 'Miguel Utrillo i Morlius', in Jean Fabris, *Utrillo, sa vie, son oeuvre* (Paris: Éditions Frédéric Birr, 1982), pp. 13–16 (p. 13).

7. John House and Anne Distel, *Renoir*, exhib. cat. (London: Hayward Gallery, 1985), p. 236. Colin B. Bailey, *Renoir's Portraits* (New Haven and London: Yale University Press, 1997), p. 200.

8. Storm, p. 71.

9. John House, *Impressionism: Paint and Politics* (New Haven and London: Yale University Press, 2004), p. 203. On Renoir's Guernsey pictures, see John House, *Renoir in Guernsey* (Guernsey: Guernsey Museum & Art Gallery, 1988). In fact, this was almost certainly a studio picture, for which studies for the background were completed on Guernsey, probably at Moulin Huet, and the figure added later in Paris. As John House remarks, 'the figure is not placed in a legible spatial relationship with what lies behind it.' House, *Renoir in Guernsey*, p. 14. We know Renoir was struggling to find a model at the time it was produced, so it seems likely that he may have drawn on earlier nude studies made of Maria before she fell pregnant. Maria referred to posing for nudes in the garden in the Rue de la Barre. See Adolphe Tabarant, 'Suzanne Valadon et ses souvenirs de modèle', *Bulletin de La Vie Artistique*, Paris, December 1921, pp. 626–7.

10. On this incident, see Storm, p. 97.

11. Robert Beachboard, *La Trinité maudite* (Paris, 1952), p. 23.

12. Storm, p. 66.

13. Storm, p. 93.

14. Suzanne Valadon, 'Suzanne Valadon ou l'absolu', n.d., MNAM.

15. On Impressionism in the 1880s, see House, *Impressionism: Paint and Politics*, pp. 187–206. An excellent overview of this period and other movements can be found in: *Post-Impressionism: Cross Currents in European Painting*, exhib. cat. (London: Royal Academy of Arts, 1979).

16. Jeanine Warnod, *Suzanne Valadon*, trans. by Shirley Jennings (Naefels, Switzerland: Bonfini Press, 1981), p. 21.

17. Storm, pp. 66–67.

18. Warnod, p. 21. Jean Fabris, *Utrillo, sa vie, son oeuvre* (Paris: Éditions Frédéric Birr, 1982), p. 6.

19. Cited in Barbara Ehrlich White, *Renoir: His Life, Art, and Letters* (New York: Abrams, 1984), p. 145.

20. Warnod, p. 32.

21. June Rose, *Mistress of Montmartre: A Life of Suzanne Valadon* (London: Richard Cohen Books, 1998), pp. 43–4.

22. On Seurat and the Salon des Artistes Indépendants, see: John Rewald, *Seurat* (London: Thames and Hudson, 1990), p. 53. John Leighton, Richard

Thompson and others, *Seurat and The Bathers* (London: National Gallery Publications Limited, 1997), p. 124.

23. The Société des Artistes Indépendants is still active. See: www.artistes-independants.fr

24. Jules Claretie, *Le Temps*, 16 May 1884, p. 3.

25. 'Le Salon de 1884', *Le Figaro*, 30 April 1884, p. 1.

26. Some studies spell Toulouse-Lautrec's full surname Montfa rather than Monfa. I have adopted the form used in *Unpublished Correspondence of Henri de Toulouse-Lautrec*, ed. by Lucien Goldschmidt and Herbert Schimmel (London: Phaidon, 1969).

27. One of the best biographies of Henri de Toulouse-Lautrec remains Henri Perruchot, *Toulouse-Lautrec*, trans. by Humphrey Hare (London: Constable and Company Ltd, 1958).

28. François Gauzi. See François Gauzi, *My Friend Toulouse-Lautrec*, trans. by Paul Dinnage (London: Neville Spearman, 1957), p. 1.

29. Perruchot, p. 71.

30. It is now widely believed that Lautrec suffered from pycnodysostosis, though the possible diagnoses of osteopetrosis, achondroplasia and osteogenesis imperfecta have also been suggested. Inbreeding is believed to have played a part in his condition. On Lautrec's deformity, see Perruchot, pp. 51–3. For recent discussions of his deformity, see: Armand Marie Leroi, 'Noble Figure', *The Guardian* (Saturday 20 November 2004), https://www.theguardian.com/books/2004/nov/20/featuresreviews.guardianreview33 [accessed 23 June 2016]; Natalie Angier, 'What Ailed Toulouse-Lautrec? Scientists Zero In on a Key Gene', *The New York Times* (6 June 1995), http://www.nytimes.com/1995/06/06/science/what-ailed-toulouse-lautrec-scientists-zero-in-on-a-key-gene.html [accessed 23 June 2016].

31. Perruchot, p. 53.

32. On Lautrec's eyes, see Gauzi, p. 27.

33. Gauzi, p. 10.

34. Gauzi, p. 10.

35. Perruchot, p. 45.

36. Perruchot, p. 47.

37. *Unpublished Correspondence of Henri de Toulouse-Lautrec*, ed. by Lucien Goldschmidt and Herbert Schimmel (London: Phaidon, 1969), Letter 25, August–September 1879, p. 51.

38. Gauzi, p. 27.

39. Gauzi, p. 27.

40. *Unpublished Correspondence of Henri de Toulouse-Lautrec*, ed. by Lucien Goldschmidt and Herbert Schimmel (London: Phaidon, 1969), Letter 66, January 1885, pp. 87–8.

41. On this, see Gauzi, pp. 59–60.

42. Gauzi, pp. 69–70.

43. Perruchot, pp. 58–9.

44. Perruchot, p. 53.

45. Gauzi, p. 59.

46. On this work, see Gauzi, pp. 61–2.

47. Rose, p. 71.

48. Perruchot, pp. 92–3.

49. Cited in Perruchot, p. 93.

50. Perruchot, p. 95.

51. Gauzi, pp. 54–5.

52. Perruchot, p. 97.

53. Perruchot, p. 126.

54. Maria speaking to art student Geneviève Camax-Zoegger, cited in Rose, p. 71.

55. Gauzi, p. 70.

56. Gauzi, p. 70.

57. *Unpublished Correspondence of Henri de Toulouse-Lautrec*, ed. by Lucien Goldschmidt and Herbert Schimmel (London: Phaidon, 1969), Letter 79, spring 1886, p. 98.

58. Perruchot, p. 111.

59. Gauzi, p. 71.

60. Gauzi recounted this episode. See Gauzi, pp. 70–1.

61. The drawing was Maria's portrait of Maurice.

62. Gauzi, p. 27.

CHAPTER 7

1. Michel Chadeuil, *Expressions et dictons Périgord Limousin* (Chamalières: Christine Bonneton, 2015), p. 178.

2. *Le Figaro*, 23 September 1886, p. 1.

3. See Maria's letter to Marie-Alix, Collection Madame Jeanette Anderfuhren, Pétridès Gallery, Paris. Cited in June Rose, *Mistress of Montmartre: A Life of Suzanne Valadon* (London: Richard Cohen Books, 1998), pp. 102–4.

4. François Gauzi, *My Friend Toulouse-Lautrec*, trans. by Paul Dinnage (London: Neville Spearman, 1957), p. 12.

5. Theo cited in Ingo F. Walther and Rainer Metzger, *Vincent van Gogh: The Complete Paintings*, trans. by Michael Hulse, 2 vols (Los Angeles: Taschen, 2010), vol. I, p. 228.

6. On Van Gogh's arrival at Cormon's see Gauzi, pp. 12–14.

7. On Anquetin, see *Post-Impressionism: Cross Currents in European Painting*, exhib. cat. (London: Royal Academy of Arts, 1979), pp. 28–9. Henri Perruchot, *Toulouse-Lautrec*, trans. by Humphrey Hare (London: Constable and Company Ltd, 1958), pp. 73–6.

8. On Bernard, see *Post-Impressionism: Cross Currents in European Painting*, exhib. cat. (London: Royal Academy of Arts, 1979), pp. 31–44. Perruchot, pp. 107–8.

9. Perruchot, p. 106.

10. Walther and Metzger, vol. I, p. 294.

11. On this project, see Walther and Metzger, vol. II, pp. 710–11.

12. Vincent van Gogh met Paul Gauguin at the end of 1887, when Gauguin arrived in Paris from Pont-Aven. See *The Letters of Vincent van Gogh*, ed. by Ronald de Leeuw, trans. by Arnold Pomerans (London: Penguin Books, 1996), pp. xxix–xxx.

13. Perruchot, pp. 116–17.

14. Gauzi, p. 95.

15. Henri de Toulouse-Lautrec and Maurice Joyant, *The Art of Cuisine*, trans. by Margery Weiner (New York, Chicago and San Francisco: Holt, Rinehart and Winston, 1966), pp. 153, 156.

16. Perruchot, p. 120.

17. Gauzi, p. 90. Susan Cope, and others, eds, *Larousse Gastronomique* (London: Mandarin, 1990), pp. 1313–14.

18. *The Letters of Vincent van Gogh*, ed. by Ronald de Leeuw, trans. by Arnold Pomerans (London: Penguin Books, 1996), Vincent van Gogh to Theo van Gogh, July 1885, pp. 306–7.

19. Recounted in Perruchot, pp. 120–1. Suzanne Valadon cited in Nino Frank, *Montmartre ou les enfants de la folie* (Paris: Calmann-Levy, 1956), cited in June Rose, *Mistress of Montmartre: A Life of Suzanne Valadon* (London: Richard Cohen Books, 1998), p.77

20. Perruchot, p. 121.

21. On Bourges, see Gauzi, p. 28.

22. This episode and its dialogue was recounted by Gauzi, pp. 64–5.

23. See the discussion of *Young Woman with a Swan*, Christie's, Lot notes, sale 2888, Lot 19, 5 November 2014 http://www.christies.com/lotfinder/paintings/

pierre-auguste-renoir-la-jeune-fille-au-5840862-details.aspx [accessed 4 July 2016].

24. Christie's, Lot notes, sale 2888, Lot 19, 5 November 2014 http://www.christies.com/lotfinder/paintings/pierre-auguste-renoir-la-jeune-fille-au-5840862-details.aspx [accessed 4 July 2016].

25. Gustave Coquiot, *Renoir* (Paris: Albin Michel, 1925), p. 98.

26. Renoir cited in *Renoir in the 20th Century*, exhib. cat. (Los Angeles: Los Angeles County Museum of Art, 2009), p. 67.

27. One of the best accounts of Maurice's childhood is found in Jean Fabris, *Utrillo, sa vie, son oeuvre* (Paris: Éditions Frédéric Birr, 1982)

28. Georges-Emmanuel Clancier, *La Vie quotidienne en Limousin au XIXe siècle* (Paris: Hachette, 1976), pp. 69–71.

29. Clancier, p. 38.
Susan Cope, and others, eds, *Larousse Gastronomique* (London: Mandarin, 1990), pp. 163, 245.

30. Rose, p. 87.

31. Maurice recalled this in Maurice Utrillo, *Histoire de ma jeunesse jusqu'à ce jour*, published in *Valadon Utrillo: Au tournant du siècle à Montmartre – de l'Impressionisme à l'École de Paris*, exhib. cat. (Paris: Pinacothèque de Paris, 2009), pp. 65–131.

32. Perruchot, pp. 131–2.

33. Georges Jeanniot, 'Souvenirs sur Degas', *La Revue Universelle*, 15 October and 1 November 1933, cited in Henri Loyrette, *Degas: Passion and Intellect*, trans. by Mark Paris (London: Thames and Hudson, 1993), p. 168.

34. Loyrette, p. 168.

35. For a biographical synopsis of Degas, see: Henri Loyrette, *Degas: Passion and Intellect*, trans. by Mark Paris (London: Thames and Hudson, 1993). *Post-Impressionism: Cross Currents in European Painting*, exhib. cat. (London: Royal Academy of Arts, 1979), pp. 63–5.

36. Jeanniot cited in Loyrette, p. 168.

37. 'Quelques conversations de Degas notées par Daniel Halévy en 1891–1893' in *Degas – Lettres*, ed. by Marcel Guerin (Paris: Bernard Grasset, 2011), p. 285.

38. Ambroise Vollard, *Degas*, 1924, cited in Loyrette, p. 158.

39. Perruchot, pp. 131–2.

40. On the Dihau family, see *Degas – Lettres*, ed. by Marcel Guerin (Paris: Bernard Grasset, 2011), pp. 15–17.

41. Cited in Perruchot, p. 132.

42. *The Correspondence of Berthe Morisot*, ed. by Kathleen Adler and Tamar Garb (London: Camden Press Ltd, 1986), pp. 170–1.

43. Perruchot, pp. 130–1.

44. On Gauguin, see *Post-Impressionism: Cross Currents in European Painting*, exhib. cat. (London: Royal Academy of Arts, 1979), pp. 71–9.

45. On Miguel's return to Paris, see Catherine Banlin Lacroix, 'Miguel Utrillo i Morlius', in Jean Fabris, *Utrillo, sa vie, son oeuvre* (Paris: Éditions Frédéric Birr, 1982), pp. 13–16.

46. Miguel's perception of Maria can be gauged from his drawing of her. Miguel Utrillo y Morlius, *Portrait of Suzanne Valadon*, 1891–2.

47. Santiago Rusiñol painted Miguel a little after this time. Santiago Rusiñol i Prats, *Portrait of Miguel Utrillo*, 1890–1891.

48. Perruchot, pp. 133–5.

49. Adolphe Tabarant, 'Suzanne Valadon et ses souvenirs de modèle', *Bulletin de La Vie Artistique*, Paris, December 1921, p. 629.

50. *Post-Impressionism: Cross Currents in European Painting*, exhib. cat. (London: Royal Academy of Arts, 1979), p. 251.

51. On Paul-Albert Bartholomé, see: *The Biography.US* http://thebiography.us/en/bartholome-paul-albert [accessed 22 July 2016]. *Encyclopaedia Britannica* https://www.britannica.com/biography/Albert-Bartholome [accessed 22 July 2016].

52. Gloria Groom and others, *L'Impressionisme et la mode*, exhib. cat. Musée d'Orsay (Paris: Skira/Flammarion, 2013), p. 111.

53. *Degas – Lettres*, ed. by Marcel Guerin (Paris: Bernard Grasset, 2011), pp. 130–1.

54. Tabarant, p. 629.

55. Formerly the Rue de Laval. It became the Rue Victor-Massé in 1887.

56. André Utter, MNAM.

57. André Utter, MNAM.

58. Tabarant, p. 629.

59. Howard Daniel and John Berger, *Encyclopaedia of Themes and Subjects in Painting* (London: Thames and Hudson, 1971), p. 217.

60. Gauzi, p. 72.

CHAPTER 8

1. Michel Chadeuil, *Expressions et dictons Périgord Limousin* (Chamalières: Christine Bonneton, 2015), p. 170.

2. This incident was recounted by Gauzi. See François Gauzi, *My Friend*

Toulouse-Lautrec, trans. by Paul Dinnage (London: Neville Spearman, 1957), pp. 72–3.

3. Adolphe Tabarant, 'Suzanne Valadon et ses souvenirs de modèle', *Bulletin de La Vie Artistique*, Paris, December 1921, p. 629.

4. Henri Loyrette, *Degas: Passion and Intellect*, trans. by Mark Paris (London: Thames and Hudson, 1993), p. 98.

5. Loyrette, pp. 66, 98.

6. *Degas – Lettres*, ed. by Marcel Guerin (Paris: Bernard Grasset, 2011), Degas to M. Brebion, 13 April 1890, pp. 154–5.

7. On the layout of the apartment, see Paul Valéry, 'Degas Dance Drawing', 1936, cited in Loyrette, pp. 155–7.

8. See Paul Valéry, 'Degas Dance Drawing', 1936, cited in Loyrette, p. 156.

9. Tabarant, p. 629.

10. On Rouart, see *Post-Impressionism: Cross Currents in European Painting*, exhib. cat. (London: Royal Academy of Arts, 1979), p. 64.

11. Paul Valéry, 'Degas Dance Drawing', 1936, cited in Loyrette, p. 155.

12. On Degas's use of media, see Loyrette, pp. 76–7.

13. On the evolution of Degas's style, see *Post-Impressionism: Cross Currents in European Painting*, exhib. cat. (London: Royal Academy of Arts, 1979), pp. 63–5.

14. Suzanne Valadon talking to Mme Camax-Zoegger, recounted in 'Pour les futurs biographes de Suzanne Valadon et d'Utrillo', *Cahiers de France*, October 1938, pp. 86–7.

15. Camille Pissarro, cited in Loyrette, p. 109.

16. Suzanne Valadon, 'Suzanne Valadon ou l'absolu', n.d., MNAM.

17. Loyrette, pp. 106–8.

18. 'Suzanne Valadon – Pensée sur l'art', cited in Robert Rey, *Suzanne Valadon* (Paris: Gallimard, 1922), p. 16.

19. Loyrette, p. 100.

20. Degas to Bartholomé, cited in Loyrette, p. 95.

21. M.G. Dortu and Ph. Huisman, 'Introduction', in Henri de Toulouse-Lautrec and Maurice Joyant, *The Art of Cuisine*, trans. by Margery Weiner (New York, Chicago and San Francisco: Holt, Rinehart and Winston, 1966), pp. 11–12.

22. Henri Perruchot, *Toulouse-Lautrec*, trans. by Humphrey Hare (London: Constable and Company Ltd, 1958), p. 167.

23. J.P. Crespelle, *Le Monde de Degas* (Paris, 1974), cited in June Rose, *Mistress of Montmartre: A Life of Suzanne Valadon* (London: Richard Cohen Books, 1998), p. 85.

24. Suzanne Valadon, cited in *Suzanne Valadon – 1865–1938*, exhib. cat. (Martigny, Switzerland: Fondation Pierre Gianadda, 1996), p. 137.

25. John Storm, *The Valadon Drama: The Life of Suzanne Valadon* (New York: E.P. Dutton & Co., Inc., 1959), pp. 93–4.

26. Robert Coughlan, *The Wine of Genius: A Life of Maurice Utrillo* (London: Gollancz, 1952), p. 45.

27. Claude Wiart, 'Utrillo Le Simple' in Jean Fabris, *Utrillo, sa vie, son oeuvre* (Paris: Éditions Frédéric Birr, 1982), pp. 121–46 (p. 126).

28. Storm, p. 102. Jeanine Warnod, *Suzanne Valadon*, trans. by Shirley Jennings (Naefels, Switzerland: Bonfini Press, 1981), p. 57.

29. Storm, p. 102.

30. Bartholomé to Suzanne Valadon, May 1891, MNAM.

31. Suzay Leudet, 'Suzanne Valadon chez les pompiers', *Beaux-Arts*, Paris, May 1938.

32. Fabris, p. 8.

33. Cited in Catherine Banlin Lacroix, 'Miguel Utrillo i Morlius', in Jean Fabris, *Utrillo, sa vie, son oeuvre* (Paris: Éditions Frédéric Birr, 1982), p. 14.

34. Ian Millman, *Georges de Faure: maître du sybolisme et de l'art nouveau* (Paris: ACR, 1992), p. 34.

35. This anecdote is recounted by Francis Jourdain, *Utrillo* (Paris: Braun et Cie, 1948), p. 3.

36. R.G., 'Autres et derniers salons', *Mercure de France*, June 1892, pp. 166–9 (p. 169).

37. Béatrice Cahors, 'Le vieux Montmartre et le théâtre d'ombres du Chat Noir: Napoléon et la Butte', *Le Vieux Montmartre*, 85 (January 2016), 16–23.

38. '*La Marche à l'Étoile*, by the Chat Noir (Black Cat) shadow theatre', Gadagne Musées http://www.gadagne.musees.lyon.fr/index.../zoom_marche_etoile. pdf [accessed 18 August 2016]

39. *Gil Blas*, 14 February 1892, p. 4.

40. Simon Shaw-Miller, 'The Only Musician with Eyes – Erik Satie and Visual Art', in *Erik Satie: Music, Art and Literature*, ed. by Caroline Potter (Oxon: Routledge, 2016), pp. 85–114 (p. 87).

41. For a good biography of Satie, see Mary E. Davis, *Erik Satie* (London: Reaktion Books Ltd, 2007).

42. Cited in Robert Orledge, *Satie Remembered* (London: Faber and Faber, 1995), pp. 10–13.

43. On *Uspud*, see Potter, p. 257.

44. Cited in Davis, p. 56.

45. Storm, p. 104.

46. Davis, p. 56.

47. Davis, p. 56.

48. An evocative impression of Satie's apartment is given in Santiago Rusiñol's *Erik Satie in his Apartment in Montmartre* (1891).

49. Storm, p. 104.

50. Storm, p. 105.

51. Suzanne Valadon, 'Suzanne Valadon ou l'absolu', n.d., MNAM.

52. *Suzanne Valadon*, exhib. cat. (Paris: Musée National d'Art Moderne, 1967), catalogue entry 3. Warnod, p. 48.

53. Erik Satie, letter to Suzanne Valadon, MNAM.

54. Potter, p. 258.

55. Banlin-Lacroix, p. 14.

56. Cited in Banlin-Lacroix, p. 14.

57. Erik Satie to Conrad Satie, cited in Ornella Volta, *Satie Seen Through his Letters*, trans. by Michael Bullock (London: Marion Boyars, 1989), p. 44.

58. Davis, p. 58.

59. Volta, p. 46.

60. Davis, pp. 40–55.

61. Parcener – someone who takes a share of something.

62. *Le Gaulois*, 17 December 1893, p. 4.

63. Cited in Davis, p. 51. Ravel and Satie met in around 1893. They had a complicated relationship. See Robert Orledge, *Satie the Composer* (Cambridge: Cambridge University Press, 1990), p. 250.

64. Potter, p. 257.

65. Mousis still gave this as his address when he got married in 1896.

66. Document supplied by M. Georges Bonne, nephew of the landlady. Collection Robert Le Masle, MNAM.

67. The MNAM archives show that Suzanne told André Utter that she lived at the former address at this time. Degas wrote to her in July 1894 at 11, Rue Girardon.

68. Two of these fascinating letters were only found in 1996. They were held in the Collection Madame Jeannette Anderfuhren at the Pétridès Gallery, Paris until the latter closed.

CHAPTER 9

1. Michel Chadeuil, *Expressions et dictons Périgord Limousin* (Chamalières: Christine Bonneton, 2015), p. 120.

2. André Utter archive, MNAM.

3. On the Société Nationale des Beaux-Arts and its history, see: http://www.salondesbeauxarts.com/snba/histoire-de-la-snba/ [accessed 4 September 2016]. *Post-Impressionism: Cross Currents in European Painting,* exhib. cat. (London: Royal Academy of Arts, 1979), p. 284. Mary Alice Heekin Burke, *Elizabeth Nourse, 1859–1938 – A Salon Career* (Washington, D. C.: National Museum of American Art and the Cincinnati Art Museum, 1983), pp. 96–7. I am indebted to Michel King and Isabelle Lawson at the SNBA for their advice and thoughts on the historical significance of the SNBA.

4. On Paul Helleu, see: Les Amis de Paul-César Helleu http://www.helleu.org. biographie.htm [accessed 9 September 2016].

5. Bartholomé to Paul Helleu, cited in *Suzanne Valadon – 1865–1938,* exhib. cat. (Martigny, Switzerland: Fondation Pierre Gianadda, 1996), p. 166.

6. Heekin Burke, pp. 96–8.

7. See *Catalogue illustré des ouvrages de peinture, sculpture, dessins, gravure et objets d'art et architecture exposés au Champ-de-Mars,* 25 April 1894 (Reissued by New York & London: Garland Publishing, Inc., 1981). Suzanne's drawings were exhibited as nos 1670, 1671, 1672, 1673 and 1674.

8. Gustave Geoffroy, *La Justice,* 19 April 1881.

9. One of the best studies of the changing role of the child in Western society remains Philippe Ariès, *Centuries of Childhood* (Harmondsworth: Penguin Books, 1986). See also: Louis Hautecoeur, *Les Peintres de la vie familiale* (Paris: Galerie Charpentier, 1945).

10. See Gerhard Gruitrooy, *Mary Cassat – An American Impressionist* (New York: Todtri, 1996), p. 65.

11. Thérèse Diamand Rosinsky provides an insightful discussion of these. See Thérèse Diamand Rosinsky, *Suzanne Valadon* (New York: Universe Publishing, 1994), pp. 25–44.

12. *Catalogue illustré des ouvrages de peinture, sculpture, dessins, gravure et objets d'art et architecture exposés au Champ-de-Mars,* 25 April 1894 (Reissued by New York & London: Garland Publishing, Inc., 1981), numbers 1670–1674.

13. Anecdote recounted to André Utter. André Utter archives, MNAM. The Salon catalogue for 1894 shows two works by Jules Valadon listed.

14. *Degas – Lettres*, ed. by Marcel Guerin (Paris: Bernard Grasset, 2011), p. 210.

15. *Degas – Lettres*, ed. by Marcel Guerin (Paris: Bernard Grasset, 2011), p. 211.

16. André Utter archives, MNAM.

17. Colin Jones, *Cambridge Illustrated History of France* (Cambridge: Cambridge University Press, 1994), p. 233. J.P. Bury, *France 1814–1940* (London: Methuen & Co., 1969), pp. 185–6.

18. Alistair Horne, *Seven Ages of Paris* (London: Pan Macmillan, 2003), p. 323. Bury, p. 188.

19. Graham King, *Garden of Zola: Émile Zola and his Novels for English Readers* (London: Barrie and Jenkins Ltd., 1978), pp. 331–2.

20. *Degas – Lettres*, ed. by Marcel Guerin (Paris: Bernard Grasset, 2011), p. 215.

21. *Degas – Lettres*, ed. by Marcel Guerin (Paris: Bernard Grasset, 2011), p. 216.

22. Degas mentioned this in an undated letter written about this time. See Ronald Pickvance, '*Terrible Maria*: Degas and Suzanne Valadon' in *Suzanne Valadon – 1865–1938*, exhib. cat. (Martigny, Switzerland: Fondation Pierre Gianadda, 1996), pp. 23–8 (p. 28).

23. On soft ground etching, see *Encyclopedia of Printmaking Art* http://www.visual-arts-cork.com/printmaking/etching.htm [accessed 4 September 2016]

24. Claude Roger Marx, cited in Jeanine Warnod, *Suzanne Valadon*, trans. by Shirley Jennings (Naefels, Switzerland: Bonfini Press, 1981), p. 55.

25. I am indebted to the ladies at l'Association Racines à Bessines for communicating the details of Marie-Alix's death certificate.

26. *État des communes à la fin du XIXe siècle – Pierrefitte* (Montévrain, 1896).

27. Maurice Utrillo, *Histoire de ma jeunesse jusqu'à ce jour*, published in *Valadon Utrillo: Au tournant du siècle à Montmartre – de l'Impressionisme à l'École de Paris*, exhib. cat. (Paris: Pinacothèque de Paris, 2009), pp. 65–131 (p. 74).

28. Maurice Utrillo, *Histoire de ma jeunesse jusqu'à ce jour*, published in *Valadon Utrillo: Au tournant du siècle à Montmartre – de l'Impressionisme à l'École de Paris*, exhib. cat. (Paris: Pinacothèque de Paris, 2009), pp. 65–131 (p. 75).

29. Letter from Marie Coca to Robert Le Masle, MNAM.

30. Cited in Catherine Banlin Lacroix, 'Miguel Utrillo i Morlius', in Jean Fabris, *Utrillo, sa vie, son oeuvre* (Paris: Éditions Frédéric Birr, 1982), p. 15.

31. Maurice Utrillo, *Histoire de ma jeunesse jusqu'à ce jour*, published in *Valadon Utrillo: Au tournant du siècle à Montmartre – de l'Impressionisme à l'École de Paris*, exhib. cat. (Paris: Pinacothèque de Paris, 2009), pp. 65–131 (pp. 77–80).

32. Suzanne and Paul Mousis's marriage certificate is reproduced in *Suzanne Valadon – 1865–1938*, exhib. cat. (Martigny, Switzerland: Fondation Pierre Gianadda, 1996), p. 250.

33. Anne Higonnet, *Berthe Morisot* (Berkeley and Los Angeles: University of California Press, 1995), p. 221.

34. Gustave Coquiot, *Renoir* (Paris: Albin Michel, 1925), pp. 61–74.

35. Adolphe Tabarant, *Utrillo* (Paris: Berheim-Jeune, 1926) cited in Rose, p. 116.

36. Suzanne Valadon, 'La Nature', MNAM.

37. John Storm, *The Valadon Drama: The Life of Suzanne Valadon* (New York: E.P. Dutton & Co., Inc., 1959), p. 124.

38. Fabris, p. 28. In the 1901 census, Paul Mousis was working for A. Founeude et Cie. I am grateful to Maeva Ballon at the Service des archives et de la documentation de Pierrefitte-sur-Seine for this information.

39. Maurice Utrillo, *Histoire de ma jeunesse jusqu'à ce jour*, published in *Valadon Utrillo: Au tournant du siècle à Montmartre – de l'Impressionisme à l'École de Paris*, exhib. cat. (Paris: Pinacothèque de Paris, 2009), pp. 65–131 (p. 81).

40. André Utter Archives, MNAM.

41. Degas to Suzanne, cited in Robert Rey, *Suzanne Valadon* (Paris: Gallimard, 1922), p. 9.

42. *Degas – Lettres*, ed. by Marcel Guerin (Paris: Bernard Grasset, 2011), 8 January, pp. 216–17.

43. *Degas – Lettres*, ed. by Marcel Guerin (Paris: Bernard Grasset, 2011), Sunday postmark, 1897, p. 228.

44. *Degas – Lettres*, ed. by Marcel Guerin (Paris: Bernard Grasset, 2011), postmark January 1898, p. 229.

45. Fabris, p. 25. I am grateful to Maeva Ballon at the Service des archives et de la documentation de Pierrefitte-sur-Seine for this information.

46. R.A.M.S., 'The International Society of Sculptors, Painters, and Gravers', *The Pall Mall Gazette*, Monday 16 May 1898, p. 1.

47. Joanna Meacock, 'Introductory Essay: The Exhibition Society' http://www.exhibitionculture.arts.gla.ac.uk/essays.php?eid=02 [accessed 22 September 2016].

48. *Catalogue of the Exhibition of International Art, Knightsbridge* (London, 1898), p. 51. Suzanne was listed as no. 63 in the catalogue.

49. Fabris, p. 25.

50. Fabris, pp. 25–6.

51. Fabris, p. 26.

52. Maurice Utrillo, *Histoire de ma jeunesse jusqu'à ce jour,* published in *Valadon Utrillo: Au tournant du siècle à Montmartre – de l'Impressionisme à l'École de Paris,* exhib. cat. (Paris: Pinacothèque de Paris, 2009), pp. 65–131 (p. 82).

CHAPTER 10

1. Georges-Emmanuel Clancier, *La Vie quotidienne en Limousin au XIXe siècle* (Paris: Hachette, 1976), p. 143.

2. On the Exposition Universelle, see Maryanne Stevens, 'The Exposition Universelle: 'This vast competition of effort, realisation and victories' in *1900: Art at the Crossroads,* exhib. cat. (London: Royal Academy of Arts, 2000), pp. 54–71. P. Morand is cited by Stevens, p. 56.

3. Stevens, p. 57.

4. Camille Pissarro, cited in Stevens, p. 59.

5. Cited in Robert Rosenblum, 'Art in 1900: Twilight or Dawn?' in *1900: Art at the Crossroads,* exhib. cat. (London: Royal Academy of Arts, 2000), pp. 26–53 (p. 29).

6. Maurice Utrillo, *Histoire de ma jeunesse jusqu'à ce jour,* published in *Valadon Utrillo: Au tournant du siècle à Montmartre – de l'Impressionisme à l'École de Paris,* exhib. cat. (Paris: Pinacothèque de Paris, 2009), pp. 65–131 (p. 83).

7. Maurice recounted the episode in his autobiography. Maurice Utrillo, *Histoire de ma jeunesse jusqu'à ce jour,* published in *Valadon Utrillo: Au tournant du siècle à Montmartre – de l'Impressionisme à l'École de Paris,* exhib. cat. (Paris: Pinacothèque de Paris, 2009), pp. 65–131 (p. 85).

8. Jean Fabris, *Utrillo, sa vie, son oeuvre* (Paris: Éditions Frédéric Birr, 1982), p. 30.

9. On Pablo Picasso's arrival in Paris, see *1900: Art at the Crossroads,* exhib. cat. (London: Royal Academy of Arts, 2000), p. 413. J.P. Crespelle, *Montmartre Vivant* (Paris: Hachette, 1964), pp. 115–52.

10. Crespelle, p. 116.

11. The drawing was sold at Sotheby's in 2014. See: http://www.sothebys.com/en/auctions/ecatalogue/2014/impressionist-modern-art-evening-sale-n09139/lot.17.html [accessed 10 October 2016].

12. *1900: Art at the Crossroads,* exhib. cat. (London: Royal Academy of Arts, 2000), p. 413.

13. Ingo F. Walther, *Pablo Picasso 1881–1973: Genius of the Century* (Greven: Taschen, 1993), pp. 90–1.

14. An insightful discussion of this work can be found in Thérèse Diamand Rosinsky, *Suzanne Valadon* (New York: Universe Publishing, 1994), pp. 109–12.

15. On this work, see Diamand Rosinsky, p. 30.

16. From a selection of Degas's letters cited in *Suzanne Valadon – 1865–1938*, exhib. cat. (Martigny, Switzerland: Fondation Pierre Gianadda, 1996), p. 29.

17. From a selection of Degas's letters cited in *Suzanne Valadon – 1865–1938*, exhib. cat. (Martigny, Switzerland: Fondation Pierre Gianadda, 1996), p. 29.

18. Maurice Utrillo, *Histoire de ma jeunesse jusqu'à ce jour*, published in *Valadon Utrillo: Au tournant du siècle à Montmartre – de l'Impressionisme à l'École de Paris*, exhib. cat. (Paris: Pinacothèque de Paris, 2009), pp. 65–131 (p. 87).

19. François Gauzi, *My Friend Toulouse-Lautrec*, trans. by Paul Dinnage (London: Neville Spearman, 1957), p. 95.

20. Henri Perruchot, *Toulouse-Lautrec*, trans. by Humphrey Hare (London: Constable and Company Ltd, 1958), p. 277.

21. Thérèse Diamand Rosinsky, 'Les multiples identités de Suzanne Valadon: Marie-Clémentine, "Biqui", ou "Terrible Maria"?' in *Suzanne Valadon – 1865–1938*, exhib. cat. (Martigny, Switzerland: Fondation Pierre Gianadda, 1996), pp. 31–53 (pp. 42–3).

22. Fabris, pp. 28–9. June Rose, *Mistress of Montmartre: A Life of Suzanne Valadon* (London: Richard Cohen Books, 1998), p. 128.

23. Maurice Utrillo, *Histoire de ma jeunesse jusqu'à ce jour*, published in *Valadon Utrillo: Au tournant du siècle à Montmartre – de l'Impressionisme à l'École de Paris*, exhib. cat. (Paris: Pinacothèque de Paris, 2009), pp. 65–131 (p. 89). On 12, Rue Cortot, see Pierre Imbourg, '12, rue Cortot', *Beaux-Arts*, 6 January 1939, p. 3.

24. This work was sold at auction in 1995. The canvas is 81 × 99cm.

25. Crespelle, p. 157.

26. Maurice Utrillo, *Histoire de ma jeunesse jusqu'à ce jour*, published in *Valadon Utrillo: Au tournant du siècle à Montmartre – de l'Impressionisme à l'École de Paris*, exhib. cat. (Paris: Pinacothèque de Paris, 2009), pp. 65–131 (pp. 89–92).

27. Robert Coughlan, *The Wine of Genius: A Life of Maurice Utrillo* (London: Gollancz, 1952), pp. 51–2. Suzanne and Paul Mousis's marriage certificate is reproduced in *Suzanne Valadon – 1865–1938*, exhib. cat. (Martigny, Switzerland: Fondation Pierre Gianadda, 1996), p. 250.

28. On the use of tubes versus ground colour in the 19th century, see Anthea Callen, *Techniques of the Impressionists* (London: Tiger Books International, 1990), pp. 22–5.

29. 'Suzanne Valadon ou l'absolu', MNAM

30. Coughlan, p. 51.

31. Maurice Utrillo, *Histoire de ma jeunesse jusqu'à ce jour*, published in *Valadon Utrillo: Au tournant du siècle à Montmartre – de l'Impressionisme à l'École de Paris*, exhib. cat. (Paris: Pinacothèque de Paris, 2009), pp. 65–131 (p. 92).

32. Rose, p. 129.

33. Fabris, p. 32.

34. Claude Wiart, 'Utrillo le Simple' in Jean Fabris, *Utrillo, sa vie, son oeuvre* (Paris: Éditions Frédéric Birr, 1982), pp. 121–46 (p. 130).

35. Richard Osborne, *Freud For Beginners* (New York & London: Writers and Readers, 1993), p. 11.

36. Maurice Utrillo, *Histoire de ma jeunesse jusqu'à ce jour*, published in *Valadon Utrillo: Au tournant du siècle à Montmartre – de l'Impressionisme à l'École de Paris*, exhib. cat. (Paris: Pinacothèque de Paris, 2009), pp. 65–131 (p. 93).

37. The rules stipulated by Sainte-Anne are just legible on a visiting card of 1926, reprinted in Fabris, p. 55.

38. Wiart, p. 130.

39. Storm, p. 133.

40. Maurice Utrillo, *Histoire de ma jeunesse jusqu'à ce jour*, published in *Valadon Utrillo: Au tournant du siècle à Montmartre – de l'Impressionisme à l'École de Paris*, exhib. cat. (Paris: Pinacothèque de Paris, 2009), pp. 65–131 (p. 93).

41. Coughlan, p. 56.

42. Coughlan, p. 55.

43. Fabris, p. 31.

44. Fabris, p. 34.

45. André Utter, 'La Carrière de Maurice Utrillo', *Beaux-Arts*, 28 October 1938, p. 2.

46. On Utter, see: Coughlan, pp. 56–7. Crespelle, p. 157. *Valadon, Utrillo & Utter à l'atelier de la rue Cortot: 1912–1926*, exhib. cat. (Paris: Musée de Montmartre, 2015), p. 119. Association Maurice Utrillo http://www.utrillo.com/fr/node/44 [accessed 15 October 2016].

47. Crespelle, p. 157.

48. Fabris, p. 34. Crespelle, p. 163.

49. Coughlan, p. 63.

50. Crespelle, pp. 186–7.

51. Fabris, p. 36.

52. André Utter, 'La Carrière de Maurice Utrillo', *Beaux-Arts*, 28 October 1938, p. 2.

53. André Utter, 'La Carrière de Maurice Utrillo', *Beaux-Arts*, 28 October 1938, p. 2.

54. Crespelle, p. 164.

CHAPTER 11

1. Georges-Emmanuel Clancier, *La Vie quotidienne en Limousin au XIXe siècle* (Paris: Hachette, 1976), p. 143.

2. *Le Figaro*, 20 February 1909, p. 1.

3. *Le Figaro*, 20 February 1909, p. 1.

4. On religious art at the turn of the century, see *1900: Art at the Crossroads*, exhib. cat. (London: Royal Academy of Arts, 2000), p. 300.

5. This similarity is highlighted by Jacqueline Munck in 'La Peinture de Suzanne Valadon: 1909–1914, une passion décisive' in *Valadon, Utrillo & Utter à l'atelier de la rue Cortot: 1912–1926*, exhib. cat. (Paris: Musée de Montmartre, 2015), pp. 29–37.

6. One of the best discussions of this painting is found in Thérèse Diamand Rosinsky, *Suzanne Valadon* (New York: Universe Publishing, 1994), pp. 84–5.

7. Letter from Suzanne Valadon to André Utter, held by the MNAM.

8. Alan Tillier, *Paris* (London, New York, Stuttgart & Moscow: Dorling Kindersley, 1999), p. 231.

9. On this work, see Robert Cumming, *Art* (London, New York, Munich, Melbourne & Delhi: Dorling Kindersley, 2005), pp. 348–9.

10. Suzanne Valadon, 'Suzanne Valadon par elle-même', *Prométhée* (Paris: Editions littéraires de France, March 1939), pp. 53–4.

11. André Utter archives, MNAM.

12. André Utter, 'La Carrière de Maurice Utrillo', *Beaux-Arts*, 28 October 1938, p. 2.

13. On the Salon d'Automne see: http://www.salonautomne.com/en [accessed 4 November 2016]

14. Louis Vauxcelles, 'Le Salon d'Automne', *Gil Blas*, 1 October 1909, pp. 1–2.

15. Jean Fabris, *Utrillo, sa vie, son oeuvre* (Paris: Éditions Frédéric Birr, 1982), p. 35.

16. This episode is recorded in J.P. Crespelle, *Montmartre Vivant* (Paris: Hachette, 1964), pp. 167–8.

17. Crespelle, p. 164.

18. Fabris, p. 29.

19. Severini described the building vividly. See Crespelle, p. 194.

20. Crespelle, p. 196.

21. On Frédé and his time at the Lapin Agile, see: Crespelle, pp. 126–8. http://montmartre-secret.com/article-frede-le-lapin-agile-et-l-ane-92424120.html [accessed 8 November 2016].

22. On this work, see: http://www.metmuseum.org/art/collection/search/486162 [accessed 8 November 2016].

23. Maurice Utrillo, *Histoire de ma jeunesse jusqu'à ce jour*, published in *Valadon Utrillo: Au tournant du siècle à Montmartre – de l'Impressionisme à l'École de Paris*, exhib. cat. (Paris: Pinacothèque de Paris, 2009), pp. 65–131 (p. 96).

24. The proceedings of the hearing are reprinted in *Suzanne Valadon – 1865–1938*, exhib. cat. (Martigny, Switzerland: Fondation Pierre Gianadda, 1996), p. 252.

25. On this work, see Thérèse Diamand Rosinsky, *Suzanne Valadon* (New York: Universe Publishing, 1994) pp. 52–4.

26. Diamand Rosinsky cites an interview with Geneviève Barrez, 11 September 1992. See Diamand Rosinsky, p. 112.

27. See 'Les Carriers de Montmagny', *L'Aurore*, 27 September 1909, p. 3.

28. On this, see June Rose, *Modigliani: The Pure Bohemian* (London: Constable, 1990), pp. 69–70.

29. On the jest, see Crespelle, pp. 126–7. 'Boronali – Aliboron', *Fantasio*, 1910, pp. 599–600. http://montmartre-secret.com/article-frede-le-lapin-agile-et-l-ane-92424120.html [accessed 8 November 2016].

30. 'Le Salon des Indépendants 25e exposition', *Le Matin*, 19 March 1910, p. 4.

31. 'Le Tableau de l'âne', *Le Journal du Dimanche*, 26 June 1910, p. 402.

32. The episode was recounted by Jourdain. See Francis Jourdain, *Utrillo* (Paris: Les Editions Braun & Cie, 1948), pp. 4–5.

33. Jourdain, pp. 4–5. Fabris, pp. 36–40.

34. Robert Coughlan, *The Wine of Genius: A Life of Maurice Utrillo* (London: Gollancz, 1952), p. 60.

35. Many of Maurice Utrillo's biographers have recorded this. Maurice himself even wrote this in a letter to André Derain in 1947. This letter is reproduced as an annexe in *Valadon Utrillo: Au tournant du siècle à Montmartre – de l'Impressionisme à l'École de Paris*, exhib. cat. (Paris: Pinacothèque de Paris, 2009), pp. 348–9.

36. Coughlan, pp. 57–8.

37. *Limoges Illustré*, 15 October 1910, p. 1.

38. On this, see June Rose, *Mistress of Montmartre: A Life of Suzanne Valadon* (London: Richard Cohen Books, 1998), p. 146.

39. *Limoges Illustré*, 15 May 1911, p. 3942.

40. 'Au Salon des Indépendants', *La Vie Artistique*, April 1911, p. 59.
41. Maurice wrote about the incident in his autobiography. See Maurice Utrillo, *Histoire de ma jeunesse jusqu'à ce jour*, published in *Valadon Utrillo: Au tournant du siècle à Montmartre – de l'Impressionisme à l'École de Paris*, exhib. cat. (Paris: Pinacothèque de Paris, 2009), pp. 97–8.
42. One of the best discussions of this piece is found in Diamand Rosinsky, pp. 84–8.
43. On 12, Rue Cortot, see Pierre Imbourg, '12, rue Cortot', *Beaux-Arts*, 6 January 1939, p. 3.
44. Saskia Ooms, 'Les Artistes-Résidents du 12–14, rue Cortot', in *L'Esprit de Montmartre et L'Art Moderne, 1875–1910*, exhib. cat. (Paris: Musée de Montmartre, 2014), pp. 19–20.

CHAPTER 12

1. Michel Chadeuil, *Expressions et dictons Périgord Limousin* (Chamalières: Christine Bonneton, 2015), p. 101.
2. On 12, Rue Cortot, see Pierre Imbourg, '12, rue Cortot', *Beaux-Arts*, 6 January 1939, p. 3. Jeanine Warnod, *Suzanne Valadon*, trans. by Shirley Jennings (Naefels, Switzerland: Bonfini Press, 1981), pp. 65–8.
3. Warnod, pp. 65–8.
4. Jean Fabris, *Utrillo, sa vie, son oeuvre* (Paris: Éditions Frédéric Birr, 1982), pp. 57–9.
5. Maurice Utrillo, *Histoire de ma jeunesse jusqu'à ce jour*, published in *Valadon Utrillo: Au tournant du siècle à Montmartre – de l'Impressionisme à l'École de Paris*, exhib. cat. (Paris: Pinacothèque de Paris, 2009), pp. 65–131 (pp. 110–112).
6. Maurice Utrillo, cited in Fabris, p. 58.
7. Libaude to Maurice Utrillo, 18 April 1912, cited in Fabris, p. 40.
8. Libaude to Maurice Utrillo, cited in Fabris, p. 40.
9. Fabris, p. 40. The sou was a unit of currency created at the time of the Revolution. It was equal to 5 centimes, or approximately a halfpenny in English currency. See Émile Zola, *The Drinking Den*, trans. by Robin Buss (London: Penguin Books, 2003), p. 433, note 5.
10. In 1912, a copy of *Le Figaro* cost 10 centimes.
11. Libaude to Maurice Utrillo, cited in Fabris, p. 49.
12. Fabris, pp. 49–50.
13. Adolphe Tabarant, 'Suzanne Valadon et ses souvenirs de modèle', *Bulletin de La Vie Artistique*, Paris, December 1921, p. 629.

14. *L'Intransigeant*, 18 May 1912, p. 2.

15. See: http://www.artist-info.com/users/publicpagegallery/19404 [accessed 1 December 2016].

16. Maurice Utrillo, *Histoire de ma jeunesse jusqu'à ce jour*, published in *Valadon Utrillo: Au tournant du siècle à Montmartre – de l'Impressionisme à l'École de Paris*, exhib. cat. (Paris: Pinacothèque de Paris, 2009), pp. 65–131 (p. 103).

17. Maurice Utrillo, *Histoire de ma jeunesse jusqu'à ce jour*, published in *Valadon Utrillo: Au tournant du siècle à Montmartre – de l'Impressionisme à l'École de Paris*, exhib. cat. (Paris: Pinacothèque de Paris, 2009), pp. 65–131 (p. 103).

18. On the history of fortune telling and the meanings typically assigned to standard playing cards, see Francis X. King, *The Encyclopedia of Fortune Telling* (London: Octopus Books Ltd, 1988), pp. 30–7.

19. This is now the Gare de Paris-Montparnasse. Fabris, p. 50.

20. Adolphe Joanne, *Itinéraire général de la France: Normandie* (Paris, 1866), pp. 116–19. On the popularity of Normandy and Brittany during the 19th century, see John House, *Impressionists by the Sea*, exhib. cat. (London: Royal Academy of Arts, 2007), pp. 13–28.

21. J. Lelarge and E. Bourdon, *Petite Histoire de la Bretagne* (Paris: Libraire Félix Juven, 1911), p. 1.

22. André Utter Archives, MNAM.

23. On Ushant, see http://www.brittanytourism.com/discover-our-destinations/brest-terres-oceanes/unmissable-sites/ushant-and-the-iroise-islands [accessed 2 December 2016].

24. Maurice Utrillo, *Histoire de ma jeunesse jusqu'à ce jour*, published in *Valadon Utrillo: Au tournant du siècle à Montmartre – de l'Impressionisme à l'École de Paris*, exhib. cat. (Paris: Pinacothèque de Paris, 2009), pp. 65–131 (pp. 104–5).

25. Maurice Utrillo, *Histoire de ma jeunesse jusqu'à ce jour*, published in *Valadon Utrillo: Au tournant du siècle à Montmartre – de l'Impressionisme à l'École de Paris*, exhib. cat. (Paris: Pinacothèque de Paris, 2009), pp. 65–131 (p. 105).

26. Libaude to Maurice Utrillo, 27 July 1912, cited in Fabris, pp. 50–1.

27. André Utter archives, MNAM.

28. Libaude to Maurice Utrillo, cited in Fabris, p. 51.

29. Marie Coca's grandson, Yves Deneberger spoke about the sitting in an interview with June Rose in August 1996.

30. On Berthe Weill, see http://www.metmuseum.org/art/libraries-and-research-centers/leonard-lauder-research-center/programs-and-resources/index-of-cubist-art-collectors/weill [accessed 5 December 2016].

31. On Corsica and its role as a French holiday destination, see Graham Robb, *The Discovery of France* (London: Picador, 2008), p. 316.

32. L. Ravel, *La Corse, resources de son sol et de son climat* (Paris: Charles Amat, 1911) p. 1.

33. Michelle Deroyer, *Quelques souvenirs autour de Suzanne Valadon* (Paris: Fayard, 1947), p. 188.

34. Deroyer, p. 188.

35. Deroyer, p. 188.

36. One of the best analyses of Suzanne's work in Corsica is found in Thérèse Diamand Rosinsky, *Suzanne Valadon* (New York: Universe Publishing, 1994), pp. 102–4.

37. Maurice Utrillo, *Histoire de ma jeunesse jusqu'à ce jour*, published in *Valadon Utrillo: Au tournant du siècle à Montmartre – de l'Impressionisme à l'École de Paris*, exhib. cat. (Paris: Pinacothèque de Paris, 2009), pp. 65–131 (pp. 106–7).

38. On Corsican cuisine, see Susan Cope and others, eds, *Larousse Gastronomique* (London: Mandarin, 1990), pp. 356–7.

39. Fabris, p. 37. On Augustin Grass-Mick, see http://augustingrass-mick. pagesperso-orange.fr/ [accessed 7 December 2016]. Augustin Grass-Mick also knew Erik Satie. See Ornella Volta, *Satie Seen Through his Letters*, trans. by Michael Bullock (London: Marion Boyars, 1989), p. 47.

40. Fabris, p. 58.

41. Fabris, p. 59.

42. Fabris, p. 55.

43. On this work, see Diamand Rosinsky, pp. 88–9. Jaqueline Munck, 'La Peinture de Suzanne Valadon: 1909–1914, une passion décisive' in *Valadon, Utrillo & Utter à l'atelier de la rue Cortot: 1912–1926*, exhib. cat. (Paris: Musée de Montmartre, 2015), pp. 36–7.

44. Richard Kendall and Jill DeVonyar, *Degas and the ballet: Picturing Movement*, exhib. cat. (London: Royal Academy of Arts, 2011), pp. 15–16.

45. *La Presse*, 4 March 1914, p. 2. *Lemouzi*, April 1914, p. 190. *L'Aurore*, 1 March 1914, p. 1.

46. On Level, see http://www.metmuseum.org/art/libraries-and-research-centers/leonard-lauder-research-center/programs-and-resources/index-of-cubist-art-collectors/level [accessed 15 December 2016].

47. On Maurice's sales at this time, see Fabris, pp. 55–9.

48. On the French mindset in 1914, see: Stéphane Audoin-Rouzeau and Annette Becker, *La Grande Guerre 1914–1918* (Paris: Gallimard, 1998), pp. 16–19. James

F. McMillan, *Twentieth-Century France: Politics and Society 1898–1991* (London, New York, Sydney and Auckland: Arnold, 1992), pp. 58–72.

49. Ernest Lavisse, *La Première année d'histoire de France, cours moyen* (Paris: Armand Colin, 1912), p. 246.

CHAPTER 13

1. Georges-Emmanuel Clancier, *La Vie quotidienne en Limousin au XIXe siècle* (Paris: Hachette, 1976), p. 145.

2. 'Appel aux Parisiennes', *Le Figaro*, 4 August 1914, p. 2.

3. 'Appel aux Parisiennes', *Le Figaro*, 4 August 1914, p. 2.

4. 'Appel aux Parisiennes', *Le Figaro*, 4 August 1914, p. 2.

5. *Art of Our Century*, ed. by Jean-Louis Ferrier, trans by Walter D. Glanze (Harlow, Essex: Longman Group UK Ltd, 1990), p. 146.

6. Suzanne and Utter's marriage certificate is reprinted in *Suzanne Valadon – 1865–1938*, exhib. cat. (Martigny, Switzerland: Fondation Pierre Gianadda, 1996), p. 253.

7. Utter has always been recorded as first joining the 158th Infantry Division. However, Heuzé (who was signed up after Utter) remembered them fighting in the 22nd Infantry Battalion together. See J.P. Crespelle, *Montmartre Vivant* (Paris: Hachette, 1964), p. 171.

8. On Paris the day after war was declared, see 'La Journée – Quelques impressions de Paris', *Le Figaro*, 4 August 1914, p. 2.

9. I am grateful to staff at the Lapin Agile for confirming the function of the venue during the First World War. June Rose, *Mistress of Montmartre: A Life of Suzanne Valadon* (London: Richard Cohen Books, 1998), p. 160.

10. Stéphane Audoin-Rouzeau and Annette Becker, *La Grande Guerre 1914–1918* (Paris: Gallimard, 1998), p. 27.

11. This was recounted by Paul Pétridès. See *L'Oeuvre complète de Suzanne Valadon*, ed. by Paul Pétridès (Paris: Compagnie française des arts graphiques, 1971).

12. Rose, p. 160.

13. Maurice Utrillo, *Histoire de ma jeunesse jusqu'à ce jour*, published in *Valadon Utrillo: Au tournant du siècle à Montmartre – de l'Impressionisme à l'École de Paris*, exhib. cat. (Paris: Pinacothèque de Paris, 2009), pp. 65–131 (pp. 110–11).

14. Maurice Utrillo, *Histoire de ma jeunesse jusqu'à ce jour*, published in *Valadon Utrillo: Au tournant du siècle à Montmartre – de l'Impressionisme à l'École de Paris*, exhib. cat. (Paris: Pinacothèque de Paris, 2009), pp. 65–131 (p. 112). On Reims

Cathedral, see Encyclopaedia Brittanica Online: https://www.britannica. com/topic/Reims-Cathedral [accessed 29 December 2016].

15. Robert Coughlan, *The Wine of Genius: A Life of Maurice Utrillo* (London: Gollancz, 1952), p. 68.

16. Letter from Maurice Utrillo to Suzanne Valadon, dated 8 December 1914, cited in Gustave Coquiot, *Des Peintres maudits* (Paris: André Delpeuch, 1924), p. 178.

17. *Art of Our Century*, ed. by Jean-Louis Ferrier, trans. by Walter D. Glanze (Harlow, Essex: Longman Group UK Ltd, 1990), p. 148.

18. On this exhibition, see Berthe Weill, *Pan! … dans l'Oeil* (Paris: L'Échelle de Jacob, 2009), p. 113.

19. Suzanne Valadon's portrait is reproduced in Jean Fabris, *Utrillo, sa vie, son oeuvre* (Paris: Éditions Frédéric Birr, 1982), p. 51.

20. Weill, p. 120.

21. Weill, p. 120.

22. Weill, p. 120.

23. Maurice Utrillo, *Histoire de ma jeunesse jusqu'à ce jour*, published in *Valadon Utrillo: Au tournant du siècle à Montmartre – de l'Impressionisme à l'École de Paris*, exhib. cat. (Paris: Pinacothèque de Paris, 2009), pp. 65–131 (pp. 110, 113). Fabris, p. 60.

24. Madeleine Valadon's death certificate is transcribed in Fabris, p. 60.

25. Suzanne Valadon talking to Mme Camax-Zoegger, recounted in 'Pour les futurs biographes de Suzanne Valadon et d'Utrillo', *Cahiers de France*, October 1938, p. 86.

26. *Bulletin municipal official de la ville de Paris*, 30 July 1915, p. 1631.

27. James F. McMillan, *Twentieth-Century France: Politics and Society 1898–1991* (London, New York, Sydney and Auckland: Arnold, 1992), p. 68.

28. Alistair Horne, *Seven Ages of Paris* (London: Pan Macmillan, 2003), p. 360.

29. McMillan, p. 70.

30. John Storm, *The Valadon Drama: The Life of Suzanne Valadon* (New York: E.P. Dutton & Co., Inc., 1959), p. 202.

31. Storm, p. 202.

32. June Rose cites a letter to Adolphe Tabarant written in 1915 in which Suzanne announced the marriage. See Rose, p. 165.

33. 'Nouvelles Diverses – La Température', *Le Figaro*, 24 January 1917, p. 4.

34. 'Nouvelles Diverses – La Température', *Le Figaro*, 24 January 1917, p. 4.

35. 'Le Froid et le charbon', *Le Figaro*, 1 February 1917, p. 2.

36. Suzanne's correspondence with Adolphe Tabarant was only discovered recently. See Rose, pp. 167–9.

37. Rose, pp. 168–9.

38. On the mutinies and General Nivelle's offensive, see Audoin-Rouzeau and Becker, pp. 88–9.

39. On the Berthe Weill exhibition, see Louis Vauxcelles, 'A travers les expositions', *Le Carnet des Artistes*, 15 March 1917, p. 19.

40. On the Galerie Bernheim-Jeune, see: http://www.bernheim-jeune.com/story/ [accessed 10 January 2017].

41. Pinturriehio, '*La Serie D* et Borgeaud', *Le Carnet de la semaine*, 5 May 1917, p. 7.

42. Louis Vauxcelles, 'A travers les expositions', *Le Carnet des Artistes*, 15 May 1917, p. 6.

43. Several of these letters are reproduced in Paul Pétridès, *Ma Chance et ma réussite* (Paris: Plon, 1978), pp. 112–15.

44. Pétridès, p. 113–14.

45. Rose, p. 171.

46. Louis Libaude wrote in response to Utter on 1 September 1917. See Fabris, p. 49.

47. Arsène Alexandre, 'Edgard Degas', *Le Figaro*, 28 September 1917, p. 1.

48. On Degas's funeral, see Albert Flamant, 'Jours de Guerre', *Le Monde Illustré*, 20 October 1917, p. 212.

49. 'Nouvelles Diverses – Le Froid', *Le Figaro*, 1 January 1918, p. 4.

50. Letter reproduced in Fabris, pp. 62–3.

51. On Big Bertha, see Horne, pp. 351–2.

52. Coughlan, p. 69.

53. Horne, p. 365.

54. On Paris on Armistice day, see: 'La Joie de Paris', *Le Figaro*, 12 November 1918, p. 2. Horne, pp. 364–5.

55. 'La Joie de Paris', *Le Figaro*, 12 November 1918, p. 2.

56. Storm, p. 202.

57. Storm, p. 204.

CHAPTER 14

1. Georges-Emmanuel Clancier, *La Vie quotidienne en Limousin au XIXe siècle* (Paris: Hachette, 1976), p. 143.

2. Colin Jones, *Cambridge Illustrated History of France* (Cambridge: Cambridge University Press, 1994), pp. 248–57.

3. On unusable agricultural land, see Jones, p. 248

4. Alistair Horne, *Seven Ages of Paris* (London: Pan Macmillan, 2003), pp. 379–85.

5. Margo Lestz, 'History of Jazz in France', *The Good Life France* http://www.thegoodlifefrance.com/history-jazz-france/ [accessed 24 January 2017].

6. Jones, pp. 255–7.

7. Berthe Weill, *Pan! ... dans l'Oeil* (Paris: L'Échelle de Jacob, 2009), pp. 130–3.

8. Jean Fabris, *Utrillo, sa vie, son oeuvre* (Paris: Éditions Frédéric Birr, 1982), p. 64. James F. McMillan, *Twentieth-Century France: Politics and Society 1898–1991* (London, New York, Sydney and Auckland: Arnold, 1992), p. 82.

9. June Rose, *Mistress of Montmartre: A Life of Suzanne Valadon* (London: Richard Cohen Books, 1998), p. 175.

10. On this work, see *Valadon Utrillo: Au tournant du siècle à Montmartre – de l'Impressionisme à l'École de Paris*, exhib. cat. (Paris: Pinacothèque de Paris, 2009), p. 292.

11. André Utter's boast has been translated variously. See for example: Robert Coughlan, *The Wine of Genius: A Life of Maurice Utrillo* (London: Gollancz, 1952), p. 86. Maximilian Ilyin, *Utrillo* (London & Paris: A. Zwemmer and Fernand Hazan, 1953), p. 5.

12. Fabris, p. 64.

13. Rose, *Mistress of Montmartre*, p. 178.

14. On Zbo, see June Rose, *Modigliani: The Pure Bohemian* (London: Constable, 1990), p. 146.

15. Rose, *Mistress of Montmartre*, p. 178.

16. 'La Peinture et la sculpture au Salon d'Automne', *Comoedia*, 4 November 1919, p. 1.

17. Weill, p. 132.

18. John Storm, *The Valadon Drama: The Life of Suzanne Valadon* (New York: E.P. Dutton & Co., Inc., 1959), pp. 200–1.

19. Fabris, p. 66.

20. On Renoir's demise, see Jacques Lassaigne, *Impressionism*, trans. by Paul Eve (London: Heron Books, 1966), pp. 190–2.

21. Rose, *Modigliani*, pp. 209–13.

22. *Le Bulletin de la vie artistique*, 15 January 1920, p. 101.

23. On the Anti-skyscraper party, see: 'Le Maire de Montmartre', *La Presse*, 12 April 1920, p. 2. Jean Émile-Bayard, *Montmartre Past and Present*, trans. by Ralph Anningson and Tudor Davies (London: T. Fisher Unwin Ltd, 1926), pp. 96–107.

24. Émile-Bayard, pp. 96–107.

25. M. Castaing, 'Le Salon des Indépendants', *Floréal*, 14 February 1920, p. 160. 'Le Salon des Indépendants', *Le Populaire de Paris*, 29 January 1920, p. 1. Morin-Jean, 'Au Salon des Indépendants', *La Gerbe*, March 1920, pp. 172–3. Clotilde Misme, 'Les Salons du Grand Palais', *La Chronique des arts*, 15 February 1920, pp. 18–19.

26. Thérèse Diamand Rosinsky, *Suzanne Valadon* (New York: Universe Publishing, 1994), p. 59.

27. Jeanine Warnod, *Suzanne Valadon*, trans. by Shirley Jennings (Naefels, Switzerland: Bonfini Press, 1981), p. 91.

28. Weill, p. 144.

29. Letter transcribed as part of the Espace Valadon in Bessines, dated by the Association Utrillo 3 May 1920.

30. Fabris, p. 55.

31. Fabris, p. 55.

32. Maurice first wrote to Robert Pauwels on 6 December 1920. See Fabris, p. 57.

33. Lucie spoke candidly to Maurice's biographer Robert Coughlan. See Coughlan, p. 101.

34. Fabris, p. 57.

35. On Berthe Weill's impressions, see Weill, pp. 141–2.

36. Coughlan, p. 103.

37. On Lucie's impressions of their friendship, see Coughlan, p. 103.

38. Suzanne to Lucie Pauwels, 21 February 1921, letter reproduced in Fabris, p. 57.

39. On this chain of events, see Fabris, pp. 55–6.

40. Letter reproduced in *Valadon Utrillo: Au tournant du siècle à Montmartre – de l'Impressionisme à l'École de Paris*, exhib. cat. (Paris: Pinacothèque de Paris, 2009), Annexes, pp. 450–1.

41. Fabris, p. 55.

42. Jeanine Warnod confirms that the picture shows Utter's mother and sister. He had no brothers, so it is assumed that the male figure is his father. See Warnod, p. 73.

43. *Le Gaulois*, 1 November 1921, p. 1.

44. Adolphe Tabarant, *L'Oeuvre*, December 1921, cited in Robert Rey, *Suzanne Valadon* (Paris: Gallimard, 1922), pp. 14–15.

45. André Warnod, *L'Avenir*, 19 December 1921, cited in Rey, p. 15.

46. Robert Rey, *L'Opinion*, 25 December 1921, cited in Rey, p. 15.

47. 'Tableaux de chevalet, ou peinture décorative?', *Bulletin de la vie artistique*, 15 February 1922, p. 78.

48. On Léon Zamaron, see *Valadon Utrillo: Au tournant du siècle à Montmartre – de l'Impressionisme à l'École de Paris*, exhib. cat. (Paris: Pinacothèque de Paris, 2009), p. 323.

49. Ilyin, p. 5.

50. Fabris, p. 56.

51. Jeanine Warnod remembers that Suzanne came on the day she was born in December 1921 to give the new parents a gift in the form of a painting by Maurice of a church. I am grateful to Jeanine Warnod for this valuable information.

52. On Utter's temper, see Paul Pétridès, *Ma Chance et ma réussite* (Paris: Plon, 1978), pp. 71–2.

53. I am grateful to the Office de tourisme in Cancale for assisting me in locating Suzanne's holiday destination. Fabris, p. 58.

54. Weill, p. 148.

55. See the letter from Maurice Utrillo to Robert Le Masle detailing this. Reproduced in Fabris, p. 59.

56. An intimate letter from Suzanne to Nora is reproduced in *Valadon Utrillo: Au tournant du siècle à Montmartre – de l'Impressionisme à l'École de Paris*, exhib. cat. (Paris: Pinacothèque de Paris, 2009), p. 319.

57. This area is now known as the Pyrénées-Atlantiques.

58. On the trip, see Storm, pp. 215–17.

59. An evocative picture of the house can be found in Suzanne's painting *Le Château de Ségalas* (1923), reproduced in *Valadon, Utrillo & Utter à l'atelier de la rue Cortot: 1912–1926*, exhib. cat. (Paris: Musée de Montmartre, 2015), p. 71.

60. Storm, pp. 215–17.

61. This is the date given to the château in *Valadon Utrillo: Au tournant du siècle à Montmartre – de l'Impressionisme à l'École de Paris*, exhib. cat. (Paris: Pinacothèque de Paris, 2009), p. 281.

62. On the château, see Fabris, pp. 61, 67.

63. Fabris, pp. 61, 67.

64. *L'Intransigeant*, 31 October 1923, p. 2. *Comoedia*, 30 October 1923, p. 4.

65. Fabris, p. 60.

66. For an account of Suzanne's spending, see Storm, pp. 226–7.

67. Suzanne, Maurice and Lucie used different spellings of the dogs' names. I have adopted the form used by Suzanne in her 1927 portrait of the animals.

68. Jeanine Warnod remembers this vividly. See Jeanine Warnod, *L'École de Paris* (Paris: Arcadia Éditions, 2004), p. 32.

69. Fabris, p. 66.

70. *Comoedia*, 1 June 1924, p. 4.

71. *L'Intransigeant*, 2 June 1924, p. 2.

72. It has often been said that this banquet was thrown to celebrate Suzanne and Maurice being offered a joint contract in 1924 with Bernheim-Jeune. However, Bernheim-Jeune holds no record of such a contract ever having existed. The archives show only a contract made with Maurice Utrillo in 1927, and there is no record of a contract ever having been made with Suzanne Valadon. I am grateful to Guy-Patrice Dauverville at Bernheim-Jeune & Cie for his scrupulous investigation into the gallery's archives.

73. On banquets, see Susan Cope and others, eds, *Larousse Gastronomique* (London: Mandarin, 1990), pp. 73–4. On Rousseau's banquet, see Jonathan Jones, 'When Henri met Pablo', *The Guardian*, 29 October 2005 https://www.theguardian.com/artanddesign/2005/oct/29/art [accessed 9 February 2017].

74. André Utter, *Entre Peintres*, MNAM, cited in Thérèse Diamand Rosinsky, 'Les multiples identités de Suzanne Valadon: Marie-Clémentine, "Biqui", ou "Terrible Maria"?' in *Suzanne Valadon – 1865–1938*, exhib. cat. (Martigny, Switzerland: Fondation Pierre Gianadda, 1996), pp. 31–53 (p. 51).

75. Cited in Cope, p. 74.

76. On this work, see Thérèse Diamand Rosinsky, *Suzanne Valadon* (New York: Universe Publishing, 1994), pp. 72–74.

CHAPTER 15

1. Bérangère Guilbaud-Rabiller, *Le Grand Almanach du Limousin 2016* (La Crèche: Geste éditions, 2015), semaine 25.

2. On the episode, see Jean Fabris, *Utrillo, sa vie, son oeuvre* (Paris: Éditions Frédéric Birr, 1982), p. 62. John Storm, *The Valadon Drama: The Life of Suzanne Valadon* (New York: E.P. Dutton & Co., Inc., 1959), p. 229. June Rose, *Mistress of Montmartre: A Life of Suzanne Valadon* (London: Richard Cohen Books, 1998), p. 199.

3. The account of Mme Annette Jacquinot regarding life at Saint-Bernard is particularly illuminating. See Fabris, pp. 67–75.

4. On Édouard Herriot, see: *Encyclopédie Larousse en ligne* – Édouard Herriot http://www.larousse.fr/encyclopedie/personnage/%C3%89douard_Herriot/123780 [accessed 20 February 2017]. *Encyclopaedia Britannica*

– Édouard Herriot https://www.britannica.com/biography/Edouard-Herriot [accessed 21 February 2017].

5. 'Suzanne Valadon', *Beaux-Arts*, 15 April 1938, p. 3.

6. Stéphane Manier, 'Quelques minutes avant de partir pour Londres M. Édouard Herriot nous a parlé du peintre Suzanne Valadon', *Paris-Soir*, 14 October 1932, p. 3.

7. See Mme Annette Jacquinot's account. See Fabris, pp. 67–75.

8. On the Boeuf sur le Toit, see: http://www.boeufsurletoit.com [accessed 23 February 2017].

9. On Paris in the 1920s, see: Alistair Horne, *Seven Ages of Paris* (London: Pan Macmillan, 2003), pp. 379–85. Colin Jones, *Cambridge Illustrated History of France* (Cambridge: Cambridge University Press, 1994), pp. 253–9.

10. Jean Émile-Bayard, *Montmartre Past and Present*, trans. by Ralph Anningson and Tudor Davies (London: T. Fisher Unwin Ltd, 1926), p. 122.

11. Émile-Bayard, pp. 125–6.

12. Heuzé recounted this episode to Paul Pétridès. See Paul Pétridès, *Ma Chance et ma réussite* (Paris: Plon, 1978), pp. 125–6.

13. This letter is reproduced in Fabris, p. 59.

14. Robert Coughlan, *The Wine of Genius: A Life of Maurice Utrillo* (London: Gollancz, 1952), p. 88.

15. The letter detailing this offer (dated 16 February 1925) is reproduced in Fabris, p. 64.

16. This exhibition ran between May and July 1925.

17. On the *Exposition internationale des Arts décoratifs et industriels modernes*, see: Luke Fiederer, 'AD Classics: Exposition Internationale des Arts Décoratifs et Industriels Modernes', *Arch Daily* http://www.archdaily.com/793367/ ad-classics-exposition-internationale-des-arts-decoratifs-et-industriels-modernes [accessed 24 February 2017]. 'Art Deco: The 1925 Paris Exhibition – Victoria and Albert Museum' http://www.vam.ac.uk/content/articles/a/ the-1925-paris-exhibition/ [accessed 24 February 2017].

18. Gustave Kahn, 'Art', *Mercure de France*, 15 July 1925, pp. 494–8.

19. Berthe Weill, *Pan! … dans l'Oeil* (Paris: L'Échelle de Jacob, 2009), pp. 160–1.

20. On Marie Laurencin, see J.P. Crespelle, *Montmartre Vivant* (Paris: Hachette, 1964), pp. 147–8.

21. Weill, p. 161.

22. Weill, p. 161.

23. See *Le Bulletin de la vie artistique*, 15 June 1925, pp. 265–6.

24. This poem is reproduced in Fabris, p. 61.
25. Fabris, p. 72. *Valadon Utrillo: Au tournant du siècle à Montmartre – de l'Impressionisme à l'École de Paris*, exhib. cat. (Paris: Pinacothèque de Paris, 2009), pp. 319–21.
26. Mary E. Davis, *Erik Satie* (London: Reaktion Books Ltd, 2007), p. 58.
27. See Fabris, p. 71.
28. André Utter to Suzanne Valadon, 15 September 1925, MNAM. Letter reprinted in Thérèse Diamand Rosinsky, 'Les multiples identités de Suzanne Valadon: Marie-Clémentine, "Biqui", ou "Terrible Maria"?' in *Suzanne Valadon – 1865–1938*, exhib. cat. (Martigny, Switzerland: Fondation Pierre Gianadda, 1996), pp. 31–53 (p. 49).
29. This letter is reproduced in Fabris, p. 65.

CHAPTER 16

1. Georges-Emmanuel Clancier, *La Vie quotidienne en Limousin au XIXe siècle* (Paris: Hachette, 1976), p. 145.
2. On the Maquis, see Sophie Krebs, 'Montmartre, colline inspirée?' in *Valadon Utrillo: Au tournant du siècle à Montmartre – de l'Impressionisme à l'École de Paris*, exhib. cat. (Paris: Pinacothèque de Paris, 2009), pp. 37–47 (p. 41).
3. On 11, Avenue Junot, see Paul Pétridès, *Ma Chance et ma réussite* (Paris: Plon, 1978), pp. 69–71.
4. Pétridès, p. 70.
5. Pétridès, p. 71.
6. Suzanne Valadon to Conrad Satie, cited in Ornella Volta, *Satie Seen Through his Letters*, trans. by Michael Bullock (London: Marion Boyars, 1989), pp. 46–7.
7. Volta, p. 47.
8. Mme Annette Jacquinot was struck by Suzanne's inattention to her appearance despite being able to afford to look good if she had wished. See Jean Fabris, *Utrillo, sa vie, son oeuvre* (Paris: Éditions Frédéric Birr, 1982), p. 75.
9. For a discussion of this work, see Thérèse Diamand Rosinsky, *Suzanne Valadon* (New York: Universe Publishing, 1994), pp. 79–81.
10. André Utter, undated letter, MNAM. Letter reprinted in Thérèse Diamand Rosinsky, 'Les multiples identités de Suzanne Valadon: Marie-Clémentine, "Biqui", ou "Terrible Maria"?' in *Suzanne Valadon – 1865–1938*, exhib. cat. (Martigny, Switzerland: Fondation Pierre Gianadda, 1996), pp. 31–53 (p. 48).
11. Anecdote recounted in Fabris, p. 35.
12. Anecdote recounted in Fabris, p. 35.

13. I am indebted to Guy Patrice Dauverville at Bernheim-Jeune & Cie for the detailed information regarding Maurice Utrillo's relationship with Bernheim-Jeune.

14. Maximilian Ilyin, *Utrillo* (London & Paris: A. Zwemmer and Fernand Hazan, 1953), p. 4.

15. André Utter to Suzanne Valadon, 16 May 1927, MNAM. Letter reprinted in Thérèse Diamand Rosinsky, 'Les multiples identités de Suzanne Valadon: Marie-Clémentine, "Biqui", ou "Terrible Maria"?' in *Suzanne Valadon – 1865–1938*, exhib. cat. (Martigny, Switzerland: Fondation Pierre Gianadda, 1996), pp. 31–53 (p. 50).

16. See Fabris, p. 71.

17. See Fabris, p. 69.

18. See Fabris, p. 75.

19. A photograph of the event is reproduced in Fabris, p. 70.

20. Robert Coughlan, *The Wine of Genius: A Life of Maurice Utrillo* (London: Gollancz, 1952), p. 97.

21. Lucie Valore, *Maurice Utrillo, mon mari* (Paris: Joseph Foret, 1956), p. 117.

22. Cited in John Storm, *The Valadon Drama: The Life of Suzanne Valadon* (New York: E.P. Dutton & Co., Inc., 1959), p. 241.

23. Robert Destez, 'Heur et Malheur de Maurice Utrillo, Chevalier de la Légion d'honneur', *L'Homme Libre*, 21 September 1928, p. 1.

24. Destez, p. 2.

25. M.R., 'Exposition Suzanne Valadon', *L'Intransigeant*, 29 January 1929, p. 5.

26. G. Charensol, 'Suzanne Valadon', *Les Chroniques du jour*, September 1929, pp. 22–5.

27. Jeanine Warnod, *Suzanne Valadon*, trans. by Shirley Jennings (Naefels, Switzerland: Bonfini Press, 1981), p. 88. John Storm, *The Valadon Drama: The Life of Suzanne Valadon* (New York: E.P. Dutton & Co., Inc., 1959), p. 222.

28. Peter de Polnay, *The World of Maurice Utrillo* (London: Heinemann, 1967), p. 168. June Rose, *Mistress of Montmartre: A Life of Suzanne Valadon* (London: Richard Cohen Books, 1998), p. 224.

29. This episode is recounted by Mme Jacquinot. See Fabris, p. 73.

30. This letter is reproduced in Fabris, p. 72.

31. See Ilyin, pp. 5–6.

32. This anecdote is recounted by Pétridès, pp. 68–71.

33. Anecdote recounted in Fabris, p. 71.

34. See Pétridès, pp. 72–4.

35. James F. McMillan, *Twentieth-Century France: Politics and Society 1898–1991* (London, New York, Sydney and Auckland: Arnold, 1992), p. 101.

36. André Salmon, *Revue de France*, January 1930, cited in Rose, p. 221.

37. See for example André Utter to Suzanne Valadon, 2 April 1930, MNAM. Letter cited in Rose, p. 224.

38. On this work and Suzanne's self-portraits, see Thérèse Diamand Rosinsky, *Suzanne Valadon* (New York: Universe Publishing, 1994), pp. 79–81.

39. René Barotte, 'Au Portique – Suzanne Valadon', *L'Homme Libre*, 11 May 1931, pp. 1–2.

40. On the depression in France, see McMillan, pp. 101–2.

41. G. Charensol, 'Les Grandes Ventes', *Formes*, May 1931, pp. 89–90.

42. On the trip, see Mme Jacquinot's account in Fabris, pp. 73–5.

43. On this work, see Thérèse Diamand Rosinsky, *Suzanne Valadon* (New York: Universe Publishing, 1994), pp. 60–5.

44. The publication was advertised in *Les Nouvelles littéraires*, 2 July 1932, p. 9.

45. This episode was recounted in *Paris-Soir*. Stéphane Manier, 'Quelques minutes avant de partir pour Londres M. Édouard Herriot nous a parlé du peintre Suzanne Valadon', *Paris-Soir*, 14 October 1932, p. 3.

46. René Barotte, 'Chez Georges Petit – Suzanne Valadon', *L'Homme Libre*, 20 October 1932, p. 2.

CHAPTER 17

1. Michel Chadeuil, *Expressions et dictons Périgord Limousin* (Chamalières: Christine Bonneton, 2015), p. 146.

2. Robert Coughlan, *The Wine of Genius: A Life of Maurice Utrillo* (London: Gollancz, 1952), pp. 101–3.

3. Maurice's letter of condolence is reproduced in Jean Fabris, *Utrillo, sa vie, son oeuvre* (Paris: Éditions Frédéric Birr, 1982), p. 74.

4. On Maurice and religion, see Lucie Valore, *Maurice Utrillo, mon mari* (Paris: Joseph Foret, 1956), pp. 65–7.

5. This and the following episode are recounted by Mme Jacquinot. See Fabris, pp. 67–9.

6. On Suzanne's flower pieces in the 1930s, see Françoise Künzi's discussion in *Valadon Utrillo: Au tournant du siècle à Montmartre – de l'Impressionisme à l'École de Paris*, exhib. cat. (Paris: Pinacothèque de Paris, 2009), p. 340.

7. See for example Louis Léon-Martin, 'Les femmes artistes modernes', *Paris-Soir*, 17 February 1932, p. 6.

8. See 'Musée du Luxembourg', *Bulletin des musées de France*, July 1933, pp. 104–5.

9. Thérèse Diamand Rosinsky, *Suzanne Valadon* (New York: Universe Publishing, 1994), p. 123. June Rose, *Mistress of Montmartre: A Life of Suzanne Valadon* (London: Richard Cohen Books, 1998), p. 229.

10. On this second version, see Fabris, pp. 67–9. Lucie Valore (subsequently Lucie Pauwels) believed Maurice was baptised when they married. See Valore, p. 66. The Association Utrillo has no record of the baptism ever having taken place. I am grateful to Hélène Bruneau for this information.

11. Peter de Polnay, *The World of Maurice Utrillo* (London: Heinemann, 1967), p. 181.

12. This document, a statement signed by Suzanne confirming the amount and terms of the loan, is held by the MNAM.

13. Valore, p. 41. Robert Coughlan, *The Wine of Genius: A Life of Maurice Utrillo* (London: Gollancz, 1952), pp. 103–4.

14. Coughlan, pp. 103–4.

15. Coughlan, pp. 104–5.

16. Valore, pp. 41–2.

17. Valore, p. 42.

18. Some accounts of the reading state that the clairvoyant gave Lucie the initial 'M'. See for example: Paul Pétridès, *Ma Chance et ma réussite* (Paris: Plon, 1978), pp. 129–130. In other accounts of the reading, Maurice was actually named. See for example: Coughlan, p. 105.

19. This card is reproduced in Fabris, p. 75.

20. De Polnay, p. 167.

21. On Gazi, see: De Polnay, pp. 187–8. 'Gazi Le Tatar' http://genealogie.lelong. pagesperso-orange.fr/curiosites/gazi_le_tatar2.htm [accessed 22 March 2017]. J.P. Crespelle, *Montmartre Vivant* (Paris: Hachette, 1964), p. 244.

22. De Polnay, pp. 187–8.

23. According to Peter de Polnay, it was 'Yvette' with whom Utter eventually settled. See De Polnay, pp. 172–3.

24. For Robert Naly's account, see Crespelle, pp. 244–6.

25. Crespelle, p. 244.

26. De Polnay, p. 228.

27. 'L'Actualité Artistique – Expositions', *Mobilier & Décoration*, 1934, p. 301.

28. Miguel Utrillo died on 20 January 1934.

29. This was the symptom that most struck Lucie. See Valore, p. 44.

30. A condition whereby the kidneys fail to properly perform their excretory, regulatory and endocrine function.

31. On Lucie's account of the visit, see Valore, pp. 43–7. See also Coughlan, pp. 105–6.

32. Valore, p. 46.

33. Valore, p. 47.

34. Coughlan, p. 98.

35. De Polnay, pp. 175–6.

36. Valore, p. 47. Coughlan, p. 107.

37. See Valore, pp. 54–5.

38. See Valore, p. 55. Fabris, p. 95.

39. Valore, p. 55.

40. Valore, p. 56.

41. De Polnay, p. 174.

42. De Polnay, p. 174.

43. Valore, p. 57. De Polnay, p. 174.

44. Fabris, p. 95.

45. De Polnay, p. 173.

46. Valore, p. 58.

47. Fabris, p. 95.

48. Letter dated 26 March 1935, reproduced in Fabris, p. 77.

49. The Association Utrillo holds no record of the baptism ever having taken place. I am grateful to Hélène Bruneau for this information.

50. Valore, p. 54.

51. René Barotte, 'A la Cathédrale de Chartres quand Maurice Utrillo peintre génial de la Butte et maniaque de la solitude, prie avec sa fiancée', *Paris-Soir*, 12 April 1935, pp. 1, 7.

52. Barotte, p. 7.

53. Valore, p. 60.

54. Rose, p. 235.

55. V, 'Les "Femmes artistes" et "Les Universitaires"', *Le Petit Parisien*, 30 May 1935, p. 4.

56. The photograph was reproduced in *Paris-Soir*, 4 May 1935, p. 14.

57. De Polnay, p. 175.

58. Valore, p. 59.

CHAPTER 18

1. Georges-Emmanuel Clancier, *La Vie quotidienne en Limousin au XIXe siècle* (Paris: Hachette, 1976), p. 143.

2. 'Thursday' is inscribed on this letter which Jean Fabris dates as 9 June 1935, reprinted in Jean Fabris, *Utrillo, sa vie, son oeuvre* (Paris: Éditions Frédéric Birr, 1982), p. 78. The 9th of June 1935 was actually a Sunday, so the letter was probably written on Thursday 6 June 1935.

3. Paul Pétridès, *Ma Chance et ma réussite* (Paris: Plon, 1978), p. 129.

4. On the house and surrounds, see Lucie Valore, *Maurice Utrillo, mon mari* (Paris: Joseph Foret, 1956), pp. 69–71. Pétridès, p. 134.

5. Peter de Polnay, *The World of Maurice Utrillo* (London: Heinemann, 1967), p. 164.

6. Fabris, p. 95.

7. Pétridès, p. 132.

8. Fabris, p. 95.

9. See Valore, pp. 70–1.

10. Letter dated 20 August 1935, cited in Pétridès, pp. 132–3.

11. Lucie Pauwels remembered that the dog died shortly before she became engaged to Maurice. See Valore, p. 49. However, in a letter dated 29 October 1935, Maurice asks if the dog is better. See Fabris, p. 79.

12. Robert Coughlan, *The Wine of Genius: A Life of Maurice Utrillo* (London: Gollancz, 1952), pp. 107–8.

13. John Storm, *The Valadon Drama: The Life of Suzanne Valadon* (New York: E.P. Dutton & Co., Inc., 1959), p. 249.

14. De Polnay, p. 187.

15. Letter dated 29 October 1935, reproduced in Fabris, p. 79.

16. J.P. Crespelle, *Montmartre Vivant* (Paris: Hachette, 1964), p. 244.

17. Episode recounted in Crespelle, pp. 244–6.

18. 'Gazi Le Tatar' http://genealogie.lelong.pagesperso-orange.fr/curiosites/gazi_le_tatar2.htm [accessed 22 March 2017].

19. Valore, p. 49.

20. Pétridès, p. 133.

21. Letter dated 6 January 1936, reproduced in Fabris, p. 80.

22. On this work and Suzanne's relationship with the Camax-Zoeggers, see Thérèse Diamand Rosinsky, *Suzanne Valadon* (New York: Universe Publishing, 1994), pp. 65–7.

23. 'L'Actualité – Les Expositions', *L'Art et les artistes*, March 1936–July 1936, p. 249.

24. Fabris, p. 89.

25. Pétridès, p. 134.

26. Valore, p. 87.

27. Many of these letters are held by the MNAM.

28. Letter transcribed in Fabris, p. 89.

29. Valore, p. 71. Fabris, p. 92.

30. Valore, p. 76.

31. Pétridès, p. 136.

32. Pétridès, pp. 137–138.

33. Pétridès, pp. 138–139.

34. On 'La Bonne Lucie' and the staff, see Valore, pp. 77–81.

35. Valore, p. 79.

36. De Polnay, pp. 189–91.

37. Geneviève Barrez (née Camax-Zoegger) in an interview with June Rose. June Rose, *Mistress of Montmartre: A Life of Suzanne Valadon* (London: Richard Cohen Books, 1998), p. 240. De Polnay, p. 187.

38. Valore, pp. 86–7.

39. Valore, p. 86.

40. Valore, p. 86.

41. G. Brunon Guardia, 'Les arts – Portraits', *L'Intransigeant*, 16 November 1937, p. 2.

42. Pétridès, p. 141.

43. On Pétridès' recollections, see Pétridès, p. 141.

44. *La Revue de l'Art*, April 1937, p. 70. Raymond Lécuyer, 'Les Femmes Artistes d'Europe exposent au Musée du Jeu de Paume', *Le Figaro*, 14 February 1937, p. 2.

45. John Storm, *The Valadon Drama: The Life of Suzanne Valadon* (New York: E.P. Dutton & Co., Inc., 1959), pp. 252–3. The exhibition Storm refers to took place in the first few months of 1937.

46. G. Brunon Guardia, 'Les Arts – Suzanne Valadon et ses satellites', *L'Intransigeant*, 15 May 1937, p. 2.

47. On this, see Fabris, pp. 68–9. The error probably came about due to Miguel Utrillo's death in 1934.

48. On this episode, see de Polnay, pp. 228–30.

49. An informative summary of these letters can be found in Rose, p. 242.

50. This card is held by the MNAM.

51. Louis Vauxcelles, 'Les Femmes Artistes Modernes', *Le Monde Illustré*, 2 April 1938, p. 16.

52. Carco is cited in Jeanine Warnod, *Suzanne Valadon*, trans. by Shirley Jennings (Naefels, Switzerland: Bonfini Press, 1981), p. 88.

53. Carco is cited in Warnod, p. 88.

54. George Besson, 'Le marchand de couleurs – Suzanne Valadon', *Ce Soir*, 20 March 1938, p. 8.

55. Claude Roger-Marx and Waldemar George, 'Suzanne Valadon' *La Renaissance*, April 1938, p. 48.

56. F.H.L., 'Suzanne Valadon (Galerie Bernier)', *Marianne*, 16 March 1938, p. 11.

57. Louis Vauxcelles, 'Suzanne Valadon', *Le Monde Illustré*, 16 April 1938, p. 14.

58. Valore, p. 87.

59. Valore, p. 88.

60. Valore, p. 88.

61. André Warnod, 'Suzanne Valadon est morte', *Le Figaro*, 8 April 1938, p. 2.

62. On the funeral, see: André Warnod, 'L'hommage des artistes à Suzanne Valadon', *Beaux-Arts*, 15 April 1938, p. 1. 'Suzanne Valadon', *Beaux-Arts*, 15 April 1938, p. 3. 'Suzanne Valadon', *Le Vieux Montmartre*, March–April 1938, p. 4.

63. Diamand Rosinsky, p. 118. The coin gives Suzanne's year of birth as 1867.

EPILOGUE

1. The following is drawn from the local paper's report of this event in Bessines in 1949. A.R. Soulier, 'D'une manière simple et touchante Bessines a honoré Suzanne Valadon', *Le Populaire du centre*, October 1949. See also A.R. Soulier, 'Après l'hommage rendu à Suzanne Valadon', *Le Populaire du centre*, October 1949. Marie-Louise Peyrat, 'Suzanne de Bessines', *Limousin Magazine*, March 1965, pp. 16–19.

2. Suzanne Valadon to Jean Vertex, cited in Jeanine Warnod, *Suzanne Valadon*, trans. by Shirley Jennings (Naefels, Switzerland: Bonfini Press, 1981), p. 89.

AFTERWORD

1. *Regards*, 21 April 1938.

2. Louis Vauxcelles, 'Suzanne Valadon', *Le Monde illustré*, 16 April 1938, p. 14.

3. 'Suzanne Valadon', *Beaux-Arts*, 15 April 1938, p. 3.

4. Yves-Bonnat, 'Suzanne Valadon – Un Grand peintre', *Regards*, 21 April 1938, p. 14.

5. On this, see: Jean Fabris, *Utrillo, sa vie, son oeuvre* (Paris: Éditions Frédéric Birr, 1982), p. 92. Lucie Valore, *Maurice Utrillo, mon mari* (Paris: Joseph Foret, 1956), pp. 112–13.

6. Text transcribed in Fabris, p. 100.

7. Robert Coughlan, *The Wine of Genius: A Life of Maurice Utrillo* (London: Gollancz, 1952), p. 122.

8. Reproduced in the last unnumbered insert in Valore.

9. Coughlan, p. 113.

10. Coughlan, pp. 113–14.

11. Coughlan, p. 115.

12. Maximilian Ilyin, *Utrillo* (London: A. Zwemmer; Paris: Fernand Hazan, 1953), p. 3.

Index